Praise for B[

"Best Places *are the best re[*
—THE SEATTLE TIMES

"Best Places *covers must-see portions of the West Coast with style and authority. In-the-know locals offer thorough info on restaurants, lodgings, and the sights.*"
—NATIONAL GEOGRAPHIC TRAVELER

". . . *travelers swear by the recommendations in the* Best Places *guidebooks . . .*"
—SUNSET MAGAZINE

"*For travel collections covering the Northwest, the* Best Places *series takes precedence over all similar guides.*"
—BOOKLIST

"Best Places Northwest *is the bible of discriminating travellers to BC, Washington and Oregon. It promises, and delivers, the best of everything in the region.*"
—THE VANCOUVER SUN

"*Not only the best travel guide in the region, but maybe one of the most definitive guides in the country, which many look forward to with the anticipation usually sparked by a best-selling novel. A browser's delight,* Best Places Northwest *should be chained to dashboards throughout the Northwest.*"
—THE OREGONIAN

"*Still the region's undisputed heavyweight champ of guidebooks.*"
—SEATTLE POST-INTELLIGENCER

"*Trusting the natives is usually good advice, so visitors to Washington, Oregon, and British Columbia would do well to pick up* Best Places Northwest *for an exhaustive review of food and lodging in the region. . . . An indispensable glove-compartment companion.*"
—TRAVEL AND LEISURE

"Best Places Southern California *is just about all the inspiration you need to start planning your next road trip or summer vacation with the kids.*"
—THE FRESNO BEE

"Best Places Alaska *is the one guide to recommend to anyone visiting Alaska for the first or one-hundredth time.*"
—KETCHIKAN DAILY NEWS

"Best Places Northern California *is great fun to read even if you're not going anywhere.*"
—SAN FRANCISCO CHRONICLE

TRUST THE LOCALS

The original insider's guides, written by local experts

COMPLETELY INDEPENDENT

- No advertisers
- No sponsors
- No favors

EVERY PLACE STAR-RATED & RECOMMENDED

★★★★   The very best in the region

★★★   Distinguished; many outstanding features

★★   Excellent; some wonderful qualities

★   A good place

NO STARS   Worth knowing about, if nearby

MONEY-BACK GUARANTEE

We're so sure you'll be satisfied, we guarantee it!

HELPFUL ICONS

Watch for these quick-reference symbols throughout the book:

FAMILY FUN

GOOD VALUE

ROMANTIC

EDITORS' CHOICE

BEST PLACES®

BAJA

★

BEST PLACES®

BAJA

The Best Restaurants, Lodgings,
and Outdoor Adventure

Edited by
LORI MAKABE

EDITION 1

SASQUATCH BOOKS
SEATTLE

Printed in the United States of America
Published by Sasquatch Books
Distributed by Publishers Group West

First edition
09 08 07 06 05 04 03   6 5 4 3 2 1

ISBN: 1-57061-359-1
ISSN: 1539-5014

Series editor: Kate Rogers
Cover and interior design: Nancy Gellos
Cover illustration/photograph: David Peevers/Lonely Planet Images
Maps: Greeneye Design

SPECIAL SALES

Best Places guidebooks are available at special discounts on bulk purchases for corporate, club, or organization sales promotions, premiums, and gifts. Special editions, including personalized covers, excerpts of existing guides, and corporate imprints, can be created in large quantities for specific needs. For more information, contact your local bookseller or Special Sales, Best Places Guidebooks, 119 South Main Street, Suite 400, Seattle, Washington 98104, 800/775-0817.

Sasquatch Books
119 South Main Street, Suite 400
Seattle, Washington 98104
206/467-4300
bestplaces@SasquatchBooks.com
www.SasquatchBooks.com

CONTENTS

Baja California

Baja California Sur

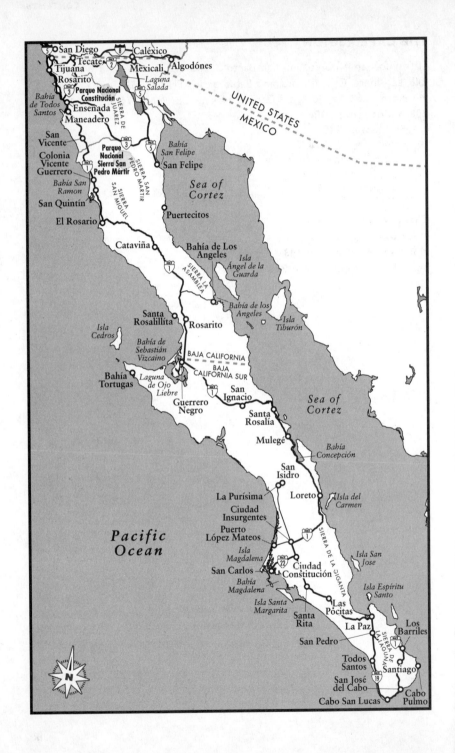

Acknowledgments

I would like to thank Linda Watanabe McFerrin for believing in me and encouraging me to stretch farther than I thought I could. Laura Gronewold, the project editor, always said the right words and helped me through some rough spots. I am incredibly lucky to have had the privilege of working with her and the series editor, Kate Rogers. Susan McCombs's assistance was invaluable, and I would also like to thank Maribeth Mellin, Jane Onstott, Carrie Robertson, Andy Sewell, and Lane Sykes for their technical, editorial, and emotional support, and Sabrina Lear for pinch-hitting with short notice.

My heartfelt appreciation goes to Lee King for first opening my eyes to the beauty of the Baja peninsula. I am also grateful to the network of folks who shared their knowledge and experience, and painstakingly answered layers of questions: Carole Scofield, Patricia Hernandez, Annalisa Valentine, Layla Aguilar, Ciro Romera, Judy Henke, Fred Jones, Don and Gayle Schenk, Bobby Van Warmer, Earl Maynard, Scott Nelson, Patty Martin, Roxanna Guttierrez, Dr. Kathleen Puckett, John Cyparski, Rita and Jean Luc Moreau, Alejandro Olvera, Spence and Carlee Rauber, Henry Obermüller, María Isabel, Marga and Tracy Bearden, Eva Garcia, Blanca Acosta, Hank and Judy Tussy, Marta Mendoza, and Jackie Reeves.

And finally I would like to thank my wonderful husband, Wayne Makabe, for seeing me through the birthing of this book. Between the cravings for fish tacos, mood swings, weight gain, exhaustion, backaches, and months of intense labor, delivering this manuscript has been the closest thing to pregnancy and childbirth that I have experienced.

Contributors

Editor **LORI MAKABE** has traveled to Baja for nearly 20 years. Her sports and adventure travel stories have appeared online and in newspapers, magazines, and travel anthologies. On her various odysseys south of the border she has collided with a cow, built a house, broke an axle, traversed the peninsula on a mountain bike, jibed over a gray whale, slept with scorpions, and lost a wheel—resulting in a ¾-mile scratch down Baja's Transpeninsular Highway. She writes offbeat lyrics for an outlaw acoustic duo, and often dangles from the end of a large power-kite. Lori currently divides her time between Northern California and Southern Baja.

Contributing editor and writer **SUSAN LYN MCCOMBS** experienced her first taste of mole, her first swim with phosphorescence, and her first kiss on a high school trip to Mexico. Inspired, she soon set out to see the rest of world, returning to Mexico whenever possible and writing about her travels along the way. The native Californian lent her fresh perspective to *Best Places Baja*; her words and wit can be found throughout this book. Susan was a contributing writer to *Best Places Northern California,* and her writing has also appeared in anthologies, newspapers, magazines, and online.

JANE ONSTOTT is a professional editor, travel writer, and translator. Since receiving a B.A. in Spanish Language and Literature from SDSU, she has lived and worked in Oaxaca, Mexico and the Galapagos Islands, Ecuador. She's written for travel guidebooks about Mexico, the U.S., and South America for years. In addition to reviewing and writing parts of The Border and the North chapter of this book, she contributed to *Best Places San Diego.*

LYNN FORD learned in 1961 that being seven months pregnant was not a handicap. When shipwrecked in the Sea of Cortez, she bobbed safely to shore at Gonzaga Bay. She is an award-winning photographer, has traveled extensively in Baja, and was a pit-crew member for the Baja 1000 off-road race for seven years. Lynn researched and contributed to portions of The Border and The North.

FRED AND GLORIA JONES have traveled extensively throughout Baja for many years. Together, they've journeyed the peninsula on roads, off roads, on water, on horseback, on foot, and by air, exploring, diving, fishing, and adventuring. Award-winning writers and photographers, they have written several books and numerous magazine and newspaper articles on Baja and other subjects. Fred and Gloria researched and contributed to portions of two chapters, North Central Baja and South Central Baja.

Photojournalist and native Texan **CARRIE ROBERTSON** spent the year 2001 exploring the Sea of Cortez and the mountains of Baja. Dividing her time between Loreto and La Paz, she worked as a windsurfing instructor, dive master, whale-watch naturalist, and kayaking guide. Before coming to Baja, she worked as a marine naturalist and underwater videographer in Maui. Her freelance photos and articles appear in magazines such as *Baja Life, Sport Diver,* and

American Windsurfer. Carrie researched and wrote the Mid-South chapter and contributed valuable information throughout this book.

TRUDI ANGELL was bit by the Baja bug in 1976 when she took a sea kayak and natural history course on the peninsula. Twenty-five years later, she's still exploring old Baja trails and missions, leading kayak tours, and organizing environmental and guide training programs for locals. Her most recent goal is to ride the entire length of the peninsula by mule! To date, Trudi and her 13-year-old daughter, Olivia, have ridden over 800 miles of Baja's most remote mountain trails. Trudi assisted with research for the Mid-South chapter.

GAIL MACLAUGHLIN first visited the southern tip of Baja in the early '70s when Cabo San Lucas was a quaint fishing village. She returned frequently to angle prize catches of marlin, *dorado, wahoo,* tuna, and other deep-sea species. With her husband, she spent two years in the early '90s exploring the remote isles of the Sea of Cortez aboard their 65-foot yacht-fisher, *Scot Free.* She now resides in Los Barriles, where she has created an exquisite indoor-outdoor palapa home. An established travel and boating writer, she also writes a weekly column syndicated by Copley News Service. Gail wrote and researched The Cape Region.

About Best Places® Guidebooks

People trust us. Best Places guidebooks, which have been published continuously since 1975, represent one of the most respected regional travel series in the country. Each guide is written completely independently: no advertisers, no sponsors, no favors. Our reviewers know their territory, work incognito, and seek out the very best a city or region has to offer. Because we accept no free meals, accommodations, or other complimentary services, we are able to provide tough, candid reports about places that have rested too long on their laurels, and to delight in new places that deserve recognition. We describe the true strengths, foibles, and unique characteristics of each establishment listed.

Best Places Baja is written by and for locals, and is therefore coveted by travelers. It's written for people who live here and who enjoy exploring the region's bounty and its out-of-the-way places of high character and individualism. It is these very characteristics that make *Best Places Baja* ideal for tourists, too. The best places in and around the region are the ones that denizens favor: independently owned establishments of good value, touched with local history, run by lively individuals, and graced with natural beauty. With this first edition of *Best Places Baja,* travelers will find the information they need: where to go and when, what to order, which rooms to request (and which to avoid), where the best music, art, nightlife, shopping, and other attractions are, and how to find the region's hidden secrets.

We're so sure you'll be satisfied with our guide, we guarantee it.

NOTE: *The reviews in this edition are based on information available at press time and are subject to change. Readers are advised that places listed may have closed or changed management and, thus, may no longer be recommended by this series. The editors welcome information conveyed by users of this book. A report form is provided at the end of the book, and feedback is also welcome via email: bestplaces@SasquatchBooks.com.*

How to Use This Book

This book is divided into five major regions, encompassing all destinations south of the Mexican border. All evaluations are based on numerous reports from local and traveling inspectors. Best Places reporters do not identify themselves when they review an establishment, and they accept no free meals, accommodations, or any other services. Final judgments are made by the editors. **EVERY PLACE FEATURED IN THIS BOOK IS RECOMMENDED.**

STAR RATINGS Restaurants and lodgings are rated on a scale of zero to four stars (with half stars in between), based on uniqueness, loyalty of local clientele, performance measured against the establishment's goals, excellence of cooking, cleanliness, value, and professionalism of service. Reviews are listed alphabetically, and every place is recommended.

★★★★	The very best in the region
★★★	Distinguished; many outstanding features
★★	Excellent; some wonderful qualities
★	A good place
NO STARS	Worth knowing about, if nearby
UNRATED	New or undergoing major changes

(For more on how we rate places, see the Best Places Star Ratings box below.)

PRICE RANGE Prices for restaurants are based primarily on dinner for two, including dessert, tax, and tip (no alcohol). Prices for lodgings are based on peak season rates for one night's lodging for two people (i.e., double occupancy). Off-season rates vary but can sometimes be significantly less. Call ahead to verify, as all prices are subject to change.

$$$$	Very expensive (more than $100 for dinner for two; more than $200 for one night's lodging for two)
$$$	Expensive (between $75 and $100 for dinner for two; between $120 and $200 for one night's lodging for two)
$$	Moderate (between $35 and $75 for dinner for two; between $80 and $120 for one night's lodging for two)
$	Inexpensive (less than $35 for dinner for two; less than $80 for one night's lodging for two)

RESERVATIONS *(for Restaurants only)* We used one of the following terms for our reservations policy: reservations required, reservations recommended, no reservations. "No reservations" means either reservations are not necessary or are not accepted.

ACCESS AND INFORMATION At the beginning of each chapter, you'll find general guidelines about how to get to a particular region and what types of transportation are available, as well as basic sources for any additional tourist information you might need. Also check individual town listings for specifics about visiting those places.

THREE-DAY TOURS In every chapter, we've included a quick-reference, three-day itinerary designed for travelers with a short amount of time. Perfect for weekend getaways, these tours outline the highlights of a region or town; the establishments and attractions that appear in boldface within the tour are discussed in greater detail elsewhere in the chapter.

ADDRESSES AND PHONE NUMBERS Every attempt has been made to provide accurate information on an establishment's location and phone number, but it's always a good idea to call ahead and confirm. Phone numbers not followed by "U.S." are local Mexican phone numbers. Please note that many Baja businesses observe seasonal closures; the establishments in this edition are open year-round unless otherwise noted.

TRAVELER'S CHECKS AND CREDIT CARDS Many establishments that accept traveler's checks also require a major credit card for identification. Credit cards are abbreviated in this book as follows: American Express (AE); Carte Blanche (CB); Diners Club (DC); Discover (DIS); Japanese credit card (JCB); Master-Card (MC); Visa (V).

EMAIL AND WEB SITE ADDRESSES Email and web site addresses for establishments have been included where available. Please note that the Web is a fluid and evolving medium, and that web pages are often "under construction" or, as with all time-sensitive information, may no longer be valid.

MAPS AND DIRECTIONS Each chapter in the book begins with a regional map that shows the general area being covered. Throughout the book, basic directions are provided with each entry. Whenever possible, call ahead to confirm hours and location.

HELPFUL ICONS Watch for these quick-reference symbols throughout the book:

FAMILY FUN Family-oriented places that are great for kids—fun, easy, not too expensive, and accustomed to dealing with young ones.

GOOD VALUE While not necessarily cheap, these places offer you the best value for your dollars—a good deal within the context of the region.

ROMANTIC These spots offer candlelight, atmosphere, intimacy, or other romantic qualities—kisses and proposals are encouraged!

EDITORS' CHOICE These are places that are unique and special to Baja, such as a restaurant owned by a beloved local chef or a tourist attraction recognized around the globe.

   Appears after listings for establishments that have wheelchair-accessible facilities.

GLOSSARY We've provided a glossary of basic Spanish terms at the back of the book.

BEST PLACES® STAR RATINGS

Any travel guide that rates establishments is inherently subjective—and Best Places is no exception. We rely on our professional experience, yes, but also on a gut feeling. And, occasionally, we even give in to a soft spot for a favorite neighborhood hangout. Our star-rating system is not simply a checklist; it's judgmental, critical, sometimes fickle, and highly personal. And unlike most other travel guides, we pay our own way and accept no freebies: no free meals or accommodations, no advertisers, no sponsors, no favors.

For each new edition, we send local food and travel experts out to review restaurants and lodgings anonymously, and then to rate them on a scale of one to four, based on uniqueness, loyalty of local clientele, performance measured against the establishment's goals, excellence of cooking, cleanliness, value, and professionalism of service. That doesn't mean a one-star establishment isn't worth dining or sleeping at—far from it. When we say that all the places listed in our books are recommended, we mean it. That one-star pizza joint may be just the ticket for the end of a whirlwind day of shopping with the kids. But if you're planning something more special, the star ratings can help you choose an eatery or hotel that will wow your new clients or be a stunning, romantic place to celebrate an anniversary or impress a first date.

We award four-star ratings sparingly, reserving them for what we consider truly the best. And once an establishment has earned our highest rating, everyone's expectations seem to rise. Readers often write us letters specifically to point out the faults in four-star establishments. With changes in chefs, management, styles, and trends, it's always easier to get knocked off the pedestal than to ascend it. Three-star establishments, on the other hand, seem to generate healthy praise. They exhibit outstanding qualities, and we get lots of love letters about them. The difference between two and three stars can sometimes be a very fine line. Two-star establishments are doing a good, solid job and gaining attention, while one-star places are often dependable spots that have been around forever.

The restaurants and lodgings described in *Best Places Baja* have earned their stars from hard work and good service (and good food). They're proud to be included in this book—look for our Best Places sticker in their windows. And we're proud to honor them in this, the premier edition of *Best Places Baja.*

INDEXES All restaurants, lodgings, town names, and major tourist attractions are listed alphabetically in the back of the book.

MONEY-BACK GUARANTEE Please see "We Stand by Our Reviews" at the end of this book.

READER REPORTS At the end of the book is a report form. We receive hundreds of reports from readers suggesting new places or agreeing or disagreeing with our assessments. They greatly help in our evaluations, and we encourage you to respond.

PLANNING A TRIP

PLANNING A TRIP

Rugged mountains, endless beaches, captivating desert landscapes, and tequila sunrises—these postcard images are only a portion of what Baja California, Mexico, has to offer. Separated from the west coast of mainland Mexico by the Sea of Cortez, this 800-mile-long peninsula is home to warm-hearted people and a deluge of diversions. Curious travelers may encounter palm-fringed canyons and ancient cave paintings, isolated shorelines and adobe mission remains, deserted islands and migrating whales. Rest and reflect at a luxury resort, taste your way through the wine country, or pump your adrenaline with extreme sports—the choices are plentiful. From the urban culinary adventures of its bustling cities to its remote canyons and pounding surf, Baja is full of discoveries.

BAJA OR BAJA CALIFORNIA?

How many Bajas *are* there, and which is the correct moniker for this desert peninsula? Baja California is the official name of the entire peninsula (see sidebar "How Baja California Got Its Name"). However, when the northern territory (above the 28th parallel), formerly known as Baja California Norte, was made a state in 1952 it was *also* officially named Baja California. In an effort to avoid confusion, many folks still say "Baja California Norte" or "Baja Norte" when referring to the northern state. The southern territory, known as Baja California Sur (South), wisely kept its original territorial name when it became a state in 1974.

Referring to the peninsula as simply "Baja" is a preference of travelers rather than natives, as the word "Baja," meaning "lower," also has an underlying translation of "inferior." The use of "Baja" in this text is used interchangeably with "Baja California" and "the peninsula," not discourteously, but we hope as acceptable terminology for all who have learned to cherish and respect this fascinating land and its inhabitants.

How to Get There

Planes, cruise ships, automobiles, buses—take your pick. With five airports hosting commercial flights, six border crossings for vehicles and pedestrians, two seaports welcoming major cruise lines as well as numerous ports and anchorages available to smaller cruise lines that frequent the Sea of Cortez, and a plethora of buses streaming from hubs along the border, travelers have many options available—it's a matter of how you wish to see the peninsula. Figure out your priorities, budget, and time frame and take to the skies, road, or sea. See the Access and Information section of each destination throughout this book for specifics. **REGULARLY UPDATED INFORMATION** with links to air, land, and sea carriers (without obtrusive advertising) is available on the web (www.bajaexpo.com; http://math.ucr.edu/~ftm/baja.html).

CROSSING THE BORDER SOUTHBOUND

There are six border crossings from the United States into Baja California, Mexico. From east to west, the border crossings are located at **LOS ALGODONES** (open 6am–10pm), **MEXICALI–CALEXICO EAST** (6am–10pm), **MEXICALI–CALEXICO WEST** (open 24 hours), **TECATE** (6am–midnight), **OTAY MESA** (6am–10pm), and **TIJUANA–SAN YSIDRO** (open 24 hours). Crossing the border heading south is usually hassle-free if you avoid weekday commuter traffic between 5–6pm. Tijuana is, by far, the largest border station, and is said to be the busiest border crossing on the planet.

Tourists are limited to the amount of goods they can bring into Mexico duty free. If driving, the total amount is $50 US; if arriving by vessel or airplane, $300 US. Large quantities of items for resale, used computers, and computer parts or monitors are not allowed into Mexico. New computers (unopened) are subject to import duties (as much as 40 percent), and laptops may or may not be subject to duty. Firearms and ammunition are not allowed without special permits. For more information regarding the latest in **CUSTOMS REGULATIONS** visit http://travel.state.gov/mexico.html.

United States citizens returning from Mexico may bring up to $400 of merchandise across the border duty free; Canadian citizens $300. Plants, fruits, animals, and Cuban cigars are prohibited, and a doctor's prescription must accompany any pharmaceutical purchases.

TOURIST CARDS AND PASSPORTS

Although officials still admit travelers with a certified birth certificate (must have a raised seal) and a photo ID, in 2000 notices were posted that in order to enter Mexico, visitors were required to have valid passports. The ruling has never been enforced, but travelers who frequent Mexico are encouraged to obtain passports as this ruling is subject to change.

If you plan to travel south of Ensenada or San Felipe, or if you plan to stay in the border area for longer than 72 hours, you'll need to pay a fee (185 pesos; approximately $20 US) and have your tourist card stamped. It is possible get your tourist card at the border and pay the required fee all in one stop, a process that can take as little as 10 minutes or as long as 30 minutes; see Access and Information in the Tijuana section in chapter 1, The Border and Northern Baja.

The duplicate form asks questions regarding your name, occupation, home address, passport number, destination, and desired length of stay in Mexico. (If you're not certain about the length of your stay, ask for the maximum allotted time of 180 days.)

Keep this document with your passport or certified birth certificate. If you're heading south across the Baja California Sur state line at Guerrero Negro, you'll be asked to show this document, and law enforcement officers may request to see it in the event of an accident.

CROSSING THE BORDER NORTHBOUND

Crossing the border heading south is usually quick and easy; returning north can be a different story, especially at the Tijuana–San Ysidro gate. Traffic there is heaviest from 6:30–8:30am and after 3pm on weekdays (Mondays and Fridays are the worst), while weekends and holidays can jam up from mid-morning until after 9pm. Wait time at this border crossing can run anywhere from 30 minutes to 3 hours. (Pedestrian wait time can also run 30–45 minutes on busy weekends.) The Otay border crossing stacks up on weekends as well, but if you can find this crossing (follow signs to "Otay Border Crossing" or "Garita de Otay" toward the airport), it's usually quicker than San Ysidro. Tecate, Mexicali, and Los Algodones wait times average 15–25 minutes. For a 24-hour, **AUTOMATED BORDER WAIT TIME REPORT** dial 619/690-8999 US (Tijuana–San Ysidro) or 619/671-8999 US (Otay). An excellent source of inside tips on crossing the border at Tijuana–San Ysidro and Otay is Paula McDonald's book *Crossing the Border Fast and Easy,* available online (meldman@primenet.com).

When to Visit

The best time to visit Baja depends on your intended activities, since many adventures are seasonal. **FISHING** and **SURFING** tend to be better in the summer and early fall (with the exception of winter swells on the Pacific), while visibility for **SCUBA DIVING** and **SNORKELING** clears remarkably in September and October. Keep in mind, however, that **HURRICANE SEASON** can begin as early as August and last through mid-November, when significant *chubascos* (rainstorms) can ruin many outdoor excursions in the Cape region. Wind junkies will find the best winds in the summer on the Pacific side, and in the winter on the Sea of Cortez side, while **KAYAKERS** and **SMALL-BOAT ANGLERS** will want to avoid these times. Wildlife watchers will find friendly **GRAY WHALES** and **MIGRATORY BIRDS** visiting December through March, while **MANGO MANIACS** will be in hog heaven July through September, when mangos drop from countless trees south of Santa Rosalía and throughout southern Baja. **SPRING BREAKERS** invade the popular beach towns (most notably Rosarito and San Felipe) from mid-March to mid-April, so make your plans overlap or avoid that time, depending on your taste for the raucous. And for the budget-focused, prices decrease from 25 to 35 percent at many hotels and resorts during the **LOW SEASON**, which begins the day after Easter and lasts through mid-October.

WEATHER

In general terms, Baja basks in sunshine most of the year. The climate in the north is very similar to that of Southern California: mild winters with occasional rains, and warm, dry summers. Winter highs average 53°F across the board, while summers range from the 70s in Ensenada (west coast) to the 90s

HOW BAJA CALIFORNIA GOT ITS NAME

A romantic legend tells of a magical island inhabited by a tribe of black Amazons led by a queen named Califia. According to historian Fernando Jordán in his book *El Otro Mexico* (1951), the legends spoke of a band of brave, strong women who kept no men among them but tamed a herd of fiery flying griffins, which they rode like horses. The women and their beasts were adorned with gold because on the island, there was no other metal. Armed with bows and arrows, the women were only occasionally visited by men. To discover this island called California became the dream of many Spanish explorers, who gained funds for future expeditions by promising the Spanish throne a treasure of women as well as gold.

The land that Cortez discovered was given the name "California" in 1535. The name California has endured, despite several changes over the years. Originally, "California" referred only to the peninsula that is now Baja California. Then in 1768, the area to the north that now comprises the U.S. state of California was given the name Nueva (new) California and the peninsula below it renamed Antigua (old) California. By 1800, the two areas were renamed Baja (lower) and Alta (upper) California. Following the Mexican-American War in 1848, the United States took possession of Alta California, naming it simply California once again, and Mexico's peninsula retained the name Baja California. In 1888 the peninsula was divided into two territories, Baja California Norte (north) and Baja California Sur (south). By 1974, both territories had been named states of the Republic of Mexico. (See "Baja or Baja California?" earlier in this chapter.)

And, while a few pockets of gold were discovered in Baja California, the legendary Amazons were never to be found.

—*Carrie Robertson*

in Mexicali (northeast). Southern Baja has hot, humid summers and dry winters. The rainy season is July through October, when occasional hurricanes pound the Cape region.

Average Baja Temperatures and Annual Rainfall

	yearly rainfall	January high low	May high low	September high low
TIJUANA	10 INCHES	65 46	71 57	77 63
LORETO	5.5 INCHES	68 52	80 64	90 81
CABO SAN LUCAS	7.7 INCHES	71 60	82 66	93 79

TIME AND MEASUREMENTS

Baja California (the northern state) is on Pacific Standard Time, while Baja California Sur (the southern state) is on Mountain Standard Time. Be sure to set your clock appropriately when crossing the state line (forward one hour heading south; back one hour heading north). Both states observe daylight savings time.

Like the rest of Mexico, Baja uses the metric system. Gasoline is sold by the liter and road signs announce distances and speed limits in kilometers. Kilometer markers (km) are used as reference points for many addresses, surf spots, and secondary roads within this book as well as on brochures and business cards. Rental car odometers are also set to measure kilometers.

Throughout Baja, weights, measurements, and temperatures are given in kilograms, meters, and centigrade, respectively. However, in this book measurements are given in U.S. units, such as yards, miles, and Fahrenheit.

What to Bring

Bring your kids! The Mexican people are very family-oriented, and they love children. Look for the 👫 icon throughout this text, referring to kid-friendly establishments.

A good English-Spanish/Spanish-English dictionary is a wise investment unless you're fluent in Spanish, and a good map (AAA carries one) will come in handy if you're driving any distance.

Your **FIRST-AID KIT** should include an antiseptic cleanser such as betadine, bandages, Band-Aids, ibuprofen and/or other painkillers, antihistamine tablets, tweezers, calamine lotion, antibiotic ointment, Pepto-Bismol, an anti-diarrhea treatment such as Imodium, rehydration solution, and hydrocortisone cream. Consult your doctor about including a course of oral antibiotics—be sure to bring copies of the prescriptions. It's also important to bring any medications and your physician's phone number in case of a medical emergency. Many Baja travelers like to go a step further, purchasing an air-ambulance membership service such as **SKYMED** (800/475-9633; www.skymed.com) for life-threatening emergency evacuations. If you plan to go to sea, Bonine (meclizine hydrochloride) prevents motion sickness without causing drowsiness. Don't forget the sunscreen, sunglasses, lip balm, and beach sandals, and it's wise, depending on what you plan to do in Baja, to bring along a flashlight (in case of power outages), bug repellant, and water purification tablets.

Most of Baja is very casual and beach attire is acceptable around the waterfront. However, it is advisable to dress modestly away from the beach, especially while visiting churches, missions, or government buildings. Many of the upscale restaurants don't allow t-shirts and shorts at dinner, and formal resort attire is requested.

General Costs

Although inflation in Mexico is high (close to 20 percent annually) and costs continue to rise, there are still some bargains to be found in Baja. As a rule of thumb, the larger tourist areas are more expensive, with the Cape outpricing many destinations within the United States. However, even in the Cape region, it is still possible to enjoy a low-budget trip by camping and preparing your own food or dining at the plethora of inexpensive eateries. More remote areas may charge more for products, although services tend to cost less. Gasoline costs about 5.5 pesos per liter (roughly $2.30 per gallon), fish tacos run 80–90 cents US each, an ice-cold beer averages $2 US, rental cars range from $60 to $90 US per day, lodging averages $52 US per night (with the exception of the luxury hotels), and campgrounds cost around $8–$10 US per night.

The peso has remained quite stable over the past few years, averaging about 9 pesos to the U.S. dollar. Check the current exchange rate online (www.oanda.com/converter/travel).

TAX AND TIPPING

The Mexican government tax (I.V.A.) is 10 percent with an additional hotel tax of 2 percent. Many hotels and resorts (most notably in Los Cabos) automatically add an additional "service tax" or service charge ranging from 10 to 18 percent of your total charges. When added to the I.V.A., additional charges can rise to a whopping 30 percent! Take this extra cost into consideration when making your arrangements.

Tipping has become expected in Baja, with 5–10 percent acceptable, 15 percent in tourist regions. It's common practice to tip waiters and waitresses, porters, and tour guides, as well as skippers and deckhands on fishing charters.

PESOS AND DOLLARS

The peso is Mexico's official currency. The small, thin silver coins are *centavos* (100 centavos equal one peso), which you may never see, since most businesses don't give them for change. Peso coins are larger and bicolored; they come in denominations of 1, 2, 5, 10, and 20 pesos. Peso paper notes come in denominations of 10, 20, 50, 100, 200, and 500. Remember that many small establishments often can't give change for larger bills.

U.S. dollars are widely used in the tourist zones, but it's more economical and easier to deal in pesos. Traveler's checks are accepted in some places, but not all; don't expect small or remote establishments to honor them, and exchange rates are not as favorable as for cash. It is wise to diversify your financial resources by using a combination of U.S. dollars, credit cards, ATM withdrawals, and traveler's checks. Prices listed throughout this book are in U.S. dollars.

BANDIDO ATMS

ATMS (signed *"cajas permanentes"*) have become increasingly common in Baja, especially in the larger cities along Mexico 1. Most machines accept cards coded with Visa, Mastercard, Cirrus, or Plus symbols. The advantage of using ATMs is that you'll get the best exchange rate (the "bank rate") without having to stand in line at the bank. Mexican banks charge a small fee for using their ATMs, and your bank may or may not charge an additional fee for this service. Be sure to inquire at your financial institution before you travel.

Some travelers use ATMs exclusively, and have never experienced a problem with this system of obtaining pesos. However, other travelers have been terribly inconvenienced by malfunctioning ATMs. Be prepared for any of the following scenarios: (1) The machine is out of pesos. This is common. (2) You hear the machine shuffle your bills, the display reads "Muchas Gracias," and a message tells you to take your pesos, but none are actually dispensed. (3) The machine keeps your card.

There are also reports of worn peso bills getting stuck in the dispenser. As the anxious patron used his or her key to free them, the bills shot out as if under pressure. A slight breeze from the cracked door then caused the money to blow around and up in the air—resembling a game show money-booth.

NOTE: It's wisest to use the ATM machines located at banks, and only during business hours. That way, if things go wrong, you have access to your card and someone who can assist you. It is also helpful to know the language or have an English-Spanish dictionary with you. Bancomer, Banamex, Bancreer, Bital, and Banca Serfín are the most common Mexican banks.

—*Lori Makabe*

EXCHANGING DOLLARS

Banks give the best rates of exchange, but they have limited hours (usually 9:30am–1pm) and long lines. *Casas de cambio* (houses of exchange), often signed "Money $exchange," are plentiful within the border areas and other tourist regions. They charge a slightly higher rate than banks do (even if they say "no commission"), but they have more convenient hours and usually no lines. Regardless of where you exchange money, always count your currency before you leave the window; errors cannot be corrected once you leave.

Some travelers prefer to exchange money before they travel. This service is offered at many U.S. banks for a fee, and advance notice is required. Thomas Cook and American Express offices also offer foreign exchange services; some are conveniently located at major U.S. airports.

CREDIT CARDS

Tarjetas de crédito (credit cards) are widely accepted at most of the larger establishments throughout Baja. The most commonly accepted cards are Visa, Mastercard, and American Express, though some establishments also take Discover. It is also possible to get cash advances at many banks using your credit card, which is helpful in case of an emergency.

NOTE: It is common policy for many establishments to charge an additional 5–6 percent when you pay with a credit card. Always ask before purchasing to avoid ticket shock.

Communications

DECIPHERING TELEPHONE NUMBERS

The telephone numbers of the establishments and services listed in this book are Mexican phone numbers unless followed by the letters "US." Many hotels have Mexican as well as U.S. numbers.

In November 2001, Mexico's telephone company, TelMex, changed the area codes throughout Mexico. Although this seemed confusing at first, what actually happened is that the one-digit area codes and five-digit numbers were changed to three-digit area codes and seven-digit numbers, making Mexican telephone numbers read like those used in the United States. The change does not, however, make phone numbers easier for U.S. citizens to interpret, because they are now written in such a variety of ways that it's very difficult to find a rhythm. You might see any combination of spaces, dashes, or groupings of numbers.

Here are some examples of how you might see the same phone number displayed: 456-78-90 or 45-6-78-90. Many still list the old, single-digit area codes: (3)456-78-90. And even with the new area codes, the numbers are listed a variety of ways: (123)45-6-78-90, (123)45-67890, or (123)4567890.

HOW TO DIAL

For local calls, dial the last seven digits of the number, regardless of how it's punctuated; in the preceding example, that would be 456-7890. For long-distance calls within the same area code, dial 01 and then the seven-digit number; in the preceding example this would be 01 456-7890. For long-distance calls to a destination with a different area code, dial 01, then the area code, and then the seven-digit number. Again, the example used above would look like this: 01 123/456-7890.

For **CALLS TO MEXICO FROM THE UNITED STATES**, you must dial 011 and the country code, 52, first. Dial 011, then 52, then the area code, and finally the seven-digit number; the example given above looks like this: 011 52 123/456-7890. To **CALL THE UNITED STATES FROM MEXICO**, dial 00, then 1, then the area code, and finally the seven-digit number; the example from above would look like this: 001 123/456-7890.

Within this book, we have omitted the 011 and the 52, listing only the new Mexican area codes and numbers. TelMex's web site offers a listing of the new **AREA CODES** in Baja and throughout Mexico (www.telmex.com/internos/nuevas claves/index.html).

To make a toll-free call within Mexico, dial 01, and then the 800 number. To dial a U.S. toll-free number, you must first dial 001, and then the 800 number. Many U.S. numbers with 877 prefixes will not work in Mexico and U.S. 888 numbers are *not* toll free from Mexico.

WHERE TO DIAL FROM

Sprinkled throughout most of the towns and cities in Baja, there are telephone offices, or *casetas de teléfono* displaying signs advertising **"LARGA DISTANCIA"** (long-distance) calling services. Within these establishments it's possible to pay a fee and use the telephone or fax machine.

TARJETAS DE TELÉFONO (phone cards) issued by LadaTel may be purchased at many local businesses. The cards, issued in 35- to 100-peso denominations, can be used in the brightly colored LadaTel telephones, which are placed around most towns. Local calls cost about 1 peso for three minutes, long-distance calls within Mexico run from 2–5 pesos a minute, and calls to the United States cost about 10 pesos a minute. Stay away from telephones with the message "Call USA With Your Credit Card Here," because this company has been known to charge exorbitant connection fees ($25 US) on top of high per-minute charges. Larger U.S. companies such as Sprint, MCI, and AT&T have the best rates, ranging from 23–50 cents US per minute if you use their prepaid, rechargeable phone cards, which will work with almost any phone that has a dial tone.

TO CELL OR NOT TO CELL

Cellular phones (analog or digital) can be activated for use throughout Baja using prepaid service plans. **TELCEL** (800/483-5235 US) and **MOVISTAR** (Baja-cellular, Norcel, and Movicel) are the most popular providers; however, it's difficult to recommend one company over the other because rates and user rules are continually changing. Quality and clarity of cellular calls are not the greatest nor is cellular service dependable. If you don't use your phone within a certain number of days, or if you don't use your prepaid minutes by a predetermined date (which is not always clearly stated in your contract), your account is closed and your credit forfeited. Always read the fine print to understand the details of your agreement before signing on. It's also possible to use your U.S.-based cell phone service in Baja, since some U.S. companies have contracts with Mexican cellular companies. Expect to pay about $1.50 US per minute. Call your cellular provider for current rates and policies.

EMAIL

Internet cafes have become quite common throughout the peninsula, and this is by far the most economical way to keep in touch. Rates range from $2 to $15 US an hour, so shop around. See the Access and Information and/or Exploring sections for each destination for a listing of Internet cafes within that area. The following web sites are helpful to both novice and longtime visitors:

WWW.BAJAEXPO.COM The most complete source of information for travel to Baja.

WWW.BAJALIFE.COM Info on fishing, diving, watersports, golf, romance, and eco-adventure tours.

WWW.BAJANET.COM Fishing reports, discussion rooms, current news, weather reports.

WWW.BAJANOMAD.COM General information, including insurance and phone rates, travel discounts, and a newsletter.

WWW.PEOPLESGUIDE.COM Accommodations, adventures, health and safety information, food, and more.

WWW.PLANETA.COM Ecotourism, online forums, scholarly reports, and education resources.

Driving Tips

Driving in Baja is very different from driving in the United States. The Carretera Transpeninsular Highway (referred to as Mexico 1 throughout the text) and the other highways are narrow (19–22 feet wide) and frequented by livestock. *Glorietas* (traffic circles, aka rotaries or roundabouts) at major intersections circulate traffic through major cities. Road signs are written in Spanish, with distances given in kilometers.

Before crossing the border, make sure your vehicle has been thoroughly inspected. Tires, brakes, belts, hoses, battery, and shocks should all be checked. Carry a useable spare tire and jack as well as spare belts, oil, cables, and tools.

When driving in Baja, always make sure to have the following items in your possession: current registration and driver's license (make sure these two documents are issued to the same person under the same name), proof of your Mexican auto insurance policy (see below), tourist card and passport, and working seat belts.

Baja Road Rules

I. GET A MEXICAN AUTO INSURANCE POLICY! Mexican authorities will not acknowledge your American auto insurance; you must purchase a separate Mexican auto insurance policy. Mexican law does not require coverage; however, Mexico's responsibility laws require the party at fault to cover all damages or injuries. If found at fault, you will need cash or Mexican liability coverage.

11

DON'T BE SHY

The people of Baja are kind, warm-hearted, patient, and polite. They are also very social, and they love to greet and be greeted. Whether or not you know the language, make an attempt to communicate with them and smile—they'll respect your efforts. A good English-Spanish/Spanish-English dictionary is recommended, and a refresher course in Spanish is also a good idea. Remember that pronunciation is much simpler than in English: (1) Each vowel is sounded, and always with the same sound: *a* sounds like the *a* in father; *e* sounds like the *e* in pen; *i* sounds like a long *e* as in peek; *o* sounds like *oh;* and *u* sounds like *ooh.* (2) A few consonants differ from English: *h* is silent; *j* sounds like an *h; ll* sounds like *y;* ñ sounds like *nyeh; qu* sounds like *k; rr* is a rolled *r; z* sounds like *s.* (3) Accent the second-to-last syllable on words ending in *n, s,* or a vowel. Otherwise, accent the last syllable or the one with an indicated accent mark. Here are some Spanish words and phrases to get you started:

GREETINGS

hello—*hola*
good morning—*buenos días*
good afternoon—*buenas tardes*
good evening; good night—*buenas noches*
good-bye—*adiós*
please—*por favor*
thank you very much—*muchas gracias*
you're welcome—*de nada* (it's nothing)
nice to meet you—*mucho gusto*
and you too—*igualamente*
very fine—*muy bien*

TO WHOM ARE YOU REFERRING?

I—*Yo*
you (formal)—*usted*
you (familiar)—*tú*
he—*él*
she—*ella*
we—*nosotros*
you (plural)—*ustedes*
they/them—*ellos* (only if they are *all* female—*ellas*)
Mr./sir—*señor*
Mrs./madam—*señora*
Miss/young lady—*señorita*

COMMON WORDS

yes—*sí*
no—*no*
good—*bueno*
not good—*no bueno*
bad—*malo*
more—*más*
less—*menos*
much; a lot—*mucho*
not much—*no mucho*
now—*ahora*
right now—*ahorita*
soon—*pronto*
a little—*un poco*
and—*y*
with—*con*
without—*sin*
here—*aquí*
there—*allí*
expensive—*caro*
cheap—*barato*
it's fine—*está bien*
so-so—*así así*
I'm sorry—*lo siento*
pardon me—*perdóneme*

I don't understand—*no comprendo; no entiendo*

I need—*necesito*

I would like—*quisiera*

the check, please—*la cuenta, por favor*

not today—*mañana*

QUESTIONS

How are you?—*¿Como está?*

What is your name?—*¿Come se llama?*

Where is (. . .)?—*¿Donde está (. . .)?*

Where is the bathroom?—*¿Donde está el baño?*

When?—*¿Cuándo?*

At what time?—*¿A qué hora?*

How much does it cost?—*¿Cuánto cuésta?*

What is this?—*¿Qué es eso?*

How do you say (. . .) in Spanish?—*¿Como se dice (. . .) en Español?*

Do you speak English?—*¿Habla Inglés?*

ON THE ROAD

bus station—*estación del autobús*

highway—*la carretera*

street—*la calle*

to the right—*a la derecha*

to the left—*a la izquierda*

straight ahead—*al derecho*

fill it up, please—*llénelo, por favor*

How many kilometers?—*¿Cuánto kilómetros?*

I need a good mechanic—*necesito un mecánico bueno*

tire repair shop—*llantera*

welder—*taller de soldadura*

tow—*remolque*

key—*llave*

—*Wayne Makabe*

Without either of these, you will be detained. Full coverage and liability insurance are available by the day, week, or month, easily purchased from home or at the border. Check into annual policies, which are usually less expensive than most two-week daily rates, and are especially wise if you plan to make multiple trips to Mexico. **REPUTABLE COMPANIES** include Instant Mexico Insurance Services (223 Via de San Ysidro, San Ysidro, CA 92173; 800/345-4701; fax 619/690-6533; www.instantmexautoinsur.com), located right at the border; International Gateway Insurance Brokers (3450 Bonita Rd, Ste 103, Chula Vista, CA 92013; 619/422-3028 or 800/423-2646; fax 619/422-2671; www.igib.com); and Lewis and Lewis (8929 Wilshire Blvd, Ste 220, Beverly Hills, CA 90211; 310/657-1112 or 800/966-6830; fax 310/652-5849; cbrettnow@cs.com; www.mexicanautoinsurance.com).

Better rates are sometimes available by joining one of the **BAJA TRAVEL CLUBS**, offering group tours, travel discounts, current road conditions, and general information. Try the Vagabundos del Mar (190 Main St, Rio Vista, CA 94571; 707/374-5511 or 800/474-BAJA; fax 707/374-6843; vags@compuserve.com; www.vagabundos.com), Baja's oldest nonprofit travel club, or the Discover Baja Travel Club (3089 Clairemont Dr, San Diego, CA 92117; 619/275-4225 or 800/727-BAJA; info@discoverbaja.com; www.discoverbaja.com).

WARNING: Drivers found under the influence of drugs or alcohol lose all insurance coverage.

2. SLOW DOWN AND PAY ATTENTION! This is the golden rule of driving in Baja. With the exception of the four-lane toll roads near the border and the Corridor in the Cape region, Baja's highways are narrow, two-lane, raised roadways with **NO SHOULDER**—*none*. Drift across that white line on your right (when there is one), and you'll probably encounter a crumbly edge and a steep little slope, perfectly designed to roll your vehicle. And if you must tow a camper or a trailer, make sure that what you are towing is not wider than your vehicle. One wheel tracking off the raised Baja highway can put a quick end to your well-planned adventure. Those extra inches in width could also make a difference when you suddenly encounter a semi or other vehicle approaching on your side of the center line.

Do not attempt to drive at the speeds you are used to in the United States. The speed limit on the open road is posted as 80 kph (48 mph) and it's seldom observed. You'll most likely encounter drivers who follow the "9 or 90 rule"— they either creep along at a frustrating 9 mph, or they bear down on you doing 90 mph. Be prepared for anything. Keep both hands on the steering wheel and watch the road at all times.

Heed the **CURVA PELIGROSA** (dangerous curve) signs that are often accompanied by yellow and black arrows. On many of these unbanked and sometimes "reverse banked" curves, you'll notice clusters of little shrines and crosses erected as memorials to loved ones who have perished there in accidents. They also serve as strong reminders for those among the living to slow down.

Baja's interior is **OPEN RANGE**, meaning there are few fences to contain livestock. Cattle, burros, horses, and goats are free to roam and feed on wild desert plants. Where fences *are* present, they seem to keep the livestock *closer* to the highway rather away from it. Since weeds are thickest along the edges of the crowned highways (especially after heavy rains), animals often feed inches from your bumper and seem totally unaffected by passing traffic. However, always slow down when approaching livestock, as they are unpredictable and may spook into your path—especially the young ones that are not yet streetwise.

Also be aware of any oncoming cars or trucks with flashing headlights or emergency flashers, or if the driver is in some way trying to signal you. This usually means there are livestock in the road ahead, or that you're approaching an accident or other road hazard. Slow down, be cautious, and then return the favor by warning others.

After heavy rains, dips in the road (*vados*) may be filled with sand or raging floodwater. Occasionally the roadway is completely washed away. Some *vados* can be bad enough to tear out your oil pan, so heed the signs (*vado peligroso*) and approach slowly. Never attempt to be the first to cross a *vado* that resembles a river. Many vehicles making such attempts have been swept away. Observe the water level on other similarly sized vehicles first.

Mexican highways have turnouts, but don't count on one being there when you need it most. Curves are sharper and unbanked, hills are steeper, and drop-offs are downright unnerving—most of them also bearing clusters of crosses as well as scattered debris from cargo trucks and other vehicles.

3. DON'T DRIVE AT NIGHT! Because of the open range, cattle, burros, horses, and goats are often drawn to the warmth of the heat-absorbing asphalt at night, when desert temperatures drop. Remote highways have no streetlights, raised reflectors, or lines of reflective paint to assist your eyes. Given these conditions, and the fact that your windshield is always dusty in Baja, you simply cannot see that cow (especially a black cow) standing near the center line chewing its cud! Add the headlights of an oncoming vehicle to the equation, and you've lost your best chance of missing ol' Bessie. And if you kill a cow, you could be held responsible for its replacement value.

Besides the danger of livestock in the road, commercial vehicles rule the highways at night. Trucks and buses often drive in the middle of the road as a precaution, avoiding the shoulderless edges. They speed on the open roadways, sneak up behind you quickly, and attempt to overtake you without missing a beat. Sharing the highway with these high-speed kamikazes is especially dangerous after dark. Realize also that many drivers have nonfunctional taillights and headlights, and are more likely to be drunk after dark. If you must drive at night, drive slowly and don't go far. Snuggle in behind another vehicle. The less time you spend on a dark highway, the better your chances of avoiding an accident.

4. OBEY TRAFFIC SIGNS AND SIGNALS, EVEN IF THE LOCALS DO NOT! Gringos who fail to follow traffic signage or signals are prime targets for the local *policía,* resulting in fines and inconveniences. Road signs are different and may or may not be present in the cities. This can be problematic when it comes to one-way streets. Before turning onto any city street, always look to see which way traffic is flowing or parked vehicles are facing. Do not assume that since there is no sign, it must be a two-way street.

STOPLIGHTS are also different. They are smaller, much harder to see, and follow a slightly different routine. Before turning yellow, the green light flashes three to six times. The yellow light is very brief, followed by red. Where there are dedicated left turn lanes, the green arrows flash four to six times and then the light quickly changes to red, with oncoming traffic rushing toward you like angry bulls charging a matador.

Also challenging your driving patience are the **STOP SIGNS** and **INTERSEC-TIONS.** Mexican stop signs say *alto.* While some stop signs are similar in size to those in the United States, others are small and obscure. Trees or branches may hide them completely. Sometimes stop signs appear on only the right side of the right lane, no matter how many lanes there are. Four-way intersections are also very different from those in the United States. Most peculiar are the locals interpretations of a four-way intersection. It seems the signs are merely placed as a suggestion. Mexican drivers rarely stop at four-way intersections. In fact, they are watching to see whether or not *you* are going to stop. There must be an unwritten rule that reads, "As long as one driver stops at a four-way stop sign, the rest of the drivers there are exempt." Proceed with caution in the cities and always drive defensively.

5. UNDERSTAND USAGE OF THE LEFT TURN SIGNAL! Sooner or later while driving the open road, you'll encounter a driver in front of you using his/her left turn signal to tell you it's safe to pass. This practice is widespread outside of the cities, and is much more common than using the left turn signal to actually indicate a left turn. If a driver truly is turning left, he/she will usually signal with a hand out the window. If you're trusting enough to pass, it's a wise practice to attempt eye contact with the driver, via his/her side mirror; then pass with caution. And don't be surprised to see caravans of motor homes from Canada and the United States using this same technique. You may even find yourself signaling this way when that fully loaded semi is breathing down your neck. Just make sure that you get out of the habit as soon as you're back in the United States.

ÁNGELES VERDES—GREEN ANGELS

Founded in 1960 by the Mexican government, the Green Angels are part of a program designed to aid tourists in need of emergency roadside assistance. Capable mechanics patrol Baja's highways in bright green trucks carrying limited auto parts, spare gasoline, cell phones, and first-aid supplies, and are capable of towing vehicles short distances if necessary.

CHECKPOINTS

The federal police, using military personnel, have set up checkpoints along the peninsula highways in compliance with the United States Drug Enforcement Agency. Some of the checkpoints are mobile; others are permanent. Young uniformed military personnel armed with automatic rifles will approach your vehicle and ask if you are carrying *drogas o armas* (drugs or weapons). They may ask to look inside your vehicle. Usually these young men are honest, but there are reports of those with sticky fingers. If possible, unlock just one door at a time. Always discreetly supervise the inspection, answering all questions politely. Keep valuables and cash well hidden. Usually you will be briefly searched or waived through without incident.

NOTE: It is illegal to enter Mexico with a firearm or even a single round of ammunition without authorization from Mexican officials.

PETRÓLES MEXICANOS—PEMEX STATIONS

Fuel is available at the government-regulated Pemex stations throughout Baja. Most Pemex stations are *not* self-service stations and an attendant will be there ready to pump your fuel. "Llénelo, por favor" (fill it up, please) is a phrase worth learning. Over the years, more stations have been added to keep up with demand, making it less likely (although still possible) to get stranded without fuel. **PRICES** are the same at all Pemex stations and cash is the only acceptable currency in most locations at press time. Use pesos instead of dollars to pay for your purchases, since you can simply read the pump and skip the lengthy calculations (there are usually long lines at Pemex stations), as well as avoid the temptations of dishonest employees. **MAGNA SIN** is the regular unleaded 87-octane gas and **PRIMA** is 92-octane premium. Diesel (*sin diesel*) is available at most of the larger stations; look for the red (*rojo*) pumps. You can calculate the number of gallons purchased by dividing the number of liters by 3.79.

RIP-OFFS at Pemex stations are common. Throughout this book, we've listed stations with the worst reputation for dishonesty, and we suggest avoiding these places if at all possible. Common tricks include but are not limited to the following: (1) The attendant quickly begins fueling without resetting the pump before you have a chance to get out of your vehicle. You can avoid this problem by having a locking gas cap. (2) The attendant manages to manipulate the pump to read higher while you're not looking. (3) The attendant shortchanges you. (4) The pumps are miscalibrated, allowing your spare 5-gallon tank to mysteriously hold 6 gallons! The best thing to do is report any of these activities to the nearest Tourism Office in hopes that if enough complaints are filed, these behaviors will stop.

When driving long distances, it's smart to top off your tank when it reads three-quarters full. This will save you the headache of arriving at your next fueling stop only to find that an RV caravan just finished off the station's supply, which could leave you stranded for a few days. This is especially true around the Christmas and Easter holidays.

POLICÍA—POLICE

Although an attempt has been made to clean up corruption within the police delegations in Mexico, many officers still line their pockets by extorting money from tourists. Law enforcement officials see *la mordida* (little bite or bribe) as an easy way to supplement their low wages. The assumption is that most tourists don't want to take the time to drive to the police station to pay a traffic violation fine (usually minimal) and would rather pay on the spot.

The officer will ask for your driver's license (or, in some instances, your front license plate) and may inform you that he can save you the time and trouble of going to the station. He may quote a price (usually high) for your infraction (real or imagined). If you don't buy in, he may lower his initial "price" or ask you to name a sum you are willing to pay. Tourists are advised to surrender their license, get the officer's name and badge number and the number on the vehicle the officer is driving (note the date and time), and go to the police station to pay the fine. If you feel that you were wrongfully stopped, try to dispute your case at the station, and then file a complaint at the local Tourism Office. Although this action won't get you reimbursed, it may draw attention to the problem and help deter such behavior in the future.

Demystifying the Km Markers

If you don't understand the secrets behind the km markers along Mexico's Highway 1, you probably think they're there only to confuse you and that the road workers who set them up were playing a cruel joke. Actually, the markers make perfect sense and are a useful navigational tool once you understand how they work. Here are the two secrets that should help demystify the km conundrum:

SECRET #1: At each end of the peninsula (Cabo San Lucas in the south and Tijuana in the north), numbers on the km markers start at 0 and *increase as you travel toward the center of the peninsula—the state line between Baja California Norte and Baja California Sur.* Conversely, *as you travel away from the state line (center), the km marker numbers decrease.*

SECRET #2: Baja California (the northern state) is divided into four sections; Baja California Sur (the southern state) is divided into five sections. At strategic locations, the km markers reset to zero, and then increase from that point again as you approach the state line (center). See the Km Markers table for a visual reference regarding the km marker mystery.

Baja California (Northern State): Km numbers INCREASE as you approach the State Line

City	Km Markers	Miles
TIJUANA TO ENSENADA	**0 TO 109**	68
ENSENADA TO SAN QUINTÍN	**0 TO 196**	122
SAN QUINTÍN TO BAHÍA DE LOS ÁNGELES JUNCTION	**0 TO 280**	174
BAHÍA DE LOS ÁNGELES JUNCTION TO STATE LINE	**0 TO 123**	76

Baja California Sur (Southern State): Km numbers DECREASE as you travel away from the State Line

City	Km Markers	Miles
STATE LINE TO SANTA ROSALÍA	**221 TO 0**	137
SANTA ROSALÍA TO LORETO	**197 TO 0**	122
LORETO TO CIUDAD INSURGENTES	**119 TO 0**	74
CIUDAD INSURGENTES TO LA PAZ	**239 TO 0**	148
LA PAZ TO CABO SAN LUCAS	**221 TO 0**	137

On Mexico 2 (the east/west highway that parallels the U.S. border), kilometer markers begin in the state capital, Mexicali, and *increase* as you travel west, resetting to 0 just west of Tecate.

Tips for Special Travelers

FAMILIES WITH CHILDREN

Minors traveling with only one parent may be asked to show a notarized consent from the other parent stating permission to travel, or the traveling parent will need a declaration of sole custody.

👫 Watch for this icon throughout the book; it indicates places and activities that are great for families.

SENIORS

Seniors traveling to Baja should be in good physical condition. Don't overdo the food, sun, activity, or alcohol, and allow time to rest between excursions. Bring along a list of any medications (generic names) you are taking, as well as your doctor's phone and fax numbers.

PEOPLE WITH DISABILITIES

Although a few resort hotels in the larger cities have wheelchair access, Baja in general isn't really set up for disabled travelers. Cruise ships are usually accessible, but once in port, disabled travelers won't find the necessary assistance. City sidewalks may have brightly painted wheelchair ramps, but they're either too narrow or too steep for realistic, safe usage. Airline boarding and disembarking takes place by crossing the tarmac and climbing or descending stairs. When making lodging reservations, always talk to the property manager rather than the hotel's reservation service to confirm accessibility. An excellent source of **INFORMATION FOR DISABLED TRAVELERS** is www.access-able.com.

WOMEN

Women traveling solo are advised to follow the same precautions as in U.S. cities. Be alert to your surroundings, avoid walking alone at night, and stay out of seedy neighborhoods. Don't wear flashy jewelry, but do consider wearing a wedding band. Use a money belt and carry only one credit card, as well as copies of your passport or other travel documents. Women are often besieged with unsolicited attention from men. Avoid responding to comments, and on buses, seek women as seatmates. If you're sexually adventurous, remember that Mexico's *machismo* attitude carries over to the bedroom, where "real men" don't use condoms.

MINOR DETAILS

Evening entertainment possibilities abound in Baja, where the legal drinking age is 18—three years younger than that of bordering California and Arizona. Many party-hungry youngsters head south every weekend to indulge. The legal age to purchase cigarettes and other tobacco products is also 18, although this ruling is rarely enforced.

—*Lori Makabe*

PET OWNERS

To bring your dog or cat into Baja, you'll need a recent health certificate (obtained within 72 hours of your crossing) and vaccination papers. Be aware of aggressive-looking stray dogs and take precautions to protect your own dogs from attack.

NOTE: Strychnine-laced meat is still the most widely accepted method used to control dog populations in many rural areas. Do not let your dog eat anything you haven't fed it. Puffer fish, an apparent delicacy in the canine world, are found along many beaches, and are also poisonous if eaten (dead or alive).

GAYS AND LESBIANS

Machismo is an important part of Mexico's culture, and although a majority of the country's population publicly rejects homosexuality, Mexico ranks as the third most popular destination among gay and lesbian travelers. Attitudes toward homosexuals are a mixed bag. While the number of gay bars in the cities increases, so does the number of hate crimes. And while such hate crime numbers are low in Baja, those who openly display their homosexuality will most likely be harassed. For more information, visit www.gaymexico.net.

Safety Tips

For medical emergencies, most of the towns and cities have hospitals and/or medical clinics that serve the local population. Some are signed from Mexico 1 (look for the cross). Cruz Roja (Red Cross) clinics are also located throughout the peninsula. In the event of a life-threatening situation, AIR AMBULANCE AMERICA (800/222-3564 US or toll free from Mexico dial 01 800/222-3564; www.airambulance.com), based in Los Angeles, has been in business for 30 years and provides emergency evacuation services throughout Baja.

State governments and medical communities are working to improve Baja's emergency response system (similar to our 911 number) for police and medical emergencies. Currently the major cities within the state of Baja California use 066. La Paz, San José del Cabo, and Cabo San Lucas in Baja California Sur respond to 060. These numbers are supposedly available 24 hours a day. Response times may differ from those in the US and there is no guarantee that the dispatcher speaks or understands English.

Safety standards in Mexico are not on par with those in the United States; stay alert to hazardous situations whenever possible.

ELECTRICAL WIRING

It is not uncommon to see exposed electrical wiring in places easily touched by passersby. In April 2002, a young boy was electrocuted when he dove into the swimming pool at luxury hotel in San José del Cabo. The accident was blamed on a faulty light fixture near the side of the pool. Be alert to potentially hazardous electrical wiring.

RIPTIDES

Many areas of Baja are known for dangerous riptides. As waves hit the shoreline, the water has to return to sea. This returning water is always channeled through the course of least resistance. The shape of the shoreline, the ocean floor, and the angle of the waves sometimes cause these back currents or riptides, which can easily carry a swimmer away from the beach. Even strong swimmers have drowned by tiring while trying to outswim riptides. Always ask someone who swims in the area about the safety of the beach in question and heed any warnings. If doubts exist, don't take the risk.

SIDEWALK TRAVEL

Even the not so adventurous traveler will find adventure just in walking the treacherous Baja sidewalks. Riddled with rebar, steep drop-offs, uneven steps, buckled surfaces, telephone poles, support cables, and broken drainpipes, these walkways require sturdy shoes and careful navigation to avoid serious injury. Pay attention and watch where you step at all times.

VIOLENT CRIME AND PETTY THEFT

You are far more likely to experience self-inflicted injury or death while adventuring in Baja than you are to fall victim to violent crime. It is, however, wise to remain alert at all times. Criminals often prey on drunken tourists. Leave your irreplaceable items at home, avoid wearing expensive jewelry, make use of hotel safes, and do not leave valuables on the beach while swimming. Camp in designated areas, with others, or close to establishments. Keep your fishing gear, bicycles, and other valuables locked and/or hidden.

TOILET TERRORS

Use the rest rooms at your hotel, campground, or restaurant instead of searching for an acceptable public rest room. Getting straight to the point, public rest rooms in Baja range from nonexistent to terribly horrific, while some stand up to U.S. standards—it just depends on where you are. Some of the newer Pemex gas stations along Mexico 1 have clean, well-maintained rest rooms, while others may well leave you in a bind. There may or may not be toilet seats or functioning toilets. And the floor will most likely be wet, with a mound of used toilet paper in the corner of each unit. Don't expect to find running water or soap, and realize that the stall doors probably won't close all the way without hitting your knees. Always be prepared with your own supply of paper and, if you feel the need, hand sanitizing gel. If you're used to thin tissue seat protectors, bring them—but don't flush them. Most Mexican septic systems cannot handle toilet paper or any paper products, and you'll usually see a note requesting that you deposit paper and feminine products in the nearby overflowing wastebasket.

NOTE: Rest rooms are referred to as *baños* or *sanitarios*. The men's rest rooms are usually labeled *hombres* or *caballeros,* while the women's rest rooms are labeled *damas.*

THE WHOLE ENCHILADA

Please don't eat at Burger King or McDonald's when you're in Mexico; you'll miss half the reason for being there! If you're really wary, take a swig of Pepto-Bismol or another stomach-coating salve, and stick with cooked foods. And remember: Never drink water from the tap. Some of the most popular south-of-the-border treats include:

BURRITOS: Flour tortillas wrapped around a wide range of fillings, from refried beans and cheese to grilled meats with guacamole.

CARNE ASADA: Marinated and grilled strips of beef served in tacos and burritos or as part of a combo plate with beans, rice, guacamole, and tortillas.

CARNITAS: Marinated pork served as above.

CHILES RELLENOS: A large semi-spicy green chile stuffed with cheese, coated with batter, fried, and covered with sauce.

ENCHILADAS: Corn tortillas wrapped around cheese, chicken, or beef and baked in a semi-spicy sauce.

FLAN: This custard-like dish with a caramel flavor is quite possibly the most popular desert in Mexico. Some chefs prepare it with tropical fruits or fancy sauces.

GUACAMOLE: Some novices call it "that green stuff"; few retain their aversion. Mashed avocados are mixed with lime, onions, tomatoes, cilantro, and all matter of ingredients following family recipes. Usually served with corn chips or in a dollop with entrees.

HUEVOS RANCHEROS: Fried eggs on corn tortillas topped with a spicy, tomato-based sauce.

Food and Water

Baja offers an amazing selection of fruits, vegetables, seafood, meats, cheeses, salsas, breads, ice creams, and beverages. Eggs are farm-fresh; chicken, beef, and milk are hormone-free; and tomatoes are almost always ripe and juicy. Salsas are made fresh daily, while flavorful chiles are roasted, mashed into delectable sauces, or pickled. *Aguas frescas* (sugary sweet fruit drinks served from large, beehive-shaped containers and pictured on this book's cover) are a refreshing treat. In traditional eateries, entrees are accompanied by beans, rice, salsas, and steaming tortillas—made from either *harina* (wheat flour) or *maíz* (corn). Instead of sticking with menu items familiar from the United States, be adventurous and try some of the more authentic Mexican creations such as *pozole* (a thick chicken or pork soup flavored with rich red chiles or pumpkin seeds) or, reflecting the colors of the Mexican flag, *chiles en nogada* (chiles stuffed with meat, fruit, and spices smothered in a puréed walnut and cream sauce).

HUITLACOCHE: It's a black fungus grown on corn, but don't let that scare you. The taste is like an earthy mushroom, especially good in quesadillas and *crepas* (crepes). It's also rumored to be an aphrodisiac. Olé!

MOLE: This blend of spices used for sauces on chicken, pork, and enchiladas comes in several varieties. Black mole includes bitter chocolate and chiles; yellow mole is seasoned with pumpkin seeds. Mole is an acquired taste worth sampling.

PAN DULCE: Sweet breads sold in bakeries, or *panaderías*. Cookies, muffins, Danish pastries, and fruit breads all taste different in Mexico; in the bakeries, preservatives are shunned and lard and butter are the favored fats. Stop by a bakery, grab a metal platter and a pair of tongs, and stockpile your snacks for the day.

SOPA DE TORTILLA: Tortilla soup is wonderful when made properly. The best ones have a spicy chicken broth and are served with a platter of crumbled cheese, chopped avocado, cilantro, and crisp tortilla strips.

TACOS: Fried or soft corn tortillas stuffed with every imaginable ingredient. Baja specialties include fish tacos and tacos al pastor, made with thin slices of rotisserie pork served with pineapple.

TAMALES: Cornmeal paste stuffed with beef, pork, chicken, veggies, or fruit and then wrapped in corn husks and steamed.

TORTA: A sandwich made on a thick, crusty roll called a *bolillo*.

—*Maribeth Mellin*

BOTTLED IS BEST

Many locals drink Baja's tap water without incident, as most of the water comes from pure underground springs. However, broken water lines often introduce bacteria into the water systems. It's safer for travelers to buy bottled water for drinking, brushing your teeth, and even washing unpeeled fruits. Many hotels have water purification systems and provide drinking water daily in your room. Restaurants and juice bars are required by law to use purified water for drinks and ice. Bottled water is readily available in markets throughout the peninsula.

Annoying Plants and Critters on Land

Baja California is full of critters and thorny plants. Some are harmful, while others are just downright annoying. It's wise to carry a **FIRST-AID KIT** (see What to Bring) as well as an anaphylaxis kit if you are allergic to bee stings. Here's a list of the most bothersome critters with suggestions for their avoidance and treatment.

DOGS

Stray dogs are usually not a problem along the well-worn tourist routes, but within the local neighborhoods and smaller villages dog bites are not uncommon. Be aware of aggressive-looking dogs and take precautions to protect yourself (and your own dogs, if you've brought them along) from attack.

INTESTINAL BUGS

It's quite possible that you could come down with a case of *turista* (an unspecified intestinal bug) while visiting Baja. Prevention is the best medicine. Use bottled water for drinking and tooth brushing and don't overdo your first few days in the country. Choose your food wisely, looking for signs of unsanitary conditions. See Food and Water, above.

If you do find yourself afflicted, it's essential to stay hydrated and rest. Drink plenty of water and consider using rehydration solutions such as CeraLyte or Rehydralite. Symptoms may include nausea and fever. Avoid greasy, spicy foods; sugary drinks; alcohol; and milk products. Pepto-Bismol or similar products allow the body to slowly rid itself of the harmful organisms. Imodium or other anti-diarrheals are sometimes necessary if you're traveling. Symptoms should gradually decrease within three or four days; however, if they persist, seek medical attention.

MALA MUJER AND SPINY CACTI

Brush up against the nasty, thistle-like **MALA MUJER** (bad woman) plant and you'll forever remember what it looks like. Also known as *caribe* (savage), this gnarly looking plant has jagged, five-lobed leaves and stalks covered with spines and stinging hairs. The stiff spines can penetrate leather gloves. This plant is common up and down the peninsula, especially in the Cape region. Victims should use tweezers to remove any hairs, wash the area with cold water, and apply calamine lotion. Pain usually increases after the initial contact and may continue for several days. **CACTI** also pose a threat to hikers and mountain bikers. Take care not to brush against or sit on any cactus lobes, as their spines are a real pain. Mountain bikers will find it necessary to use tire liners such as Mr. Tuffy as well as a tire sealant such as Slime to avoid continuous flats.

MOSQUITOES AND NO-SEE-UMS

Bloodsucking mosquitoes and **NO-SEE-UMS** (better known in Baja as *jejenes* or *bo-bos*), are present year-round along the peninsula's coastline and inland watering holes. In the months following heavy rains and hurricanes, hiking in the backcountry requires a strong repellent, since standing water in the *arroyos* (small canyons) harbors mosquitoes. Even more annoying are the pesky no-see-ums, whose bites cause an intense itch and often leave welts that tend to fester and scar. These critters fly right through household screens and regular mosquito netting, often driving travelers away from infested areas. Mosquito repellent is not necessarily effective for no-see-ums, even those containing high amounts of

Deet (di-ethyl-toluamide). Some travelers report relief from rubbing exposed skin with lime juice (followed by a shake of salt and a shot of tequila, perhaps?) instead of repellent, while others swear by a few drops of pennyroyal oil (available at health food stores; not recommended for pregnant women) mixed in with repellent. One product worth trying is an insect "discourager" called Crocodile made from natural ingredients (603/357-5050; www.dancingroots.com), which many have found to be effective on no-see-ums as well as mosquitoes.

RATTLESNAKES

They say that the first person startles the rattler, and the second person is the one who gets bit—so offer to take the lead when hiking. To avoid being bit, stay alert; wear leather boots in the desert; and if you do spot a rattler, leave it alone. Always look before placing your hands and feet while rock climbing or hiking. If a bite does occur, here are some important things to remember: Seek medical attention as quickly as possible, but do not allow the victim to exert him/herself. Wrap (snugly but not tightly) and immobilize the affected limb, keeping it lower than the heart. Keep the victim calm, cool, and hydrated. Do not apply ice or a tourniquet, and do not attempt to "cut and suck" the wound. Do not allow the victim to drink alcohol. Identify the snake if possible.

ROOSTERS

You might have thought that roosters crow only at dawn. An overnight in Baja will teach you otherwise. Roosters crow whenever they feel like it—throughout the day, throughout the night. This is not a problem for those who can sleep right through the fowl concert, but it's terribly annoying to light sleepers or insomniacs, who hear every crow and can often distinguish between roosters by learning upon which syllable of the *cock-a-doodle-doo* the accent is placed. Earplugs are recommended for light sleepers in Baja, because if it's not roosters keeping you awake, it could very well be dogs, all-night fiestas, the crashing of the waves, or traffic.

SCORPIONS

More than 60 species of scorpions are found throughout Baja. Related to spiders, they are nocturnal, and can be found at night by using a black light, which makes them glow in the dark. Scorpions may sneak into your vacant bed, shoes, wet suit, or the folds of your towels. They can be under your tent, on the ceiling of your hotel room, or hidden within that piece of wood you carefully place on the campfire. And speaking of campfires, many stings occur either while gathering firewood or while enjoying the fire, as scorpions hastily retreat from the heat and climb right up your pants leg. Their stings (often multiple) are extremely painful, as neurotoxins are released into your system. Intense pain at the site as well as in the groin, swelling, tingling, fever, and nausea are all reactions to scorpion encounters. For treatment, keep the victim calm. Clean the site and apply a cold compress. Elevate the limb to heart level if possible. Painkillers and/or antihistamines should relieve pain. Although scorpion stings are rarely life threatening, babies and the elderly run higher risks of serious illness and even death if not treated. Bark scorpions, found in northern Baja, inflict the strongest venom, while in southern Baja, small "blondies" are usually more toxic than the larger California browns found in the region.

Sea Creatures

JELLYFISH
The Portuguese-man-of-war (bluebottle) is one of the more common jellyfish found in the waters around Baja. These invertebrates travel with the wind and currents and are often blown onshore. Beach walkers need to be on the lookout for the bubbles and bright blue tentacles, while swimmers should look on the surface for the clear bubblelike bladders. The attached tentacles carry venomous stinging cells (nematocysts), which are triggered by touch whether the creature is dead or alive. Immediate intense stinging occurs upon contact. Avoid touching the tentacles, even to remove them from the victim; use a stick or blunt object. Advised treatment is to rinse the area with seawater, and then remove tentacles as quickly as possible. Do *not* rinse with vinegar! Apply an ice pack and, if needed, hydrocortisone cream. In severe cases, breathing difficulties and allergic reactions may occur. Always seek medical attention if symptoms persist or worsen.

SEA URCHINS
One step onto a spiny little sea urchin can put a real damper on your vacation. Sea urchins are round, prickly invertebrates covered with purple or red spines. They are found in the water among the rocks on both coastlines of the peninsula. Sea urchin spines will penetrate even the toughest aqua booties. If you see evidence of urchins on the beach, there are most likely urchins in the water nearby. When in doubt, carefully snorkel the area in question. Puncture wounds from sea urchins can become infected. The brittle spines break apart, making their removal difficult and often requiring surgery. If you step on sea urchins, do not make the mistake of sitting down on or touching the nearby rocks. It's not uncommon for a victim to be inflicted with subsequent spines in the buttocks or hands as well as the feet. Treatment includes rinsing with fresh water, followed by immersion in hot water for 30–90 minutes (as hot as the victim can stand without being burned), followed by the prompt removal of any spines (if possible) using tweezers. Vinegar in the water helps neutralize the stinging. Scrub the wound(s) with soap and water and do not cover. Apply an antibiotic cream and take painkillers as needed. Seek medical attention if symptoms persist.

STINGRAYS

Hidden on the sandy bottom of those gorgeous, aquamarine coves are stingrays. In the summer and fall, they bury themselves just under the sand where it's nice and warm. Unsuspecting bathers can easily step on a stingray, causing the animal to strike with its barbed tail, inflicting a nasty wound coupled with an even nastier toxin, which is released through its spiny tail. The best way to avoid contact with a stingray is to do the "stingray shuffle"—shuffle your feet to give these critters some warning that you're on your way—scaring them off. If you are unfortunate enough to get nailed by a stingray, treatment includes rinsing with fresh water, followed by immersion in hot water for 30–90 minutes (as hot as the victim can stand without being burned). Next is the prompt removal of any tail pieces (if possible) using tweezers. Scrub the wound(s) with soap and water and do not cover. Apply an antibiotic cream and take painkillers as needed. Larger, more serious strikes may require stitches and/or surgery. Seek medical help if the victim shows signs of shock, or if symptoms persist.

LIBROS EXCELLENTES

Adventure Kayaking Baja, Andromeda Romano-Lax, 2001

Almost an Island, Bruce Berger, 1998

Antigua California, Harry W. Crosby, 1996

The Baja Adventure Book, Walt Peterson, 1998

Baja Camping, Fred and Gloria Jones, 2000

The Baja Catch, Neil Kelly and Gene Kira, 1997

Baja Fever, Greg Niemann, 1999

The Cave Paintings of Baja California, Harry W. Crosby, 1997

Eye of the Whale, Dick Russell, 2001

The Grinning Gargoyle Spills the Beans, J.P Smith, Jr., 2001

Into a Desert Place, Graham Mackintosh, 1988

A Dying Sea, Tom Knudson, 1995, in the *Sacramento Bee*
    (www.sacbee.com/news/projects/dyingsea/index95.html)

King of the Moon, Gene Kira, 1997

The Log from the Sea of Cortez, John Steinbeck, 1941

The Magnificent Peninsula, Jack Williams, 1998

Searching for Steinbeck's Sea of Cortez, Andromeda Romano-Lax, 2002

The Unforgettable Sea of Cortez: Baja California's Golden Age 1947–1977: The Life and Writings of Ray Cannon, Gene S. Kira, 2001

THE BORDER AND
NORTHERN BAJA

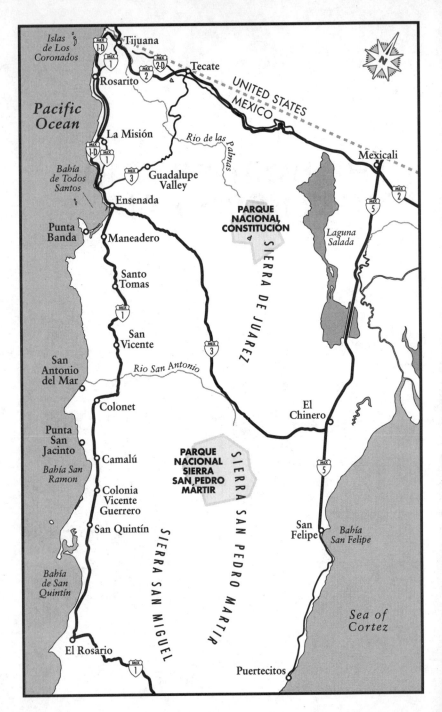

THE BORDER AND NORTHERN BAJA

The border is just the beginning of a fascinating journey into Mexico's Baja Peninsula. The 850-mile-long strip of ever-changing desert scenery, seemingly endless beaches, and rugged mountains is firmly anchored between the Pacific Ocean and the Sea of Cortez. This chapter covers the northern section of the state of Baja California (often referred to as Baja California Norte or Baja Norte), one of the fastest-growing regions in all of Mexico.

Development has spread south from Tijuana to the coastal community of Rosarito and on to the port city of Ensenada. Hundreds of U.S. citizens live in this portion of Mexico; hundreds more have vacation homes in private communities. Along the border, nearly 450 *maquiladoras* (manufacturing plants) employ well over a million workers. Vineyards thrive among the fertile valleys cooled by marine breezes and nourished by runoff from the highest mountains on the peninsula. Macadamia nuts, asparagus, olives, and baby vegetables are cultivated and sold to northern markets.

Farther east, the state capital, Mexicali, is a bustling business center rich with the diversity brought by savvy entrepreneurs from Mexico City, multinational investors, local farmers, and a Mexican-Chinese population that's been melting into the local scene for generations. College students, off-roaders, and beach bums migrate to San Felipe, south of Mexicali, for holiday weekends and spring breaks. Many North American retirees maintain second homes there as well.

Northern Baja is home to two national parks—both snuggled deep within the peninsula's tallest mountains—where granite peaks rise above ponderosa, lodgepole, and incense pines. Parque Nacional Constitución de 1857 harbors Baja's highest summit—Picacho del Diablo (Devil's Peak), soaring 10,154 feet—while astronomers study the night sky at Mexico's national observatory located inside Parque Nacional Sierra San Pedro Mártir.

The region's temperatures vary with the terrain. While the mountains and, to a lesser degree, the coast provide relief from oppressive desert temperatures in the summer, those same desert settings make desirable winter destinations. Yearly rainfall can be as much as 10 inches in Tijuana to almost nonexistent in the flat, scrubby deserts near San Felipe.

This is also the region where fried fish was first stuffed inside a steaming-hot tortilla, creating the fish taco, and violin-sized lobsters, sliced lengthwise, were cooked Puerto Nuevo–style (briefly dipped in bubbling oil, then grilled). The caesar salad was born in a climax of culinary desperation, and Tecate beer first cooled the throats of thirsty gringos in the '40s.

Area attractions are not exclusively land-based. The Pacific coast stacks up some of the best swells on the entire west coast of North America, and surfers dig in at their favorite breaks. Diving and sportfishing are just as popular here, as is whale watching: gray whales cruise these waters on their way to southern lagoons. For two-legged travelers, however, northern Baja is more than just a place to pass through. With so much to see, so much to do, and so much to consume, and all so close to the border, many people never feel the need to venture farther south.

The Northwest

Tijuana

The busiest border crossing in the world connects San Ysidro, California, and Tijuana, Baja California. Locals from both sides of the border cross frequently to visit family and friends, attend concerts and sporting events, shop for groceries and gifts, and dine in favorite restaurants.

Miles before you reach the Mexican border, signs on roadways and storefronts combine Spanish and English instructions and descriptions. Soon the spoken language slips into Spanglish, a combination of the two languages with its own special slang. The border itself assaults the senses with congested traffic, a significant police presence, and entirely foreign sights and smells. The aromas of meat, onions, and chiles sizzling on grills at taco stands immediately set your stomach growling. Shops and souvenir arcades get your fingers twitching. And your eyes are constantly challenged by fascinating distractions.

With Tijuana's proximity to Southern California, it's not surprising to find a similar climate—occasional morning fog, and warm afternoons with the highs ranging between 60 and 80°F from winter to summer. Some U.S. residents have even chosen to live in this middle-class city by the border. Most noncitizens, however, come to Tijuana—nicknamed TJ—for just a day trip or a short stay.

Though bullfights, bars, hawkers, and velvet paintings are as much a part of Mexico's fourth-largest city as they ever were, Tijuana has grown beyond its reputation as a hard-drinking shantytown. Poverty still plagues parts of the city, but visitors will also find an international airport, several universities, a thriving arts and culture scene, and hotels and restaurants befitting business travelers and wealthy Mexican families. Unfortunately, the city has for years been a base for the infamous Arrellano Felix drug cartel. Ramón Arrellano Félix was gunned down in Mazatlán in February 2002, and his brother Benjamín was arrested shortly thereafter. Authorities fear that rival cartels will be moving in to fill the void left by what was formerly Mexico's largest drug-running operation. Although ordinary citizens and tourists have little to fear from this drug trade, it's wise to be aware of the situation. And unless you're a seasoned and savvy foreign traveler, stick to the central parts of the city. In any case, there's little to lure you from downtown and the Zona Río.

ACCESS AND INFORMATION

If you're visiting Tijuana for a day trip, a clever plan is to drive to the border and park in the huge **BORDER STATION PARKING** (take the last U.S. exit; 4570 Camino de la Plaza; 619/428-1422 or 619/428-6200 US), a fenced, lighted parking lot with security cameras and 24-hour attendants. This lot has a 500-car capacity, and it's only a short walk (15–20 minutes) over the elevated pedestrian walkway to the north end of the famous Avenida Revolución—Tijuana's tourist zone. By walking, you reduce the hassles and expenses of Mexican auto insurance and parking, and you avoid traffic and delays at the border on your return to the United States. Parking at Border Station costs $7 US a day.

You can also leave your car in San Diego and take the **SAN DIEGO TROLLEY** (619/233-3004 US), which departs every 15 to 30 minutes beginning at 4:30am. Orange-line riders should transfer to the blue line at the 12th Street/Imperial Avenue station; the trolley reaches the U.S. side of the border in another 20 minutes. The last trolley leaves San Ysidro at 11:30pm; but double check if you're planning to take the last one of the day. Cost depends on the length of your ride. The maximum fare is $2.50 US.

Another alternative is to take the bus across the border from Border Station Parking. Comfortable, bright red **MEXICOACH BUSES** (619/428-9517 US) depart every 15 minutes(8:30am–9pm). These buses drop off and pick up at the downtown Tijuana Tourist Terminal on Avenida Revolución and cost $2 US round-trip.

DRIVING ACROSS THE BORDER

Before you drive into Mexico, make sure that you have your **PASSPORT** or a certified copy of your **BIRTH CERTIFICATE** (uncertified copies may or may not be accepted) as well as a **PHOTO ID.** You'll also need **MEXICAN AUTO INSUR-ANCE,** since American policies are not honored in Mexico. It's also advisable to have pesos, especially if you're heading south on the toll roads or plan to get fuel before you change money. (U.S. dollars are widely accepted in Baja's major tourist destinations, but you'll save money if you deal in pesos.) A convenient stop for auto insurance and money exchange before crossing the border is **BAJA-MEX** (358 E San Ysidro Blvd; 619/428-8508 US), an easy in and out from the San Ysidro Boulevard exit off Interstate 5.

Entering Mexico at the San Ysidro/Tijuana border crossing (open 24 hours) is fairly easy. More than 30 million vehicles pass through these gates each year. Interstates 5 and 805 both route you directly into a five-lane, sheltered crossing. Mexican officials will generally just wave you through, although there is sometimes a short wait, especially on weekends.

Remember that crossing the border in Tijuana heading south is a piece of cake; returning north is a different story. Traffic is heaviest from 6:30–8:30am and after 3pm on weekdays (Mondays and Fridays are the worst) while weekends and holidays can jam up from mid-morning until after 9pm. Wait time at this border crossing can run anywhere from 30 minutes to 3 hours. Make sure your car has plenty of gas and coolant, avoid peak hours, and consider using an alternate border crossing such as Tecate or Otay on the trip home. If you must join the lineup at San Ysidro, pack plenty of patience and remember that drinking water, air-conditioning (summer), and a visit to *el baño* are essential.

Favored by truckers, the **OTAY BORDER CROSSING** is usually less congested than San Ysidro and is open 6am–10pm daily. From downtown Tijuana or the Zona Rio, this border crossing can be a bit tricky to find, so it's best to have a co-pilot. From Avenida Cuauhtémoc, follow signs to the Rodríguez International Airport, Otay Border Crossing, or Garita de Otay. After the airport, follow signs to the Otay Border Crossing. For a **24-HOUR, AUTOMATED BORDER WAIT TIME REPORT** for Otay dial 619/671-8999 US.

TOURIST CARDS

To get your tourist card and pay your bank fee at the border, stay in the far right lane, park, and walk through the first building on your right. Continue to your right down the cement walkway to the very end and look for the **OFFICE OF IMMIGRATION** on the left. Officials there will give you a tourist card (form) to fill out. (Bring a pen.) Take your completed form to the cashier and pay the 185-peso fee, and they will stamp your form. Another stamp from the Office of Immigration and you're ready to roll; they will stamp your passport as well if you have one. Keep the tourist card with your passport or certified birth certificate. You will be asked to show it at the state line if you plan to go south of Guerrero Negro, and law enforcement officers may request to see your tourist card at any time.

ACROSS THE BORDER

Once you are finished with the maze at the border, you'll be faced with many distractions—narrow streets, faded lane lines, cars belching black exhaust, and aggressive drivers—so be ready. An attentive copilot is extremely helpful at this time. If you're heading **DOWNTOWN TO THE TOURIST ZONE**, stay in the center lanes and follow signs to "Downtown/Centro." If you want to **HEAD SOUTH** and bypass as much of the city as possible, follow signs that read "Scenic Route, Rosarito-Ensenada" or "Ensenada Cuota."

BUS, AIR, AND TOURIST INFORMATION

There are three **BUS TERMINALS** in Tijuana. Camionera de la Línea is located at the border with service by Autotransportes de Baja California (also known as ABC; 664/686-9010) and Estrellas del Pacífico (664/683-5022). The downtown terminal, Antigua Central Camionera (Calle 1 at Madero; 664/688-0752) services Autotransportes Águila, Greyhound (664/688-0165 or 800/231-2222

US), ABC, and Línea Elite (664/688-1979). The Central de Autobuses (Lázaro Cárdenas at Alamar; 664/621-7640), is Tijuana's primary terminal servicing Mexico's major bus lines (see above) with the most frequent bus service to mainland Mexico as well as daily service to cities south and east on the peninsula.

Tijuana's airport, the **ABELARDO L. RODRÍGUEZ INTERNATIONAL AIRPORT**, is located about 5 miles east of central Tijuana. This modern facility houses currency exchanges, liquor and crafts shops, and an information kiosk. Airlines currently serviced here include Aeromexico (664/685-4401 or 800/237-6639 US), Mexicana (664/634-6566 or 800/531-7921 US), and Aero California (664/684-2876 or 800/258-3311 US). The Tijuana airport is an official port of entry for Mexico.

For **TOURIST INFORMATION** or maps of Tijuana and the surrounding region, visit the Comité de Turismo y Convenciones de Tijuana (Tijuana Convention and Tourist Bureau; Calle Mina and Paseo de los Héroes; 664/684-0537; www.tijuanaonline.org). The office is open weekdays (9am–2pm and 4–7pm). The **TOURIST INFORMATION BOOTH** (corner of Av Revolución and Calle 1; 664/688-0555) has a bilingual staff that's friendly and helpful. They're open daily (9am–7pm).

The Camara Nacional de Comercio, Servicios y Turismo (Av Revolución at Calle 1; 664/685-8472), sometimes referred to as CANACO, is Tijuana's **CHAMBER OF COMMERCE**. This office is just opposite the SECTUR booth. They will assist with tourist information, and offer a public telephone and public rest rooms; open weekdays (9am–6pm). The **TIJUANA TOURISM TRUST** (9365 Paseo de los Héroes; 888/775-2417 US; www.seetijuana.com) has a helpful website and can be reached by phone from the United States before your trip. If you're traveling farther south in the state, you might pick up some information at the **BAJA CALIFORNIA STATE SECRETARY OF TOURISM OFFICE** (Paseo de los Héroes 10289; 664/634-6330). **TIJUANA INFORMATION** (888/775-2417 US) can help you with hotel reservations and suggested itineraries.

INTERNET CAFES are scattered throughout the downtown area along Avenida Revolución as well as the business district (Zona Río) along Paseo de los Héroes. The average cost is about $6 US per hour.

EXPLORING

Many tourists come to Tijuana just to experience **AVENIDA REVOLUCIÓN**, the traditional tourist zone. This eight-block strip is lined with shopping arcades, franchise restaurants, and a few truly Mexican restaurants. Its bars have always catered to a rowdy crowd. These days, sleazy topless clubs (usually down a dark stairway) compete with rock-and-roll bars (usually up a stairway to a rooftop terrace). Up and down the avenue, you'll see zebra-striped burros that seem to have been standing in the same spot for decades, waiting for tourists to pose with them for souvenir snapshots. Women and kids beg for change, hawkers shout: it's always a carnival scene on La Revo. Wander the parallel and cross streets to see shops patronized by the locals amid less hype and bluster.

Not too far from the border is Tijuana's **MUSEO DE CERA** (Wax Museum; Calle l; 664/688-2478). Inside you'll find cheap entertainment (admission $2; children under 6 free) and a cool place to visit on a hot afternoon. Open daily 10am–8pm. The kids will love **MUNDO DIVERTIDO** (Calle José María Velasco 2578 at Av Paseo de los Héroes; 664/634-3213), with its miniature golf course, batting cages, roller coaster, and enormous video-game arcade. Open daily (Mon–Fri noon–8:30pm, Sat–Sun 11am–9:30pm). Rides are inexpensive, and stands offer fast food.

The amusement park and several of the city's finer restaurants are located in the **ZONA RÍO** (between Blvd Agua Caliente and the border) on and around Avenida Paseo de los Héroes. The avenue runs parallel to the dry Tijuana River and is a main thoroughfare with large statues of historical figures, including one of Abraham Lincoln, in the center of the *glorietas*. The heart of the Zona Río is the **CENTRO CULTURAL DE TIJUANA** (Tijuana Cultural Center; Av Paseo de los Héroes at Av Independencia; 664/687-9600), which houses the **MUSEUM OF THE CALIFORNIAS** (664/687-9650). The museum gives an overview of the peninsula's history and is appealing to children as well as adults: there are artifacts from 19th-century Russian and French immigrants, and reproductions of rock art and a willow *wa* (hut) used by the peninsula's first inhabitants. Signage is in English and Spanish. Admission is $2; open Tuesday through Sunday 10am–8pm. Next door, the **OMNIMAX THEATER** (Av Paseo de los Héros at Mina St; 664/684-1111), with its 180-degree screen, shows a variety of interesting films—with at least one daily in English. Admission is $3.50; open Tues–Sun. The films often complement the center's rotating art and culture exhibits. The bookstore has a fine selection of art and history books (although most are in Spanish), and the coffee shop is a great place to take a break.

Tijuana has a zoo, administered by the city and established quite by accident. Authorities needed housing for the numerous exotic pets confiscated from smugglers and drug lords and decided to keep them at **PARQUE JOSE MORELOS** (Blvd Insurgentes 1600, La Mesa; 664/625-2469 or 664/625-3886). It's a tidy, well-run operation with large enclosures, healthy animals, and a caring staff. See Billy the tiger, a lioness, ostriches, a golden eagle, and the aviary, and don't miss the albino python, taken from a lap dancer who was using the snake in her act. With shade trees and grassy lawns, the park is a nice place for a picnic. Admission is 10 pesos per car and 5 pesos per adult. Open Tues–Sun 9am–5pm.

Learn about Baja California's great wine-making tradition at the **L.A. CETTO WINERY** (Cañón Johnson 2108; 664/685-3031). The beautifully restored, 80-year-old facility houses the winery's headquarters, aging vats, and warehouses. Tours are led by bilingual guides, and end with generous wine tastings. Pick up souvenirs and vintages at the winery gift shop. Cetto may even send its minibus to pick you up from the border, your hotel, or anyplace in Tijuana. Open Mon–Sat; tasting fee, starting at $2. Call for more information and to check the current tour schedule.

Another alcohol-related attraction is the recently established **CERVECERÍA TJ,** also known as the **TJ BREWERY** (Blvd Fundadores 2951; 664/638-8662). This great little microbrewery began production in 2000, using hops, malts, and know-how imported from the Czech Republic and formulated by a Czech brewmeister. The resulting three lagers—a dark *morena,* a pale *güera,* and the lighter *bronca*—are bold and extremely popular. The brewery has an elegant cantina, paneled with wood imported from, yes, the Czech Republic. Tours of the facility are possible if the brew staff is not too busy.

Although considered gruesome and barbaric by many non-Mexicans, *corridas de toros,* **BULLFIGHTS,** are an important aspect of the Mexican heritage, via Spain. There are two large bullrings in Tijuana, where both tourists and locals await the outcome of the raging-bull-versus-brave-and-graceful-matador showdown. The bull usually loses. **EL TOREO DE TIJUANA** (2 miles east of downtown on Blvd Agua Caliente; 664/686-1510) hosts bullfights May through October, generally on Sunday. During the summer months, you can see these fights at **PLAZA DE TOROS MONUMENTAL,** also known as Tijuana's **BULLRING BY THE SEA** (6 miles west of downtown off Mexico 1-D; 664/680-1808). This massive arena has a seating capacity of 25,000 and is one of the largest bullrings in Mexico. If it's your first time, it's easiest to book tickets through your hotel or in San Diego through **FIVE-STAR TOURS** (1050 Kettner Blvd, at Amtrak station; 619/232-5049 US). Admission cost depends on seating location and the matador's fame.

There are two **GOLF COURSES** in the Tijuana area. In town you'll find **CLUB CAMPESTRE,** also known as the **TIJUANA COUNTRY CLUB** (Blvd Agua Caliente 4500; 664/681-7852). Located next to the Grand Hotel, and occasional home to the **MEXICAN OPEN,** this club offers a championship 18-hole course with a par 72, measuring 6,500 yards. Greens fees run $35 US. **REAL DEL MAR** (10 miles south of Tijuana on Mexico 1-D; 664/631-3401) is a challenging par 72, 18-hole golf course within a spectacular setting offering breathtaking views of the Pacific. Greens fees range from $60 to $70 US.

For years, thoroughbred greyhounds ran at the **AGUA CALIENTE RACETRACK** (3 miles east of downtown along Blvd Agua Caliente; 664/681-8088 or 619/231-1910 US), and thousands of Americans still remember the thrill of picking the winning horse. Eventually a drawn-out labor dispute ended the era of horseracing in Tijuana. Today, greyhounds run nightly at the Caliente Racetrack, in their relentless pursuit of the mechanical rabbit. This is the only greyhound track in Baja and is the headquarters of **CALIENTE RACE AND SPORTS BOOK,** a chain of off-track betting parlors with subsidiaries in major cities throughout the country. Greyhounds run every night of the week (at 7:45pm), with additional afternoon races on Saturday and Sunday (at 2pm). General admission is free.

¡VIVA EL CHARRO!

You've heard of "grabbing the bull by the horns," and maybe even taken that advice to heart during difficult situations. But have you ever grabbed a bull by the *tail?* And flipped it over? Mexico's cow flippers are not tipsy cow tippers out for a midnight prank, but elegantly dressed men practicing the official national sport, *charrería.*

La cola or *coleadero,* the move mentioned above, is just one of many tasks (called *suertes*) seen during the *charreada,* rather inadequately translated as "Mexican rodeo." Practiced mainly by the upper-middle class and wealthy, the sport is a far cry from a typical rodeo seen in the United States. In Baja as elsewhere in Mexico, teams of women and men practice and compete in the *lienzo charro,* a key-shaped arena with a long, narrow rectangle emanating from a round show ring. Events include bronco and bull riding, *piales* (roping the back legs of a galloping horse, while either on horseback or standing), and rope tricks, among others. The most impressive, and dangerous, is *el paso de la muerte,* in which a rider attempts to switch from his own horse, ridden bareback, to an unbroken horse—at full gallop. Women's events are generally performed as a team and stress elegance and riding ability rather than dangerous feats. Men participate individually and as teams. Both men and women are judged on the gait, speed, appearance, and comportment of their mounts.

A *charro*'s most valuable possession is his horse. Quarterhorses are prized for their graceful movements and the ability to remain calm and focused during the demanding *suertes.* After his horse, a *charro*'s next greatest concern is his clothes: from the broad-brimmed felt hat to the tips of fine leather boots, each piece is an elegant work of art. Even in the simplest *traje de faena* (work outfit), worn when riding, *charros* cut a handsome figure. Men wear a short jacket, tapered trousers, a dress shirt, and fabric tie. Women's dresses vary in style, from peasant-type dresses with lots of lace and ribbons to more elegant suits with long, narrow skirts and jackets stitched in gold. Spectators also don their finest apparel, and as *charreadas* are always accompanied by music—of mariachis, brass bands, or other types—they make for a very festive occasion.

The season runs from May through September and events take place on weekend afternoons, usually Sunday. In Tijuana, one of the most popular public *lienzos charros* is the **CORTIJO SAN JOSÉ** (Av del Agua and Paseo Ensenada, Tijuana; 664/630-1825). For more information on upcoming *charreadas* and their locations, contact the **TIJUANA TOURISM BOARD** (664/684-2854 or 888/775-2417).

—*Jane Onstott*

SHOPPING

Between Calle 1 and Calle 8, **AVENIDA REVOLUCIÓN** is lined with shops selling trinkets, mementos, and crafts from cheap and tacky to elegant and expensive, including silver jewelry, *sarapes* (colorful ponchos), blankets, embroidered dresses and blouses, figures carved in onyx and wood, *huaraches* (leather sandals), and more. Artisans' stands line Calle 2 between the border and Revolución. Bargaining is expected on the streets and in less formal shops, but not in the nicer stores. Shopkeepers throughout Tijuana generally speak excellent English and accept dollars; some take credit cards.

Some shoppers find the hawkers, shills, and touts who loudly beckon and proclaim from outside the storefronts a little disconcerting. If you're one of these folks, you may feel more comfortable in the mini-malls and modern arcades. **BAZAAR DE MEXICO** (Av Revolución at Calle 7; 664/638-4737) is clean (it even has decent public rest rooms) and packed. You'll find some quality arts and crafts tucked among the more tacky souvenir-quality items. **SANBORN'S** (Av Revolución at Calle 8; 664/688-1462), a classy coffee shop/restaurant/department store popular with middle- and upper-class Mexicans, also has folk art from throughout the county, excellent books and CDs, and a delectable assortment of chocolates, cakes, and pastries. **TOLÁN** (Av Revolución 1471, between Calles 7 and 8; 664/688-3637) is a high-end arts and antiques boutique with the latest designs by artist Sergio Bustamante, beautiful Christmas ornaments and decorations, Talavera pottery from the state of Puebla, and lots of other elegant and rustic items from throughout Mexico. For gifts and housewares, and lots of wrought iron, visit **MALLORCA** (Calle 4a 8224, between Revolución and Madero; 664/688-3502). A finer selection of housewares and gifts can be found at **CASA MEXICANA** (Blvd Salinas 11111, Frac Aviación; 664/686-5491), near the Grand Hotel.

More orderly shopping can be found at **PLAZA RÍO TIJUANA** (Av Paseo de los Héroes between Avs Cuauhtémoc and Independencia; 664/684-0402), a full-scale mall with department stores, boutiques, a Sanborn's coffee shop, and a multiplex theater. Closer to the border, **PUEBLO AMIGO** (Vía Oriente 9211) is home to bars rather than shops, but here you'll find **LEY,** a grocery that sells real Mexican delicacies such as candied papaya and fresh spicy sauces for seafood and meat. If you'd like to visit a real Mexican market, head for the **MERCADO HIDALGO** (Avs Independencia and Sánchez Taboada, 5 blocks east of Revolución). The souvenirs here are of a practical bent—sandals, piñatas, soaps, and potions with intriguing labels—and the market is a great place to people-watch or take discreet photos and see life outside the tourist zone. On Calle 2 near the border are several shops selling massive unglazed ceramic pots and planters, stone birdbaths, and other pieces for rustic gardens. Most are large, heavy, and inexpensive.

ADVENTURES

DIVING / The islands off the coast just south of Tijuana, **ISLAS DE LOS CORO-NADOS**, are off-limits to commercial fisherman, making them an excellent destination for diving. Coronado del Norte (the north island) is one of the most frequently dived sites on the peninsula as well as home to a thriving sea lion colony, where playful pups often frolic and interact with divers. (Don't get too close to the huge bulls, especially when they are protecting a harem.) Dive operators from San Diego bring anxious novice divers to the protected eastern side of the island for their open-water checkout dives. **LOIS ANN DIVE CHARTERS** (800/201-4381 US; loisann@aol.com; www.loisann.com) and **HORIZON CHARTERS** (858/277-7823 US; divesd@aol.com; www.earthwindow.com/horizon), both based in San Diego, offer day trips here, as well as longer diving excursions aboard their fully equipped dive boats.

FISHING / The commercial fishing ban around **ISLAS DE LOS CORONADOS** also makes them prime recreational fishing grounds. Catches include bonito, barracuda, and seabass, with occasional runs of yellowtail from April through mid-October. Most of the fishing trips to these islands are scheduled through operators based in San Diego. **CORTEZ YACHT CHARTERS** (619/469-4255 US) charters private yachts in the 44- to 66-foot range. Trips usually run from 10pm to 5pm or 5am to 5pm and cost $1,400–$1,500 US, depending on the vessel. **FISHERMEN'S LANDING** (2838 Garrison St, San Diego; 619/221-8500 US) takes 30–40 people out (11pm–5pm) on their 57- to 124-foot vessels for $90 US per person. **H&M LANDING** (2803 Emerson St, San Diego; 619/222-1144 US; www.hmlanding.com) covers all preferences, with private charters as well as 80-foot party boats that leave daily (at 6am). Prices vary, but party-boat fishing costs $70 US plus $12 US rod rental and includes your Mexican fishing license.

GUIDES AND OUTFITTERS

BAJA CALIFORNIA TOURS (based in La Jolla, California; 800/336-5454 US; www.bajaspecials.com) has been around since 1990 offering day trips, 3- to 4-day excursions, and extended trips throughout Baja in their comfortable motor coaches. Buses depart from the King's Inn in the Mission Valley area of San Diego. Their Winery Tour ($75 US) is a day trip that visits three wineries in the Guadalupe Valley—L.A. Cetto, Domecq, and Chateau Camou—complete with tours of the facilities and wine tasting. Another popular tour is the Lobster Lunch, which includes a driving tour of Tijuana, lobster lunch in Puerto Nuevo, and a few hours of shopping in Rosarito. Other tours focus on the arts, the missions and Baja history, whales, and spas.

NIGHTLIFE

Tijuana still merits its reputation as a serious party town, and several discos carry on long and hard, especially on weekend nights. Casual dressers beware: Many of Tijuana's discos have dress codes—no T-shirts, jeans, or sandals allowed. The best-known dance club in Zona Río, which has a hip, well-heeled, and generally youngish following, is **BABY ROCK** (corner of Paseo de los Héroes and Diego Rivera; 664/634-2404), the trendy little sister of the original Acapulco disco. It gets pretty wild after midnight as the high-powered acoustics blast techno-tunes and rock 'n roll. Thursday is ladies' night and on Saturday nights you can boogie until morning to tunes in Spanish and English. **AH! JIJO TORTILLAS Y ROCK** (Plaza Fiesta Shopping Center; 664/634-1640) offers lively music and weird drinks in a color blast motif. On the small corner stage, Tijuana musicians perform Latin rock on Tuesday and Wednesday, with mariachi music the rest of the week.

Several groovy clubs can be found in the somewhat dilapidated Pueblo Amigo Shopping Center, which looks decidedly better by night, when crowds of reasonably hip youths slouch around in search of a good time. **GALAXY MARTINI LOUNGE** (Pueblo Amigo Shopping Center; 664/607-3833) specializes in creative martinis, with electronic music spun by internationally known disc jockeys. This club doesn't start rocking until after 11pm, so plan accordingly. Almost next door is **ZOO'LL BAR-GALERÍA** (Pueblo Amigo Shopping Center; 664/683-6255), a disco that sometimes features live bands. Downtown, **CAFÉ JUGLAR** (Plaza Nexx, Calle 8 between Pío Pico and Quintana Roo; 664/685-5361; jjuglar@telnor.net) is a tiny, mellow bar/art space featuring art shows and live Dylan-type folk music on weekend nights. For special occasions, owner Jaime Carrillo can arrange for mariachis to liven up the evening. Order a homemade *sangrita,* a mixture of tomato, chile, and lemon juice that accompanies a shot of tequila.

EL LUGAR DE NOPAL (downtown at corner of Calle 6 and Av Cinco de Mayo; 664/685-1264; www.el-lugar-del-nopal.arts.xs2.net) is a venue for local performing artists. Exclusively in Spanish, the entertainment menu ranges from poetry readings to movie screenings and classical guitar. Expect to tip the attendant who watches your car. For a relaxed drink in an upscale cantina, head for **MARÍA BONITA** (in Hotel Camino Real; 664/633-4000). Modeled after the famous Bar L'Opera in Mexico City, it has etched-glass windows and a highly polished wood bar that boasts 130 brands of tequila.

Tijuana's **RED-LIGHT DISTRICT** does still exist, although city officials would like visitors to think otherwise. Nicknamed "Zona Norte," it is near the border and west of Avenida Revolución, with its center near Calle Coahuila between Avenidas Martínez and Niños Héroes. This area is thick with drug dealers and prostitutes and is not recommended, especially after dark.

FESTIVALS AND EVENTS

For more information or schedules regarding these or any other Festivals and Events in the Tijuana area, contact the **TOURIST OFFICE** (Calle Mina and Paseo de los Héroes; 664/684-0537; www.tijuanaonline.org).

If you happen to be in Tijuana, or any port city, during the nine days before Ash Wednesday (usually around mid-February), you'll hit **CARNAVAL**, a precursor to the Lenten Season and the Latin American version of New Orleans's Mardi Gras. Wear comfortable shoes and be prepared to join in the costumed parades and portable parties winding down Avenida Revolución. Festivities include music, food, and all-night parties.

SEMANA SANTA (Holy Week) occurs during Easter week, and is as important in Mexico as Christmas, and this is as true in Baja as throughout the country. A fun custom at this time is breaking *cascarones*—colored, hollowed-out eggs stuffed with confetti—over the heads of friends. You can buy these colorful eggs anywhere in town during this time of year. Easter is also a time for Mexican and American family vacations, so many Baja locations can be extremely crowded at this time.

CINCO DE MAYO (May 5th) celebrates the defeat of French troops invading Mexico in 1862. The city of Tijuana holds street fairs and celebrates with a parade and plenty of traditional music and dancing.

The days surrounding July 11 celebrate the **FOUNDING OF THE CITY OF TIJUANA** with live music, food booths, and dancing. It all takes place at various locations throughout the city.

The **FERIA DE TIJUANA** (Tijuana Fair) in late August (or sometimes mid-September) is a traditional Mexican fair held at the Agua Caliente Racetrack featuring carnival rides, contests, performing artists, food booths, dancing, and cockfights.

FIESTA PATRIA DE LA INDEPENDENCIA is the most celebrated secular holiday in all of Mexico: Mexican Independence Day, observing Mexico's independence from Spain on September 16, 1821. Festivities actually begin in the evening of the 15th and continue through the following day. There are fireworks, parades, *charreadas* (Mexican-style rodeos), music, and *folklóric* dancing. Street vendors selling traditional foods and *cerveza* (beer) line the tourist section of town.

Commemorating Tijuana's place in history as the home of the original, the **CAESAR SALAD FESTIVAL** in mid-October is a culinary celebration tossed with food booths, music, recipe contests, caesar salads, and caesar salad ice cream (just kidding).

The **FEAST OF OUR LADY OF GUADALUPE** is a religious feast day and national holiday on December 12 honoring the Virgin of Guadalupe, Mexico's patron saint.

RESTAURANTS

Caesar's / ★

AV REVOLUCIÓN AND CALLE 5, TIJUANA; 664/685-1666 Overlooking the busy shopping scene of Avenida Revolución, this small, unassuming restaurant on the second floor of the Hotel Caesar is the acclaimed birthplace of the caesar salad. Back in 1924, a crowd of Hollywood celebrities dropped by for a light dinner. The chef on duty, Caesar Cardini, threw together what was, at the time, a very unconventional salad consisting of romaine lettuce, garlic-infused olive oil, eggs, a squeeze of lemon, and some crusty bread. He tossed this salad right at the table and his legendary recipe became the caesar salad as we know it today. Nowadays, young waiters wheel double carts with large wooden bowls to your tableside, apportion the ingredients over crisp romaine, then toss, fold, and scramble for what seems like an eternity, and *voila!* your salad is presented on a chilled plate. The menu also includes steaks, fish, and Mexican favorites for those who aren't particularly fond of salad, but the salad-making performance itself is well worth the price. *$; MC, V; traveler's checks OK; lunch, dinner every day; full bar; no reservations; corner of Revolución and Calle 5.*

Café La Especial / ★

AV REVOLUCIÓN 718, TIJUANA; 664/685-6654 Café La Especial offers a dependable menu of Americanized Mexican favorites in a clean, cheerful setting. Colorfully painted tables and chairs adorn the large dining room with paintings of bullfighters gracing the walls. Breakfast specials include fresh pastries and a spicy Tex-Mex version of ham and eggs, served with beans, tortillas, and salsa. For lunch or dinner, try the mild carne asada or the chicken enchiladas, both served with soup, beans, guacamole, fresh salsas, and a beverage. La Especial is famous for its tasty steamed tacos—pork, beef, or bean—that come with all the trimmings. The atmosphere is casual and can be very quiet or very noisy, depending on the season and the day of the week, but overall this is a pleasant place to drop in for a late lunch after shopping. For dessert, don't miss the *bombón glacé*, a caramel-centered scoop of vanilla ice cream smothered with chocolate and topped with pecans, or the *limón helado especial* (lemon ice cream special) served in a lemon. Café La Especial also runs a street-level take-out window where you can order their popular steamed tacos to go. *$; Cash only; breakfast, lunch, dinner every day; beer and wine; no reservations; between Calles 3 and 4, downstairs.*

Café La Libanesa / ★★

CALLE TAPACHULA 10, INTERIOR 4, TIJUANA; 664/686-2923 This authentic Lebanese deli is a great place to grab take-out for a picnic lunch or, if you don't mind the tiny dining area, enjoy it amid the savory aromas of a genuine deli. Five years ago, Samiá del Danaf opened her doors, offering Middle Eastern alternatives along this busy tourist zone. Sample the cheese and spinach empanadas served with Lebanese flatbread, or one of the gyro sandwiches with freshly baked pita bread. Other lunch offerings include falafel, club sandwiches, and fresh salads with feta cheese and olives. Coffee addicts can choose from espressos and cappuccinos, or try the Café Arabé, a thick, rich, exotic blend. For dessert, the baklava and date or custard pie are hard to beat. *$; Cash only; breakfast Mon–Sat, lunch, dinner every day; beer and wine; no reservations; across from NW corner of Agua Caliente Racetrack.*

Chiki Jai / ★★

AV REVOLUCIÓN 1388, TIJUANA; 664/685-4955 Olé, matadors and bullring aficionados! Bullfighting is the theme at Chiki Jai, a small but popular eatery serving tasty Basque and Mexican food at reasonable prices. See the antique matador cape preserved behind glass within clear view of the mounted bull's heads guarding the front wall. Manuel Monje and his charming wife, Paquita, both from Madrid, settled in Tijuana in 1947 and opened this Basque restaurant near the Jai Alai Fronton Palacio. Start your meal with a cold beer, served in a chilled pewter mug with fresh-baked bread and generous portions of Roquefort cheese and salsa. Then dive into their most requested dish, paella, with portions almost large enough for two. The *filete de pescado al ajillo* (fish prepared with olive oil and garlic) is accompanied by fried calamari rings. If you (and your waistline) can handle more, ask for the Spanish rice pudding or a slice of their perfectly textured flan. *$$; Cash only; lunch, dinner every day; full bar; no reservations; corner of Calle 7 and Revolución.*

Cien Años / ★★★

CALLE JOSÉ MARÍA VELASCO 2407, TIJUANA; 664/634-6262 Cien Años is one of Tijuana's most elite restaurants. The menu offers authentic Mexican recipes employing ingredients dating back to pre-Spanish days; for example, ant eggs in garlic butter or crispy *chinicuiles* (fried maguey worms—the ones commonly seen at the bottom of tequila and mezcal bottles) served on hot tortillas with guacamole and salsa. Bite through the tortilla and taste the lemony avocado and the garlic crunch of the worm casing. No, this is not a scene from *Survivor!* Wash it down with a serving of spine marrow soup, or if you need something stronger, a shot of tequila. If you'd rather not go the route of the ancients, try the Oaxacan mole pollo en salsa Cien Años, a house specialty of tender chicken in light chipotle chile mole sauce. The rack of lamb is tender and moist; the beef fillets are cooked to order. And if you can find a little bit of courage, take a small dining adventure into the flavors of *huitlacoche* (black fungus grown on corn), nopal (prickly pear cactus), or sauces made with tamarind (a seed pod with a sweet-and-sour flavor). The bar is stocked with more than 35 tequilas and a full range of Baja California wines. *$$$; MC, V; traveler's checks OK; lunch, dinner every day; full bar, reservations recommended; next to Hotel Real del Rio.*

El Rincón / ★

PRIVADA VALENCIA RIVERA 157, TIJUANA; 664/686-2491 Got a carload of hungry kids? Bring them on over to El Rincón, a brightly decorated restaurant with a menu to please the entire family. The owners are from Mexico City and have found a niche in Tijuana, serving affordable, reasonably quick meals. Try the *gorditas,* fat little corn cakes slathered with butter and cheese and heaped high with salsa, sour cream, and meat, or *sopes,* a smaller version with beans, fresh lettuce, and tomato. The flautas are tacos rolled pencil-thin and fried—crispy and delicious, especially when dipped in the salsa of your choice. Portions are large and include rice and beans. Service is good and the prices are very reasonable. *$; Cash only; lunch, dinner every day; beer only; no reservations; just north of Blvd Agua Caliente.*

La Casa de Mole / ★★★

PASEO DE LOS HÉROES 10511, TIJUANA; 664/634-6920 Holy mole! This place serves it up—green mole, sweet mole, brown mole, and spicy mole. Just what *is* mole? Mole is an extremely rich sauce stewed with a multitude of spices including cinnamon, cloves, and cumin. The sauce is then poured over meat, often poultry. Different moles require different ingredients, including roasted chiles, ground sesame or pumpkin seeds, broth, and bitter chocolate. Herminia Hamador and her son Efrain Lere started La Casa de Mole in 1996 using recipes from the family kitchen. Highly recommended house specialties include mole poblano, a chicken breast or leg smothered with a rich, chocolate brown mole; mole verde, a spicy mole with cilantro, jalapeño, and serrano peppers, also over chicken; and mole *almendrado,* a delightful almond-based mole. For lunch or a lighter fare, try the brown mole tamales served over a bed of seasoned rice and corn. Filet mignon tops the list of more than 20 beef favorites along with tamales, chicken, and a large selection of enchiladas. A pianist at the back of the room softly serenades customers, sometimes accompanied by guitar and mellow drum. *$–$$; Cash only; breakfast, lunch, dinner every day; full bar; no reservations; right on traffic circle near Zaragoza monument.*

La Diferencia / ★★★

BLVD SÁNCHEZ TABOADA 10611-A, TIJUANA; 664/634-3346 OR 664/634-7078 La Diferencia is, in fact, different. The fare, although odd, is delicious. Have you had your fried worms today? How about rattlesnake or crispy crickets? What makes La Diferencia different is not the Moorish architecture, elegant decor, or the lovely blue and white glazed pottery from San Miguel de Allende—it's their traditional recipes and unorthodox menu selections. Rattlesnake fillets are smoked and served beside vegetables; crickets are baked until crispy for texture; maguey worms (found by the roots of agave plants) are delicately grilled with garlic and butter and then served with mashed avocado on green tortillas. If you're not into the creepy-crawly choices, try the *salmon fresco* (fresh grilled salmon) served with a mango and roasted chile sauce, or the *camarón en salsa de chile de árbol y guayaba* (shrimp in tree chile and guava sauce). Whether you choose to experience these delicacies firsthand or watch others partake, your overall dining experience will be pleasant and educational. Service is attentive and the wine list offers vintages from Baja California's wine region. *$$$; AE, DIS, MC, V; traveler's checks OK; lunch, dinner every day; full bar; reservations recommended; ladif@telnor.net; on the right, 1½ blocks past Hotel Hacienda.*

Los Arcos / ★★

BLVD SALINAS 1000, TIJUANA; 664/686-3171 Los Arcos is a Tijuana treasure, packed with locals and savvy gringos on the weekends and serving up a boatload of seafood dishes. Fresh fish is prepared almost any way you can imagine, along with 13 variations of shrimp. You've got your fried shrimp, your garlic shrimp, your shrimp *a la veracruzana,* your shrimp in herbs and butter; you've got your boiled shrimp, shrimp tacos, and shrimp fajitas. Between September and February, you've even got giant shrimp from San Felipe. The seafood stew is outstanding, overflowing with scallops, shrimp, and octopus in a rich broth, served with fresh lime and steaming tortillas. The decor is naturally fish related, with colorful seashore murals, tropical fish, and fishnets hanging on the walls. There's plenty of off-street parking and enough menu choices to please even the pickiest of eaters. *$$; MC, V; traveler's checks OK; breakfast, lunch, dinner Tues–Sun; full bar; no reservations; 1½ blocks west of Grand Hotel Tijuana (twin towers).*

Sanborn's / ★

AV REVOLUCIÓN 100, TIJUANA (AND BRANCHES); 664/688-1462 Sanborn's is an institution in Mexico—a chain of classy coffee shop/restaurant/department stores patronized by middle- and upper-class Mexicans and knowledgeable gringos. There are four of them in Tijuana, so you won't have to travel far to find one. The menu includes standard Mexican favorites, but also offers steaks, seafood, salads, sandwiches, and tasty soups that change daily (try the sopa de pollo con arroz—chicken soup with rice). Fresh juices, omelets, hotcakes, and waffles round out the breakfast menu. The coffee is perked, not instant, the rest rooms are clean, and there are separate smoking and nonsmoking sections. Other Tijuana locations include Plaza Rio, Avenida Revolución (between Calles 3 and 4), and Avenida Revolución 737. *$; MC, V; traveler's checks OK; breakfast, lunch, dinner every day; beer and wine; no reservations; one block south of Jai Alai Palace.*

Vallarta Natural Restaurant Vegetariano / ★★

BLVD AGUA CALIENTE 1252, TIJUANA; 664/686-1560 This pumpkin-colored building with bright mushrooms and plants painted on the exterior walls sits squarely on its corner, resembling a transplant from Taos, New Mexico. Owners Ana Corona and Luis Alcántar have nourished this delightful vegetarian restaurant from its inception five years ago. The Saltillo-tiled dining room is tidy, with rustic furniture and a collection of decorative suns covering the walls. The vegetarian menu offers a wide selection of Mexican-style entrees such as *taquitos panzones* (fried corn tortillas stuffed with mushrooms, soy chorizo, and scallions), and *chiles rellenos* stuffed with Chihuahua cheese. Crisp salads, including the spinach, with mushrooms, avocado, and tomato, as well as flavorful soups, are made with fresh produce—mostly grown by Ana and Luis. The breakfast menu includes eggs, fresh fruit salads, bananas with sweet cream, and yogurt. For a midday pick-me-up, try the Enzymatic superdigestive smoothie (banana, apple, and papaya). This 100 percent nonsmoking eatery has reasonable prices, good service, and off-street parking. *$; Cash only; breakfast, lunch, dinner every day; no alcohol; no reservations; at Agua Caliente and Río Yaqui, across from bullring.*

Villa Saverios / ★★★

ESCUADRÓN 201, TIJUANA; 664/686-6502 OR 664/686-6442 One of the latest additions to Tijuana's upscale dining scene, Villa Saverios quickly earned a reputation for serving the finest Mediterranean food in town. Start your evening with a visit to their extensive downstairs wine cellar. Choose a Baja wine or a vintage from California, Europe, or Chile. Upstairs, the quiet atmosphere is accompanied by the clink of glassware and low conversations. Dark mahogany panels the walls while a wrought-iron French provincial staircase winds gracefully from the reception area to upper-level dining rooms. The intimate lounge, with its ornate wooden bar, is set off from the dining room with etched glass and large gilt-framed mirrors that reflect the carved, dark wood. House specialties include *risotto de Verano con champiñón porcini*, a rich, creamy mushroom pasta, and fresh halibut grilled over a mesquite fire. Meat eaters can choose from the beef medallions served with rice and a choice of three different marinades, or the rib eye à la Lena prepared with a cabernet sauvignon reduction and surrounded by fresh baby vegetables. After your meal, consider a snifter of five-star cognac or head downstairs for a Cuban cigar. *$$$; AE, MC, V; traveler's checks OK; lunch, dinner Mon–Sat; full bar; reservations recommended; www.saverios.com; in Zona Río, corner of Sánchez Taboada and Escuadrón.*

LODGINGS

Fiesta Inn / ★★★

PASEO DE LOS HÉROES 18818, TIJUANA; 664/634-6901 OR 800/504-5000 US, FAX 664/634-6912 Moorish-Spanish architecture defines the exterior of this hotel with elaborate stucco designs and intricate flowing patterns of tile and carved wood. Ornate wrought-iron chandeliers hang in the otherwise unimpressive lobby, which is cramped by a recently enlarged dining room. A member of the Fiesta Americana chain of business-class hotels, the Fiesta Inn prides itself on the quality of its business center, which is actually rather small and sometimes unstaffed. The second floor is a designated nonsmoking floor—something rare in Mexico. Rooms are spacious and comfortable, and set up with data ports, desks, and coffee makers amid a tasteful aqua and mauve color scheme. Thermal water from an underground spring is piped into a tiny outdoor whirlpool as well as the Vita Spa on the third floor, where you can get massages, facials, pedicures, and other spa treatments. Guests can use the sauna, steam, or whirlpool at no extra charge. There's a small swimming pool, squished like an afterthought behind the glass-walled restaurant, and secure off-street parking. *$$$; MC, V; traveler's checks OK; www.fiestainn.com; next to BMW dealership.*

Grand Hotel Tijuana / ★

BLVD AGUA CALIENTE 4500, TIJUANA; 664/681-7000, FAX 664/681-7016 Conveniently located near the financial district, shopping, and the Tijuana Country Club, the 22-story steel and glass structure reflects tequila sunrises and magenta sunsets. One of Tijuana's landmarks, the twin towers of the Grand Hotel Tijuana were the city's first and highest skyscrapers—but their sleek 1980s sophistication has worn a bit thin. The 422 rooms and suites are looking a bit worn too, although still colorfully decorated with soft pastel walls and comfortable furniture. Choose from two queens or one king-size bed. Larger suites have guest rooms, multiple bathrooms, and views of unimpressive cityscapes or the nearby golf course. A few floors are designated as nonsmoking areas. For on-site recreation, there are tennis courts, a fitness center, a heated swimming pool, a hot tub, and a sauna. An extensive shopping gallery at the twin towers' base houses a Caliente Race-and-Sports betting lounge, three restaurants, two bars, and convention facilities. The bilingual staff is friendly and helpful. Underground parking is secure and your stay here includes continental breakfast and complimentary airport transportation. *$$$; AE, MC, V; traveler's checks OK; ghotel2@telnor.net; right next to Club Campestre.* &

Hotel Camino Real / ★★

AV PASEO DE LOS HÉROES 10305, TIJUANA; 664/633-4000 OR 800/722-6466 US, FAX 664/633-4001 Ideally situated close to shopping and the Cultural Center, this relatively classy hotel is accustomed to accommodating business and upscale travelers. Bright colors—purple, orange, and blue—identify the wings of the 250-room complex, although the colors become softer inside. The domed atrium is capped with wrought-iron filigree and glass. Explore the corridor to the left of the reception desk, where you'll find enlargements of sepia photos taken during the Mexican revolution. The guest rooms have recently been renovated and include data ports, satellite TV, and direct-dial phones to help travelers keep in touch. The top floor is a dedicated executive center with business facilities and meeting rooms. There are also two restaurants, a bar, a travel agency, and a rental car desk. Located 10 minutes from the border and 15 minutes from the international airport. *$$$; AE, DIS, MC, V; traveler's checks OK; tij@caminoreal.com; www.caminoreal.com/tijuana/; corner of Paseo de los Héroes and Av Cuauhtémoc.* &

Hotel Lucerna / ★

PASEO DE LOS HÉROES 10902, TIJUANA; 664/633-3900, FAX 664/634-2400 Although a large Italian-style fountain with sculpted fish guards the main entrance to this hotel, the Lucerna is built along traditional Mexican lines with a central, palm-lined courtyard, arched walkways, and a hacienda feel. However, the 156 rooms and 9 suites overlooking the pool and patio could use a face-lift. Amenities include air-conditioning, fully tiled bathrooms, satellite TV, direct-dial telephones, and data ports. The business center offers computers, copiers, and conference rooms; there are two restaurants, a piano bar, a travel agency, and a small gym. Hotel Lucerna is located in the Zona Río, just a few miles from the border and within walking distance of many of Tijuana's attractions. *$$–$$$; AE, DIS, MC, V; traveler's checks OK; lucerna@telnor.net; www.hotel-lucerna.com.mx; across from Plaza Río North.*

Pueblo Amigo / ★★

VÍA RÁPIDA ORIENTE 9211, TIJUANA; 664/683-5030 OR 800/386-6985 US, FAX 664/683-5032 There are several reasons to stay in this modern, medium-rise hotel. First, at less than 10 years old, facilities are newish and well maintained. Architecture and decoration are modern and somewhat sleek, yet still warm and welcoming. Spacious and comfortable rooms have such perks as direct-dial phones and mini-bars. The large indoor pool is heated, and the hotel has its own water purification plant, so clean water flows from the taps in guest rooms. The location is ideal for those attending events at the Cultural Center. It's also close to Pueblo Amigo and the Plaza Río shopping mall, and a 10- to 15-minute walk from Avenida Revolución. In addition to the covered patio restaurant, which serves international and Mexican food, the hotel has a gym, Caliente Race and Sports Book, and 24-hour room service. *$$$; AE, MC, V; no traveler's checks; htlpuebl@telnor.net; www.puebloamigo.com; north end of Pueblo Amigo Shopping Center.* &

TIJUANA AND TECATE THREE-DAY TOUR

DAY ONE: Arriving in Tijuana midmorning, drive to the **CENTRO CULTURAL DE TIJUANA (TIJUANA CULTURAL CENTER)** and visit the museum for a summary of Baja's fascinating history. Walk toward the downtown area along Independencia, stopping at **MERCADO HIDALGO** (Avenidas Independencia and Sánchez Taboada), an authentic Mexican market with mounds of dried and fresh chiles, herbs, fresh produce, and colorful piñatas.

When you get hungry for lunch, head for Calle Revolución where you'll find **CAFÉ LA ESPECIAL,** an easy entry into Mexican cuisine, with good food and waiters who understand English. Stroll busy **AVENIDA REVOLUCIÓN,** nicknamed "La Revo." If you've got a superstitious streak (or just a quirky curiosity), check out the soaps, perfumes, and powders used to attract lovers or defeat enemies at **EL TEXANO,** a few blocks east of Calle Revolución at Calle 6 (Flores Magón 8143; 664//688-1955).

Check in at the brightly colored **HOTEL CAMINO REAL;** be sure to ask the concierge to make your dinner reservation for tonight at **CIEN AÑOS** and for late-afternoon spa treatments tomorrow at **FIESTA INN'S VITA SPA.** Mexicans rarely dine before 8pm, so delay dinner with a drink in the hotel's charming bar, María Bonita.

By the time you finish a late dinner at Cien Años, **BABY ROCK,** TJ's hottest disco, should be starting to gear up. If you can't deal with their dress code, head for the more casual **ZOO'LL BAR-GALERÍA** (still, no tennis shoes).

DAY TWO: For breakfast, belly up to the busy bar at the nearest **SANBORN'S** or settle into a comfy booth and order a hearty full breakfast or just a coffee and pastry. Thus fortified, shop at Sanborn's for CDs or tapes of the tropical tunes you heard at last night's clubs. If you've got kids with you, take a short cab ride to **MUNDO DIVERTIDO,** with its miniature golf and all sorts of games. Otherwise, tour the **L.A. CETTO WINERY** (it's easiest to take a cab), ending with a tasting and visit to the gift shop.

Back on Avenida Revolución, have a light late lunch at the informal Spanish restaurant **CHIKI JAI.** Spend the afternoon getting spa treatments at **FIESTA INN'S VITA SPA,** where you can also use the steam, sauna, and whirlpool spa.

Thus exfoliated and polished, have dinner at lovely **VILLA SAVERIOS.** If you're looking for a party, head for the boisterous upstairs bar at **SEÑOR FROGS** in Plaza Pueblo Amigo (Via Oriente 60; 664/682-4962). It's enormously popular with the locals as well as gringos.

DAY THREE: Take advantage of the Hotel Camino Real's generous buffet breakfast in Restaurant Azulejos before checking out, then head out of town on Avenida Cuauhtémoc, which becomes Calle 16 and then Carretera Aeropuerto. Follow the signs to Highway 2-D, the toll road to **TECATE,** a border town that doesn't feel like one. It's about a 20-minute drive. In downtown Tecate, park your car near the square and people-watch in the tree-lined plaza.

Have lunch at **LA MISIÓN,** several miles west of town on the free road to Tijuana. Continue west another mile or so to check out the beautiful Talavera tiles and house-wares at **LOS AZULEJOS,** and then return to downtown Tecate for a visit to the Beer Gardens at the **TECATE BREWERY.** You can head back to the United States through the Tecate border crossing (closes at midnight), or spend the night at **RANCHO OJAI KOA** (km 112, Mexico 2; 665/653-3014), about 13 miles east of Tecate on the free road to Mexicali. For dinner try the quail or rack of lamb at the contiguous **EL ENCINO** (km 112, Hwy 2; 665/655-3016), adjacent to the KOA campground and cabins.

Rosarito

Rosarito Beach, as it's most commonly called, is northern Baja California's newest boomtown. Once just a tiny beach hamlet pertaining to the municipality of Tijuana, Rosarito has a population approaching 100,000 and growing. Also growing is its reputation as party central among die-hard young fans of dancing, drinking, and general rabble-rousing. Spring breaks, holidays, and summer weekends pack the town and the alcohol flows like a river in a *chubasco.*

The young and the restless aren't the only ones attracted to Rosarito, whose 5-mile-long beach stretches without interruption from the power plant at the town's northern border all the way to the Rosarito Beach Hotel. The climate here is pure Southern California with lots of sunshine and little rain. Surfers have their secret breaks, and snowbirds flock to private residences, trailer parks, and condos in search of respite from Canadian and Midwestern winters. Twentieth Century Fox built a studio south of town in 1995, which it used as a base for filming the hit movie *Titanic* in 1996 and 1997, increasing Rosarito's prestige and growth. Scenes for other films, including *Pearl Harbor,* have also been shot at the studio.

Despite recent hobnobbing with Hollywood glamour-pusses, Rosarito isn't synonymous with sophistication or culture. It's about sun and sea, relaxing and boogying. Although you can visit Rosarito on a day trip from San Diego, many adopt the Mexican mañana attitude and delay their return home for one or more days. It's certainly worth considering, since there's enough shopping, outdoor activities, and good restaurants to keep you busy throughout the day and on into the night.

ACCESS AND INFORMATION

Rosarito lies about 19 miles south of Tijuana on the Pacific Coast. If you're driving, you can take the **TOLL ROAD** (Mexico 1-D; follow signs to "Ensenada Cuota," or "Ensenada Scenic Route") or the **FREE ROAD** (aka Mexico 1 or "the Old Highway;" follow signs to "Ensenada Libre"). The free road is slower and longer (by about 3-1/2 miles) but perfectly acceptable. If you choose the toll road (four lanes and well maintained), there is one toll station between Tijuana and Rosarito ($2.30 US). The free road eventually crosses over the toll road and becomes Rosarito's main street, **BOULEVARD BENITO JUÁREZ**—although you may never realize this, since street signs are almost nonexistent in Rosarito.

You don't have to drive to Rosarito—you can take a bus from the border. The comfortable, bright red **MEXICOACH ROSARITO BEACH EXPRESS** (619/428-9517 US; www.mexicoach.com) will pick you up at the **BORDER STATION PARKING** (4570 Camino de la Plaza, San Ysidro; 619/428-1422 US) located at the last U.S. exit from I-5 or I-805. This large parking lot is well lit and has a perimeter fence, security cameras, and 24-hour attendants. The bus takes you first to the **TIJUANA TOURIST TERMINAL** on Avenida Revolución ($3 US round trip), and departs for Rosarito soon thereafter with a drop-off in front of the Rosarito Beach Hotel. These buses run every two hours (9am–7pm); $8 US round trip, children 4 and under are free. Other transportation options include the ubiquitous **YELLOW AND WHITE STATION WAGON TAXIS** that travel north and south (Tijuana to Puerto Nuevo). Once in Rosarito, look for **WHITE TAXIS** for local service, and the small, economical buses that travel up and down Boulevard Benito Juárez, Rosarito's main drag.

The **COMITÉ DE TURISMO Y CONVENCIONES DE ROSARITO (TOURIST OFFICE)** at Oceana Plaza (Blvd Juárez 907; 661/612-0396 or 800/962-2252 US; www.rosaritobch.com) is located two blocks north of the Festival Plaza Resort on the beach side of the street and has a helpful bilingual staff; it's open daily (Mon–Sat 9am–7pm, Sun 10am–4pm). **BAJA INFORMATION** (800/522-1516 from California, Nevada, Arizona; 800/225-2786 from rest of U.S.; impamexicoinfo@juno.com) can assist with hotel reservations for Rosarito and Ensenada as well as destination information for northern Baja.

Local Internet cafes include **EL TUNEL.COM** (Blvd Juárez 208; 661/613-1297) and **BAJACHAT.COM CYBER CAFÉ** (north entrance to Rosarito Beach Hotel, Blvd Juárez 31; 661/612-1008). Both are reasonably priced at about $3 US an hour.

EXPLORING

Rosarito careens haphazardly along both sides of the Old Ensenada Highway (Mexico 1), in town more commonly known as **BOULEVARD BENITO JUÁREZ**. This street is strewn with restaurants, bars, and shops in a rather incongruous mix of building styles.

The small but informative **ROSARITO BEACH HISTORICAL MUSEUM** (south entrance to Rosarito Beach Hotel, Blvd Juárez 31) offers a look into Rosarito's indigenous, ranching, and political history with artifacts and photo journals. Look for the large sign reading "Wa-Kuatay," the Indian word for water. Open Thursday through Sunday (10am–4pm); admission is free.

Although shells are not as plentiful as they were in the past, **BEACHCOMBING** is still a major attraction, as are walks on the long, wide beach. **SWIMMING** is also a popular activity, although the line of beachfront hotels and condominiums has contributed to spills of questionable materials along the high tide mark. If you have any doubts about the cleanliness of the water, check with the Tourist Office (661/612-0396).

GAMBLING has long been a significant source of revenue for Rosarito and the state, from tourists and locals alike. In fact, the Rosarito Beach Hotel owes its existence to gambling, as Americans came in droves to its poker, faro, and crap tables. In 1930, the Mexican government outlawed casino gambling, but today race and sports betting are permitted here as elsewhere in Mexico. At **CALIENTE RACE AND SPORTS BOOK** (Quinta Plaza; 664/633-7300 ext 6005 or 619/231-1910 US) you can wager on horse races as well as any major sporting event.

If you're curious about movie making, visit **FOXPLORATION** (3 miles south of Rosarito on Mexico 1; 661/614-9444 or 866/369-2252 US; www.foxploration. com). Unlike Universal Studios, Foxploration is not an amusement park with rides but, rather, an interactive journey through the magic of moviemaking. Twentieth Century Fox built the huge indoor/outdoor studio complex in 1996 for the filming of its blockbuster film **TITANIC**. A giant saltwater tank was constructed to house a model of the doomed ship. Tours include audience participation in all facets of moviemaking with actual studio setups. The *Titanic* exhibit will tempt you to abandon ship pronto as live rats scurry past your feet. The sound stage demands your attention as you attempt to insert the correct soundtrack to a movie clip with no sounds; the special effects studio reveals camera tricks and screening effects. Fox Studios leases part of the 37-acre complex to other film studios; portions of *Deep Blue Sea, Monkey Bone, Pearl Harbor,* and *Anna and the King* were filmed here. Wander through authentic sets from *Romeo and Juliet* and *Bedazzled*. Open Thursday through Sunday (10am–5:30pm). Admission is $12 US; children under 12, $9 US.

GOLFERS should check out the secluded **MARRIOTT REAL DEL MAR RESIDENCE INN** (km 19.5 Mexico 1-D; 661/631-3675 or 800/803-6038 US; www.realdelmar.com.mx), 6 miles north of Rosarito Beach. The resort has a beautiful 18-hole golf course with expansive views of the Pacific. The par 72 course measures 5,949 yards, and greens fees range from $60 to $70 US.

SHOPPING

Rosarito has a respectable number of stores selling indoor and outdoor furniture, pottery, and other interior decor items. Small souvenir and T-shirt shops are sprinkled along **BOULEVARD JUÁREZ,** and the larger hotels have shopping arcades and crafts stores. A good place to start is the small collection of vendors right in front of the **ROSARITO BEACH HOTEL** (see Lodgings). A couple of blocks south, **EL MERCADO DE ARTESANÍAS** (Artisans Market; Blvd Juárez 306) is packed with more than 100 vendors peddling everything from tacky curios to wonderful handcrafts from all regions of Mexico. Just south, beyond the Pacífico Hotel, **LA MISIÓN DEL VIEJO** (Blvd Juárez 139; 661/612-1576; open Thurs–Tues) sells Mexican handcrafts and rustic furniture.

Before its numerous restaurants and Johnny-come-lately hotels sprang up, Rosarito was known for the pottery stands lining the highway. You can still find shops (generally at the north and south extremes of town) selling huge ceramic planters and pots as well as rustic furniture and accessories. Among the most interesting of these are **APISA** (Blvd Juárez 2400; 661/612-0125), with a 15,000-square-foot inventory of fancy furnishings, carved wooden frames, and iron sculpture from Guadalajara, and **FÉLIX FURNITURE** (Blvd Juárez 316; 661/612-0091), where you can purchase rustic-looking furniture made to order. At the south end of town, you can also watch carvers create these popular wooden pieces on the premises at **CASA LA CARRETA** (km 29 Mexico 1; 661/612-0502).

ADVENTURES

HORSEBACK RIDING on the beach has been a popular tourist activity since the 1920s. Along the Rosarito shoreline, individual entrepreneurs have horses for rent—some bored and boney-looking, others raring to go, but all looking rather wilty at high noon on a hot day. Look for signs along Boulevard Juárez, or clumps of horses standing in the shade along the beach. Most of the animals take a bit of prodding to amble slowly down the beach but show amazing recovery as they eagerly gallop back to their handlers. Prices vary according to your bargaining skills, but usually run $5–$8 US an hour.

The best **SURFING** beaches in the area are south of Rosarito on the Old Ensenada Highway (free road, aka Mexico 1), which runs parallel to the toll road, Mexico 1-D here. Beaches are usually designated by, and sometimes even named after the nearest kilometer markers. Locals and Southern Californians habitually check the waves at **POPOTLA** (km 32.5), **CALAFIA** (km 35.5), and just beyond at **COSTA BAJA** (km 36), as well as **KM 38**. For current conditions and equipment rentals, try the **INNER REEF SURF SHOP** (km 34.5 Mexico 1; 661/615-0841), where surfboards rent for $2 US an hour or $20 US a day. They also rent boogie boards and wet suits.

NIGHTLIFE

MTV and *Playboy* magazine both touted Rosarito as a perfect spot for the **SPRING BREAK PARTY SCENE**, and college kids raced down to test the waters—and the firewaters. Since then, government-sponsored advertising blitzes have warned young revelers of the consequences of too many tequila shooters, but the party rages nonetheless during school holidays and on hot summer weekends. Rosarito has boisterous bars, piano lounges, and more sedate restaurant bars. Drinking-and-driving laws are strictly enforced—take a cab or assign a designated driver if you plan to imbibe.

Adjacent to the carnival-like Festival Plaza Hotel (see Lodgings), **EL MUSEO CANTINA TEQUILA** (661/612-2950 ext 144) is a bar-cum–tequila museum where you can literally choose your poison. There are more than 300 brands of the agave-based liquor at this bar frequented by party-hungry locals and tourists. The eight-story hotel has other bars and cantinas, including the **CHA CHA CHA BAREFOOT BAR, ROCK & ROLL TACO,** and **JAZZ GROTTO. SEÑOR FROG'S** (next door to Festival Plaza Hotel; 661/612-4375) pumps out high-voltage dance music as tequila servers pace the crowd. Two blocks toward the beach, the enormous indoor/outdoor installation of **PAPAS & BEER** (Av Eucalipto at Av Mar Adriático; 661/612-0444; www.papasandbeer.com) generally attracts a boisterous younger crowd and hosts international beach volleyball tournaments, often televised from their sand courts.

You'll find a mixed crowd of old and young revelers at the **ROSARITO BEACH HOTEL** (see Lodgings), which has live music on weekends and during the week when things are hopping. For a sunset cocktail, nothing beats **CALAFIA** (km 35.5 Mexico 1; 661/612-1580 or 877/700-2093 US), where the small tables are set down the cliff—each overlooking the ocean on its own miniature terrace. Live music is sometimes performed at a dance floor near the base of the cliffs. Calafia is a 10-minute ride south of Rosarito by car or cab.

FESTIVALS AND EVENTS

For information on any of these events, contact the Tourist Office (661/612-0200; www.rosaritobch.com, or www.toomuchfun.com.mx/events).

In February of each year, there's an exciting display of horsemanship at the **CABALGADA POKER RIDE** (gathering of riders). In great swirls of dust, vaqueros (cowboys) run their trusty steeds in short, sometimes disorganized races, and stage other events to show off their riding abilities and their swift-footed mounts.

April brings the **ROSARITO-ENSENADA 50-MILE FUN BICYCLE RIDE,** which draws nearly 10,000 pedalers who leave Rosarito, pump the coastline, crank through the foothills, and glide across the finish line just outside of Ensenada. A huge fiesta in Ensenada follows, featuring live music, food, massages, dancing, and souvenirs. The entry fee is $20 US (call 619/424-6084 US; www.rosaritoensenada.com).

If that's not enough biking, May brings hundreds of hard-core mountain bikers to town for the annual **MONTAÑA GRANDE CHALLENGE.** The grueling 20-mile course climbs and descends the steep hills east of Rosarito before ending in town. For more information contact the Convention and Visitors Bureau (800/962-2252 US).

In July, scores of howling motorcycles scream up and down the sand dunes, often flying high in the air and digging themselves into the sand in the **ROSARITO OFF-ROAD RACE.** Helpful spectators run across the track to assist in the dig-out, dangerously dodging oncoming traffic and providing extra thrills and spills.

August delivers the prestigious **INTERNATIONAL SEAFOOD FAIR** held along hotel row in Rosarito Beach with a wonderful assortment of food booths, cook-offs, and seafood galore.

The Rosarito City Council presents an authentic taste of the real Mexico with the **MEXICAN INDEPENDENCE DAY CELEBRATION** on September 16.

Another authentic-flavored event presented by the Rosarito City Council is the **ANNIVERSARY OF THE MEXICAN REVOLUTION** on November 20.

RESTAURANTS

El Nido / ★★★

BLVD JUÁREZ 67, ROSARITO; 661/612-1430 Brick walls and arched windows define the exterior of this ranch-style restaurant, but traditional Mexico best defines the treasures that leave the kitchen. Established in 1974, and with branches in both San Felipe and Loreto, El Nido is known for its mesquite-grilled entrees and recipes that have been in the family for more than 100 years. Fresh seafood, tender beef shipped from the beef-producing state of Sonora, quail, and venison (both from the family farm) highlight the menu. Try the *filete adobado,* a tender steak marinated with a paste made from ancho and *guajillo* chiles, vinegar, and spices and grilled to order. Dinners are served with El Nido's thick and hearty bean soup, salad, and a baked potato. The wine list is extensive, showcasing many of Baja California's premier wines. Breakfasts are also noteworthy, including specialties such as their venison *machaca* scramble and their omelets made with quail eggs and nopal (cactus). Service is great and the coffee is some of the best around. *$$; Cash only; breakfast, lunch, dinner every day; full bar; no reservations; www.loreto.com/elnido; one block north of Hotel Fantastic.*

La Casa de Langosta / ★

BLVD JUÁREZ, ROSARITO; 661/612-0924 La Casa de Langosta (the Lobster House) is a small yet comfortable restaurant that caters to families and serves a reasonably priced lobster dinner. Order your lobster grilled or Puerto Nuevo style, where the live crustacean is dipped in hot oil before it's moved to the grill. Servings come with beans, rice, flour tortillas, plenty of salsa, and fresh *limón.* The menu also includes lobster omelets and lobster burritos. Their Sunday brunch is an all-you-can-eat buffet and is also reasonably priced. *$; Cash only; breakfast, lunch, dinner every day, brunch Sun; beer and wine; no reservations; northern end of Blvd Juárez (west side of street).*

La Flor de Michoacán / ★★

BLVD JUÁREZ 291, ROSARITO; 661/612-1858 For a taste reminiscent of Mexico's colonial heartland, visit this popular, casual spot at the north end of town. Martín Ochoa and his sister, Lupita, have taken over the family-run business that has specialized in *carnitas* (little meats) since 1950. Order this pork special by the kilo (2.2 pounds) or *medio kilo* (about a pound). Wrap the succulent steamed meat in a fresh, hot tortilla and garnish with onions, salsa, and cilantro. Meals are accompanied by beans, rice, and fresh guacamole. Or have them wrap up the whole meal so you can take it for a picnic on the beach. Other menu choices include tostadas, tacos, tortas, and burritos made with beef or their famous pork. If you have room for dessert, they usually offer a half dozen choices, including a fresh coconut pudding and a wonderful chocolate flan. The service is excellent and La Flor is an affordable and comfortable place to bring the kids. *$–$$; Cash only; breakfast, lunch, dinner Thurs–Tues; beer, wine, and tequila; no reservations; 2-story building north of town.*

Le Cousteau / ★★

BLVD JUÁREZ 184, ROSARITO; 661/612-2655 One of Rosarito's newest and certainly most elegant restaurants is this cozy bistro on the boulevard. Both owner Philippe Chauvin and his maitre d' are Frenchmen who married local women and immigrated to rustic Rosarito Beach. Their passion for cooking is evident in the French and Mediterranean dishes they prepare with attention to detail and an ever-evolving menu (in English and Spanish). There are a number of pasta dishes, including lasagne and a four-cheese fettuccine, as well as grape leaves and veggie crepes. The spinach and goat cheese salad has just the right amount of vinaigrette dressing. Meat lovers: try the filet mignon or a humble club sandwich. A fireplace takes away any winter chill, while in the evening, candlelight bounces off burgundy table linens and knotty pine walls to reflect a warm light. There's a different continental menu daily so the regular clientele—foreign and Mexican residents—will not become bored. For dessert treat yourself to chocolate mousse à l'orange, chocolate crepes, or a poached pear served with vanilla ice cream and warm chocolate sauce. Peruse the wine list for Chilean, Mexican, or French vintages. *$–$$; No credit cards; traveler's checks OK; lunch, dinner Tues–Sun; full bar; reservations recommended; across the street from El Nido.*

Rincón San Román / ★★★

KM 19.5 MEXICO 1-D, ROSARITO; 664/631-2241 Chef Martín San Román of Mexico City owns this excellent ocean-view restaurant on the grounds of the Real del Mar resort complex with its Marriott Hotel and 18-hole golf course. The enthusiastic, boy-faced chef was trained in Paris and taught at Le Cordon Bleu. Although the underlying influence is French, Román's seasonings and recipes are contemporary Mexican and American. For appetizers you'll find scrumptious breaded and fried *panela* cheese with fruit compote along with salmon carpaccio with capers. Many recipes are upgrades of plebeian fare such as the duck *taquitos* served with orange marmalade and salsa of fiery *pequín* (a tiny, dried chile), or the less expensive beef *machaca* (shredded, air-dried meat) burrito. Try the Alaskan salmon crusted with sesame seed in a sweetened *tomatillo* salsa, or the tender beef fillet in escargot sauce. The French pastries and desserts come highly recommended, especially the chef's special *pastel de* *crepas Tijuana,* a "pie" of 21 thin crepes topped with a mousse of white chocolate—light and delicious but not overly sweet. The restaurant is small without being crowded, the wine list is adequate, and service is friendly and professional. *$$; V; traveler's checks OK; lunch, dinner every day; full bar; reservations recommended; between Tijuana and Rosarito off the toll road.*

Vince's Seafood Restaurant / ★★

BLVD JUÁREZ 97-A, ROSARITO; 661/612-1253 Long before Rosarito was a bona fide tourist destination, Vince's was serving the town's freshest seafood to locals and gringos in the know. Don't come for the ambience: the smallish restaurant is beyond plain and has a cafeteria-like feel. Plates are institutional plastic, although at least you get flatware instead of plastic forks and knives. What folks flock here for is the food. The Pimentel family, who own it, has long-standing connections with area fishermen. (Head for the back of the restaurant for a look at the day's catch, sold to hotels and restaurants all over Rosarito.) Portions are large, which is great because the shrimp, halibut fillets, and fresh ceviche (raw seafood marinated in lime juice) are all excellent. Order a dozen oysters for less than $10 or the house special: steamed fish fillet served with soup, salad, tortillas (made on the premises), and rice or potatoes for around $6. *$; Cash only; breakfast, lunch, dinner every day; full bar; no reservations; several blocks north of Hotel Festival Plaza.*

LODGINGS

Just a few of the following listings are in the town of Rosarito proper; others are north or south along the highway, facing the beach. Most of those in town are on Boulevard Benito Juárez, which outside of town translates as the "Old Ensenada Highway" (Mexico 1).

Festival Plaza Hotel / ★☆

BLVD JUÁREZ 107-1, ROSARITO; 661/612-2950 OR 800/453-8606 US, FAX 661/612-2836 The Festival Plaza is the most amazing structure in Rosarito, with a brightly colored eight-story exterior and a Ferris wheel in its backyard. Within or adjacent to the carnival-like complex are 110 rooms, myriad restaurants, and a multitude of clubs, cantinas, and spaces for group parties. The centerpiece of the plaza, behind the main hotel, is a giant black-and-white snake devouring a watermelon. The plaza is crammed with a heated, free-form swimming pool (with swim-up bar and hot tub), an outdoor performing stage, and the working Ferris wheel. Economy-minded partiers should consider the Rock 'n' Roll Bungalows, which sleep up to six people, with a nearby pool and bar for their sybaritic pleasures. Casitas sleep four and have two bathrooms, while roomier suites, villas, and townhouses give you a choice of a king or two queen-size beds. Horseback riding and ATV rentals are available nearby for those who'd rather venture away from the bars. This venue is always noisy, often rowdy, and most often packed with 30-and-under party animals. *$; DIS, MC, V, traveler's checks*

OK; *crosettew@hotmail.com; www.festival-plaza.com; toward south end of Blvd Juárez but north of Rosarito Beach Hotel.*

Hotel Calafia / ★

KM 35.5 MEXICO 1, ROSARITO; 661/612-1581 Calafia sits on the 1773 boundary line between the Dominican and Franciscan orders. Designed to look like an authentic mission, this sprawling tile-roofed property is perched along a cliff at the ocean's edge. The complex does appear authentic in that it's rather dilapidated. The small parking lot is crowded with miniature replicas of missions, examples of Baja's cave paintings, and a 16th-century galleon. The entire resort is mazelike, with terraced cement walkways leading up and down and around. To check in, walk down and through the sloped tunnel leading to a closet-sized reception area. The 60 standard rooms and five indoor/outdoor restaurants are all in need of some TLC, with the exception of a few that have been newly renovated for oceanfront weddings. The outstanding feature here is the location. Sit at the verandah cafe looking out over the rugged coastline of the Pacific; from January through April, gray whales can be spotted passing between the islands and the beach. *$; MC, V, traveler's checks OK; calafia1@telnor.net; www. calafia.com.mx; 6 miles south of Rosarito on the free road.*

Las Rocas Resort and Spa / ★★★

KM.38.5 MEXICO 1, ROSARITO; 661/614-0354 OR 888/527-7622 US The striking, white-on-white Mediterranean-style structure against the azure sea draws you into the gated entrance of Las Rocas (the rocks). Uncluttered white walls continue throughout the property, where large rocks emerge from lush landscaping. Although it's looking a bit worn, this resort has all the trappings of a first-class retreat. The 72 suites are spacious and well appointed with fireplaces, kitchenettes, satellite TV, rustic Mexican furniture, and stylish accessories. Enjoy a drink on your private terrace and watch the sunset or listen to the waves crashing on the rocky point below. Choose a standard suite or a larger luxury suite with sunken bathtub, private hot tub, and king-size bed. The two restaurants specialize in seafood, steaks, and Mexican favorites; the full-service spa offers a wide range of treatments including hydrotherapy, aromatherapy, facials, wraps, and massage. A steam room, two pools, and classes such as yoga and aerobics are available for guests. Las Rocas is also headquarters to the **AQUARIUS TRAINING AND DEVELOPMENT CENTER,** an exemplary adventure and problem-solving program used by many top U.S. corporations and universities to develop team-building. Other facilities include an infinity-edged swimming pool, terrace bar, three hot tubs, complete fitness center, tennis courts, arts-and-crafts center, gift shop, and piano bar. For those who crave the waves, the resort is near the popular surf break **KM 38.** *$$$–$$$$; MC, V; traveler's checks OK; reservations@lasrocas.com; www.lasrocas.com; 6 miles south of Rosarito on the free road.*

LUSCIOUS LANGOSTA

Plucked fresh from the Pacific and split in two, Puerto Nuevo–style **LOBSTERS** are dipped in fat and steeped in history. According to local legend, the recipe for this coastal delicacy came from the cooking pots of three fishermen living on the bluffs above the Pacific Ocean where Puerto Nuevo resides today. The tiny village, located 12 miles south of Rosarito, now hosts more than 30 restaurants, all featuring the spiny crustacean, dipped in oil and grilled to perfection. With a nod to the weight-conscious, some restaurants also offer lobster boiled in water.

In case you are planning to fire up your own pot of lard (or water) on the beach, you should know it is against the law for foreigners to catch their own lobsters. Fortunately, this sweet, succulent entree is served up and down the peninsula. Puerto Nuevo also hosts an annual **FESTIVAL DEL VINO Y LA LANGOSTA** (Lobster and Wine Festival) each October. The celebration features cook-offs, folklóric dancing, wild mariachi music, and crazy foot races, including one where swift (and sometimes drunk) waiters carry serving trays with 3 wine glasses and a bottle of vino. Baja wineries also participate, offering samples of their latest vintages. Wherever you dine on Baja California's luscious langosta, remember its humble beginnings—bubbling in a clay pot above a fisherman's fire. For more information on the Festival del Vino y la Langosta, contact **ROSARITO'S TOURIST OFFICE** (661/612-0396).

—Susan McCombs

Rosarito Beach Hotel / ★★★

BLVD BENITO JUÁREZ 31, ROSARITO; 661/612-0144 OR 800/343-8582 US, FAX 661/612-1125 Manuel Barbachano was the visionary who more than 76 years ago acquired this property, with its wide, pristine beach and run-down hunting lodge. When the hotel was built in 1926, its on-site gambling casino attracted people from around the world, including Hollywood celebrities. Today greatly expanded, the facility retains at least a little of its original charm and allure. The large lobby has the original Spanish tile floors and 1930s-era murals, while colorful Mexican tiles pattern the hallways and lobby walls. Its 280 rooms vary widely in price depending on the day of the week, the season, and their location. Choose from oceanfront suites, garden or oceanfront rooms, or two-bedroom suites. Rooms are comfortably furnished and even the older section, which was looking a bit worn, has recently been refurbished and updated with fresh paint, carpets, drapes, and colorful accessories.

Adjoining the hotel, the original owner's mansion has been fully restored and converted into **CHABERT'S RESTAURANT,** where diners feast under glittering crystal chandeliers in opulence that seems quite out of place in blustery, youth-oriented Rosarito. Within the hotel, the **BEACH SPORTS SHOP** rents diving, fishing, and sports equipment, and on adjoining grounds, **CASA LA PLAYA** offers spa treatments and massage. Other facilities include a 500-yard fishing pier, two swimming pools, three hot tubs, and a children's playground. The beach is wide and wonderful for beachcombing, swimming, and bodysurfing. Horseback riding is available nearby and if that's not enough to keep the kids busy, in the summer the hotel offers them supervised activities including arts and crafts, sand castle contests, and swimming pool games. *$$–$$$; MC, V; traveler's checks OK; rositorr@telnor.net; www.rosaritobeachhotel.com; near south end of town.* &

Ensenada

One of Mexico's largest seaports, Ensenada (Spanish for "cove" or "inlet") has grown slowly but steadily since the bay on which it lies, Bahía de Todos Santos (All Saints' Bay), was first seen by Portuguese explorer Juan Rodríguez Cabrillo in the 16th century. Later, whalers and pirates discovered the bay, the latter hiding their ships inside its sheltered waters. Queen Elizabeth I sent Sir Francis Drake to crush the competition; he hijacked the pirates and carried away most of their booty on his ship, *The Pelican*.

Since then, the town has supported ranchers, gold miners, vintners, fishermen, and a slew of partiers in search of a good time. A prosperous fishing fleet and fish-processing industry thrives along the boulevard fronting Ensenada's perfect, fishhook-shaped harbor, where you'll find boat repair docks, fishing fleets, and commercial shipping warehouses.

Today Ensenada is a metropolis of some 325,000 souls, and the peninsula's largest port. With warm days and cool, occasionally foggy nights, the city is one of the most popular destinations for weekend tourists from Southern California, which shares a similar climate but lacks the laid-back attitude and less-expensive prices.

Every summer an estimated 4.5 million visitors invade Ensenada, including those who briefly pass through town on cruise ships in from Southern California. Since it's just 68 miles from the international border at Tijuana, both dollars and pesos are acceptable currency and everyone speaks at least a little English. The city's main tourist/shopping zone is compact and easy to cover on foot. It consists of two parallel streets, Boulevard Costero (also known as Boulevard Lázaro Cárdenas) and Avenida López Mateos, which hosts the most interesting concentration of shops, restaurants, and clubs.

There are no beaches in Ensenada proper, and burgeoning beach facilities and accommodations to the north at Rosarito over the last decade have siphoned off a substantial amount of Ensenada's tourist trade. Most of those who choose Ensenada over Rosarito are seeking a glimpse of the "real Mexico" as close to the U.S. border as possible.

Though there is plenty of entertainment to be found within Ensenada, there are several worthwhile excursions waiting just beyond the city limits. Less than an hour's drive away are two golf courses, a blowhole, the remnants of a Russian settlement, and Mexico's oldest surviving winery. Of course, if a beer or a tequila shooter is more your style, you can stay in Ensenada and sing along with the mariachis in historic Hussong's Cantina.

ACCESS AND INFORMATION

BY CAR, Mexico 1-D, the toll road to Ensenada (follow signs to "Ensenada Cuota" or "Scenic Route") from Tijuana, is a faster ride than the old Mexico 1— it's also one of the most scenic drives on the peninsula. Frothy breakers beat the shore as sunshine and ocean mist alter the Pacific's colors from deep blue to steely gray or sometimes aquamarine. Three tolls are required (about $2.30 US per toll) to travel the 90-minute drive from the border. Mexico 1 is the free road, also called Ensenada Libre, Old Road, or the Old Ensenada Highway. While it's only two lanes and undivided, it is nonetheless a perfectly acceptable road, which heads inland about halfway to Ensenada, returning to the coast to become Boulevard Costero at the northern entrance to town. Ensenada can also be reached from Tecate along Mexico 3, which passes through wine country, Valle de Guadalupe. Mexico 3 resumes at the south end of Ensenada, winding east and south across the Sierra de Juárez to join Mexico 5 near the Sea of Cortez. If you're heading south of Ensenada, or staying longer than 72 hours, make sure that you have a validated tourist card (see the Planning a Trip chapter).

The best way to get to downtown is to follow signs toward "Ensenada Centro," which will lead you along the waterfront. The easiest route for those continuing south is to follow signs toward San Quintín (keep hugging the waterfront). This is Boulevard Costero (also known as Boulevard Lázaro Cárdenas). After passing the manicured lawns of Plaza Cívica (Civic Plaza; also known as Tres Cabezas), get into the left lane. At the naval base (on your right), turn left onto Calle Sandinés (which may or may not be signed). On this stretch, keep a close watch for stop signs, which are not always clearly visible (look for *alto* painted on the road as well as stop signs). Mexico 1, disguised as Ejército Nacional (which may or may not be marked), is at the second stoplight (look for the huge Gigante grocery store) and turn right (south). The km markers in this region reset in Ensenada and increase as you head south; see Demystifying the Km Markers in the Planning a Trip chapter.

Technically, there is no direct **BUS SERVICE** from the United States to Ensenada; however, Greyhound buses take passengers from downtown San Diego to downtown Tijuana, where a connecting bus can deliver them to Ensenada. Ensenada's main bus station, Central de Autobuses (Av Riveroll at Calle 11a) is serviced by Autotransportes de Baja California (ABC; 664/178-6680) with daily bus routes as far south as La Paz and east to San Felipe and Mexicali. Autotransportes Aragón (664/178-8521), Transportes Norte de Sonora, Elite, and

Estrellas de Oro (664/178-6770), which serve mainland Mexico, all operate out of a terminal on Avenida Riveroll and Calle 8a.

On a local level, **CITY BUSES** serve most of the popular downtown destinations. Look for them along Boulevard Costero, Avenida Juárez, and Avenida Reforma. **TAXI SERVICE** centers around the tourist zone, major hotels, and the bus stations. Most prevalent are the green and white **TAXIS VERDE Y BLANCA**.

Aeropuerto El Ciprés, the **ENSENADA AIRPORT** (south of town on Mexico 1; 664/176-6301), is a military airport and official Mexican Port of Entry with a paved airstrip suitable for only small planes. It is frequently used by Doctors Without Borders and is the headquarters of Baja Helicopters (Obregón 527-6 at Calle 4; 664/178-8266) for chopper charters throughout Baja California.

If you plan to travel south of Maneadero (a town about 12 miles south of Ensenada) and you did not obtain a tourist card at the border, tourist cards are available at the Ensenada **IMMIGRATION OFFICE** (on Blvd Azueta at north entrance to town via Mexico 1, next to Port Captain's office; 646/174-0164). Beyond Ensenada, tourist cards are hard to come by, and if it's requested and you do not have a legal one in your possession, you could be fined and/or sent back to the border.

For tourist information and questions about the city, visit the **CONVENTION AND VISITORS CENTER/COTUCO** (Blvd Costero 540 con Azueta; 646/178-3675; cotucoe@telnor.net). For up-to-the-minute information and maps, contact the Secretaria de Turismo de Estado, the **STATE OFFICE OF TOURISM** in Ensenada (Blvd Costero and Calle Las Rocas; 646/172-3022, fax 646/172-3081; otucoe@telnor.net; www.sdro.com/cotuceda). The English-speaking staff is friendly and helpful; it's open daily (Mon–Fri 8am–5pm, Sat–Sun 10am–3pm). The **TOURISM TRUST** (Blvd Costero 609-5 between Macheros and Miramar; 800/310-9687 US; info@enjoyensenada.com) offers information about restaurants, hotels, and other places of interest in Ensenada. It's open weekdays (8am–5pm).

CYBERCAFES are a recent addition to the Ensenada scene. **INTERNETCAFÉ** (Av Juárez 1449-8 between Espinoza and Guadalupe; 646/172-5051) is about the most reasonable (15 pesos per hour) and centrally located. Other choices include **LA CASA DEL INTERNET** (Av Macheros 275-1 at Calle 3; 646/178-1584), **KFE INTERNET** (Av Riveroll 724; 646/178-3870), and **CAFÉ INTERNET** (Blvd López Mateos 582, upstairs; 646/175-7011).

EXPLORING

Although Ensenada can be visited as a long day trip, many choose to spend one or more nights in this bayside city. Start your tour by walking along the **MALECÓN** (waterfront walkway) to the enormous **MERCADO DE MARISCOS** (seafood market, *malecón*). As you make your way past the vendors selling everything from giant Gulf shrimp to tiny anchovies and octopus with dangling tentacles (as well as sailfish, marlin, corvina, yellowtail, *dorado,* mackerel, tuna, sculpin, halibut, snapper, sharks, rays, and squid), you may be tempted to stop

ROSARITO, ENSENADA, AND GUADALUPE VALLEY
THREE-DAY TOUR

DAY ONE: Head south on Mexico 1-D (toll road) toward Rosarito. Take the La Paloma/Popotla/Calafia/Las Rocas exit. Continue south on the Old Ensenada Highway (Mexico 1, the free road) for about 3 miles and look for the signs to **FOXPLORATION**, where you'll tour the Fox Movie Studios. See authentic movie sets from the films *Titanic* and *Bedazzled*. Afterward, drive north on Mexico 1 to **ROSARITO**. Stop for lunch at **EL NIDO**, where the ambience is as delightful as the food. After lunch, check into the historic **ROSARITO BEACH HOTEL**, where the party all began. Spend the afternoon **EXPLORING** this popular party town on foot while **SHOPPING** up and down Avenida Juárez. If you'd rather be a seaside vaquero, go for a **HORSEBACK RIDE** on the beach. After a sunset stroll along the shoreline, drive or take a cab to downtown Rosarito for dinner at **LE COUSTEAU**. After dinner, check out Rosarito's rather rowdy nightlife at **PAPAS & BEER,** right on the sand. (If you're planning to imbibe, it's best take a cab into town from the Rosarito Beach Hotel.)

DAY TWO: Rise early and, after a quick breakfast at the hotel, check out and drive south on Mexico 1-D (toll road) to Ensenada. Enjoy the rugged shoreline along this scenic stretch of highway. Once in Ensenada, follow the waterfront past shipyards and huge boats in dry dock. After the road curves to the right, begin looking for a place to park. Walk toward the waterfront and enjoy Ensenada's **MALECÓN** (waterfront walkway), exploring the **MERCADO DE MARISCOS** (seafood market) and the sportfishing piers. For lunch, you can enjoy a typical Ensenada meal of fish tacos at the Mercado de Mariscos or, if you prefer something more formal, the seafood at **MARISCOS DE BAHÍA DE ENSENADA** is highly recommended. After lunch, shop for locally made handcrafts: intaglio prints at **GUADALUPE GALERÍA DE ARTE** (Calle 1 850-A, Hotel Bahía; 646/175-9122) or stained glass at **SANTA PAULA BAZAR** (Av López

and haggle over the already low prices. But unless you have somewhere to cook such maritime prizes, take a dive instead into one of the handful of outdoor eateries selling Ensenada's legendary fish tacos (spawned in this region and copied by fast-food Mexican restaurants everywhere). These original Baja beauties are made with piping-hot corn tortillas, fresh deep-fried fish, chopped cabbage, a squeeze of lime, and salsa. Add an inexpensive beer to your meal and you're in heaven. Clean public rest rooms are available near the seafood market for a nominal fee. Continue south to the **SPORTFISHING PIER** (*malecón* at Av Alvarado), where **FISHING** and **WHALE-WATCHING** boats depart, the latter during winter months only. The best fishing is generally April through November; see the Adventure section for details.

Mateos between Gastelum and Miramar). If you'd rather work out than shop, walk north on Calle 2, and then west (toward the ocean) up Boulevard Miguel Alemán for an aerobic workout. High above downtown are the homes of some of Ensenada's wealthiest residents, as well as great views of the ocean, town, harbor, and the enormous Mexican flag above it all. Reward yourself for all this walking or shopping with an ice cream cone (try the avocado or corn flavors) at **LA MICHOACANA** (Calle Ruíz between Calles 1 and 2). After checking into the **POSADA EL REY SOL**, freshen up and relax in your room before heading out for the night. For dinner, stroll down to **CASAMAR**, where trios croon romantic tunes. As the evening wanes, visit Ensenada's historic **HUSSONG'S CANTINA** for a nightcap. If you prefer coffee and dessert, **PUEBLO CAFÉ BAJA** (Av Ruíz 96; 646/178-8742) is just half a block from Hussong's.

DAY THREE: Grab a coffee and croissant at **CAFÉ KAFFA** or a more ample breakfast at **LONCHERÍA LA HOLANDESA**. Then spend the day in the **VALLE DE GUADALUPE**, where many of Mexico's leading vineyards are found. From the north end of Ensenada, follow signs saying "Carretera a Tecate" to Mexico 3 and Valle de Guadalupe. About half an hour from Ensenada, visit the **L.A. CETTO WINERY** (km 75 Carretera a Tecate; 646/155-2264). Free tours and tastings are offered daily. You might opt to buy a bottle of olive oil as well as your favorite reserve vintage at the winery shop. Return toward Ensenada (or see Day Three of the Tijuana/Tecate tour, and spend the rest of the day following the itinerary laid out for Tecate). About halfway between L.A. Cetto winery and the northern edge of Ensenada, enjoy a delicious lunch of quail and grilled veggies at **RESTAURANTE CAMPESTRE LOS NARANJOS,** or, Wednesdays excepted, at the fancier **LAJA**. After lunch, continue south on Mexico 3 to its junction with Mexico 1. Head south through Ensenada and another 10 miles through Maneadero to State Highway 23. Take this highway west to **PUNTA BUFADORA** (the blowhole), one of the region's most visited attractions. Hit the road before dark, arriving back in Ensenada in time for dinner at **GASTELUM 57.**

Continue along the *malecón* toward the enormous Mexican flag: at 130 feet by 160 feet long (and weighing 550 pounds), the tricolor icon is easy to spot. It waves above **PARQUE VENTANA AL MAR** (Window-to-the-Sea Park; *malecón*). This aptly named park affords a nice view of the port and the sea beyond.

Hitch a ride in a horse-drawn carriage on the opposite side of the Mercado at the **PLAZA CÍVICA** (Blvd Costero at Av Riveroll) where you'll find **PLAZA DE LAS TRES CABEZAS** (Blvd Costero at Av Riveroll), home to the enormous bronze busts of Benito Juárez, Miguel Hidalgo, and Venustiano Carranza, three of Mexico's best-known freedom fighters.

CATEDRAL NUESTRA SEÑORA DE GUADALUPE (Our Lady of Guadalupe Cathedral; Av Floresta at Av Juárez) with its prominent twin towers is noted for its lovely stained-glass windows and impressive marble columns.

COFFEEHOUSES are brewing throughout Ensenada. Two of the most popular are **CAFÉ KAFFA** (1090-12 Blvd López Mateos; 646/674-0259) and **CAFÉ TOMÁS** (Blvd López Mateos at Calle Ruíz), both specializing in tasty pastries and perfect espressos. **ESPRESSO BAR** (Blvd López Mateos 496) is a friendly place that usually offers live music on Saturday night. **LA ESQUINA DE BODEGAS** (Av Miramar at Calle 7; 646/678-2509) is one of the few cafe/galleries in the city. In addition to wines, coffee, and tiramisu, the small restaurant serves a fixed-price lunch menu, soups, salads, and sandwiches.

And don't miss Baja California's oldest winery, **LAS BODEGAS DE SANTO TOMÁS** (Av Miramar at Calle 7; 646/178-3333; bstwines@telnor.net; www.santo tomas.com.mx). Tours are available Monday through Saturday (at 11am, noon, 1pm, and 3pm); avoid Wednesday and Saturday, when cruise-ship passengers receive priority. The normal tour costs $5 US, and includes samples of 10 wines; for $10 US, taste 16 vintages (including a special reserve) and receive a commemorative wine glass souvenir. **CAVAS VALMAR** (Av Riveroll 1950 at Ambar; 646/178-6405; valmar@telnor.net; www.cavasvalmer.com), a small-production winery, buys most of its grapes elsewhere, but its varietals are worth following. Tours and tasting are by appointment only. For more on Baja's other wineries, see the "Beyond Tequila" sidebar in this chapter.

German immigrant John Hussong established **HUSSONG'S CANTINA** (Av Ruíz 113; 646/178-3210) in 1892. The once rough-and-tumble bar, now owned by John's son Ricardo, essentially looks like it did the day it opened more than 100 years ago. Sawdust still covers the floor of this long, one-room cantina. Hussong's was originally a stagecoach stop frequented by miners and cowboys who rode their horses right up to the bar. Today, Hussong's is the most famous watering hole in Ensenada and the oldest in continuous operation in Baja. Expect a crowd and belly up to the bar if you can—sip a cold one, people watch, and enjoy the music of mariachis and *ranchero* groups. Open daily (10am–1am).

For a taste of Prohibition-era luxury and style, head over to **RIVIERA DEL PACÍFICO** (Blvd Costero and Av Riviera; 646/176-4310), formerly known as the Playa Ensenada Hotel and Casino. At its grand opening in 1930, dignitaries and Hollywood celebrities listened to Bing Crosby croon to the sounds of the Xavier Cugat Orchestra. Originally owned by world boxing champion Jack Dempsey, the Riviera closed shortly after its inauguration, when gambling was outlawed. Now a cultural center, the restored building remains a glamorous reminder of Ensenada's past. Glance upward at the painted ceilings as you walk through the mansion's echoing corridors and tour its ballrooms. Enjoy a relaxing drink downstairs at the **BAR ANDALUZ**, where life-size nudes still gracefully recline behind the elaborately carved mahogany bar. Or head upstairs to the gift shop and the small **MUSEO DE HISTORIA DE ENSENADA** to learn about Ensenada's colorful past. Before leaving, take a moment to visit the flower gardens and stroll the landscaped grounds full of exotic palms and subtropical plants surrounding this impressive white-walled building declared a "World Historical Monument" by the United Nations. Currently, the rooms are used for wedding receptions and other social and civic events. Unless rented for one of these occasions, the venue is open weekdays (8:30am–8pm). Admission $1 US.

If you've ever wanted to peek inside a Mexican jail (from the law-abiding side), sneak over to the **MUSEO HISTÓRICO REGIONAL** (Historical Museum of Ensenada; Av Gastelum between Blvd Costero and López Mateos; 646/178-2531). Built in 1886 as an army barracks (and still retaining its corner guard posts), it later served as the city jail. Step into one of the small, windowless cells, close the door, and imagine life inside with four or five other unfortunates. Across from the remaining cells is a small collection of historical photos, military and farm equipment, and native Indian artifacts (labeled in Spanish only). Open daily (10am–5pm). Donations are welcome.

Ensenada boasts several fine **GOLF COURSES** within a half hour's drive of the city. Ten miles south on Mexico 1 is the **BAJA COUNTRY CLUB** (646/177-5523), an 18-hole, par 72 semiprivate course. Tucked in a small valley just north of Maneadero and east of the highway, greens fees here run about $40 US. Twenty-one miles north of Ensenada on Mexico 1, the **BAJAMAR OCEANFRONT GOLF RESORT** (km 77.5 Mexico 1; 888/311-6076; info@golfbaja.net; www.golfbajamar.com) has three 9-hole courses with spectacular ocean views. Play ranges in difficulty among the three courses. You'll see the entrance on the west side of the freeway. Greens fees run $45–$80 US.

SHOPPING

For souvenirs from your trip, visit Ensenada's main shopping zone, which runs about eight blocks along **AVENIDA LÓPEZ MATEOS** (also called **CALLE PRIMERA** along this stretch) between Avenidas Castillo and Obregón. Restaurants and bars share the sidewalk with street cafes. Among the nicest shops is the two-story **BAZAR CASA RAMÍREZ** (Av López Mateos 496; 646/178-8209), where traditional techniques and materials are used in the creation of innovative objects d'art. **LOS CASTILLO** (Av López Mateos 815; 646/176-1187), which has franchises throughout Mexico, sells a nice selection of silver jewelry from Taxco at this and several other locations along López Mateos. Just down the block, **MARIOS SILVER SHOP** (Av López Mateos #1090) also features Taxco silver along with knockoff handbags, leather goods, glassware, and guitars.

Jammed between several **GOLD DUCK** stores selling knockoffs of Gucci handbags are vendors selling Cuban cigars and cheap Mexican art. Also nearby are shops such as **VALENCIA** (Av López Mateos 1084; 646/178-8938), with hundreds of lambskin leather goods from Italy and Spain, and the classy **SARA BOUTIQUE** (Av López Mateos 1090-15; 646/178-2966), noted primarily for selling duty-free perfumes. Farther down the street, **COLORES DE MÉXICO** (Av López

Mateos 1094; 646/178-8194) displays Gucci and Prada handbags, ceramics, onyx vases, and the signature black pottery of Oaxaca.

One of Ensenada's newest shops is worth seeking out even if you don't spend a peso inside. **ORÍGENES** (Av Gastelum 55-4; 646/178-1080) is the most unusual craft store in Ensenada. Prices here reflect the quality of the one-of-a-kind home furnishings and crafts from throughout the country, including metal art, wall hangings, lamps, and furniture.

Closer to the waterfront, trade ebbs and flows at the **CENTRO ARTESANAL DE ENSENADA** (Artisans Center of Ensenada; Blvd Costero 1094), as the cruise ships dock and unload. Some tenants have fled as cruise ship traffic has been diverted from the area in recent years; others, such as **GALERÍA DE PÉREZ MEILLÓN** (646/174-0394), stick it out. This small gallery has been in business for 13 years, carrying museum-quality folk art, including rustic but elegant pottery from Chihuahua; pit-fired pottery made by the Paipai Indians; and willow baskets made by the Kumayaay. Most of the better downtown and oceanfront hotels also have **GIFT SHOPS** if you still haven't found what you're looking for.

ADVENTURES

PARQUE NACIONAL CONSTITUCIÓN DE 1857 / One of four national parks in Baja, the Parque Nacional Constitución de 1857 stretches over 12,335 acres amid the Sierra de Juárez mountains southeast of Ensenada and southwest of Mexicali. The washboard dirt road (sometimes graded) climbs 26 miles before reaching the gate at nearly 4,000 feet elevation. Watch the surrounding landscape change in texture and color from the desert's thorny scrub to low junipers, gradually becoming forests of Parry, piñon, ponderosa, and Jeffrey pines. At the top, several granite peaks rise above 5,000 feet and the forest forms a protected woodland area, certainly one of the most impressive in Baja California. Summer temperatures in the park offer relief from the oppressive heat of the surrounding desert communities, while winter months always bring the possibility of snow.

Near the center of the park is **LAGUNA HANSON**, Baja's only natural lake and a stopover for migratory waterbirds. The shallow lake was named after an American miner who mysteriously disappeared here in 1880. Clusters of ducks and coots inhabit the water and surrounding marshlands every fall. Hunting is prohibited, but **FISHING** is allowed and the lake can hold a substantial stock of largemouth bass and catfish. Large boulders surround the basin, framing it with tall ponderosa pines and the granite outcroppings to the north and west, where **CLIMBING** is popular. A 6-mile walking path follows the shoreline. Nearby **CAMPSITES** ($7/night) are well-tended, with tidy fire pits, grills, tables, and sometimes firewood.

To reach the park, take Mexico 3 south of Ensenada. Travel about 20 miles and then turn left onto the secondary (dirt) road 200 yards east of km 55 (look for signs to Laguna Hanson) near Ojos Negros. Continue on this road for approximately 25 miles. **ECOLOGICAL & ADVENTURE TOURS OF BAJA CALIFORNIA** (Blvd Costero 1094, Ensenada; 646/178-3704; ecoturbc@

ens.com.mx; www.mexonline.com/ecotur.htm) leads trips into the park from Ensenada. See the Guides and Outfitters section for more information.

There is another entrance to this park between Tecate and Mexicali that is passable (to a certain point) via passenger cars. This eastern entrance offers access to hiking trails, scenic canyons, and hot springs. See Mexicali's Adventures section for more information.

DIVING AND SNORKELING / The eastern shores of **ISLAS DE TODOS SANTOS**, 30 minutes by boat from Ensenada, are great for snorkeling and diving. Thick kelp forests are home to barracuda, kelp bass, and occasional schools of yellowtail. The summer months offer the best visibility (50–60 feet) and warmer water temperatures (60–63°F), but thick wet suits are recommended year-round. The **PUNTA BANDA** peninsula, 16 miles south of town, offers excellent scuba diving and snorkeling. For do-it-yourselfers, **JUANITO'S BOATS** (*malecón;* 646/174-0953) is the best place to hire a *pangero* (*panga* with driver) to take you out to these dive sites. If you need to rent dive gear and fill tanks, or prefer to go with an experienced divemaster, **LA BUFADORA DIVE** comes highly recommended; see Guides and Outfitters.

HORSEBACK RIDING / Are you a *vaquero* (cowboy) at heart? If you or the kids have an itching to spend a few hours or even a few days on horseback, contact **BAJA BANDIDOS** (646/174-6767; bandidos@bajabandidos.com.mx; www.bajabandidos.com.mx). Though Bandidos offers two trail-ride locations, the closest is the centuries-old **RANCHO LA MENTADA**, located just a few miles north of Ensenada. At this working ranch, you can ride through the rolling foothills alongside *vaqueros* who have worked cattle and trained horses all their lives.

FISHING / Fishing the Ensenada waters is very similar to fishing in Southern California, with the best season running from late June through early September. When the albacore tuna are running, the town buzzes with "fishing energy," since Ensenada has convenient access to the albacore's migratory path near the Todos Santos Islands. Many charter companies (see Guides and Outfitters) offer 14-hours trips during albacore season, traveling as far as 30 miles to find these schooling tuna. Lingcod, barracuda, and *bonito* can strike any time of the year. Seven-hour fishing trips usually run about $40 US per person, with an additional fee for your Mexican fishing license ($24 a week; $35 a month; $45 a year).

SURFING / The most popular surfing destination in the region is about 3 miles north of Ensenada—the small bay known as **SAN MIGUEL**. Mexico's first surfboard manufacturing company was named after this bay. Consistent waves and typically uncrowded lineups draw surfers from Southern California. **EL RINCÓN** ("the Nook"), a favorite spot within the bay, is known for its fast-moving, right-hand point break. Look for the turnoff to San Miguel just south of the third toll station from Tijuana. Other popular surfing destinations include the area around **SALSIPUEDES** (near km 88, north of the third toll plaza), and all along the shoreline south of Ensenada.

ISLAS DE TODOS SANTOS is the site of some of the largest surf on the west coast of North America. The twin islands, located about 12 miles west of Ensenada, are known for their monster winter waves with 30-foot faces. Experienced, hard-core surfers will need to hire an experienced *pangero* to reach these breaks. Try **JUANITO'S BOATS** (*malecón*; 646/174-0953). Their 20-foot skiffs are large enough to hold a half dozen surfers plus their equipment. The total cost is about $150 US per day and the trip out to the waves takes about 30 minutes. The **SAN MIGUEL SURF SHOP** (Av López Mateos and Calle Ruíz; 646/178-1007), near famous Hussong's Cantina, is the home of the reputable San Miguel Surfboards and a great place to see the latest in surfboards, check current conditions, have a ding repaired, or for any other equipment needs.

WHALE-WATCHING / Ensenada is a good place to watch California gray whales as they migrate from the Arctic Ocean to their mating and birthing grounds in the coastal lagoons of Baja California Sur. Accompanied by adult and yearling males, females hug the coast and seem to favor the waterway between the shoreline and the Todos Santos Islands. The rugged, volcanic headlands to the north and south of Ensenada are both excellent locations for spotting these magnificent creatures as they pass close to shore. For a closer look, book a whale-watching excursion from **GORDO'S SPORT FISHING AND WHALE WATCHING BOATS** (*malecón*; 646/178-3515; www.gordos.8m.com) or **SERGIO'S SPORT-FISHING AND WHALE WATCHING** (*malecón*; 646/178-2185 or 800/336-5454 US; www.sergios-sportfishing.com). Tours typically last from three to four hours and cost about $20 US for adults, $15 for children 11 and under. The season runs from mid-December through late March and reservations are required.

GUIDES AND OUTFITTERS

For new diving equipment, annual equipment servicing, repairs, and tank fills ($3 US), see Memo Almaraz at the **ALMAR DIVE SHOP** (Av Macheros 149; 646/178-3013). **LA BUFADORA DIVE** (end of State Hwy 23; 646/154-2092; divebc@telnor.net; www.labufador.com/dales/Dales.htm) in Maneadero, 16 miles south of Ensenada, is the most experienced outfitter in the region, offering guided dive trips around Punta Banda. The owner, Dale Erwin, also rents kayaks and can give useful tips regarding local dive sites; see Maneadero's Adventures section for more information on Punta Banda.

For ecologically conscious expeditions in the area and throughout the peninsula, contact **EXPEDICIONES DE TURISMO ECOLÓGICO Y AVENTURA—ECOLOGICAL AND ADVENTURE TOURS OF BAJA CALIFORNIA** (Blvd Costero 1094; 646/178-3704; ecoturbc@ens.com.mx; www.mexonline.com/ecotur.htm). Affable owner Francisco Detrall is certified by the Outdoor Leadership Council and has Wilderness First Response training. His staff of bilingual guides lead adventure-based excursions on foot, by mountain bike, sea kayak, four-wheel-drive vehicles, *pangas* (skiffs), and creative combinations of all of the above.

SERGIO'S SPORTFISHING CENTER (*malecón*; 646/178-2185 or 800/336-5454 US; sergios@telnor.net; www.sergios-sportfishing.com) is a modern, open-party outfitter and one of the best equipped in the Ensenada area. For more than 10 years, this operation has maintained full electronic fish-finding, navigation, and communication systems with knowledgeable captains and crews. The seven-vessel fleet ranges from the sleek 30-foot **PROBE**, holding up to six passengers ($300–$450 US charter price) to the 85-foot **ENSENADA CLIPPER** ($1,500–$3,000 US charter price) with full accommodations for up to 50 passengers. If you don't need a charter, they can book you on a day trip out to the San Miguel Reef for $45 US; prices include Mexican fishing license, gear, and bait. They'll even shuttle you to and from your hotel. Sergio's also offers whale-watching excursions from January through March.

Founded in 1953 by Isaac Ptacnik, **GORDO'S SPORTFISHING** (*malecón;* 646/178-3515; fax 646/174-0481; www.gordos.8m.com) is now run by Isaac Jr. The four-ship private charter service can accommodate 15–35 fishermen. Twelve-hour day trips (2am–4pm), popular during albacore season, run about $100 US per person. Half-day trips (7am–2pm) run $40 US per person. Both include Mexican fishing license, gear, and live bait. What's more, the deckhands will fillet your catch. Bring your own cooler with food and beverages for these trips. Gordo's also offers a **HARBOR TOUR** with a bilingual local guide. The 40-minute tour glides past warships, cruise ships, and tuna boats, and then visits seals and sea lions that make the harbor their home ($2.50 US for adults, $1.50 for children). During the winter, a 4-hour whale-watching trip is offered ($20 US for adults, $15 for children), and for surfer dudes, Gordo's will motor you out to Todos Santos Islands, wait for you to rip it up, and bring you back ($200 US for six surfers).

The modern **HOTEL CORAL MARINA** (3421 Zona Playitas; 646/175-0000 or 800/862-9020 US; marina@hotelcoral.com; www.hotelcoral.com) offers sportfishing charters with fully equipped 35-foot boats and bilingual guides. Half-day trips cost $400 US for six people. Sito Espinoza, a native Tijuanan and experienced fisherman, has managed charters here for more than seven years. If you're not into fishing, Sito can set you up with a 25-foot sailboat for the day ($75 US), or 10- to 16-foot kayaks for $10–$20 per hour. Located 3 miles north of Ensenada at Mexico 1 km 103, the marina has modern conveniences and 350 slips for 30- to 135-foot yachts.

Ensenada's newest sportfishing outfitter is **WE HOOK 'EM ENSENADA SPORTFISHING CHARTERS** (at Hotel Coral and Marina, km 104 Mexico 1; 646/174-5182 or 866/934-6653 US; wehookem@aol.com). Linda Kuhar runs the **MAR DIOSA**, a 40-foot, eight-passenger yacht with full electronics and walk-around decks as well as the smaller **SCHATZI**, a 38-footer set up for six fisherpersons. Summer prices run $1,200–$1,350 US for six to eight people for a 14-hour trip and $800–$950 US for a 10-hour trip. Winter prices are considerably less, starting at $500 US. Price includes tackle, crew, bait, fish cleaning, and boxed lunch, but you must provide your own Mexican fishing license. During the whale-watching season (January–March), excursions for 8 to 12 people cost $350.

NIGHTLIFE

Ensenada's bars and nightclubs have long been a magnet for gringos, young and old. Mix the legal drinking age of 18 with the draw of tequila shooters and higher-octane Mexican beer; add some black leather, a little electronic disco, a touch of mariachi, and some loud rock 'n' roll, and you'll start to get a picture of Ensenada's nightlife scene. If you're doing the town, **HUSSONG'S CANTINA** (Av Ruíz 113; 646/178-3210), Ensenada's most famous bar and the cornerstone of the town's partying past, is a great place to start. Across the street, **PAPAS & BEER** (Av Ruíz 102; 646/174-0145) is a huge multilevel entertainment complex popular among surfers and the dedicated party set. The blasting hip-hop, industrial, or acid rock goes on until 3am and the dancing and partying never seem to slow down. Next door, **OXIDOS** (Av Ruiz 108; 646/178-8827) radiates live pop, jazz, or rock 'n' roll on weekend nights. The club's bar, barstools, tables, and even the bathroom fixtures border on modern pieces of art: classy and innovative.

If none of this is your scene, try **BAR ANDALUZ** (at Rivera del Pacífico; 646/177-1730), a quiet and dignified place to nurse a glass of wine and enjoy conversation with a classical music background, or **PUEBLO CAFÉ BAJA** (Av Ruíz 96; 646/178-8055), where locals sip hot tea and drink coffee after hours, and on weekends listen to local jazz, pop, or soft rock groups.

FESTIVALS AND EVENTS

Nine days before Ash Wednesday (usually around mid-February), Ensenada hosts one of the largest **CARNAVAL** festivals on the peninsula. Streets are closed from the port to the cathedral, and visitors are swept into a genuine Mexican celebration and sensory overload. Music resonates through huge sound systems, mouth-watering aromas of barbecued chicken and chorizo assault the olfactories, and confetti showers fill the streets as colorful parades—some serious, some funky—promenade the downtown sector of this waterfront city. If you're into it, *carnaval* is a fun time to visit Ensenada; if you're not, the celebration can be an inconvenience within the 10- to 12-block area of downtown. For exact dates and more information, contact the Tourism Office (Blvd Costero and Calle Las Rocas; 646/178-2411).

The 50-mile **ROSARITO-ENSENADA FUN BICYCLE RIDE** down the Baja coast culminates in a large fiesta in Ensenada. See Rosarito's Festivals and Events section (www.rosaritoensenada.com).

Also in April, the **NEWPORT-ENSENADA YACHT RACE** (949/664-1023; www.nosa.org) begins near the outside jetty at Newport Harbor, California, and ends at the mouth of the Ensenada Harbor, covering 125 miles of ocean sailing. Some 500 vessels enter this prestigious race, one of the largest competitive sailing events on the west coast, now in its 50th year.

The grueling **BAJA 500** off-road race (little brother to the Baja 1000) is held in June and sponsored by SCORE International (818/853-8068; www.scoreinternational.com) and Tecate Beer. More than 15 different vehicle classes compete in this desert and mountain loop, which starts and finishes in Ensenada.

Also in June, the **ESTERO BEACH VOLLEYBALL TOURNAMENT** (www.estero beach.com) celebrates the beach volleyball lifestyle. The blind-draw tournament attracts some 2,000 participants for three days of serious competition and three nights of serious parties.

Despite the name, **MEXICALI EN LA PLAYA** is a multifaceted event (www.too muchfun.com.mx/events/melp/) held in Ensenada near the cruise ship terminal in July. It features volleyball, beach soccer, motocross and Jet Ski races, music, food, and a bikini contest.

Beginning the first Friday in August, the classy **FIESTA DE LA VENDIMIA (WINE HARVEST FESTIVAL)** features regional cuisine, wine tasting, live jazz and classical music, *folklórico,* and street fairs. Hosted by the **ASOCIACIÓN DE VINICULTORES** (Winegrowers Association; López Mateos 582-208, Plaza Mauina; 646/178-3038; brac@telnor.net; www.ensenadawines.com), this 10-day event is usually a sellout, so it's wise to purchase tickets in advance. Since the finest chefs in the region make this an annual pilgrimage, don't miss the cook-offs and the paella contest. Call for tickets (646/178-3136) at least two weeks in advance.

L.A. Cetto (Tijuana office, 664/685-3013) also hosts a similar one-day **BLESSING OF THE GRAPES CEREMONY** in August with grape crushing, concerts, tours, and wine tasting.

JUAN HUSSONG'S INTERNATIONAL CHILI COOK-OFF AND SALSA CONTEST offers entertaining chili challenges, arts and crafts, plenty of music, and samplings of some fine chili creations. Held north of town at Quintas Papagayo Resort, this event (www.hussongs.com/chilicookoff.html) is the largest and oldest chili contest in all of Mexico.

Big waves mean big fun for surfers in October at the **O'NEILL TECATE MEXICAN SURF FIESTA** (619/585-9173). Four days of surfing, parties, and competition take place at San Miguel Beach, just north of Ensenada.

The "granddaddy" of off-road racing is the hard-core **BAJA 1000**, a desert survival test sponsored by SCORE International (www.score-international. com) and Tecate held each November. More than 20 different vehicle classes, including ATVs, motorcycles, trucks, and autos, compete in this marathon race, which starts in Ensenada and travels south through 1,000 miles of rugged desert terrain before finishing in La Paz (or sometimes looping back to Ensenada).

December 12 marks the **FEAST OF OUR LADY OF GUADALUPE,** a religious feast day and national holiday honoring Mexico's patron saint. Dress warmly, bring the kids, and watch as processions of faithful children, dressed as Juan Diego (the peasant boy who first saw the virgin in a vision) parade the streets. Ceremonies take place from midnight to midnight, centering around Catedral Nuestra Señora de Guadalupe (Av Floresta at Av Juárez).

RESTAURANTS

Bronco's Steakhouse / ★★

AV LÓPEZ MATEOS 1525, ENSENADA; 646/172-4892 The Russian-descendant owners of this steakhouse have created a western, ranch-style eatery with a home-cooked menu that is popular with townies and tourists alike. For lunch and dinner, you can't go wrong with their mesquite-grilled steaks and ribs. If you're really hungry, order one of their traditional specials such as carne asada, beef tips, or their most popular steak, the *vaquero*—a large, marinated rib eye cooked to order and served with potatoes and steamed vegetables. Light eaters might try the *sopa de tortillas*. Most plates come with rice, beans, steaming tortillas, and salsas. Wednesday buffet dinners, which change each week, offer cuisine from throughout Mexico. Their dessert specialty is a moist and rich chocolate cake, or have a scoop of vanilla ice cream topped with Kahlúa. Their reasonably priced, all-you-can-eat weekend brunch features omelets, breakfast enchiladas, hotcakes, fresh fruits, and juices. During the week, the breakfast menu includes steak and egg dishes, a fried apple-cinnamon flatbread, and tasty *huitlacoche* (a black fungus that grows on corn) crepes. Service is good and off-street parking is available. *$–$$; AE, MC, V; traveler's checks OK; breakfast, lunch, dinner every day, brunch Sat–Sun; full bar; no reservations; broncos@telnor.net; www.broncossteakhouse.com; across from San Nicolas Hotel.*

Casamar / ★★

BLVD LÁZARO CÁRDENAS 987, ENSENADA; 646/174-0417, FAX 646/174-0887 High ceilings and large windows create an airy, open feeling at this quiet and reputable restaurant with a second-floor view of the Port of Ensenada and the bay. Linens adorn the tables and diners can choose their own sizable, fresh crustacean from a tank of live lobsters. The menu features an extensive selection of seafood dishes, including *camarónes al mojo de ajo* (shrimp in garlic sauce); fried or sautéed scallops; grilled lobster, squid, or shrimp; and a broiled fillet of shark, halibut, or seabass covered with a mango and tequila salsa. The house special—butterflied shrimp stuffed with crab, cheese, and mushrooms and served in a cream sauce—is delicious if incredibly rich. Lunch and dinner entrees include soup, salad, and fresh-baked rolls. Service is quick and friendly and there is convenient parking next door. In the evening, a musical trio creates a romantic mood. *$; MC, V; traveler's checks OK; lunch, dinner every day; full bar; no reservations; casamar@telnor.net; www.sdro.com/casamar; opposite the big flag.*

El Charro / ★★

AV LÓPEZ MATEOS 454, ENSENADA; 646/178-2114 Perfect rotating rotisserie chickens lure first-time diners in; good food and reasonable prices bring them back again. The restaurant moved to its present location in 2001 after 47 years at the address across the street, and some of the ancient waitresses appear to be originals. Eat your beans, rice, chicken, and salsa with a basket of the delicious handmade tortillas (corn or flour) for which the restaurant is known. Breakfasts are hearty and reasonably priced, such as *chilaquiles,* served with potatoes and bacon, Sonoran beef *machaca* (shredded, air-dried meat), refried beans, guacamole, and tortillas for under $7. But most folks come later in the day for the chicken: simple rotisserie-style, or served in one of several piquant, unusual sauces. Tables and chairs are made of chunky dark wood, and each heavy table is draped in a bright orange, pink, or yellow cloth. The restaurant is festive without being the least bit fancy. Menus are printed in English and Spanish, and wait staff is accustomed to dealing with English-speakers. *$; No credit cards; traveler's checks OK; breakfast, lunch, dinner every day; full bar; reservations recommended; half a block from Hussong's Cantina and Calle Ruíz.*

El Rey Sol / ★★★★

 AV LÓPEZ MATEOS 1000, ENSENADA; 646/178-1733 For the best dining in Ensenada, don't miss the French-inspired El Rey Sol. The restaurant was created by chef doña Pepita Geffroy and her husband, who met while studying at the renowned Cordon Bleu culinary academy. Together they opened this French-international restaurant in 1947. Doña Pepita is no longer with us; the chef who continues her tradition of excellence is Candido Pacheco. Start off with a bowl of authentic French onion soup or a puff pastry shell stuffed with chicken, ham, and fresh mushrooms and topped with a delightful béchamel cream. Entree choices are exquisite, such as the New York steak sautéed in a spicy green peppercorn and cognac sauce, or the crab crepes stuffed with delicate crabmeat, topped with cheese and seasoned bread crumbs. Shrimp Medallions Doña Pepita arrive butterflied and smothered with a white wine sauce and capers. The menu also includes chicken chipotle cooked in brandy and port wine with chiles, prunes, and fresh cream; as well as a selection of Mexican specialties. All meals are served with a hearty bread and fresh vegetables grown on the family's farm in Santo Tomás. Try to save room for dessert, featuring fresh-baked pastries, or top your meal with their imported cheese plate and a glass of port. Service is professional, and your dining experience here will be memorable. *$$–$$$; AE, MC, V; traveler's checks OK; breakfast, lunch, dinner every day; full bar; reservations recommended; corner of López Mateos and Blancarte.*

Gastelum 57 / ★★★☆

LAS DUNAS 118, ENSENADA; 646/177-1480 If you crave something more exotic than burritos and beer, and like decor that is over-the-top Old World, head for this fashionable restaurant owned and operated by the Pacheco family. Ceilings and walls are painted with portraits of fat pink cherubs, tiny chandeliers sparkle from the ceiling, and chairs are upholstered in mauve brocaded material. Stained-glass windows are framed in lavish drapes; reproductions of European paintings hang on the walls. It's *muy* fashionable or terribly fussy, depending on your point of view. The food is distinctive as well, employing such exotic ingredients as coconut, mango, and *huitlacoche* (a black fungus that grows on corn). Entrees, served with soup or salad, are eclectic, ranging from pork ribs with apple and mint relish to beef tongue in peanut and chile sauce. Recommended dishes include fish fillet stuffed with seafood and the curried rice with grilled shrimp. Service is somewhat formal, and fellow diners are bound to be dressed up. This is the place for your glad rags. Located just outside downtown, the restaurant will usually send a car to your hotel or yacht to pick you up. *$$; No credit cards; traveler's checks OK; lunch, dinner Tues–Sun; full bar; reservations recommended; gastelum57@hotmail.com; one block from Blvd Costero.*

La Embotelladora Vieja / ★★★

AV MIRAMAR AT CALLE 7, ENSENADA; 646/174-0807 Dine among 35-foot wine casks and racks of aging vintages at La Embotelladora Vieja—The Old Bottling Plant. Housed within the Bodegas de Santo Tomás winery complex, which was established in 1888, this romantic jewel is comfortably cool and dark with thick brick walls, an expansive ceiling with exposed wooden beams, and high, opaque windows. Candlelight encourages a peruse through the wine list for a varietal to accompany crisp bread served with herbed butter. Chef Ivan Cedeño creates a changing menu with starters such as salmon carpaccio or a delicate Moroccan pastry stuffed with spinach, raisins, and pinenuts. For an entree, choose from swordfish with a coriander and cascabel chile sauce, filet mignon with mushrooms and port, or a spicy tamarind shrimp. Desserts include imported cheeses, cheesecake, or an option for chocoholics. *$$; MC, V; traveler's checks OK; lunch, dinner Mon–Sat; full bar; no reservations; on E side of Miramar at 7th.*

Lonchería La Holandesa / ★

AV RUÍZ 57, ENSENADA; 646/178-1915 Locals dive into this, well, "dive" to eat good food at bargain prices, not to see or be seen. The term *lonchería* signals food without frills, and in this case the food is great. Seat yourself at the long orange bar, where friendly, efficient waitresses dispense giant shredded-beef burritos singly or by the pair. Or sit at one of the round or rectangular tables with thick red plastic tablecloths and order a burger with fries or a *torta* (a sandwich served on a thick, crusty roll). This location—the original and one of the most central—is run by José Sánchez Bernal, the grandson of the popular restaurant's creator. This is a good place to bring the kids, as it's relaxed and no one minds a little extra noise. For breakfast try the *desayuno vegetariano* (vegetarian breakfast), with *nopal* (cactus), mushrooms, and a mildly piquant red sauce served with corn or flour tortillas. *$; Cash only; breakfast, lunch every day, dinner Mon–Sat; no alcohol; no reservations; half a block from Blvd López Mateos.*

Mariscos de Bahía de Ensenada / ★★★

AV RIVEROLL 109, ENSENADA; 646/178-1015, FAX 646/178-3185 Mariscos is one of the best places in town for seafood. Its decor is old-fashioned, but the quality and quantity of seafood selections overshadow any lack of aesthetic detail. Choose a rich and filling fisherman's soup or sample abalone, clams, oysters, shrimp, or giant squid fried or sautéed with or without garlic. Seabass, albacore tuna, and shark are among the fresh fish specials cooked just right (without overcooking) and accompanied by piles of seasoned rice, fresh flour tortillas, and a side salad. Portions are large, so come hungry. Servers, many who have worked here for 15 to 20 years, can give recommendations and are friendly and attentive. The traditional favorite is whole fish (head, tail, and all) cooked to your liking and served with rice, beans, and corn or flour tortillas, both made fresh on the premises. Secure parking is available behind the restaurant. *$; MC, V; traveler's checks OK; lunch, dinner every day; beer and wine; no reservations; mbahia@cafeinternet.net.mx; www.mariscosbahia.com; corner of López Mateos and Riveroll.*

The Restaurant at Punta Morro / ★★★

KM 106 MEXICO 1, ENSENADA; 646/178-3507 OR 800/526-6676 US, FAX 646/174-4490 Dining at Punta Morro is a feast for the senses. Perched on a rocky point, this is a prime location to feel, hear, and witness the mighty Pacific as it pounds the rocks below. Windows shield diners from the spray, but there's no barrier between you and the fabulous meals sent from the kitchen. Arrive in time to watch the sun set and order a vintage from their wine cellar—reputably the finest collection in the region—including labels from the nearby Guadalupe and Santo Tomás vineyards. Start your evening with a mixed green salad topped with almonds, a few anchovies, and grilled skewers of shrimp and chicken, drizzled with a tangy tamarind dressing. Chilly nights might require something warmer, such as their cream of chile poblano and apple soup. For an entree, choose from the blackened tuna steak with peppers; baked pork shanks with sweet pineapple; or a moist fillet of halibut marinated with fresh orange juice, butter, and a hint of tequila. Among the house specialties are the grilled calamari steak and the salmon steak with a delicious herb sauce. A perfect closure might be a cup of freshly ground coffee with a snifter of cognac. The service here is professional yet not overbearing. *$$$; AE, MC, V; traveler's checks OK; breakfast Sat–Sun, lunch, dinner every day; full bar; reservations recommended; pmorro@telnor.net; www.punta-morro.com; on the toll road 2 miles north of town.*

LODGINGS

El Cid Best Western / ★

AV LÓPEZ MATEOS 993, ENSENADA; 646/178-2401 OR 800/352-4305 US, FAX 646/178-3671 Centrally located and affordable, El Cid was built in the 1970s and retains that old-fashioned air. Desk clerks chat and watch TV in the small lobby warmed by dark ceramic floor tiles and a comfortable sofa and chairs. Tall palms shade the plastic chaise lounges surrounding the small, unheated pool, which is sandwiched between the parking garage and meeting rooms. The 52 rooms and 2 suites are basic but clean with heavy, creosote-colored furniture, clock radios, telephones, satellite TV, and wet bar with mini-fridges. Choose two doubles or one queen size bed—you'll pay substantially more for two beds. Bathrooms have noisy fans and funky dispensers for shampoo, conditioner, soap, and shaving cream. The restaurant serves decent meals and covered parking is available. Continental breakfast is included with your rate; children under 12 stay free. *$; AE, MC, V; traveler's checks OK; elcid@telnor. net; www.hotelelcid.com.mx; across from Villa Fontana Days Inn.*

Estero Beach Hotel and Resort / ★★★

KM 14 MEXICO I, ENSENADA; 646/176-6230, FAX 646/176-6925 This beautifully landscaped, 98-room Spanish mission–style complex is spread out along an uncrowded beach on the south shore of Bahía Todos Santos. Popular among families as well as the younger set of partiers interested in outdoor activities, this facility is home to the famous and widely televised Estero Beach International Beach Volleyball Tournament (see Festivals and Events). Rooms range from standard with two double beds to luxury suites with king-size beds and ocean views; none of the rooms have telephones. There's a swimming pool and a children's playground on-site as well as tennis, basketball, and sand volleyball courts. An exhibit center displays an interesting collection of pre-Columbian artifacts, as well as a collection of fossilized marine life found in Baja California. Also located on the property are a recreation hall, an RV park with full hookups, a beachfront restaurant serving breakfast, lunch, and dinner, and a happening bar with refreshing margaritas and a nice selection of local wines. You'll find horseback riding, kayaks, and wave runners for rent, an off-road, short-course racetrack, and plenty of beachcombing and bird-watching opportunities. You can safely swim in the bay here if you don't mind walking out for some distance on mudflats at low tide. Nonguests can use the hotel's facilities for a small fee. *$–$$; MC, V; traveler's checks OK; estero@telnor.net; www. hotelesterobeach.com; 6 miles south of town.*

Hotel Coral and Marina / ★★★

KM 103 MEXICO 1, 3421 ZONA PLAYITAS, ENSENADA; 646/175-0000 OR 877/233-5839 US, FAX 646/175-0005 Built in 1995, the Hotel Coral combines Mediterranean architecture with a full-service marina that can accommodate up to 350 boats. The 147 roomy suites located in three eight-story towers are decorated in contemporary Mexican designs with seating areas that open onto balconies overlooking the marina or the ocean. All of the suites feature direct-dial telephones, cable TV, and refrigerators. Take a break from the kids and have the hotel arrange for babysitting services while you enjoy the 5,000-square-foot European spa offering massages, facials, and aromatherapy treatments. For recreation there are two lighted tennis courts, an exercise room, heated indoor and outdoor pools, and two hot tubs. A dive shop is also on the premises, and fishing and diving excursions can be organized on-site. The hotel also features a restaurant, a bar and nightclub, several gift shops, and a secure parking garage. *$$$; AE, MC, V; traveler's checks OK; reservations@hotel coral.com; www.hotelcoral.com; 3 miles north of downtown—exit at "Ensenada Centro."*

Las Rosas Hotel / ★★★

KM 102 MEXICO 1, ENSENADA; 646/174-4310, FAX 646/174-4595 True to its name, The Roses Hotel is pretty and pink. Elegant touches are found throughout the lobby: marble floors, windows looking out over the sea, and a green glass ceiling above the atrium. All of the 48 well-appointed rooms overlook either the pool or the Pacific; some have fireplaces. A flagstone terrace surrounds the infinity-edged swimming pool, a perfect spot for morning coffee or a salty margarita at sunset. Take a dip in the heated pool or relax in the hot tub after a game of tennis. There's a restaurant and bar where live jazz is featured every Friday night. Las Rosas is one of the few hotels in Baja with wheelchair access. Weekend visits require a two-night minimum stay, while holidays require a three-night minimum. This classy establishment is often booked up months in advance, so make arrangements early. *$$; AE, DIS, V; traveler's checks OK; las rosa@telnor.net; www.lasrosas.com; north of Hotel Coral and Marina.* &

Paraíso Las Palmas Hotel / ★

AV SANGUINÉS 206, ENSENADA; 646/177-1701, FAX 646/176-0985 This 15-year-old, American-style hotel caters to families. Recently renovated (with the exception of the carpets), each of the 53 rooms features either two queens or one king-size bed, air conditioning, telephones, and cable TV. The small pool is perfect for the kids and there's a children's playground, along with a restaurant and bar. A large green parrot resides by the pool and a fountain is surrounded by beautiful gardens. The staff is bilingual and helpful, and secure parking is available. *$; MC, V; traveler's checks OK; paraiso@telnor.net; www. paraisolaspalmas.com; about 1 mile south of downtown.*

Posada El Rey Sol / ★★

AV BLANCARTE 130, ENSENADA; 646/178-1601, FAX 646/174-0005 Owned by the same family that runs the popular El Rey Sol restaurant around the corner (see review), this low-rise, Mediterranean-style hotel has recently been remodeled and is spic-and-span clean. Located in the downtown area, the 38 rooms are modest yet nice, with blue and green Mexican tile and multicolored accessories splashing color and complementing the soft pastel walls. Rooms are outfitted with one queen or two full-size beds, minibars, cable TV, hair dryers, and coffeemakers. The property has an elevator and ramp for wheelchair access. Facilities include a small business center, two restaurants, a bar, a swimming pool and hot tub, and a small gym; off-street parking is secure. *$; AE, MC, V; traveler's checks OK; poreysol@telnor.net; www.PosadaElRey Sol.com; one block east of López Mateos on Blancarte.* &

Punta Morro Resort / ★★★

KM 106 MEXICO 1, ENSENADA; 646/178-3507 OR 800/526-6676 US, FAX 646/174-4490 Punta Morro is a secluded hideaway as recommended for its charming restaurant as its 30 suites, all with fully equipped kitchenettes and terraces facing the bay. Built in 1989, the setting is cozy and romantic with great views of the Pacific, and has gradually acquired a following among couples and small family groups who appreciate the comforts of an intimate oceanside resort. All of the units have fireplaces, coffeemakers, minibars, hair dryers, and satellite TV. Choose between one, two, or three-bedroom suites with king-size beds. Continental breakfast is delivered to your room each morning. Although Punta Morro is located on the beach, the surf is rough and swimming is not recommended; enjoy the resort's pool and hot tub instead. The Restaurant at Punta Morro (see review) specializes in international cuisine, and the bar has one of the best-stocked wine cellars in Ensenada, offering local and imported vintages. *$$$; AE, DIS, V; traveler's checks OK; pmorro@telnor.net; www.punta-morro.com; 2 miles north of town.* &

Villa Fontana Days Inn / ★

AV LÓPEZ MATEOS 1050, ENSENADA; 646/178-3434 OR 800/329-7466 US Built in 1986, this Days Inn has a generally tidy appearance and is located in the heart of town near shops and restaurants. High-pitched roofs and balconies define the outside of the peach-colored stucco structure bordered with potted plants. All of the 66 rooms and suites have air conditioning and heat, telephones, satellite TV, and balconies, and some have bathtubs. Some face the street and can be noisy; others have a musty smell. Although all have pressed-wood furnishings and rather plain decor, some have newer curtains and carpet, so ask to see another if you're not happy with the first one you're shown. Standard rooms have two double beds, or pay a bit more and have two queens or a king. Junior suites have vaulted ceilings and private Jacuzzi tubs. Midweek rates are some of the best in town. There's a good-size pool and hot tub in the back; continental breakfast is included with your stay. Some private parking is available, so try to reserve a space with your room. *$; AE, DC, MC,V; traveler's checks OK; villafontana@microsol.com.mx; www.villafontana.com.mx; across from El Cid Best Western.*

Guadalupe Valley

EXPLORING

Many travelers stop to see the **COLONIA RUSA,** the remnants of a **RUSSIAN SETTLEMENT** about 20 miles northeast of Ensenada on Mexico 3 (follow signs to the adjacent village of Francisco Zarco, near km 78). Russian families fled to the Guadalupe Valley at the turn of the last century to escape religious persecution in their homeland. Called Molokans (Russian for milk drinkers) by the locals, they lived in the valley until 1938 when Mexican President Cárdenas confiscated all foreign-owned lands. After this edict, the previously aloof immigrants and their offspring began to marry into Mexican families in order to obtain land titles. Some still live in the community; others with Russian last names are prominent business owners in Ensenada.

A tiny museum, **EL MUSEO COMUNITARIO DEL VALLE DE GUADALUPE** (Calle Principal 276) contains some old farming implements, Russian-language Bibles, and keepsakes of the original Russian settlers. Next door, **COCINA RUSA** (Calle Principal 276; 646/155-2030) has an abbreviated menu (expanded on weekends) of traditional Russian food. They also sell fresh-baked bread, local cheese, and a robust, homemade wine. The museum and restaurant are open Tuesday through Friday (9am–5pm), Saturday and Sunday (10–6pm).

For an interesting day trip from Ensenada, visit one or two of the **WINERIES** in the Guadalupe Valley. Both L.A. Cetto and Pedro Domeqc (see the "Beyond Tequila" sidebar) offer tours for groups or individuals without appointments. The smaller wineries generally accommodate only groups and require prior arrangement. Things get liveliest around harvest, when you can see picking, loading, pressing, and other seasonal activities.

RESTAURANTS

Laja / ★★★

KM 24 MEXICO 3, VALLE DE GUADALUPE; 646/155-2556 Laja is a trendy, upscale gem located in the wine-producing Valle de Guadalupe. Jair Téllez and his wife, Laura Reinert, have created a fine venue for their talents with this classy eatery. The restaurant's understated interior provides for a romantic dining experience. Glossy hardwood floors and a stained alderwood ceiling bring an earthy ambiance as light filters through the windows. The inter-

BEYOND TEQUILA

If you thought Mexico was only about tequila—think again. There are two major wine-producing regions on the peninsula, both of them located in the northern state of Baja California. Several of Mexico's finest wineries reside in the vine-laden **VALLE DE GUADALUPE,** just north of Ensenada on Mexico 3; **VALLE DE SANTO TOMÁS,** 30-miles to the south, is home to a lineage of vineyards dating back to the 1700s when Dominican monks brought grapes and religion to this wild and fertile land. Both valleys benefit from cool ocean breezes, while the arid land basks in the warm sun. Although cabernets and merlots tend to dominate the list of award-winning varietals from this region, many other vintages and blends carry good credentials including Nebbiolos, chardonnays, Petite Sirahs, Tempranillos, Fumé Blancs, and Barberas. You can familiarize yourself with the Baja California wines by visiting **SÉDEVINO** (Calle Ruiz 138; 646/178-3433), Ensenada's trendy new wine bar, or **SANO'S** (Blvd Azueta, Ensenada; 646/174-4385), an upscale chop house (too new to review) with a complete wine shop. Both establishments feature vintages from all of Baja California's wineries. Here's a rundown on the local wineries and their specialties:

Once owned by former Mexican President Abelardo Rodríguez, **BODEGAS DE SANTO TOMÁS** (Av Miramar at Calle 7, Ensenada; 646/178-3333; bstwines@telnor.net; www.santotomas.com.mx) is the oldest continuously operating winery and business in Baja. Facilities are presently split between Santo Tomás, where its vineyards still

nationally trained chefs, Téllez and Hector Peniche, prepare an imaginative cuisine integrating the fine wines produced in the surrounding valley. Fresh vegetables and herbs from Laura's garden highlight entrees such as the seared scallops in a chanterelle mushroom and wine sauce, and the herb-laced, house-made pastas. Fresh vegetable soups change regularly and salads are crisp and refreshing. And don't skip dessert! A recent choice included their wine-poached pear tart drizzled with rich, dark chocolate. Service is splendid and their wine list features the best of the local vintages. *$$$; Cash only; lunch Thurs–Sun, dinner Fri–Sun; full bar; reservations required; about 10 miles north of El Sauzal, just north of San Antonio de las Minas.*

Restaurante Campestre Los Naranjos / ★

KM 24.5 MEXICO 3, VALLE DE GUADALUPE; 646/155-2450 Located about 15 minutes' drive northeast of Ensenada in the Guadalupe Valley, this restaurant is hidden in a grove of orange trees. Owner and chef Cuauhtémoc Santana, a native Ensenadan, and his staff do a fine job preparing country-style meals; service is friendly if a bit slow. Menu choices include range-fed poultry, quail, steaks, juicy hamburgers, chicken and beef enchiladas, and taco platters. The thrive, and their downtown Ensenada facilities. Santo Tomás produces an excellent Petite Sirah, and is currently working on Dueto—the result of a joint venture between Santo Tomás and Wente Brothers, the well-known California winery. Tours are available ($2 US) at the Ensenada site Monday through Friday at 11am, 1pm, and 3pm and culminate with wine tasting accompanied by an assortment of breads and cheeses. Groups of 12 or more can tour the Santo Tomás facility (about 75 minutes south of Ensenada; $6 US), where advance reservations are necessary.

French-trained oenologist Hugo D'Costa specializes in two wines at **CASA DE PIEDRA** (km 94, Mexico 3; cpiedra@telnor.net; www.vinoscasapiedra.com), a small winery located just south of the Guadalupe Valley in the scenic Valle de San Antonio de las Minas: Casa de Piedra Red (a Bordeaux blend), and a rich Casa de Piedra Chardonnay. Tour the beautiful rock buildings, and, if you're up to it, try the artisanal *mezcal* produced in small batches here. Tasting and tours are by appointment only; contact them by email.

CAVAS VALMAR (Av Riveroll 1950 at Ambar, Ensenada; 646/178-6405; valmar@telnor.net; www.cavasvalmer.com) is a small-production winery that buys most of its grapes elsewhere, but its varietals are worth following. One of the first Baja California wineries to export to the United States, their specialty is a bold cabernet sauvignon. Tours and tasting are by appointment only.

CHATEAU CAMOU (Mexico 3 north to Francisco Zarco; 646/177-2221 or 619/233-8466 US; mexwine@hotmail.com; www.chateau-camou.com.mx), a small,

roasted quail is delicately presented on a plate of steamed broccoli and accompanied by baked potato and grilled peppers, onions, and tomatoes. Hearty breakfasts—such as the country veggie omelet with sautéed vegetables, mushrooms, and cheese—are served in the western-style dining rooms, one with a small fireplace to warm you on chilly days. The property has two large unheated pools, picnic tables, and grills available to campers, RVers, and those renting sparse but presentable cabins (bring your own sheets and towels). *$; Cash only; breakfast, lunch every day; full bar; no reservations; about 20 miles northeast of Ensenada at Rancho Mariateresa.*

LODGINGS

Adobe Guadalupe / ★★★

CAMINO A CHATEAU CAMOU, FRANCISCO ZARCO; 646/155-2094 Don't expect loads of company if you come to this isolated bed-and-breakfast in the middle of wine country. Bring your significant other, a great novel, and the desire to hear the wind blowing through the vines. The six spanking-clean guest rooms have 16-foot ceilings, adobe-colored tile floors, and comfortable furnishings.

high-end winery, has gained the respect of master winemakers such as Robert Mondavi. Formulated by Dr. Victor Torres Alegre, who studied in Bordeaux, the vintages produced here are earning a reputation as some of the finest in the region, if not the country. Their El Gran Vino Tinto, a blend of cabernet sauvignon, cabernet franc, and merlot has won numerous international awards. Tours and tasting ($2 US) are possible by appointment Monday through Friday 10am–2pm and Sunday 10am–noon.

Paramount among the Guadalupe vineyards, **L.A. CETTO WINERY** (km 73.5 Mexico 3; 615/155-2264; www.lacetto.com.mx) has collected more than 70 international awards. Their Nebbiolo has consistently been one of their best vintages for a number of years. The winery has recently released a line of reserve wines under the new label Don Luis, whose merlot, Viognier, Bordeaux blend, and cabernet-Syrah blends are stirring excitement within the wine industry. Row upon row of vines, some more than 60 years old, cover the valley floor and slope gently up the low hills surrounding this photogenic winery located about 35 minutes north of Ensenada on the Ensenada–Tecate Highway. Free tours and tasting are led by certified viticulturists Monday through Friday 10am–4pm and Saturdays 10am–1:30pm.

From grapes grown and bottled at Rancho el Mogor (km 86.5, Mexico 3; phone/fax 646/177-1484) in the Guadalupe Valley, **MOGOR-BADAM** released its first wine in 1987. Today the small-production winery, owned by oceanographer Antonio Badam, is beginning to gain recognition in the region. Its single red wine is a Bordeaux blend; the most impressive white is a *chasselas* grape from Switzerland, the land of Badam's ancestors. Tours and tasting are by appointment only.

Each room's small sitting area features *equipale* (popular woven-wood and leather style) chairs surrounding a diminutive table; the handmade quilts on comfortable beds have a wedding band design. There's a telescope in the large library, a great room with a domed ceiling, and a more formal living room; the latter two have large fireplaces. The kitchen is the warmest of the communal rooms, with a thick-legged farm table where breakfast is served between 8 and 10am. For dog lovers, the resident Weimaraners are a friendly touch, but the spare central patio, with beautiful fountain, would benefit from some potted plants, and the pool area is equally unadorned. Dinner, at $50 per person, must be arranged in advance so the chef can be spirited over to the premises. *$$$; MC, V; no traveler's checks; adobegpe@telnor.net; www.adobeguadalupe.com; from Calle Principal Francisco Zarco, turn right at stop sign (adjacent to Unidad Médica Familiar building) and continue ½ mile; Adobe is on the right.*

MONTE XANIC (Calle Principal Francisco Zarco; 646/174-7055 or 646/155-2080; montexanic@telnor.net; www.montexanic.com), overlooking acres of vineyards 45 minutes from Ensenada in the Guadalupe Valley near Francisco Zarco, is a highly respected boutique winery rumored to have elevated the quality of all Mexican wines with their inaugural release in 1988. Selling internationally, their cabernet sauvignons and merlots have won numerous awards; their Viña Kristel, a refreshing blend of sauvignon blanc and sémillon, is considered a superb accompaniment to oysters and other seafood, and is one of the most popular Mexican wines in the United States. Tasting ($3 US) and tours are by appointment only.

One of the larger wineries in the Guadalupe Valley, **VIDES DEL GUADALUPE DOMECQ** (km 73.5 Mexico 3; 646/155-2249; domecq@compuserve.com.mx; www.vinos-domecq.com.mx) bottles a fine Chateau Domecq Wine Cellar Reserve, a tasty Los Reyes vintage red table wine, and a nice Blanc de Blanc. Tours are offered Monday through Friday 10am–4pm and Saturday 10am–1:30pm. The winery is located opposite L.A. Cetto Winery.

Retired Tijuana businessman Eduardo Liceaga has developed a lovely property and winery, as well as a fine merlot. Located within the small Valle de San Antonio de las Minas, en route to Valle de Guadalupe on Mexico 3 about 25 minutes from Ensenada, the bright yellow **VIÑA DE LICEAGA** (km 93 Mexico 3; 664/684-1184; elibac@telnor.net; www.vinoliceaga.com) winery is hard to miss; look for the yellow buildings and the sign. Tours and tastings are by appointment only.

—*Lori Makabe*

Maneadero

A prosperous farming community, Maneadero is located 12 miles south of Ensenada on Mexico 1. This is the southernmost town within the Ensenada Tourist Zone, and travelers heading south of Maneadero are required to have a valid visitors permit or tourist card (see the Planning a Trip chapter). There are two Pemex stations along Mexico 1 as it gradually pulls away from the traffic of Ensenada. The highway is lined with rows of vendors selling olives, olive oil, and fresh produce. Some sell tamales stuffed with chicken or beef, or perhaps sweet potato or pineapple. Olives are the main crop here; also important are onions, strawberries, squash, and tomatoes. Recently, Maneadero has filled a niche by growing and exporting tons of baby vegetables. Minuscule corn, green beans, asparagus, and tomatoes are shipped to American, Asian, and European markets where this petite produce is in high demand.

As you drive south, the mountains appear to wrap around the bay, which can be distracting to drivers. But pay attention to the road! Maneadero is also notorious for its *topes* (speed bumps). Although they have improved from the axle-breakers of a few years back and they're now well marked, these *topes* can still sneak up on you.

At the north end of Maneadero is the signed turnoff for State Highway 23 and one of the area's most popular tourist destinations—**LA BUFADORA** (The Blowhole)—and the **PUNTA BANDA** peninsula. Along this stretch there's a pretty beach called **LA JOYA** where the locals like to hold moonlight picnics called *lunadas,* especially when the weekend and the full moon coincide. The **LA JOYA BEACH CLUB** (Km 12.5 Carr a Punta Banda; 646/154-2005) is a trailer and RV park with campsites, a public rest rooms, a restaurant, a taco shop, a mini-mart, and a boat launch. Across the street, you can purchase sweet or savory tamales and jars of olives, olive oil, and honey at roadside stands. Just beyond, **VILLARINOS RV PARK** (Km 13 Carr a Punta Banda; 646/154-2045) has picnic tables, public rest rooms, and showers as well small restaurants and shops, a boat launch (you can rent boats here too), and even a thermal spring near the ocean.

But most day-trippers to the area come to see La Bufadora, a rather capricious wave-induced geyser. When a sizable wave pushes seawater through the submerged cave in the volcanic cliff, it forces a column of water to shoot skyward—sometimes 100 feet high—with a thundering roar. If the waves are big and the wind is right, the resulting spray mists the spectators—particularly pleasant on a hot summer day. The viewing platforms nearby provide plenty of room for great photos. The drive to La Bufadora takes about 30 minutes from downtown Ensenada. The paved, two-lane road winds its way up the Punta Banda peninsula, providing excellent panoramic views of Todos Santos Bay. During the winter, this is one of the best places in northern Baja to spot gray whales and a great place for photos any time of the year. Paved parking is available at the blowhole for $1 US, and vendors lining the long walkway sell postcards, trinkets, leather goods, seashells, cigars, jewelry and *churros*: long sticks of fried, sweet dough rolled in coarse white sugar and handed to you in a twist of wax paper.

Six miles south of Maneadero on Mexico 1 is the recently expanded **LAS CAÑADAS RV PARK** (km 30 Mexico 1; 646/153-1055, fax 646/153-1056; www. lascanadas.com). The imposing entrance leads to a restaurant, campground, RV park with full hookups, a water park, a private lake for fishing, and four rental cabins.

Just south of the turnoff to Las Cañadas, the federal police have set up a **CHECKPOINT** in compliance with the United States Drug Enforcement Agency. Young, uniformed policemen armed with automatic rifles will approach your vehicle and ask if you are carrying *drogas o armas* (drugs or weapons). They may ask to look inside your vehicle. Usually these young men are honest, but there are reports of those with sticky fingers. If possible, unlock just one door at a time. Always discreetly supervise the inspection, answering all questions politely. Keep valuables and cash well hidden. Usually you will be briefly searched or waived through without incident.

ADVENTURES
Besides La Bufadora, the Punta Banda peninsula offers excellent SCUBA DIVING, SNORKELING, and KAYAKING. This rugged peninsula has rocky outcroppings and pristine, unpeopled sand beaches. Dive sites include numerous sea caves and an underwater hot spring. Colorful hydrocorals and sea anemones harbor schools of fish and help conceal the area's large population of lobsters. Dale Erwin of LA BUFADORA DIVE (end of State Hwy 23; 646/154-2092 evenings) is the local divemaster, offering guided dive trips and lots of useful information. The shop also has equipment rentals and sales, air fills, and rental kayaks.

Santo Tomás
South of Maneadero, Mexico 1 climbs the low, meandering hills and at 31 miles from Ensenada descends into the broad agricultural Valle de Santo Tomás (Santo Tomás Valley) with a small, eponymous settlement at its center. This stretch of highway is in excellent condition, but travel is slow as the road follows the contour of the terrain. Miles of olive groves, grain fields, green pastureland, and vineyards blanket the valley floor, which stretches for nearly 5 miles. The town of Santo Tomás has a Pemex station, two RV parks, and a winery, as well as several markets and restaurants.

EXPLORING
Some of the vines in this region are descendants of those planted by the Dominican missionaries who settled here in 1791. MISIÓN SANTO TOMÁS DE AQUINO was once one of Baja California's most prosperous missions, supporting large herds of cattle and sheep and with a population of nearly 1,000 Indians. Wine produced by the friars was transported to other missions throughout Mexico and used as altar wine. The BODEGAS DE SANTO TOMÁS winery (see the "Beyond Tequila" sidebar) still produces varietals from the offspring of those original mission vineyards, and is Baja's oldest continuously operating winery. Groups of 12 or more can tour the facilities ($6 US) with advance reservations.

Besides the winery, the town of Santo Tomás has a Pemex station and two RV parks, as well as several markets and restaurants. The eroded ruins of MISIÓN SANTO TOMÁS DE AQUINO can be viewed north of the olive orchard within El Palomar Motel and RV Park (see Lodgings) or from the east side of Mexico 1 by walking just north of the Pemex station. This is a preferred stopping point for many Baja-philes who, eschewing the more touristy cities such as Rosarito and Ensenada, still have a distance to travel down the peninsula.

THE MISSION POSITION

In their zeal to convert what they considered to be hedonistic, pagan inhabitants of Baja's inhospitable and harsh corner of Mexico, the Dominican, Jesuit, and Franciscan orders left a stinging reminder that good intentions do not necessarily guarantee good results. Dispatched from Spain, the *padres* built 30 missions from 1697 to 1834, while native populations decreased from an estimated 40,000 to a mere 1,000 souls 150 years later. The wholesale decimation from smallpox, syphilis, dysentery, measles, and frontier violence was rationalized as God's will for the sins of the unbaptized heathen.

The Jesuits founded **MISIÓN NUESTRA SEÑORA DE LORETO** in 1697, and from there established almost two-thirds of Baja's missions, spanning 527 miles. In 1767, **SANTA MARÍA DE LOS ÁNGELES** (near Cataviña) was the last mission founded by the Jesuits. For all their efforts, they were rewarded with suspicion and expulsion, and replaced by the Franciscans, who built one mission and then had the good sense to hand things over to the Dominicans and head north to Alta California. Their heirs erected another nine missions and fortified many Jesuit structures before the mission system completely fell apart, due to depopulation and secularization after Mexico gained independence from Spain.

Of the mission structures, 7 have been reclaimed by the very land they were intended to conquer; 15 are in ruins; and of the remaining 8, 5 are still in operation with much of each original structure intact. **SAN FRANCISCO DE BORGA** and **SANTA GERTRUDIS** are remote, serving but a handful of humble residents, while **SAN IGNACIO, SAN JAVIER,** and **LORETO** are thriving parishes, each towering over their respective communities like a mother over a wee child, constant reminders of the sheer power of a determined faith.

Our modern society attaches a romantic ideal to the missions. We contribute money

RESTAURANTS

El Palomar / ★★

KM 154 MEXICO 1, SANTO TOMÁS; 646/178-2355 This large, family-run restaurant opened in 1948 and the decor hasn't changed since. The spacious dining room has a definite Old West feel, with heavy wooden chairs and tons of space between tables. Portions are large, the food is good, and the menu surprisingly varied, given that this place is fairly isolated. One of the house specialties is lobster tacos, served with a nice lineup of fresh condiments; or order your lobster as an entree. Try their thick abalone chowder—perfect on a cool evening. Other menu choices include Cornish game hens, breaded shrimp, steaks, and grilled quail (in season). The margaritas are just right, the beer is cold, and the wines are a nice selection of local vintages. Entering the restaurant to their restoration and maintenance through private initiatives and publicly funded organizations such as Historic Corridor of the Camino Real Missions of the Californias (Carem), and National Institute of Anthropology and History (INAH). With a contemporary educated perspective, walkways, tourist information booths, and chain-link fences are added, designed with the historical and ecological well-being of the physical and social landscape in mind.

INAH has worked to keep the patrimony of the missions alive throughout the peninsula, with Carem providing regular maintenance and restoration of the mission sites of Baja California along El Camino Real (the King's Road), which linked Baja (Lower) and Alta (Upper) California during the colonization period. In recent years, Carem has excavated **SAN VICENTE DE FERRER** (54 miles south of Ensenada), the largest northern mission site and former military and administrative center of the border missions, and **SANTO DOMINGO** (124 miles south of Ensenada). An information center is currently being built at the popular San Vicente site, along with other improvements for public use. Protection and conservation work continues at six other mission sites as well, ranging from maintenance to enhancements including guard huts, fencing, public seating, and sidewalks.

What would Baja be like today if the 40,000 original inhabitants had been allowed to evolve naturally as a people and a culture? Would they have flourished and survived, or were they indeed so pathetic, as the missionaries would have us believe, that eventually someone would have conquered and subjugated them? Today, with the exception of a few pockets in the extreme north, the indigenous faces one sees in Baja are that of the transplanted mainlanders. The true legacy of the missions lies buried with the people, who are now little more than a footnote in the tourist's serendipitous day trip.

—Sabrina Lea

can be a challenge, as the front door is located at the back of their touristy curio shop; another entrance is hidden around the side of the building. *$; MC, V; traveler's checks OK; breakfast, lunch, dinner every day; full bar; no reservations; east side of highway.*

LODGINGS

El Palomar Motel and RV Park / ★

KM 154 MEXICO 1, SANTO TOMÁS; 646/178-2355 Located right on the highway and sprawling a little bit north each year, the El Palomar complex offers just about everything a traveler might need: Pemex station, restaurant, RV park, motel, market, liquor store, water park—heck, there's even a small zoo. The comfortable motel perched above the restaurant houses eight modest but adequate rooms with double beds, heat, and hot showers. Highway noise can be a problem; light sleepers will be wise to carry some earplugs. Across the highway, the RV park sits in an olive grove and has 50 spaces (25 with full hookups), hot showers, and scores of recreational facilities including a swimming pool, water park, small zoo, tennis and volleyball courts, barbecue pits, and a children's playground. Motel clients, campers, and day-trippers are all welcome to use the facilities. The ruins of Misión Santo Tomás de Aquino are nearby—ask for directions. *$; MC, V; traveler's checks OK; east side of highway.*

San Vicente

On Mexico 1 just south of km 88, a well-packed dirt road leads ½ mile west to the ruins of the Dominican stronghold **MISIÓN SAN VICENTE FERRER** and a nearby 18th-century cemetery. This mission is slated for eventual reconstruction as part of a joint effort between the National Institute of Anthropology and History (INAH) and the California Department of Parks and Recreation, so you could find some activity here.

A few miles south of the mission turnoff is the town of **SAN VICENTE**. The town has a Pemex station, a mechanic, a *llantera* (tire repair shop), a bike shop, a *panadería* (bakery), a *tortillería,* a doctor, and a pharmacy as well as numerous cafes and markets to resupply your cooler. There is also a small museum, **MUSEO COMUNITARIO,** displaying a nice collection of Indian artifacts, farming tools, and mission history.

Colonet

A string of small agricultural centers stretches out along Mexico 1 south of Ensenada. *Granjas* (farms) line the highway and spread from the foothills of the Sierra San Pedro Mártir (home of Baja's highest peak) to the Pacific. Macadamia nuts are grown here, as are olives, *nopales* (prickly pear cactus), tomatoes, squash, onions, peppers, and broccoli. Much of this produce is shipped to U.S. markets. Pismo clams and farm-raised abalone also fuel the local economy.

At km 126, just north of Colonet, there's a signed junction with a dirt road leading west to **SAN ANTONIO DEL MAR,** a beachside settlement. This road is in pretty good shape and passenger cars should have no trouble navigating the 5 miles to the waterfront. Sand dunes and rugged cliffs border this unspoiled stretch of sand, formed by a tidal estuary. **SURF FISHING** (good for halibut and bass), **CLAMMING, BIRD-WATCHING,** and **BEACHCOMBING** are all enjoyable here. Beach camping is possible, but come prepared, as services are minimal.

Colonet is about 34 miles south of San Vicente, 76 miles south of Ensenada (43 miles north of San Quintín). The town itself isn't the focal point of this area, but it's a good place to stock up on provisions for excursions to the mountains or the coast. There's a Pemex station here that usually has gas, a number of markets and restaurants, and a small hotel, all easily accessible and visible from Mexico 1.

South of Colonet, between km 140 and 141, there is a Pemex station and a **NATIONAL PARK ACCESS ROAD** with a sign pointing east. This well-graded dirt road passes through the settlement of **SAN TELMO** (gas is usually available), then climbs up the foothills and beyond into the wild and beautiful **SIERRA SAN PEDRO MÁRTIR**. Rancho Meling (see Lodgings), a working ranch with guest facilities, lies 26 miles along on this winding road, at about 2,500 feet, where the view goes on forever. The ranch is a wonderful place to explore and serves as an excellent base camp for excursions into the mountains. Another 1½ hours along the steep and narrow graded road, you'll eventually reach the entrance gate to the Parque Nacional Sierra San Pedro Mártir, one of Baja's four national parks.

ADVENTURES

Named after Misión San Pedro Mártir, the Dominican mission that struggled for 12 long years and then failed in 1824 due to lack of supplies, **PARQUE NACIONAL SIERRA SAN PEDRO MÁRTIR** (Park Administration Office, 1711 #l Montegano, Mexicali; 686/566-7887, fax 686/566-7867; sanpedro@sys.net. mx) sits in the center of the highest mountain range on the peninsula. Not surprisingly, this is also the location of Baja's highest summit, **PICACHO DEL DIABLO** (Devils Peak). Snowcapped in the winter, the summit measures 10,154 feet, towering over the western edge of the San Felipe desert.

The park consists of 170,000 acres of roadless wilderness, thick with Douglas firs; lodgepole, piñon, and sugar pines; incense cedars; and a sprinkling of aspens. Mule deer, raccoons, and foxes make appearances, as do rabbits, songbirds, woodpeckers, and occasionally mountain lions and bighorn sheep. In the spring, park meadows are blanketed in wildflowers, while fall, winter, and spring can bring snow. Summer temperatures are pleasant, but afternoon thunderstorms may obscure the views.

Hunting and off-roading are prohibited within the park boundaries, preserving its pristine beauty, crisp clean air, and serenity. Although San Pedro Mártir has no major bodies of water, there are several year-round running streams where **FISHING** can often yield a tasty rainbow trout. Only a few hundred people visit San Pedro Mártir each year, primarily hikers, climbers, and backpackers. Although **HIKING** trails are abundant, inexperienced hikers are cautioned not to wander too far without a guide, since these trails can easily be confused with livestock and wildlife paths.

Within the park, the **OBSERVATORIO ASTRONÓMICO NACIONAL** (National Astronomic Observatory) features Mexico's largest telescope, an 84-inch reflector. Future plans involve a new cluster of telescopes at this site, which would make it the largest such cluster in the world. Guided observatory tours are given (in Spanish) every Saturday (11am–1pm). If you can't make the tour, the view from the observatory walkway is still worth the trip, offering spectacular views of the Pacific, the Sea of Cortez, Picacho del Diablo, Cañon del Diablo, and even the Mexican mainland.

It is possible to get to the national park and the observatory with a two-wheel-drive passenger car, although the road is often closed during winter due to snow. To get there, from Mexico 1 at 8.5 miles south of Colonet, between km 140 and 141 (look for the national park sign), turn east on the secondary road. Follow this graded dirt road up into the foothills, beyond Rancho Meling at 31 miles and up to the park entrance gate at about 53 miles). A ranger station is located near the park entrance with rough maps of the area. Admission is $7 US per vehicle. To get to the observatory, continue through the park on the access road to its end. Walk the final 1½ miles (paved) to the observatory.

LODGINGS

Rancho Meling / ★★★

NEAR SIERRA SAN PEDRO MÁRTIR NATIONAL PARK, COLONET; 646/179-4106, 646/176-4159 PHONE AND FAX This 2,500-acre spread was founded by a gold miner in the late 1800s, trashed by rebellious Indians in the early 1900s, and rescued by a Norwegian family—the Melings—who turned it into a successful cattle ranch in 1913. Duane Barre Meling has recently reopened the ranch, and now steers a thriving business on the land that bears her family's name. There are no TVs, telephones, or computers here—just plenty of fresh air, a view that won't quit, and at night a gazillion stars. The 12 guest rooms have potbelly stoves, hardwood floors, paneled walls, and handsome wood furniture with rustic hardware. Choose from bunk beds, twins, or doubles. Your stay here includes three hearty meals a day with fresh-baked bread, homegrown veggies, and occasionally beef from the ranch stock. Hire a horse for the day ($5 US) and explore on your own—pan for gold, swim in the spring-filled pools, or just relax and curl up with a good book. There's hiking, fishing, and quail hunting—or if you'd rather shoot with your camera, photo opportunities abound. A 3,500-foot private airstrip accommodates small planes. The ranch doesn't have ice or alcohol, so guests are reminded to bring your own—and a little extra—just in case you decide to extend your stay. *$$; Cash only; chiledog@telnor.net; http://meling-ranch.ensenada.net.mx; 31 miles from Mexico 1, on dirt road leading east from Colonet at km 140.5, toward Sierra San Pedro Mártir National Park.*

Camalú and Punta San Jacinto

From the Colonet area, Mexico 1 descends a long, steep hill into Camalú, a small village with a Pemex station, a *panadería* (bakery), a telephone office, several markets, a *llantera* (tire repair shop), a mechanic, several taco stands, and a few restaurants. On the flat plain northwest of town is a dry lakebed that has become a playground for local **SAIL-CAR ENTHUSIASTS**. If the wind is blowing, this is a fun activity to watch.

Farther south, between km 149 and km 150, a signed dirt road leads 5½ miles to Punta San Jacinto and a popular point break known as "Freighters," named for the huge freighter that went aground here in 1982. There's a nice beach for **CAMPING**, good **FISHING** (thresher shark, yellowtail, bass, and halibut), and a classy bed-and-breakfast called El Milagro (see Lodgings). **PUNTA CAMALÚ**, accessible by the dirt road to the north of San Jacinto, also offers a decent point break and a more isolated environment.

Just south of Colonia Vicente Guerrero, near km 178 on Mexico 1, the **SECRETERIA DE TURISMO DEL ESTADO** (State Tourist Information Office; km 178 Mexico 1; 616/166-2728) serves the Camalú area and the surrounding region, offering maps, tourist assistance, information, and before long, email access.

LODGINGS

Camp Quatro Casas

PLAYA SAN JACINTO, CAMALÚ; 616/165-0010 For modest but adequate accommodations, try this friendly hostel. Located right on the beach with a prime location for water sports, the facility has recently been remodeled and is completely solar powered. Owner Richard Stevens is a retired commercial diver who knows the best local dive sites. Quatro Casas has satellite TV, sleeps up to 20 people (they provide clean bedding), and rents fishing equipment, Jet Skis, and surfboards. Lodging runs $15 US per person per night, with shared bathrooms and kitchen privileges, and if you'd like to buy your meals, breakfast is $5 and dinner $10. *$; Cash only; from Mexico 1 between km 149–150, take the dirt road west and follow signs to El Milagro; turn right and continue 1 mile.*

El Milagro / ★★★

PLAYA SAN JACINTO, CAMALÚ; 616/162-4490 Built by former restaurateurs Rick and Maria Howe of San Clemente, California, this upscale, hacienda-style bed-and-breakfast sits on a small rise overlooking the Pacific Ocean. The two-story, 4,000-square-foot house was completed in November 2000. Vaulted ceilings, Saltillo tile floors, Mexican pottery, and handicrafts accent the living and dining areas, while prints by Frida Kahlo adorn the earth-tone walls. Two tastefully decorated bedrooms come with ocean views; king, queen, or double beds; and satellite TV. The courtyard cafe, where meals are served, is filled with colorful, flowering bougainvillea, azalea, and hibiscus and offers a stunning ocean view. Lodging prices include gourmet breakfast; dinner is available for an additional $20 US per person. *$$; Cash only; from Mexico 1 between km 149–150, take the dirt road west and follow signs.*

Colonia Vicente Guerrero

Five shallow rivers meander through the countryside surrounding Colonia Vicente Guerrero, another settlement along the string of small agricultural centers stretched out along Mexico 1. This is the perfect climate for olive trees, but lately groves of macadamia nut trees are more prominent. Fields of strawberries vie with tomatoes and other vegetables on the patchwork of flat terrain spreading from the ocean to the foothills. Yumano Indians once lived on this peaceful plain, fishing and hunting. Archaeological finds, including rock paintings and petroglyphs, indicate their presence in this area about 2,500 years ago. During September and October, a heavy morning fog rolls in from the ocean, blanketing Vicente Guerrero and the region south to San Quintín.

ACCESS AND INFORMATION

Colonia Vicente Guerrero is a fast-growing nucleus for the surrounding area and a central transportation hub for both produce and people. There's an Auto-transportes de Baja California (ABC) **BUS TERMINAL** (west side of Mexico 1) that connects travelers with other destinations in Mexico, as well as a 24-hour Pemex station, a small hospital, a post office, several markets, two banks (including a Banamex with an ATM), several eateries, a *butano* (propane) plant, and two RV parks. Establishing its prosperity, Vicente Guerrero also has a traffic signal—the first one south of Maneadero.

A few miles south of town on the west side of the highway is the **SECRETARIA DE TURISMO DEL ESTADO** (State Tourist Information Office; km 178 Mexico 1; 616/166-2728), which offers tourist assistance, maps, and information regarding the surrounding area.

EXPLORING

The partially preserved ruins of **MISIÓN SANTO DOMINGO** can be found near Colonia Vicente Guerrero. The signed turnoff from Mexico 1 is a dirt road passable by passenger cars that leads 5 miles to the ruins. In this rough country, horses are the preferred means of transportation and cowboys are frequently seen checking their livestock in the surrounding foothills.

The mission was first established in 1775 a little farther east along the *arroyo*. However, floodwaters were a constant threat so it was moved to the present location in 1782. The mission was closed in 1839 as the population of local Indians was reduced by epidemics. Portions of the foundation and 3-foot-thick adobe walls are still standing. Donations of a few pesos are appreciated.

FESTIVALS AND EVENTS

Fiesta de Santo Domingo takes place here each August, with plenty of rodeo-type action and lots of food, dancing, and music. For more information contact the Tourist Office (616/166-2728).

RESTAURANTS

Posada Don Diego / ★★

KM 174 MEXICO 1, COLONIA VICENTE GUERRERO; 616/166-2181 Located only a mile from the ocean, Posada Don Diego has been serving up seafood specialties and steaks since 1971. Owners Irene and Jose Martinez operate the clean, comfortable eatery with good service and reasonable prices. Fish, shrimp, and steaks are grilled and served with beans or potatoes and a small salad. Abalone, squid, and Pismo clams are the house specialties (in season), and if you'd like to bring in your own clams, Irene will cook them for you. On Sundays, Jose grills baby-back ribs with his spicy secret sauce and serves them with corn on the cob, salad, and beans. Breakfasts are hearty and include the standard Mexican choices such as huevos rancheros and *huevos a la mexicana*. *$; Cash only; breakfast, lunch, dinner every day, brunch Sun; full bar; no reservations; posadadondiego@yahoo.com; from Mexico 1 turn west onto dirt road just north of propane station and proceed past RV park about 1 mile.*

LODGINGS

Posada Don Diego RV Park and Camping / ★★

KM 174 MEXICO 1, COLONIA VICENTE GUERRERO; 616/166-2181, FAX 616/166-2248 This RV park is set up nicely with 100 full-hookup campsites, some shaded areas, and concrete pads. Facilities include a disposal station, flush toilets, showers, a Laundromat, and a children's playground. The nearby beach is good for clamming and fishing, and ice is available in case you catch more than you can consume. The grounds here are spacious enough to handle large groups, which is good if you like large groups but bad if you try to avoid them. *$; Cash only; posadadondiego@yahoo.com; from Mexico 1 turn west onto dirt road just north of propane station and proceed to the RV park.*

Tecate

Tecate sits on the U.S. border in a fertile albeit dry valley 34 miles east of Tijuana. Rock-studded hills surround the town, while Mount Cachumá—a sacred mountain with powerful significance to the indigenous Kumeyaay Indians—looms to the west. Tecate's namesake brewery, the largest structure in town, generates the malty aroma of fresh-baked bread that lingers through the city streets.

Tecate's roots go back to the early 1800s, when the settlement served as an important supply station for regional farmers. Completion of the Tijuana-Tecate-Mexicali-Tucson railroad in 1915 opened more than just an east-west rail thoroughfare—it created a steady, dependable supply route for area produce. The railroad also helped establish Tecate as a town—the oldest border town in Baja California.

Among the town's attractions are its relatively traffic-free border crossing, its famous brewery, and Rancho La Puerta (see Lodgings), a high-end, earthy resort and spa with a celebrity clientele and a focus on the body-mind-spirit connection. Multinational *maquiladoras* (manufacturing plants) provide much of the population's income, producing everything from instant coffee to automobiles and televisions. The Tecate brewery, agriculture, brick- and tile-making, and tourism also fuel the town's economy, along with a large number of *farmacias* (pharmacies) and *dentistas* (dental offices), providing low-cost pharmaceuticals and dental care for visitors from the north. Olives, grapes, wheat, and alfalfa are grown in the region, with the remaining countryside used for cattle grazing. The Universidad Autónoma de Baja California (University of Baja California) has an extension in Tecate, with an engineering emphasis as well as other opportunities for higher learning. There are also a growing number of artists living in town, and art shows, exhibits, and performances have become weekly events.

Due to its elevation (around 1,700 feet), Tecate's summers don't boil the mercury as much as they do in the lower desert regions, but temperatures can still reach the century mark. Winter highs tend to hover around 55°F, occasionally dipping down to lows in the 20s when cold weather systems move through the region.

With no neighboring U.S. city sharing the border, Tecate basks in commuter-free traffic, mostly drawing travelers in search of an alternative to the northbound border station delays faced in Tijuana. Drivers crossing into the U.S. at Tecate do avoid a major wait at the border, but may spend more time on U.S. freeways if their destination is near the coast. One way to have your cake and eat it too is to drive down the scenic Tijuana–Ensenada Toll Road (Mexico 1-D) to Ensenada and return to the United States via the Guadalupe Valley and Tecate (Mexico 3).

ACCESS AND INFORMATION

From Southern California, the easiest way to reach Tecate is to simply take State Highway 94 east out of San Diego, then head south briefly on State Highway 188, which leads across the border and into Mexico. **NOTE:** Tecate's border crossing is open from 6am to midnight only.

Once in Mexico, Highway 188 becomes Calle Lázaro Cárdenas, which leads directly to Tecate's main plaza. Parallel to Lázaro Cárdenas on the other side of the plaza, Calle Ortiz Rubio leads to the start of Mexico 3, which stretches south through the Guadalupe Valley for about 70 miles to the city of Ensenada on the Pacific coast. Crossing Lázaro Cárdenas and facing the square, Avenida Juárez is Tecate's main street. Here you'll find many useful services, including banks, a medical clinic, the **BUS TERMINAL** (Avs Juárez and Rodríguez; 665/654-1221), telephone/fax offices, and Internet cafes. At the outskirts of town, Avenida Juárez becomes the free road (Mexico 2), leading both to Tijuana (31 miles to the west) and Mexicali (90 miles to the east).

To reach Tecate from Tijuana, you can either take Mexico 2-D, the Tijuana-Mexicali Cuota (toll road; $6 US to Tecate; $7 additional toll to Mexicali), or Mexico 2, also called the Carretera Libre a Tecate (free road).

EXPLORING

Calle Cárdenas leads to the center of town from the border crossing, funneling you easily to Tecate's tree-studded central plaza, **PARQUE HIDALGO** (Av Juárez between Calle Ortíz Rubio and Calle Cárdenas). Covering a city block with large shade trees, clean wooden benches, a colorful raised gazebo, and a monument to Benito Juárez, the plaza is lively by Baja standards and a good place to reconnoiter. The rather uninformed **STATE SECRETARY OF TOURISM** (Callejón Libertad 1305; 665/654-1095; fmptkt@telnor.net; www.tecate mexico.com) borders the south edge of the park; next door is El Jardín (see review), one of the town's only outdoor restaurants. A number of banks with ATMs are sprinkled along the plaza's western edge. Ice cream shops, taco stands, and other small stores also surround the park, and on weekends local craft vendors line the plaza's wide cement walkways. Just two blocks east of the plaza, visit the 24-hour **PANADERÍA EL MEJOR PAN DE TECATE** (331 Av Juárez) for the best pastries and bread rolls in town. You probably won't encounter any panhandlers in Tecate—which lacks the desperation felt in Tijuana—but you'll more than likely be approached by eager shoe polishers and children asking you to purchase items to help support their schools.

If you're in town early on Sunday morning, you might go to mass at the **MONASTERIO DE LAS BRIGIDINAS** (km 12.5 Mexico 3, toward wine country), a convent with an interesting, modern cement church located about a mile past Rancho Tecate. The rest of the week, you can stop in to buy *rompope* (liqueur of eggs, milk, and sugar), cookies, or other treats made by the nuns.

An alternative way to travel from the United States to Tecate is to hop aboard the vintage **CARRIZO GORGE RAILROAD** (contact the Rail Adventure Center of the San Diego Railroad Museum; 619/938-1943 US; cgrailway@yahoo.com; www.sdrm.org). The refurbished train chugs out of the (U.S.) townlet of Campo's depot, arriving an hour later in Tecate's Estación Ferrocarril Tecate (Tecate Railroad Station) just behind the centrally located Tecate Brewery (Av Hidalgo and Calle Carranza). You'll have a couple of hours to tour the brewery (see below), explore the town, and eat lunch before you hear "All aboard!" and the train returns to Campo. This trip is offered year-round on select Saturdays and reservations are required. Trains usually depart at 10am and return at 3:30pm October through May), while June through September trips are scheduled from 3pm to 8:30pm to avoid the midday heat. Round-trip tickets run $40 US for adults, $20 for children. There's also first class seating, which offers a champagne brunch featuring Pullman style service, afternoon hors d'oeuvres, and desserts; $100 US per person. These trips often fill up weeks in advance.

Arguably, the most popular beer in Baja is Tecate. The golden beverage was named for the town where Alberto Aldrete first brewed his malt beverage in 1943. The **TECATE BREWERY** (Av Hidalgo and Calle Carranza; 665/654-9478, fax 665/654-9476; basanfra@ccm.femsa.com.mx; www.tecate.net.mx) is now part of **CERVECERÍA CUAUHTÉMOC-MOCTEZUMA**, a large corporation with seven breweries throughout Mexico. Headquartered on the mainland in Monterrey, the company produces several other suds familiar to beer lovers, including Bohemia and Superior. Besides its namesake brew, Tecate's brewery produces Dos Equis, Equis Lager, Carta Blanca, and Sol. In the past, the Tecate Brewery filled only bottles and kegs. With the recent addition of their state-of-the-art filling machine, they now also fill 4,000 cans per minute, processing some 90,000 cases per day.

One-hour tours with English-speaking guides are free, but run only when groups are scheduled. (Call ahead for information.) Walk among huge, stainless-steel tanks in the brewhouse, taste the pungent air of the fermentation rooms, and witness the bottling process before quenching your thirst with samples of Tecate's celebrated brews. The touring department is under new management, and promises to be well organized, something that was lacking in years past. However, if you don't have firm reservations, it's wise to come with alternative plans. If you don't get a tour, the Beer Gardens (where you can get two free beers) and gift shop—**SOUBEERNIR**—are open to the public and are worth visiting. Open Monday through Friday (10am–5pm) and weekends (10am–2pm).

SHOPPING
Although a few souvenir shops cluster around the main square, most of Tecate's bargains are in the form of unglazed or glazed tiles and Talavera-style pottery, found in pottery yards toward the outskirts of town on roads heading west to Tijuana or east to Mexicali (Mexico 2) or south to Ensenada (Mexico 3). If you're in the market for tiles, both locally made and imported from Spain and Italy, visit **TECATE CERAMIC TILE** (Av Juárez 690; 665/654-3898). On the same street but several miles in the opposite direction, **LOS AZULEJOS** (Av Juárez 745; 665/654-4141) sells a smaller selection of Talavera tiles along with painted sinks, home accessories, and wooden furniture. A third shop, **CERÁMICA J.R.** (km 139 Mexico 2 to Tijuana; 665/654-2750), has a large selection of tile; it's located several miles beyond Azulejos on the free road.

RESTAURANTS

La Misión / ★★☆

AV BENITO JUÁREZ 1110, TECATE; 665/654-2105 Entry to this pleasant restaurant is through an enclosed patio and past a central fountain. Oak wainscoting and high ceilings define the interior, and colorful paintings of sleepy towns adorn the walls. Start off with a bowl of tortilla soup—a rich broth with boneless chicken and thin tortilla strips—or if you're in the mood for shrimp, have a cocktail. Entrees include lobster (cooked Puerto Nuevo–style), fried shrimp, vegetarian and seafood pastas, and cheese, beef, or chicken enchiladas topped with *crema* (sour cream). The tender filet mignon comes with mushroom sauce and served with baked potato and steamed vegetables. Most entrees are preceded by a small caesar salad. Try the chocolate cake for dessert, and if you order a margarita here, beware—they run heavy on the tequila. *$; MC, V; traveler's checks OK; breakfast, lunch, dinner every day, brunch Sun; full bar; no reservations; about 3 miles west of the central plaza.*

Restaurant El Jardín / ★

ANDADOR LIBERTAD 274, TECATE; 665/654-3453 Tecate's only sidewalk cafe, El Jardín is a simple, no-frills restaurant patronized mainly by locals. White umbrellas with the Tecate beer moniker shade white plastic tables and chairs overlooking the shady central square. Inside, the ambience is decidedly dinerlike and portions are small, but this simple restaurant offers a nice selection of specials, which are served quickly and change daily according to the mood of the cook. Recent choices included enchiladas with beans and rice, and a steaming plate of *chile verde* (pork in a green chile sauce). Also on the menu are seafood dishes and soups served with fresh tortillas. This is a great place to order a beer or soft drink and a meal while you people-watch. On weekends, roving musicians come around to offer mariachi or *norteño* music on ancient guitars. *$; No credit cards; traveler's checks OK; breakfast, lunch, dinner every day; beer only; no reservations; next to Tourist Office on south side of central plaza.*

Restaurant Rancho Tecate / ★★★

KM 10 MEXICO 3, TECATE; 665/654-0011, FAX 665/654-0241 Housed in a vintage building within Rancho Tecate Resort and Country Club, this restaurant is an elegant choice for a romantic evening. The restored structure is a former winery, established here 100 years ago. Dine by the windows for a panoramic view of the small golf course and the surrounding countryside, where dramatic granite boulders bulge from rolling hills. Choose a vintage from the nearby wine region (see Guadalupe Valley section). For a starter, order a mixed green salad, clam chowder, or the house special: *sopa de tortilla* garnished with fresh avocado and sour cream and served with warm, fresh-baked bread. Lemon-basil butter, delicately steamed vegetables, and a baked potato accompany the grilled lobster plate, while shrimp are either marinated and grilled or sautéed in a rich garlic sauce. Baked quail is a house specialty, stuffed with mushrooms, minced vegetables, and rice. For dessert, order their amaretto cake or the flaming crepe suzette. If you crave coffee rather than sugar, watch your red-coated waiter prepare a specialty coffee such as *café Diablo* (coffee, tequila, and whipped cream) tableside. Service is prompt and unobtrusive and the wine list is impressive. Although this restaurant is refined, semi-casual attire is acceptable. *$$; MC, V; traveler's checks OK; breakfast, lunch, dinner every day, brunch Sun; full bar; reservations recommended; rgrosaiii@aol.com; 6 miles southwest of town.*

LODGINGS

Motel El Dorado

AV JUÁREZ 1100, TECATE; 665/543-1101, FAX 665/654-1333 This reasonably priced two-story stucco motel on the western edge of town has 40 large, basic, but clean rooms with either one queen or two double beds, air conditioning, wall heaters, telephones, and cable TV. Secure off-street parking is available, and you're only a short walk to shopping, restaurants, and services. *$; MC, V; traveler's checks OK; at Juárez and Calle Esteban.*

Rancho La Puerta / ★★★★

KM 135.5 MEXICO 2, TECATE; 760/744-4222 US OR 800/443-7565 US, FAX 760/744-5007 US Rancho La Puerta was founded in 1940 by an immigrant family whose objectives were to enrich body and soul with healthful food, beautiful surroundings, and plenty of strenuous exercise. These principles still form the foundation of the greatly expanded health spa, and the lovingly tended grounds have been shaped over the years into acres of gorgeous gardens—with rosemary, thyme, sage, *palo verde,* and other native plants. The resort is one of the most famous spas in this part of the world and is not open to the public as simple lodgings. The prices tend to limit the clientele, and the resort discourages any visits except weeklong stays, Saturday through Saturday. However, if you have money to burn, this is the place to burn it, along with those unwanted pounds of fat. Myriad activities are available, and all are enticing: mountain hikes, breakfast walks to the retreat's organic gardens, power yoga, tai chi, swimming, and Pilates. All meals are included and served buffet-style, featuring fresh, healthful, low-fat foods, many of which come from the organic garden. Various gyms with sliding glass walls are situated throughout the lush grounds. Guest cottages have fireplaces and comfortable sitting rooms decorated in brick, warm wood, and Mexican furnishings. On the property are several swimming pools, whirlpools, saunas, and four lighted tennis courts. First-timers soon learn it's best to sign up for massages, facials, pedicures, and body treatments *before* arriving at the resort, as the most popular treatments and times get snatched up early by savvy returnees. *$$$$; AE, DIS, MC, V; traveler's checks OK; reservations@rancholapuerta.com; www. rlp.com; several miles west of town.*

Rancho Los Chabacanos / ★✩

KM 12.5 MEXICO 2, TECATE; 665/655-1624 OR 665/655-0150 In 2002, Nellie Gallardo opened to the public the ranch where she'd played as a child. Although the ranch caters mainly to corporations sponsoring team-building events, it is open to any group of 20 or more. Individuals are welcome as overnight guests when groups are there, but reservations are required. Ten rustic cabins accommodate four to six guests each and feature fireplaces and small kitchenettes. Guests bring their own food, or may order meals and eat in the attractive dining area, which is also used by groups for their presentations and exercises. Ask for a bag of vitamin-packed mud, slather it on, and after you dry in the sun, rinse off in one of the property's cool-water springs. Advance reservations are required for meals as well as activities such as yoga classes, ritual sweat baths in the *temezcal* (a sauna made of a stick frame covered in reed mats), or massages. *$$; No credit cards; traveler's checks OK; closed Nov–Mar; rancho_ loschabacanos@hotmail.com; 8 miles east of town.*

Rancho Tecate Resort and Country Club / ★★★

KM 10 MEXICO 3, TECATE; 665/654-0011, FAX 655/654-0241 Rancho Tecate offers an affordable resort experience in a peaceful setting in the scenic Tanama Valley, just south of Tecate. The road passes several small vineyards before it turns into a sweeping drive, reaches the gated entrance, and leads down a palm-lined avenue to the reception area. Owned by the Alesio family (heirs of the former Mr. A's, of San Diego), the resort is surrounded by cropped hills and boulder-strewn mountains. The estate was a winery more than 100 years ago and, although enlarged, the renovated property has retained its traditional hacienda style. The enormous lobby has cathedral ceilings with exposed beams and chandeliers, while the comfortable sitting area is scattered with couches and enough antiques to start another business. Area rugs cover the wood flooring, and windows frame the view toward the golf course. Rooms offer your choice of one king or two queen-size beds; larger suites have views of the grounds or the surrounding hills. Recreational facilities include a 3-hole golf course, swimming pool, hot tub, tennis courts, barbecue pits, and a man-made lake stocked with fish. This resort is often booked solid during the summer months, so make reservations well in advance. *$$; MC, V; traveler's checks OK; rgrosaiii@aol.com; 6 miles southwest of town.* &

The Northeast

Mexicali

One of Baja's youngest major cities and the capital of the state of Baja California, Mexicali is the center of the peninsula's industrial and agricultural industries. Much different from its larger border cousin, Tijuana, Mexicali is geared for commerce as opposed to tourism, and its citizens enjoy one of the highest standards of living in the state. Nearby agricultural areas have become major producers of asparagus, green onions, and broccoli.

The main source of the city's revenue, however, has gradually shifted from agriculture to manufacturing. More than 400 thriving *maquiladoras* (manufacturing plants) are concentrated northeast and south of town. Companies such as Rockwell International, ITT, Sony, Hughes Aircraft, and Kenworth Trucks are only a few of the multinational corporations with facilities in or around Mexicali. Most of these companies retain a workforce of more than 3,000 employees with production lines running 24 hours.

Also contributing to Mexicali's wealth are the massive **GEOTHERMAL RESER-VOIRS** found under the eastern Mexicali Valley. The Cerro Prieto Electric Complex, located 18 miles southeast of the city, is currently Mexico's largest geothermal facility. Near the dormant volcano Cerro Prieto (Dark Hill), the surrounding area is seismically active, often having three or four small earthquakes a day. Another nearby geothermal plant provides electricity to Tijuana, while farther north, on the U.S. border, construction of the enormous La Rosarita Power Plant is projected to be productive sometime in 2002, and is expected to supply power to most of the southwestern United States.

It's certainly not the weather that attracts businesses to this capital city. Mexicali has the most extreme temperatures on the peninsula—summers are long, hot, and arid enough to suck your eyeballs dry, while winters are cold enough that you look forward to that cup of hot coffee. The average yearly rainfall totals drip in around 3½–4 inches. Vacationers usually pass right through Mexicali, focused on waterfront escapes farther south, such as San Felipe and Puertecitos.

Mexicali's city limits are enormous, encompassing 5,254 square miles and consisting of 14 neighborhoods. Along its wide and sunny streets, you'll find *taquerías* (taco stands), *cervecerías* (beer depots), and *abarrotes* (groceries) interspersed with McDonalds, Smart & Final, Blockbuster Video, and Home Depot. Cívico Centro-Comercial de Mexicali, the financial and government district, is the core of the city's thriving business sector, while La Chinesca, Mexico's only legitimate Chinatown, is home to scores of Chinese eateries and Asian markets.

This capital city has been rated one of the cleanest cities in Mexico. The strategy of the city planners is to maintain and reinforce the city's image as a prosperous, business-oriented, safe, and clean place to visit. The current mayor has implemented a strict program to clean up the town, using student and community volunteers who paint sidewalks, cover graffiti, and pick up litter. Business owners are fined if their premises are not clean. Security guards patrol downtown areas, public parking lots, and city parks.

Mexicali has a number of schools, including a branch of the Universidad Autónoma de Baja California, which began as a teacher's college and has developed into an internationally recognized educational facility. The university has reputable foreign-language, architecture, and anthropology departments along with one of the finest libraries in Mexico. There are also several museums in town, including a children's museum and an outstanding museum of anthropology, sponsored by the university. Within the city there's also a bold and thriving arts scene where cultures collide, offering a refreshing blend of expression—something unique to Mexicali.

ACCESS AND INFORMATION

Mexicali now has two border crossings with Calexico, California, its U.S. neighbor. The old downtown crossing (California State Highway 111) is open 24 hours and leads you onto Mexicali's main drag, Calzada López Mateos, which later becomes Mexico 5. This is the principal artery for travel to San Felipe and other points south on the eastern side of the Baja peninsula. To avoid the sometimes congested border commute (southbound in the morning; northbound in the afternoon), consider using the newer border crossing, 6½ miles east of downtown at the junction of Avenida Argentina and Boulevard Rodríguez. **NOTE:** While Mexicali's Western Border Crossing is open 24 hours, the Eastern Border Crossing is open only 6am–10pm.

If you plan to go farther south than San Felipe, you'll need a tourist card, available in the United States at the office of the **MEXICAN CONSULATE** (331 W 2nd St, Calexico; 760/357-3863 US) or across the border at the **MEXICAN TOURISM AND CONVENTION BUREAU-COTUCO** (Calle Camelias and Calzada López Mateos, Mexicali; 686/557-2561 or 888/268-8262 US), headquartered in the orange building across from Museo del Niño. If you're driving to mainland Mexico, you'll need a vehicle permit as well—also available at either location.

Decent maps and other tourist information are available at the **SECRETARIA DE TURISMO DEL ESTADO** (State Tourism Office) more commonly known as SECTUR (Blvd Benito Juárez 1; 686/566-1116).

If you don't feel like driving into Baja, you can take a **BUS** from the United States. The Greyhound station (123 1st St; 760/657-1895 US) in Calexico is within walking distance of the pedestrian border bridge. Or, leave your car in one of Calexico's secure parking lots and walk across the border. To get around the city, you can catch one of the **CONVERTED SCHOOL BUSES** from Calle Altamirano, downtown. If you prefer to take a cab, **PRIVATE TAXIS** are common and more expensive, but faster.

For destinations throughout the peninsula by bus, Autotransportes de Baja California (ABC, 686/557-2440; http://abc.com.mx) runs scheduled bus service out of the **INTERCITY BUS TERMINAL** known as Central de Autobuses (south side of Calzada Independencia, between Calzada López Mateos and Centro Civico; 686/557-2421).

Mexicali's international airport, **AEROPUERTO INTERNACIONAL GENERAL RODOLFO SÁNCHEZ TABOADA** (km 23.5 Mesa Veandrade; 686/553-5071), has recently cancelled its service to both Tucson and Phoenix, Arizona. For the time being, you must first travel to Mexico City to be routed to Mexicali by air. Aeroméxico (Pasaje Alamos 1008-D, Mexicali; 686/557-2551) and Mexicana (Madero 833, Mexicali; 686/553-5401) both fly to Mexicali from Mexico City. **RENTAL CAR AGENCIES** located at the airport and in town include Budget (airport; 686/552-3550; and downtown at Holiday Inn Crowne Plaza; 686/556-0888) and Hertz (1223 Blvd Benito Juárez, downtown; 686/568-1973).

EXPLORING

PLAZA DE SANTA CECILIA, often referred to as **MARIACHI PLAZA** (Calle Mexico and Zuazua) is worth a visit if you like traditional music. Around the outside edge of this grassy park is a line of benches where professional mariachi musicians sit in full costume, holding their instruments, waiting for clients—hire a small group or an entire band for your celebration. Neighborhood elders congregate at the park's interior to listen and watch the action. **PARQUE DE JARDENS**, also known as Hippie Park, is located on Benito Juárez a few blocks south of the Avarita Hotel. On the weekends, locals relax in the grass while vendors peddle tie-dyed clothing and folk art.

BOSQUE DE LA CIUDAD (Forest of the City; Av Ocotlán and Calle Alvarado; 686/555-2833) is a sprawling park southwest of town, very popular with local families, especially on weekends and holidays. Within the boundaries, you'll find one of the three **ZOOS** on the peninsula, along with a small **NATURAL HISTORY MUSEUM**, narrow-gauge **TRAIN**, children's playground, and scores of picnic areas and shade trees. Gates are open Tuesday through Sunday (9am–5pm); admission is free.

PLAZA DEL TOROS CALAFIA (Bullring Calafia; Calle Calafia and Blvd de los Héroes; 686/557-3864) is Mexicali's most recognized landmark. This massive, 26-year-old bullring was built like the traditional bullrings; great brick-lined arches encircle the white exterior with six entrances leading directly into the center arena. The Plaza del Toros Calafia holds 9,450 people and is the second-largest bullring in Baja. Admission ranges from $5 for a seat in the top section (in the sun) to $45 for a seat closer to the action (in the shade). These prices can change drastically, depending on the popularity of the matadors, whose managers carefully select the bulls to fight, and cleverly choreograph the *corridas* (bullfights) in an attempt to manipulate the performance as well as the outcome. **BULLFIGHTS** are frequently preceded by flamenco dancers or *charros* (demonstrations of horsemanship) with entertainment starting at 2pm and the main event running from 6pm to 8pm. The season usually runs from September through May with events scheduled at least once a month. For tickets, event information, or schedules, call the ticket office (686/557-3864) or the Tourist Office (686/566-1116).

If **GOLF** is your game, try the challenging 50-year-old **MEXICALI COUNTRY CLUB** (Mexico 5; 686/563-6170, fax 686/563-6171; 07club@yupi.com). This professional, 18-hole, par 72 course runs 6,630 yards and blankets 25 acres of manicured, tree-studded greens just 15 minutes from the center of town. Other facilities include a swimming pool and wading pool, tennis courts, multiple-sports court, snack bar, ballroom, full bar and restaurant, a cafeteria for children, picnic areas, and a children's playground. Greens fees are $25 US in the summer, $50 US in the winter, and include a cart. Reservations are required. To get there, take Mexico 5 south of Mexicali 2.5 miles through the Laguna Campestre Colony and look for signs.

More than 80 years ago, Chinese immigrants were brought to Mexicali to build an irrigation system and to work in the cotton fields. The colorful downtown **LA CHINESCA (CHINATOWN)** is the result of that era. Today it's the only significant Chinese community in Mexico. About 4 percent of the city's total residents have Chinese lineage. Explore La Chinesca, a fusion of cultures where *taquerías* have Chinese names, Chinese restaurants serve tortillas and salsas, and patron saint votive candles share shelf space with statues of Buddha. Although some of the restaurants and businesses are in need of repair and don't compare to Chinatowns elsewhere in the world, a stroll among this historic amalgamated community is a worthwhile experience. The heart of La Chinesca is on Calle Altamirano near Av Juárez, just south of the U.S. border.

The **MUSEO DEL NIÑO** (Children's Museum; Blvd López Mateos; 686/554-9595; sol.mxl@mail.com; www.soldelnino.com) is an excellent learning experience for kids and adults with a focus on science, technology, and daily practicalities. Housed in a 100-year-old soap manufacturing plant, the building has been remodeled to include an enclosed, expanded-metal catwalk (three stories up) that overlooks the 200-foot, single-room exhibit hall as well as the surrounding city. The interactive displays are well staffed with bilingual personnel to assist with the learning experience (and maintain order). Play piano with your feet, build a Lego space station, and learn how modern conveniences such as telephones, bicycles, and the Internet work. One exhibit allows visitors to experience how disabled citizens must face everyday challenges by simulating blindness and paralysis. Don't miss the wave-generating machine (15 feet tall, 35 feet long), the bubble area with large trays to let the kids stand inside of the bubble, or the shape-shifting mirrors. The large facility can handle more than 1,000 visitors at a time and has a cafeteria and a well-stocked souvenir shop. Open Tuesday through Sunday (9am–5pm); admission $3.50 US, $2.50 for children.

The **MUSEO REGIONAL DE LA UNIVERSIDAD AUTÓNOMA** (University Regional Museum; Av Reforma and Calle L; 686/552-5715; museo@info.rec. uabc.mx) is an anthropology and natural history museum—the biggest and best of its kind in Baja—sponsored by the Universidad Autónoma de Baja California. Opened in 1975, this facility was originally managed by the federal government. Ten years later, the architectural department of the university took over the failing project and transformed the eight-room museum into a world-class exhibition hall. Permanent displays focus on geology and fossils, the Mission period, and the peninsula's nomadic Indians, featuring a life-size photographic display of the region's indigenous people taken in the 1890s by Carl Lumholtz, a Norwegian photographer who lived with the tribes. The museum also features traveling exhibits from the United States and Europe. Open Tuesday through Friday (9am–6pm) and Saturday and Sunday (10am–4pm); admission $1 US.

SHOPPING

Near the border (Avenida Melgar) is where you'll find rows of shops selling typical Mexican souvenirs. **EL ARMARIO** (Calzada Justo Sierra 1700; 686/568-1906) has better-quality goods including furniture, blown glass, and ceramics. The colorful **PLAZA LA CACHANILLA SHOPPING CENTER** (Calzada López Mateos) is the largest shopping center in Mexicali and a good place to spend a hot afternoon. The 12-year-old mall houses more than 300 stores, including a **DORIAN'S DEPARTMENT STORE** (Blvd López Mateos Centro; 686/553-5304) and four movie theaters. Art collectors and admirers will appreciate the fine art exhibited at the privately owned **GALERÍA DE LA CIUDAD** (Av Obregón 1209; 686/553-5044).

For a wonderful authentic **FRUIT AND VEGETABLE MARKET** not too far from the border, head for **BRAULIO MALDONADO** (Calles Azueta and Altamirano), a three-block section of narrow street that's packed with vendors and bursting with fresh produce from the surrounding fields. To get there, head south on Altamirano until you hit Calle Azueta.

ADVENTURES

BIRD-WATCHING AND FISHING / A great place for bird-watching, fishing, and waterskiing is **CAMPO RIO HARDY,** located about 25 miles south of Mexicali on Mexico 5. The Río Hardy is a short extension of the Colorado River (usually dry) that has formed an estuary. Several fishing *campos* have spawned along its banks. Your daily catch might include perch, catfish, and largemouth or striped bass. RV and camping facilities line Mexico 5 en route, and small, fully equipped houses at Campo Río Hardy rent for $50–$60 US a night. Rowboats and Jet Skis are also available for rent. The Río Hardy area is perfect for bird-watchers, as the tall grasses and reeds attract a wide variety of wading birds such as egrets and herons, as well as ducks, coots, doves, and even pelicans. The warm, glassy water is also a haven for serious waterskiers and wakeboarders.

PARQUE NACIONAL CONSTITUCIÓN DE 1857—EASTERN ACCESS / Stretching over 12,335 acres amid the Sierra de Juárez southwest of Mexicali, this national park is home to Baja's only natural lake (Laguna Hanson) and an incredible expanse of uncrowded wilderness. The park can be accessed from the east off Mexico 2 near km 28, 22 miles west of Mexicali. (See San Felipe, Guides and Outfitters section, for guided trips.) Several **HIKEABLE** canyons studded with blue fan palms, huge granite boulders, and sheer cliffs rib Constitución's eastern edge. The most accessible of these, and well worth the effort to get there, is the stunning Cañón de Guadalupe, a geothermal hot spot with steam vents, bubbling mud, and a **CAMPGROUND** that's cashing in on the soothing, lithium-laced mineral water. Near the canyon, granite escarpments are riddled with caves embellished with ancient petroglyphs.

To reach the campground at Cañón de Guadalupe you'll need a high-clearance vehicle (four-wheel-drive is not necessary). From km 28 on Mexico 2 (heading west), look for the secondary (dirt) road leading south on the opposite side of the highway (watch for the large sign to Cañón de Guadalupe). Once you reach the turnoff, travel south along the washboard road for roughly 27 miles until you see the next sign to the campground. Turn right and follow this road for about 7 miles to Campo 1/Arturo Y Roberto. This is camp 1 of the **GUADALUPE CANYON HOT SPRINGS AND CAMPGROUND** (www.guadalupe-canyon.com). Each of the 20 campsites has a shade *palapa* and its own rock-rimmed hot tub filled with clean geothermal water. Trees provide additional shade and privacy. Shower facilities, rest rooms, and a small market are available. Car camping is not cheap ($60 US a night), and the campground no longer takes reservations. They are operating on a first-come first-served basis and it's wise to arrive early to assure a site. Cash only; visit their web site for more information.

If you do not have a high-clearance vehicle, **BAJA SAFARIS** (888/411-2252 US; www.bajasafari.com) leads trips into the canyon from San Diego and **ECOLOGICAL & ADVENTURE TOURS OF BAJA CALIFORNIA** (Blvd Costero 1094, Ensenada; 646/178-3704; ecoturbc@ens.com.mx; www.mexonline.com/ecotur.htm) guides trips into the park from Ensenada. See Ensenada, Adventures and Guides and Outfitters sections, for more information and details. You can also access a separate area of this park (no hot springs) on your own, without a high-clearance vehicle, from the western entrance at km 55 on Mexico 3, south of Ensenada.

At the northeastern edge of the Park is **MIKE'S SKY RANCH** (PO Box 1948, Imperial Beach, CA 92032; 664/681-5514; mikes@telnor.net), a popular destination for dirt bikers and other **OFF-ROAD ENTHUSIASTS**, as well as **HIKERS** and **MOUNTAIN BIKERS**. The mountain ranch features clean, simple lodging with family-style meals and camping. To reach Mike's, take the 22-mile rough dirt road (passenger cars OK) south near km 138.

NIGHTLIFE

You'll find live music (mostly Latin pop) at most of the major hotel bars after 10pm. Try **LA CAPILLA** (Juárez 2151; 686/566-1000), a popular dance club that rocks on weekends, or the **FORUM VIDEOTHEQUE** (Av Reforma and Calzada Justo Sierra; 686/553-5091), which is usually crammed with gyrating college students. It's open Thursday through Sunday and takes a hefty $8 US cover charge to enter. **MOLCAJETES BAR AND GRILL** (Calle Montegano 1100; 686/556-0700) gets hopping after 11pm Wednesday through Saturday.

FESTIVALS AND EVENTS

Headquartered along Nuevo Río Boulevard, the annual **FIESTA DEL SOL** is the most popular fair in Mexicali. More than 400,000 people visit this border town and capital city in celebration of its founding in 1904. There's a large circus, *folklóric* dancers, music, art exhibits, horse races, and a city of food and craft booths. The fiesta always begins during the third week in September and lasts for 21 days. Several large parking lots are guarded and well lit for this celebration. For more information regarding this event or others, as well as maps and brochures, call the Mexicali Tourist and Convention Bureau (686/557-2561 or 888/268-8262 US).

RESTAURANTS

Chalet Restaurant / ★★

JUSTO SIERRA 899, MEXICALI; 686/568-2001, FAX 686/568-2305 The Chalet has a distinctly western motif with heavy wooden doors and furnishings with leather accents. The menu features well-prepared Mexican dishes as well as grilled seafood and steaks. The chicken mole is tender and slightly spicy, served with steaming rice and mixed baby vegetables. Grilled seabass is seasoned with garlic and oregano and served with a salad and shredded carrots. The dessert of choice is the *flan de la casa*. Portions are large, so come hungry. On occasion, a pianist quietly serenades diners. Service is quick and prices are reasonable. *$; MC, V; traveler's checks OK; lunch, dinner every day; full bar; no reservations; near the Tourist Office.*

El Vaquero / ★★

AV DE LOS HÉROES 476, MEXICALI; 686/557-5741 OR 686/557-5652 If you're craving a good steak, El Vaquero is probably the best steakhouse in Mexicali. Sonoran beef, brought over from the mainland's beef region, is their specialty, prepared on their impressive grill located behind the restaurant. As you enter the dining room, the first assault on your olfactory senses is not the grill—it's the bread. Piping-hot sourdough is baked continuously and your basket stuffed full. The decor is strictly rustic ranch-style, with large front and side windows looking out on the surrounding green lawn. Order a cold beer to sip while you await your porterhouse, rib eye, sirloin, or T-bone. Salads are fresh, served with a vinegar dressing, and meals are served with rice or potatoes. Ribs are also served on occasion, and halibut and albacore tuna sometimes make appearances (when fresh), but generally, this is a meat and potato establishment. *$$; AE, MC, V; no traveler's checks; lunch, dinner every day; full bar; no reservations; in front of City Hall.*

La Misión Dragon / ★★

BLVD LÁZARO CÁRDENAS 555, MEXICALI; 686/566-4400 La Misión Dragon offers a pure Mexicali experience—a blending of cultures. The decor is elaborate, a mix of Chinese pagoda with Mexican hacienda; the menu, a mixed bag. Choices include a wide selection of Chinese fare, some with a Mexican twist. House specialties are jalapeño peppers stuffed with shrimp; and crispy (and a bit greasy) egg rolls filled with your choice of spicy meats and packed with veggies. You'll have to decide whether to dip into the Mexican hot sauce or the Chinese hot mustard. The *camarónes a la mariposa* (butterfly shrimp) are served in a light garlic sauce. Also worth trying are the sweet and sour pork or the wonton soup. Most dishes are available by the half order, which is nice for smaller appetites and great for diversifying your order. This eatery is also popular for take-out meals, and they're open until midnight. *$; MC, V; no traveler's checks; lunch, dinner every day; full bar; no reservations; one block east of Cárdenas monument on Calzada Benito Juárez.*

Los Arcos / ★★☆

CALAFIA 454, MEXICALI; 686/556-0903 One of Mexicali's most popular restaurants, Los Arcos specializes in fresh seafood. Located in the financial and government sector (Cívico Centro), the colorful restaurant is popular among the business crowd as well as gringos in the know. Menu items include lobster served Puerto Nuevo–style (sliced lengthwise, dipped in oil, and then grilled), a marinated seabass, *camarónes al mojo de ajo* (shrimp cooked in garlic sauce), and their house specialty—a delightfully rich seafood stew with fish, shrimp, squid, and octopus in a tomato and lemon broth. On the weekends, trios play requested ballads and love songs. The wine list is adequate and service is prompt. *$$; MC, V; traveler's checks OK; lunch, dinner every day; full bar; no reservations; north end of Calafia near López Mateos.*

Molcajetes Bar-Grill & Pawnshop / ★★

CALZADA MONTEGANO 1100, MEXICALI; 686/557-0600 This small eatery is usually pretty crowed and tends to get stuffy on hot summer nights, but you'll understand the tolerance when you try their fajitas. Order these with chicken, shrimp, or fish—they'll come to you on a sizzling platter surrounded by peppers, onion, tomatoes, and chiles with a scoop of guacamole and a bowl of *limón* to squeeze on top. Their *tortas* (large sandwiches) are also worth trying, but skip the coffee here. This small building was formerly a pawnshop—hence the pawnshop tag on the establishment name. *$; Cash only; lunch, dinner every day; full bar; no reservations; across from the Tourism Office.*

Sakura / ★

BLVD LÁZARO CÁRDENAS 2004, MEXICALI; 686/566-4848 If you're craving sushi and wasabi, head to Sakura, Mexicali's only Japanese restaurant, where Rosamaria Tsutsumi has been rolling sushi for more than 16 years. Schooled in San Diego, Mexicali-born Tsutsumi trained her faithful team of Mexican sushi-chefs and teppanyaki chefs. Under her watchful eye, they've invented Mexicali's version of a California roll that's a big hit with locals, adding hot peppers to the filling along with fresh avocado, egg, vegetables, and cream cheese. If you're not crazy about sushi, order a steaming plate of fish, chicken, or shrimp teppanyaki and tempura vegetables. Sake and Japanese beer are available, and on weekends the bar is a popular spot for karaoke. *$; MC, V; traveler's checks OK; lunch, dinner Tues–Sun; full bar; no reservations; Lázaro Cárdenas at Calzada Montejano.*

LODGINGS

Araiza Inn / ★★★

BLVD BENITO JUÁREZ 2220, MEXICALI; 686/564-1100 OR 877/727-2492 US, FAX 686/564-1113 Relatively new on the scene, Araiza Inn Mexicali belongs to a small chain of upscale hotels that cater to business travelers. Located close to the border and government buildings, the unassuming exterior harbors a fine choice in luxury lodging. The marbled lobby is open and bright with opulent leather furnishings and rich wood accents. The 269 units are modest in decor, with a choice of one king or two double beds, tile bathrooms and showers, and practicalities such as air conditioning, cable TV, direct-dial telephones, and large desks. Executive suites are roomier and clients have access to the Executive Business Center with Internet service, computers, copy machines, and meeting rooms with audiovisual equipment. For recreation there's a fitness center, a swimming pool and hot tub, and tennis courts. Golf lovers have access to Mexicali's Country Club, one of the oldest golf courses in Baja. There's an on-site restaurant, Calafia, with a Mexican menu, and a car rental agency, and a travel agent to cover most of your travel needs. *$$; AE, MC, V; traveler's checks OK; www.araizainn.com.mx; just south of the Benito Juárez monument.* &

Colonial Hotel / ★★

BLVD LÓPEZ MATEOS 1048, MEXICALI; 686/556-1312 OR 800/437-2438 US, FAX 686/556-1141 Located near the Plaza de Torros Calafia (the bullring) and Cívico Centro (Civic Center), this 16-year-old, two-story hotel is quite popular with tourists as well as business travelers. A grassy lawn surrounds the swimming pool and hot tub, which offers views of Mexicali's famous bullring. On bullfight weekends, listen as the crowd roars with each pass of *el toro*. The 145 rooms are spacious with king-size beds, satellite TV, and telephones. Near the lobby you'll find a comfortable reading area and a small guest bar. This hotel is very well maintained and offers a pleasant, economical stay in Mexicali. *$; MC, V; traveler's checks OK; next to Sanborns.*

Holiday Inn Crowne Plaza / ★★★

AV DE LOS HÉROES 201, MEXICALI; 686/557-3600 OR 800/465-4329 US, FAX 686/577-0555 Located 5 miles from the border and within walking distance of Vicente Guerrero Park, the Crowne Plaza has been recently renovated and has the amenities expected in a moderately luxurious hotel. Rose-colored stone walls and majestic palms tower over the porte cochere, with its peaked, white-tile roof. Guaranteed to give the best service in town, the staff is friendly and helpful, and many are bilingual. Eight floors contain 151 spacious rooms and 7 junior suites, with new carpeting, tiled bathrooms and showers, and handsome furnishings. Climate control, satellite TV, modem ports, and direct-dial telephones keep you comfortable and connected. The on-site business center has copy machines and meeting rooms, while a swimming pool and hot tub allow guests to recreate and relax. There's also a restaurant, sports bar, and travel agency on the premises. Your stay includes a buffet breakfast. Some non-smoking rooms are available, something not always easy to find. *$$$; AE, DIS, MC, V; traveler's checks OK; venta@crowneplaza.com; www.6c.com; corner of Av de los Héroes and López Mateos.*

Hotel del Norte / ★★

 CALLE MELGAR 205, MEXICALI; 686/552-8101 This four-story downtown hotel offers a clean, affordable stay within walking distance of the border as well as Mexicali's Chinatown, La Chinesca. The 56 rooms are well kept and comfortable, with air conditioning, color TV, telephones, and different combinations of single and double beds. There's a restaurant and bar on the premises, and off-street parking is available. You might consider using earplugs here, as sometimes traffic and street noise can keep you awake. *$; MC, V; traveler's checks OK; at Madero.*

Lucerna Hotel / ★★★★

BLVD BENITO JUÁREZ 2151, MEXICALI; 686/564-7000 OR 800/582-3762 US, FAX 686/566-4706 The Lucerna is a rambling, colonial-style establishment, surrounded by lush gardens, making it Mexicali's most attractive hotel. Arched entryways lead to several courtyards with tiled fountains; carvings by the famous Coronado Ortega adorn the walls. Among the 195 well-appointed rooms are 20 individual bungalows, tucked amid dense greenery and palm trees. Bungalows and rooms have either balconies or patios and are equipped with refrigerators, climate control, fully tiled bathrooms, satellite TV, direct-dial telephones, and data ports. On one side of the lobby is El Acueducto Restaurant, featuring international cuisine and a melt-in-your-mouth rib eye steak. Another restaurant, Mezzosole, serves tasty Italian cuisine. The health-conscious will enjoy the fitness center, two swimming pools, and sauna. For a really fun workout, boogie all night at the Lucerna's trendy nightclub, La Capilla, often packed on the weekends and very popular among locals as well as visitors. The hotel also has a piano bar (for quieter evenings) and a gift shop. *$$$; AE, MC, V; traveler's checks OK; lucernam@telnor.net; www.hotel-lucerna.com.mx; corner of Blvd Benito Juárez and Calzada Independencia.*

Los Algodones

Tucked into the northeast corner of Baja, and the peninsula's easternmost border crossing, Los Algodones (the cotton) is the commercial center of a once-thriving cotton-producing region. One hour east of Mexicali on State Highway 8, and 10 minutes west of Yuma, Arizona, on US Interstate 8, Los Algodones is a meeting place: California meets Arizona, Mexico meets the United States, and Baja California meets mainland Mexico, all within miles of this tiny community.

Most travelers don't stop here, but pass through on their way south to San Felipe. It's a matter of opinion as to whether or not this border town has much to offer. These days the town's economy is fueled not by the cotton fields or *nopal* (cactus) farms that manage to survive its furnacy summers, but by the large population of snowbirds who flock to this city of 15,000 for its affordable dental and medical care. Thousands of U.S. and Canadian citizens cross the border every winter to escape the northern chill. Many of them frequent the dental, medical, and optometry offices as well as the pharmacies that line the business district, conveniently compressed into a few blocks near the border. Within this district are some 40 dentist offices, charging 35 to 50 percent less than the prices currently charged in Arizona.

Gas is available in town at the Pemex stations, but remember that it's usually cheaper to fill up in the United States, before crossing the border. There are plenty of coffee bars, *cervecerías* (beer depots), restaurants, and taco stands in town as well as vendors selling fruit cups and *elotes* (corn on the cob). Try **LA CONQUISTA** (Av B) for excellent coffee and the best fruit smoothies around (try the strawberry mango). **EL PARAISO** (Calle 1; 658/517-7956) and **EL RANCHERITO** (Calle 1) are two popular eateries serving tamales, enchiladas, and tacos with fresh salsas, at affordable prices.

The **MEXICAN TOURISM OFFICE** (Av International; 658/517-7635) is a short block past the border crossing on the south side of the street. **NOTE:** The border crossing at Los Algodones is open daily 6am–10pm.

San Felipe

Miles of undeveloped beaches and close proximity to the U.S. border have made the growing village of San Felipe one of Baja California's most popular tourist destinations. Holidays, spring break, and weekends bring a flurry of activity to the otherwise laid-back town. As many as 5,000 visitors can invade this sleepy resort town on a single weekend, bumping the population to nearly 25,000. California and Arizona residents often arrive in time to watch the sunset on Friday, party all weekend, and return back to work (hung over) on Monday. Though hotels are available, most returning visitors have either purchased second homes here or stay at one of the many campgrounds, whose facilities range from primitive to deluxe—with satellite TV hookups and hot tubs.

Situated on the shallow Bahía San Felipe, the town and beaches are shouldered by the Sierra San Pedro Mártir mountain range to the west, the sparkling Sea of Cortez to the east, and protected from northerly winds by the 700-foot Cerro El Machorro (Barren Hill) with its landmark lighthouse. Summers can be slow and hotter than a jalapeño, while winters offer plenty of sunshine but cool temperatures. Though the weather tends to be the most pleasant in the spring and fall, San Felipe's golden beaches draw motor-homers, car campers, fishermen, and off-road enthusiasts throughout the year. Bathwater sea temperatures in both the summer and fall attract water buffs, with swimming, Jet Skiing, sailing, windsurfing, kayaking, and paddle boating among the favorite activities.

San Felipe was once known for its excellent fishing. In the late 1960s, as San Felipe was recovering from a tropical storm that nearly wiped out the town, the Mexican government signed a lease authorizing Japanese fishing fleets to work the northern Sea of Cortez. Using long-lining methods and a destructive "sea vacuum," these fleets scooped and sucked up anything and everything from the bottom, destroying the bounty of marine life and devastating the delicate ecosystem. The government eventually banned such methods, but these waters may never fully recover.

Today San Felipe is famous for its huge shrimp, known locally as "Big Blues." Rusty shrimp boats anchor in the deeper waters south of town, and local fishermen park their *pangas* along the wide, sandy beaches. Many refer to this town with no streetlights as "Cabo 25 years ago," where the locals know each other by name and English is as prevalent as the U.S. dollar. An active American community holds raffles to raise money for local schools. Retirees buzz around on ATVs as their principal means of transportation. Enjoy the small-town, big-party feel of San Felipe, and if you'd rather skip the party scene, find a quiet hotel outside of town or a campground on the beach and let the Mexican sunrise greet you in the morning.

ACCESS AND INFORMATION

There are two ways to reach San Felipe **BY CAR**. From Mexicali, San Felipe lies 124 miles south on Mexico 5. This paved route is well maintained and a straight shot, so travel time usually runs about 2½–3 hours from the U.S. border. Beware of the steep *vados* (dips) along the way. They will damage your car if taken at high speeds. The drive is dramatic, with barren wastelands, irrigated farmlands, bone-dry lakebeds, rugged mountains, and views of the turquoise Sea of Cortez.

Another route to San Felipe is from Ensenada on Mexico 3. This scenic drive covers 127 miles of plateaus and valleys as it climbs the Sierra de Juárez, sneaks between two of Baja California's national parks, and then coasts into flatter terrain near the junction with Mexico 5. Road conditions are unpredictable since this stretch of highway is always in need of repair and washouts are common. This route is not recommended after dark, and allow plenty of time for the traverse; expect anywhere from 3½ to 5 hours to reach the junction with Mexico 5. (There is a Pemex station at this intersection). From there, it's another 31 miles south to San Felipe.

At the junction of Mexico 3 (the route from Ensenada) and Mexico 5 (about 93 miles south of Mexicali), the federal police have set up a **CHECKPOINT** in compliance with the U.S. Drug Enforcement Agency. Young, uniformed policemen armed with automatic rifles will approach your vehicle and ask if you are carrying any *drogas o armas* (drugs or weapons). They may ask to look inside your vehicle. Usually these young men are honest, but there are reports of those with sticky fingers. If possible, unlock just one door at a time. Always discreetly supervise the inspection, answering all questions politely. Keep all valuables and cash well hidden. Usually you will be briefly searched or waived through without incident.

About 31 miles south of this checkpoint, Mexico 5 turns into a four-lane divided highway where a pair of tall, white arches welcome visitors to San Felipe. After negotiating the town's second *glorieta* (traffic circle), continue straight ahead toward the water. This road becomes Calzada Chetumal, which dead-ends at the one-way (north) Paseo de Cortez—San Felipe's *malecón*.

San Felipe is quite small and it's easy to get around. The north-south streets are named after the world's seas; the east-west streets are named after Mexican ports. The two main streets, Mar de Cortez and Paseo de Cortez (the *malecón*) are both one-way (Paseo runs north; Mar runs south).

The Autotransportes de Baja California (ABC) **BUS TERMINAL** (Av Mar Caribe; 686/577-1516) services San Felipe with buses heading south to Puertecitos twice daily as well as scheduled bus service to Mexicali, Ensenada, and Tijuana. Local **TAXIS** can be found along the *malecón* and at the resort hotels around town.

AEROPUERTO INTERNATIONAL DE SAN FELIPE (International Airport; Av Camino del Sur; 686/577-1386) is 5 miles south of San Felipe. The first female aeronautical commandant in Mexico, Marta López Bueno, is in charge. There are currently no commercial flights into San Felipe; however, the 5,300-foot runway can accommodate commercial carriers and it's only a matter of time before flights are scheduled to this waterfront destination. Private planes are welcome during daylight hours and aviation fuel is available. The Flying Samaritans and off-road racing officials of SCORE have used this facility for many years.

There are 3 **PEMEX STATIONS** in San Felipe, two on Calzada Chetumal, the main drag into town, and one on Avenida Camino del Sur, heading south. **BANKS** and **ATMS** are found on either end of Avenida Mar de Cortez. The **STATE TOURISM OFFICE** (Av Mar de Cortez at Calle Manzanillo; 686/577-1155; turismosf@yahoo.com.mx) has brochures and city maps, and the staff can assist you with fishing licenses and day-trip information. They're open Monday through Friday (8am–8pm) and Saturday and Sunday (10am–1pm).

Need to check your **EMAIL**? It's not cheap in San Felipe. The **NET** (Plaza Canela; 686/577-1600; visitor@canela.sanfelipe.com.mx) is tucked between the Peoples Gallery and the El Cortez Hotel, and you'll need close to $4 US for each 15-minute block.

EXPLORING

The wide, sandy **BEACHES** are the main attractions of this popular resort town, along with **FISHING** and water activities. The tide ebbs as much as 22 feet in this section of the Sea of Cortez, and at low tide, the water recedes up to ½ mile offshore, making boat launching next to impossible. Take advantage of low tide for **BEACHCOMBING, CLAMMING,** and **TIDEPOOLING**.

For a great view of Bahía San Felipe and the town, follow the *malecón* to the north end and cross the new pedestrian bridge that leads to Boom Boom (restaurant and disco) and up toward the **LIGHTHOUSE** (closed). Climb the stairs up to the large **SHRINE** of the Virgin of Guadalupe, Mexico's most popular icon. Following Mexican custom, light a votive candle, make a wish, and then take in the spectacular scenery. If you're not into the walk, take Calle Guaymas and park near the shrine (you'll still have to climb those steps). Baja's highest mountains, including the peninsula's tallest—**PICACHO DEL DIABLO** (Devils Peak), tower in the distance behind San Felipe, set off by the azure Sea of Cortez. The island that is sometimes visible (south of town and 17 miles offshore) is **ROCA CONSAG,** a 286-foot pinnacle that's a popular fishing destination.

Along the beach that extends north of the lighthouse, tiny jets of hot water bubble up from **UNDERGROUND GEOTHERMAL** forces beneath the sand. This is evidence of the region's history of volcanic activity. When the tide is out, shallow pools are formed, holding the warm therapeutic water. South of San Felipe, such hot-water pools are even more extensive.

San Felipe has a great selection of **TACO STANDS** and small open-air eateries along the *malecón*. Some of these places serve only tacos, while others serve up tasty treats such as steamed or breaded clams, thick chowders, ceviche, and *cockteles* (seafood cocktails). Cachanillas, Tony's, Marisco's Norma, and Tacos y Cockteles Blanca are all worth trying and are clean, consistent, and popular among tourists.

SHOPPING

Most of the shopping in San Felipe is concentrated along **AVENIDA MAR DE CORTEZ,** one block west of the *malecón*. Souvenir shops are packed like sardines along several blocks. Most of the goods here are of lower quality and you'll see San Felipe's collection of T-shirts bearing messages that you wouldn't show your mother. For a nicer selection of artwork and handmade gifts, try the **PEOPLES GALLERY** (5 Mar de Cortez).

ADVENTURES

FISHING / Although the fishing in the San Felipe area has seen better days, it is rumored that some species are starting to make a comeback. April and October seem to be the best months for fishing as well as weather. You can expect to bring in corvina, croaker, cabrilla, white seabass, and occasionally sierra. Shore casting is best from the beaches either north or south of town.

You'll probably have the best luck fishing offshore. For a day on the water, hire a local *pangero* (*panga* driver). Guided fishing trips usually run about $45 US per person for 5 hours. Look for the *pangas* (skiffs) along the north end of the *malecón,* or contact **KIKO** (686/577-2293), who keeps his small fleet of *pangas* at the Hotel El Cortez (Av Mar de Cortez; 686/577-1055).

Do-it-yourselfers need to be wise about the tides in the area, as coming in at the wrong time could leave you high and dry. Always consult a current tide table and observe the local fishermen—they know what they're doing. **BOAT LAUNCHING** is available in town at the Hotel El Cortez, and just north of town at the Club el Pesca campground, as well as Ruben's RV Park. There's a croaker hole about 3 miles off of the lighthouse, and seabass sometimes run close to shore near Punta Estrella to the south. Roca Consag, 17 miles offshore, offers some of the better fishing in the region, and is also home to sea lions and numerous bird species. Minimarket Las Americas (at the marina south of town) and Proveedora de Equipos de Pesca (Av Mar de Cortez; 686/577-1802), also near the marina, both sell tackle and Mexican fishing licenses, and can offer advice. **NOTE:** A Mexican fishing license is required to fish anywhere in Mexico.

HORSEBACK RIDING / Horses are available for rent by the hour ($5 US) or the day (negotiable) along the beach near the entrance to Costa Azul Hotel. Guided trips can be arranged as well, but need to be scheduled in advance.

OFF-ROAD ADVENTURES / Off-road enthusiasts dig the surrounding desert and dunes where they can cut loose. Modified vehicles, dirt bikes, souped-up ATVs, dune buggies, sand rails, and HumVees buzz the streets and beaches around San Felipe. You can rent ATVs from a number of independent operators along Mar Blanco (6 blocks up from the *malecón*). Helmets (provided) are required for street travel, but not on the beach. Prices start at about $40 US per hour, but you might be able to bargain for less. Guided tours are also available.

Twelve miles south of San Felipe is **EL VALLE DE LOS GIGANTES** (Valley of the Giants). This narrow valley is home to hundreds of huge *cardón* cactuses—some as tall as 40 feet and weighing in at 10 tons! These magnificent specimens are federally protected; some are estimated to be more than 650 years old. Access is via a sandy road heading west at km 13, opposite Campo Estrella (a small American development). Four-wheel-drive is recommended at times, so inquire at the Tourism Office (686/577-1155) for current road conditions.

GUIDES AND OUTFITTERS

CASEY'S BAJA TOURS (Calle Mar Y Sol, next to El Cortez Hotel; 686/577-1431; casey@sanfelipe.tv; www.lovebaja.com) offers guided expeditions in four-wheel-drive Suburbans equipped with GPS, cell phones, and first-aid-certified English-speaking guides. Tours include visits to the centuries-old cactus at El Valle de los Gigantes, a sulfur mine, waterfalls, and/or the nearby Petrified Forest. Prices start at $25 US for a 3½-hour tour.

For an extended fishing adventure, contact **TONY REYES FISHING TOURS** (Av Mar Bermejo; 686/577-1120; treyes@canela.sanfelipe.com.nx; www.sanfelipe.com.mx/treyes). Their 86-foot **JOSÉ ANDRES,** a live-aboard vessel based in San Felipe, is outfitted for serious, weeklong fishing excursions to the Midriff Islands, 250 miles south.

NIGHTLIFE

If you've got spring break fever and can't get enough partying, head to **ROCK-ODILE** (Av Mar de Cortez 199; 686/577-1219), a multilevel disco and entertainment complex that packs a crowd on weekends with dancing, sand volleyball courts, and pool tables. A pedestrian bridge near the lighthouse links bar-hoppers to the **BOOM BOOM ROOM** (Calle Guaymas), a popular disco with a great view. Nearby, the **LIGHTHOUSE** (Calle Guaymas 152; 686/577-2540) has a happening rooftop bar/disco that rocks until 2am and is a favorite hangout during spring break. If you're sick of the spring break rowdies, head for one of the quieter lounges in San Felipe's upscale hotels, such as **LOS PELICANOS BAR** at the Hotel Las Misiones (Av Misión de Loreto 148; 686/577-1282).

FESTIVALS AND EVENTS

For information regarding any of these events, contact the **TOURISM OFFICE** (Av Mar de Cortez at Calle Manzanillo; 686/577-1155; turismosf@yahoo.com.mx).

Nine days before Ash Wednesday, **CARNAVAL** takes place in the port cities throughout Mexico, and San Felipe is no exception. Their version begins with the crowning of the Carnaval Queen and King and culminates with a grand masquerade ball on the following Tuesday. The festivities include music, food booths, costumed dancing, cockfighting, and even some amateur boxing.

Around the same time, Hobie West holds its midwinter regatta on Bahía San Felipe for three days of **ONE-DESIGN HOBIE CAT RACING** centered near the waters in front of the Hotel El Cortez.

March brings the SCORE **SAN FELIPE 250**, a 250-mile off-road race that starts and finishes in town, while April brings the SCORE **GRAN CARRERA DE SAN FELIPE** (San Felipe Grand Prix), another 250-mile off-road race that starts and finishes within the city limits.

In the midst of high octane excitement from mid-March through mid-April, San Felipe gears up for **SPRING BREAK**, as college and university students from the United States and Canada descend upon this resort town.

Festivities cool down during the hot summer, but start back up in early November with the **FERIA DE CAMARÓN** (Shrimp Festival), which is close to its 10th year. Celebrations include recipe contests, live music, food booths, wine tasting, carnival rides, and a parade.

RESTAURANTS

El Nido / ★★

AV MAR DE CORTEZ 348, SAN FELIPE; 686/577-1028 The ranch-style atmosphere at El Nido is almost overshadowed by the aroma of their specialties: mesquite-grilled Sonoran beef, local chicken, and fresh local seafood. Sip one of Baja California's wines as you watch the chefs prepare your tender cuts or succulent shrimp kebabs. And come hungry. Dinners are served with bean soup, salad, and a baked potato. A trio of musicians often serenade diners. If you have room, try a slice of their delightful flan. Service is prompt and helpful. *$$; MC, V; traveler's checks OK; lunch, dinner Thurs–Tues; full bar; no reservations; south of Calle Manzanillo.*

Las Dunas / ★★★

KM 4.5 CARR SAN FELIPE AEROPUERTO, SAN FELIPE; 686/577-1455 EXT 285 Located within the luxurious Hotel San Felipe Marina Resort & Spa (see Lodgings), Las Dunas sits up on a rise, just high enough to offer sweeping views of the bay. Large windows front the spacious dining room with its vaulted ceilings, white linen tablecloths, and candlelit romantic ambience. Arrive early enough to watch the sky change colors at sunset while relaxing with a fine wine or an icy margarita. Make sure someone in your party orders the tequila shrimp in chipotle sauce, as this dish recently won top honors at the local

Shrimp Festival. Other choice specialties include fresh fish smothered with garlic and scallops in a cilantro pesto. A breakfast buffet is set up daily. Although service tends to be on the slow side overall, this is a wonderful place to melt into "Baja time." *$$; MC, V; traveler's checks OK; breakfast, lunch, dinner every day; full bar; reservations recommended; snmarina@telnor.net; www.sanfelipe. com.mx/sfemarina/index.htm; 3 miles south of downtown.*

Lighthouse Restaurant and Bar / ★★

CALLE GUAYMAS 152, SAN FELIPE; 686/577-2540 Standing above the old boatyard and across from the real lighthouse, the Lighthouse Restaurant offers the best view in town, looking out over San Felipe and across the bay. Owner-operator Ron Ledrer has modernized this former harbormaster's house into a popular eatery and nightclub. The menu is eclectic and includes pizza, steaks, taco salads, seafood, and pastas. Don't miss the Lighthouse's rich chipotle (roasted jalapeño) salsa with blackened tomatoes and garlic—so popular, people come in just to buy it by the pint. Order their signature dishes— *camarónes vino,* succulent shrimp cooked in a butter, garlic, and wine sauce—or the *camarónes barracho*—shrimp in a butter, garlic, and tequila sauce. Their fish comes in fresh, right from the beach below, where local *pangeros* bring in the catch of the day. For dessert, try their wonderful flan or a slice of cheesecake. After dinner, boogie on their 1,400-square-foot rooftop dance floor. *$–$$; MC, V; traveler's checks OK; breakfast, lunch, dinner every day; full bar; no reservations; ronriko@yahoo.com; across from the lighthouse.*

Rice and Beans / ★

PASEO DE CORTEZ 262, SAN FELIPE; 686/577-1770 Owned and operated by Richardo Romo Cota, Rice and Beans is an affordable waterfront eatery and a great place to bring the family. Portions are hefty, and include—you guessed it—rice and beans (dinner entrees are also served with a baked potato and tortillas). Order your clams, fish, or shrimp as a ceviche, a soup, in tacos, *a la veracruzana,* breaded, or grilled—or spring for a *hamburguesa,* burrito, or fajitas. The Mexican combo is a belt buster including chile rellenos, quesadillas, enchiladas, and tacos. Large windows allow great viewing from inside the air-conditioned green dining room, or dine outside and soak up the sun. This is one of the only restaurants in town with a ramp suitable for wheelchair use. The Cota family also runs International Rice and Beans Oasis, a similar restaurant with a small hotel and campground in the town of San Ignacio, more than 500 miles south of Tijuana on Mexico 1. *$; MC, V; traveler's checks OK; breakfast, lunch, dinner every day; beer and wine; no reservations; www.sanfelipe.com.mx/restrnt/randb.htm; across from the malecón between Zihuatanejo and Acapulco.* &

LODGINGS

Costa Azul Hotel / ★☆

AV MAR DE CORTEZ 247, SAN FELIPE; 686/577-1702 Conveniently located on the south end of the *malecón,* this eight-year-old, three-story hotel is surrounded by lush greenery and bordered by the wide sandy beach. Walkways and a terrace surround their heated outdoor pool and *palapa* bar. The 140 rooms are modest but clean, outfitted with air conditioning, telephones, and satellite TV. There's off-street parking, plus an on-site restaurant, bar, and coffee shop. With its large capacity, this hotel can get noisy and it's not as well maintained as other hotels in town. *$$; MC, V; traveler's checks OK; at Calle Ensenada.*

Hotel Las Misiones / ★★★

AV MISIÓN DE LORETO 148, SAN FELIPE; 686/577-1282 OR 800/464-4270 US, FAX 686/577-1283 Colonial architecture highlights this charming hotel, built in 1979 and remodeled in 1984. Las Misiones is a well maintained, sprawling beachfront hotel with mature palms, flawless desertscape, and the feel of an oasis. Rooms are adequately sized and light, with colorful accessories and tile bathrooms, air conditioning, telephones, and satellite TV. Palms and subtropical greenery also surround the resort's two swimming pools, both with swim-up bars. Volleyball, basketball, and tennis courts are on the premises, and when you've played too hard, waterfront massage is available to work out the knots. The in-house restaurant, La Teraza, serves breakfast and dinner with Mexican and seafood choices. The adjacent Club Misiones is comprised of 24 suites with fully equipped kitchens and large bathrooms with tubs. The suites also have balconies, but unfortunately the building is set perpendicular to the water so that none have a great view. The club has its own swimming pool, but for other facilities you must walk over to the hotel. All-inclusive family plans are available at both locations, with two- and three-night options. Although Las Misiones is a bit too far for a quick walk into town, taxi service is readily available in front of the lobby. Secure, off-street parking is also available. *$$$; AE, MC, V; traveler's checks OK; www.hotellasmisiones.com; just over a mile south of town.*

Hotel San Felipe Marina Resort & Spa / ★★★☆

KM 4.5 CARR SAN FELIPE AEROPUERTO, SAN FELIPE; 686/577-1455, FAX 686/571-1569 Built in 1993, this secluded resort has a casual elegance that's complimented by its high, sloping roof and baked-pumpkin façade. Sixty luxury suites are large with tall, beamed ceilings and are tastefully decorated with simple furnishings, colorful woven artwork, and traditional basketry. All have tiled floors, fully equipped kitchenettes, and large patios offering splendid panoramic views (best from the upper floor), as well as air conditioning, telephone, and satellite TV. There's a heated indoor pool, an infinity-edged outdoor pool, a fitness center, sauna, hot tub, and lighted, tartan-top tennis courts that have a fantastic view of the Sea of Cortez. The on-site restaurant, Las Dunas (see

119

review), is one of the best in town. The resort does not have a marina of its own; however, they do have a very nice RV park with full hookups (even cable TV) at 143 spaces. There's a mini-market and laundry facility located within the compound, as well as secure parking. Adventurous visitors can pay beach vendors and rent Jet Skis, or take a thrilling, scenic ride on an ultralight. Prices for lodging vary greatly according to the season. *$$–$$$; AE, DIS, MC, V; traveler's checks OK; snmarina@telnor.net; www.sanfelipe.com.mx/sfemarina/index; 3 miles south of town.*

CAMPING AND RV PARKS

San Felipe has a plethora of campgrounds, most of them right on the beach. Some are quiet and mellow, others party central; some are extremely primitive and inexpensive, others luxurious and costly. For a great introduction to the area, **PLAYA BONITA RV PARK** (Av Golfo de California, north of Ruben's; 626/967-8977 US; playabonita@aol.com; www.sanfelipebeachcondos.com) offers full hookups (for tenters and RVs), clean, tiled rest-rooms with hot showers, shade *palapas,* and good security.

RUBEN'S RV PARK (Av Golfo de California 703; 686/577-1442) is a very popular spot on the same expansive beach. The boat launch ramp makes Ruben's popular among boaters. Tent campers often pitch their tents on top of the beachfront shade structures. This place gets quite rowdy on weekends, holidays, and spring break.

For upscale camping away from the middle of the action, try **SAN FELIPE MARINA RV PARK** (3 miles south of town on Airport Road; 686/577-1455; www.sanfelipe.com.mx/sfemarina/index).

Puertecitos

To avoid the crowds of San Felipe and get away from it all, some travelers prefer the tiny hamlet of Puertecitos, 56 miles south. The road is passable by passenger cars, but careful driving is necessary; allow about 2 hours for the drive. This section of road is in disrepair, and often washboard sections are interspersed with sections of crumbling asphalt. Watch out for the series of steep *vados* (dips) and potholes that can wreak havoc with your shocks and alignment as well as your nerves. Remember also that road conditions can change drastically from year to year, and it's always wise to ask for current road conditions before setting out.

Along the way you'll pass through scenic desert landscape with mesquite bushes, red-tipped ocotillo, elephant trees, and sagebrush while the turquoise shimmer of the Sea of Cortez is ever present to the east. When you come to the end of the road, you've reached **PUERTECITOS**. The town is like a maze, with narrow, winding streets weaving in and out of neighborhoods. Services include a cafe and bar, a small general store, a Pemex station (frequently closed), a *llantera* (tire repair shop), and an airstrip. The village consists of renovated trailers, rusted vehicles, and small homes clustered together on a bluff overlooking the sea.

Besides the isolation, the big draw to Puertecitos is the **FISHING**, which is considerably better than in San Felipe. Local *pangeros* are often more motivated to guide paying guests than to untangle their nets. **PUERTECITOS CAMP-GROUND** offers 20 campsites with electricity (from sundown to 10pm only) and has the only restaurant in town as well as a boat launch ramp where you'll find the local *pangeros*.

There are also **HOT SPRINGS** in the area, some located right on the beach. From the boat ramp, walk about ¼ mile north to the point and look for walkways leading to three rocky pools by the water's edge. Water temperatures vary according to the tides. Try to time your visit with high tide, giving seawater a chance to cool the scorching spring water.

Beyond Puertecitos, the road deteriorates considerably and four-wheel-drive with high clearance, extra gas, water, and provisions are highly recommended.

NORTH-CENTRAL BAJA

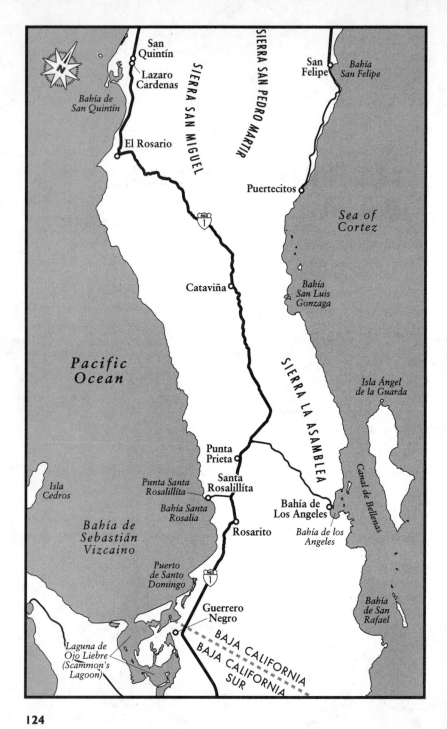

NORTH-CENTRAL BAJA

San Quintín to the State Line

Baja begins to show its true colors in the north-central region of the peninsula. Slowly the irrigated fields of the San Quintín Valley and the sheltered bays of the Pacific Ocean give way to cactus and desert scrub as Mexico 1 heads south toward the unassuming town of El Rosario, the last place to refuel before entering the Desierto Central (central desert). *Cirio* and *cardón* cactus loom over the elephant trees, agave, and barrel cactus prickling the low-lying mesas. Rising from the desert floor like a giant's rock garden, the Cataviña Boulder Fields mark the entrance to the Parque Natural Desierto Central, home to a large concentration of ancient Indian rock art. It is almost impossible not to stop at the settlement of Cataviña to take a photograph of this strange but enchanting scenery. Sadly, too many travelers have also stopped to tag the rocks with graffiti.

In this region, there are not many towns where travelers pause for more than a few hours. For fisherfolk, water enthusiasts, and those seeking a remote destination, Bahía de los Ángeles on the Sea of Cortez is one of the exceptions. The jarring, semi-paved road to this fishing village begins 65 miles south of Cataviña off Mexico 1. Besides the Historical, Nautical and Cultural Museum, there is little of interest in town. Visitors spend their time along the 10 miles of beach and on the waters of the island-dotted bay. Whales and dolphins play in the deep channels throughout the year. Back on Mexico 1, the highway continues southwest down the peninsula toward the state line and the next region, South-Central Baja.

ACCESS AND INFORMATION

Reaching north-central Baja is essentially limited to Mexico 1 by **AUTOMOBILE** or bus unless you own a private plane. The highway is usually in good condition, but realize that few of the streets are named in this section of the peninsula. **NOTE:** Remember that in the northern state (Baja California), the km marker numbers increase as you travel from north to south; see Demystifying the Km Markers in the Planning a Trip chapter.

Presently the road to Bahía de los Ángeles (near km 44 on Mexico 1) is a rough one, beginning with 5 miles of new pavement, which soon turns into 36 miles of crumbling asphalt requiring careful navigation. This portion of the "paved" road is pitted with deep, unavoidable potholes. Slow down and take your time. Twenty-two miles south of the Bahía de los Ángeles junction, the first 3 miles of the 10-mile washboard road leading west to the Pacific fishing village of Santa Rosalillita have also been paved. These paved segments are the first phase of Fonatur's proposed *Escalera Náutica* (the Nautical Ladder), with plans to link these two small villages using a cross-peninsular "boat highway," and a grandiose vision to add new seaports, develop existing port cities, and rebuild airports around the peninsula as well as on mainland Mexico. (See sidebar "The Phantom Escalera Náutica.")

The primary **BUS** carriers, Autotransportes de Baja California (ABC; http://abc.com.mx) and Autotransportes Águila, are accessed through the **MAJOR TERMINALS** near San Quintín (Mexico 1, Lazaros Cardenas; 616/165-3050) and Guerrero Negro near the state line (Blvd Zapata; 664/157-0611).

AIRSTRIPS are located in the San Quintín area, at Cataviña, in Bahía de Los Ángeles, and on the Pacific near Santa Rosalillita. Contact **BAJA BUSH PILOTS** (480/730-3250 US; fax 530/730-3251 US; www.bajabushpilots.com) for information regarding runways and private aircraft.

Tourist information is available 8 miles north of San Quintín at the **STATE GOVERNMENT TOURISM OFFICE—SECTUR** (km 178 Mexico 1; 616/166-2728), with numerous brochures and a friendly bilingual staff who can update you on current events and road conditions. They're open Monday through Friday (8am–5pm) and Saturday and Sunday (9am–1pm). In Bahía de los Ángeles, the **MUSEO DE HISTORIA NATURAL Y CULTURA** (behind the plaza) acts as an unofficial tourist office.

Winters are fairly mild throughout north-central Baja, with December through March bringing the most rainfall. In the summer, the Pacific coast can be cool and foggy, with highs in the mid-70s. Inland areas and the Sea of Cortez coast can be extremely hot and humid, but at the same time water temperatures are very conducive to water sports, so plan your trip accordingly.

San Quintín

In the late 1800s, an English company established a wheat-growing colony at San Quintín, though year after year the crop was destroyed by drought. Remnants of this era can still be seen today—a gristmill (*Molino Viejo,* Old Mill), a loading pier (*Muelle Viejo,* Old Pier), a railroad, and an English cemetery. Modern irrigation has enabled this flat, arid coastal plain to thrive. Today, row after row of tomato plants, grown mainly for U.S. consumption, are visible for miles on both sides of Mexico 1.

Though the town of San Quintín is nothing to write home about, the region, with its proximity to the Pacific Ocean and bays, has become a popular place for Southern Californians to set up first or second residences. Being an easy day's drive from the border makes San Quintín a great weekend destination for those who enjoy surfing, windsurfing, bird-watching, beachcombing, swimming, fishing, clamming, and crabbing for delicious blue crab. Serious hikers and rockhounds can explore the line of volcanic cinder cones that stretches northwest across the land into the Pacific Ocean.

The villages of San Quintín and neighboring Lázaro Cárdenas make up a population center of roughly 25,000—spreading out on both sides of Mexico 1. With two Pemex stations, a bank, a clinic, scores of markets and taco stands, *cervecerías* and *tortillerías,* plus an Internet cafe, it's a good place to stock up and connect before continuing in either direction. **WARNING:** The Pemex stations in San Quintín are notorious for rip-offs. Always get out of your vehicle and pay attention. Use pesos to purchase your fuel and know what bill denomination you hand the attendant. Make sure the pump is cleared before they begin fueling (this is not always easy, as they sometimes start before you have a chance to get out of your car).

Unfortunately, visitors to the area have been the victims of theft and more serious violent crimes in recent years. Two Nevada men were brutally murdered in the late '90s while camped on a remote beach just south of San Quintín. Petty theft and reports of armed robbery have also occurred in the region. Try to avoid situations that may encourage such crimes. Camp in designated areas, with others, or close to establishments. Keep your fishing gear, bicycles, and other valuables locked and/or hidden.

The weather here is fairly moderate, void of extreme hot or cold temperatures (with the exception of unusual weather patterns). Count on cool mornings and evenings throughout the year, although strong winds are also common. Summers are pleasant, cooled by coastal fog with temperatures hanging in the 68- to 72°F range. Winters highs can reach the 60s but tend to hover in the mid-50s. Winter also brings the most rain, often concentrated into short periods of time. Although Mexico 1 has been greatly improved, highway washouts do occur in this region, especially south of San Quintín.

EXPLORING

Only a few of the *calles* (streets) are officially named, so you'll need to rely on your own sense of direction and the kindness of strangers to navigate the dusty roadways. The **PEMEX** station (corner of Mexico 1 and Luis Alcerriga) is a convenient stop to multitask. After refueling, park at the plaza on Luis Alcerriga. A Banamex, telephone office, pharmacy, and Mercado Alejandra (a good place to stock up on groceries) are all within walking distance. **THE INTERNET CAFÉ** (100 feet north of Mercado Alejandra and upstairs; 616/165-3984) offers quick email access for about $2 US an hour. Nearby, numerous taco stands serve a variety of seafood, carne, and pork tacos. For dessert, have an ice cream at **PALETERÍA LA REYNA DE MICHOACÁN** (just behind the Pemex station).

The inner bay of San Quintín is one of Baja's best places for **BIRD-WATCHING**, especially in the winter when migratory species such as black brant geese are in the area. The bay is a large salt marsh frequented by great blue herons, snowy egrets, sandpipers, terns, ducks, and loons that feed on the multitude of fish, crab, shrimp, and mollusks. So far, conservationists have managed to stave off development schemes that would destroy this delicate marshland. To get there, drive west on the rough dirt road that leaves the highway just south of the military base in Lázaro Cárdenas and keep to the left as the road forks. Park and walk to get to the shoreline. Be careful to avoid the thick mudflats at low tide.

Families will be drawn to the wide, sand **BEACHES** and gentle surf of the outer bay, but swimmers need to watch out for an undertow. Surf perch, corvina, and calico bass are easily caught by casting out from knee-deep water—the kids love **SURF-FISHING**. Beaches in the San Quintín area are thick with **PISMO CLAMS**. Walk out to the waterline and as the waves recede, you may feel them beneath your feet. Gather them up for a seaside meal. To make a perfect day on the sands, don't forget to bring a lunch basket and cooler. This is also a good place to explore the volcanic cinder cones. To get to the outer bay from Mexico 1, turn west on the dirt road just south of the military base (toward Campo San Ramón). Travel about 4 miles to the waterfront.

ADVENTURES

DIVING / The best dives in the area are the seamounts south of **ISLA SAN MARTÍN**. Both **JOHNSTON'S SEAMOUNT** and **ROCA BEN** rise to within 10–12 feet of the surface during low tide and are known for their healthy populations of giant mussels. Visibility can be excellent and the area is especially popular with underwater photographers. Roca Ben is considered by some to be one of the most colorful dives in Baja. Huge lobsters, abalone, *bonito,* yellowtail, and vibrant nudibranches can be found among the red sea stars and green sea grass. Both dives should be arranged as drift dives. Diving here is recommended only on extremely calm days and with a divemaster or an experienced, dive-oriented *pangero;* see Guides and Outfitters for more information.

FISHING AND HUNTING / Good fishing can be found offshore in the Pacific Ocean around Isla San Martín and in a number of shallow spots, such as Roca Ben, where you can **BOTTOM FISH** for halibut, rockfish, and lingcod. More exciting game fish come in seasonally—yellowtail, yellowfin tuna, *bonito,* and white seabass. **WATERFOWL HUNTING** is also popular, as is **QUAIL** and **DOVE HUNTING** on surrounding ranches. **TIBURON'S PANGAS** (Old Mill Rd; 616/170-0821 or 616/165-2768) guides hunters and fishermen, and can give helpful information regarding permits. See Guides and Outfitters for more information.

Some adventurers bring their own boats and launch them at the **PUBLIC BOAT RAMP** next to the Old Mill. Remember that seas can be calm at departure time and build to small craft advisories within hours. Sandbars, eelgrass, and breaking waves at the mouth of the bay must all be negotiated. It's wise to know the area and pay attention to signs of changing conditions.

SURFING, WINDSURFING, AND KITEBOARDING / Surfing, bodysurfing, kiteboarding, and windsurfing can be good all along the expansive **BAHÍA SANTA MARÍA**, the northern section of Bahía de San Quintín, just south of the entrance to the inner bay. A long, gentle, mushy wave comes in when there's a north/northwest swell. For windsurfing and kiteboarding, this spacious, unpeopled beach, combined with side-onshore winds and wave direction, make this a playful, nonintimidating spot to work on skills or learn new tricks. **PLAYA SAN RAMÓN**, just north of Lázaro Cárdenas, is a favored surf spot with a long, well-

NORTH-CENTRAL BAJA THREE-DAY TOUR

DAY ONE: After an overnight at the **OLD MILL MOTEL** in San Quintín, rise early for breakfast at the hotel. Then walk to the waterfront to board your vessel for your pre-booked fishing trip (try **DON EDDIE'S LANDING** or **EL CAPITAN SPORT-FISHING**), and spend the day on the water. Or, if you prefer to stay on land, enjoy a day of bird-watching near the Old Mill while learning about the area's history—visit the deteriorating flour mill, the loading pier, and the old English cemetery, or take a long walk on Santa María beach, a few miles south. For lunch, head over to **CIELITO LINDO** restaurant and ask for their house specialty, cracked crab. With plenty of daylight left, start your drive to Cataviña, 112 miles south (allow at least 2½ hours for this drive). Because there is no fuel available in Cataviña, be sure to top off your tanks at El Rosario before heading farther south. Check in for the night at the **HOTEL LA PINTA** in Cataviña, then enjoy dinner at their **LAS CAZUELAS RESTAURANT.** A moonlit stroll through the blue palms near the hotel caps off the evening.

DAY TWO: After breakfast at the hotel's restaurant, ask the hotel manager for directions to the Indian rock art locations in the area or, better yet, inquire about a guide the night before. Take your camera and walk among the huge boulders and desert cacti, where photo opportunities abound. If you're hungry, grab a taco at **CAFÉ LA ENA-MADA** (east side of Mexico 1) before you leave Cataviña, or wait for greater variety at your next destination. Hit the road, heading south on Mexico 1 for 65 miles. Look for the junction to **BAHÍA DE LOS ÁNGELES** and then drive an additional 42 miles on this broken, pitted road heading east. Allow 1½–2 hours of drive time from the main highway. Check into your room on the beach at **GUILLERMO'S MOTEL** and RV park. Ask the staff at Guillermo's to help you contact a bilingual guide (Dr. Abraham Vasquez at **CAMP GECKO** comes highly recommended) for tomorrow's adventure on the water, then enjoy your evening repast at **GUILLERMO'S RESTAURANT.**

DAY THREE: Have breakfast at **GUILLERMO'S,** and ask them to pack you a lunch. After breakfast, visit the **MUSEO DE NATURALEZA Y CULTURA** (Museum of Natural History and Culture) to see whale skeletons, fossils, Indian artifacts, and to learn about the local history and marine life. With your packed lunch, camera, and sunscreen, you're off to see the beauty of Bahía de los Ángeles. Head out into the bay in a comfortable cruiser and, if you're lucky, your guide will be able to show you a whale shark or a pod of resident fin whales. If it's springtime, ask to go to Isla Raza, south of Bahía de los Ángeles, to marvel at the thousands of elegant terns and Heerman gulls nesting cheek to beak. If fishing is your thing, your guide will know where to take you. Return to **GUILLERMO'S** for a cold beer and a hot shower. For dinner, take a stroll over to **COSTA DEL SOL** and dine on their view patio.

defined wave, especially when there's a northwest swell. To get there from Mexico 1, turn west on the dirt road just south of the military base (toward Campo San Ramón). Travel about 4 miles to the waterfront. Another good surf spot still reachable by passenger car is a few miles south of San Ramón near the second cinder cone. To reach the best spot in the area you'll need an experienced *pangero* (skiff driver) or four-wheel-drive. This westernmost point break, located near the mouth of the inner bay, is simply known as **CABO SAN QUINTÍN**. See Guides and Outfitters for information on *pangeros* in the area.

GUIDES AND OUTFITTERS

BAJA SURF ADVENTURES (800/428-7873 US; bajabill51@aol.com; www.baja surfadventure.com) offers prearranged surfing adventures and highly successful learn-to-surf lesson packages from their rustic resort 3 miles north of San Quintín. Rooms can accommodate up to four surfers, and guests are provided three meals a day. No drop-ins.

DON EDDIE'S LANDING (Old Mill Rd; 616/162-3143, 616/162-2722 or 616/162-1244; www.doneddies.com; doneddie@hotmail.com) has their own fleet of three *pangas* and two cruisers. Day trips run $180–$280 US for *pangas,* while their 22- to 24-foot cruisers run $320 US. Prices do not include tackle, bait, or licenses. Captains usually know enough English to communicate fishing lingo. On Mexico 1 at the military base in Lázaro Cárdenas, go 2.5 miles south then turn west at the Old Mill sign and take the rough dirt road 3.5 miles.

Kelly Catian of **EL CAPITAN SPORTFISHING** (Old Mill Rd; 616/162-1716 or 800/376-8787 US; www.elcapitansportfishing.com), based at the Old Mill, is an experienced American guide who knows exactly where to take you for the best surfing, diving, and fishing. Day trips (6:30am–3pm) on his 26-foot, center console "Attack" boats run $360 US a day July through October and $320 US a day the rest of the year. Fishing trips include bait and guide, but you need to purchase your own fishing license. Each custom-built boat comfortably holds four fishermen or five surfers. Kelly has recently begun giving bird-watching/nature tours for $80 US around the marshes.

Located at the Old Mill, **PEDRO'S PANGAS** (Old Mill; 562/599-5430 US or 888/568-2252 US; www.pedrospangas.com; pahillis@aol.com) offers day trips in their 22- to 24-foot *pangas* ($180 US for three people) or if you prefer a larger boat, they have cruisers including a 26-foot, walk-around diesel with a center cabin and head ($280 US for up to five people). When the albacore are running, there's an additional fuel charge ($30 US) since the boats travel farther. If your Spanish isn't great, ask for an English-speaking captain. Pedro's also caters to divers (nearby seamounts) as well as kayakers who enjoy paddling the Pacific or within the bay.

HORIZON CHARTERS (858/277-7823 US; divesd@aol.com; www.earth window.com/horizon) based in San Diego offers dive trips to Johnston's Seamount and Roca Ben, as well as longer diving excursions aboard their fully equipped dive boats.

FESTIVALS AND EVENTS

After failed recent attempts to have another Clam Festival in San Quintín, the long-standing **EXPO-FERIA** (616/165-2792) is the region's major annual event, usually held the last two weeks in August. Highlights include a large carnival, bicycle races, off-road races, cockfighting, food booths, and live entertainment. For more information call the Tourism Office (616/166-2728).

RESTAURANTS

Cielito Lindo Restaurant / ★★

HOTEL LA PINTA RD, SAN QUINTÍN; 616/162-1021 OR 619/593-2252 EXT 2 US Roll up your sleeves and get ready—you've come to *the* place for cracked crab claws! This world-famous house special is well worth the price as well as the cholesterol. Your fresh, generous portion of stone crab is served in a deep dish, dripping with a blend of melted butter, spicy paprika, lemon pepper, and garlic. Squeeze on some fresh *limón* and dig in. You'll need some serious cleanup after the feast, but bets are that you won't mind the mess. Other menu options include *camarónes rellenos*—shrimp stuffed with crabmeat; *almejas*—clams served with garlic, grilled in foil, or sautéed; and broiled quail. They will also grill, fry, or bread your fresh catch and serve it family style with rice, beans, tortillas, and soup for 45 pesos per person. Monthly fiestas as well as pig roasts (on Mexican and American holidays) have made Cielito Lindo popular among the local population as well as those just passing through. Half-priced drinks are offered at happy hour daily (4–5pm) and there's a dance party every Friday night. *$; No credit cards; traveler's checks OK; breakfast, lunch, dinner every day; full bar; no reservations; www. bajasi.com; 8 miles south of San Quintín on Mexico 1 to km 11, then west at La Pinta sign for 3.5 miles.*

Don Eddie's Landing Restaurant / ★★

CALLE MOLINO VIEJO, SAN QUINTÍN; 616/162-3143 Formerly known as Ernesto's, Don Eddie's is now owned and operated by Heriberto Marquez and his family from Tijuana. The newly renovated restaurant and bar offer a 180-degree view of the Bahía San Quintín—a great place to revel in the sunset with an ice-cold margarita. An outdoor patio can seat up to 200 and still have room for the band. The grounds are attractive and well maintained, interspersed with small palms and brick planters. An old railroad bridge abutment is visible—a remnant of the early English settlement here. The menu features steamed lobster, platters of succulent fried shrimp, steamed stone crab claws in paprika and butter, fresh fish, and oysters served as many ways as you can imagine. If seafood doesn't sound appetizing, they also serve steaks, carne asada, *machaca* (shredded dried meat), linguine, and chicken. Try the crab omelet for breakfast; it's a real treat. *$$; No credit cards; traveler's checks OK; breakfast, lunch, dinner every day; full bar; no reservations; doneddie@hotmail.*

20

com; www.doneddies.com; on Mexico 1 go 2.5 miles south from military base in Lázaro Cárdenas, then turn west at Old Mill sign and take rough dirt road 3.5 miles.

Jardínes Baja Restaurant / ★★

OLD MILL RD, SAN QUINTÍN; 616/162-4970 OR 616/160-1616 (CELL) This new restaurant has already earned a fine reputation for their creative dishes and outstanding service. Snuggle near the fireplace on cool winter nights and try the house specialty—*camarónes borrachos* (drunken shrimp) grilled with olive oil and garlic, then flamed with tequila and topped with cilantro and *limón.* Another recommended dish is the shrimp stuffed with local *jaiba* (blue crab—the same delicious critter as that found on our eastern seaboard). If shrimp are not your thing, try the *pescado Jardínes*—delicate grilled fillets smothered with house-made mango salsa. *$; Cash only; breakfast, lunch, dinner Tues–Sun; full bar; no reservations; on Mexico 1 go 2.5 miles south from military base in Lázaro Cárdenas, then turn west at Old Mill sign and take rough dirt road 1 mile (look for Jardínes sign), then ½ mile south.*

Misión Santa Isabel Restaurant / ★★

KM 192 MEXICO 1, SAN QUINTÍN; 616/165-2309, FAX 616/166-8282 Convenient, clean, and highly recommended by travelers as well as local residents—what more could you ask for when hunger strikes? The house specialty is *carne tampiqueña*—a small portion of meat piled high with beans, guacamole, lettuce, and chiles. Hotcakes, eggs with chorizo, and omelets are featured for breakfast. For something different, order the eggs Oaxacan style—scrambled and topped with tomato sauce and chiles. Another dish worth trying is the *pescado veracruzana*—baked fish with tomato sauce, chiles, green pepper, and capers. *¡Delicioso! $; AE, MC, V; traveler's checks OK; breakfast, lunch, dinner every day; beer only; no reservations; on north end of town.*

Restaurante Viejo San Quintín / ★

LÁZARO CÁRDENAS, SAN QUINTÍN This simple rectangular restaurant is popular among the gringo community as well as Mexican locals, which is always a good sign. A low counter separates the kitchen from the dining area, while decorative tiles and tablecloths splash bright colors against the green of the interior. The breakfast menu runs through the full range of American selections, such as oatmeal and hotcakes, to traditional Mexican specialties, such as *huevos con nopales* and *chilaquiles.* Lunch choices include their special *sincronizada*—a pan-fried flour tortilla stuffed with ham, cheese, and beans—*tortas de machaca,* and quesadillas. For dinner try their fresh clam chowder or fried clams, or order a fish or shrimp platter, filet mignon, or T-bone steak, all served with beans, rice, and tortillas. *$; Cash only; breakfast, lunch, dinner every day; beer only; no reservations; south end of highway divider on east side of highway.*

LODGINGS

Cielito Lindo Motel / ★★☆

HOTEL LA PINTA RD, SAN QUINTÍN; 616/162-1021 OR 619/593-2252 US Located just behind the dunes and surf on beautiful Santa María beach, Cielito Lindo is a perfect spot for clamming, fishing, beachcombing, or watching the sunset. Under new ownership, the entire complex has been improved and updated. The 13 modest rooms are spacious and clean with queen-size beds and tiled bathrooms. The tap water is briny, but purified bottled water is available for sale in the restaurant. Children can play at Niñolandia, a small, on-site playground, or visit the nearby petting zoo with its goats, burros, rabbits, and horses. Horseback riding is available, and the motel also has its own sportfishing fleet. Well-supervised pets are welcome, and there's supposedly 24-hour security. The on-site restaurant (see review) serves a sizable platter of delicious cracked crab, and is a popular dinner spot. *$; No credit cards; traveler's checks OK; www.bajasi.com; 8 miles south of San Quintín on Mexico 1 to km 11, then west at La Pinta sign for 3.5 miles.*

Don Eddie's Landing Hotel / ★

CALLE MOLINO VIEJO, SAN QUINTÍN;
616/162-3143 Formerly known as Ernesto's, Don Eddie's is a popular location for fishermen and waterfowl hunters. The new owner, Heriberto Marquez, has made many improvements since he purchased the hotel in 1999, and customer satisfaction is his top priority. Situated next to the narrow inlet between the inner and outer bays, the property is flanked on either side by old railroad bridge abutments. The main attraction here is Bahía San Quintín, so those arriving with their own boats will appreciate the large parking area (with security), boat wash, and the public launch ramp next door. Fishing charters are easy to book nearby, but guests can also cast their lines into the bay from shore, just outside their hotel rooms. There's even a barbecue to grill your own catch of the day. The 17 units are set up with different combinations of twin and double beds, and there's one spacious junior suite. Rooms have clean bathrooms with shower stalls, closets, fans, and satellite TV. *$; No credit cards; traveler's checks OK; doneddie@hotmail.com; www.doneddies.com; on Mexico 1 go 2.5 miles south from military base in Lázaro Cárdenas, then turn west at Old Mill sign and take rough dirt road 3.5 miles.*

Hotel La Pinta / ★★☆

HOTEL LA PINTA RD, SAN QUINTÍN; 616/165-9094 OR 800/263-4500 US This branch of the La Pinta chain of hotels was built on choice beachfront property. Walkways lead to beautiful Santa María beach where you'll find a 100-yard-wide, 30-mile-long stretch of sand, perfect for fishing, clamming, beachcombing, or walking the beach. Watch the sunset from your room and at night let the sound of the waves breaking on shore lull you to sleep. Mexican handicrafts adorn the walls of the 58 spacious rooms with ocean views, satellite TV, clean bathrooms, and somewhat comfortable beds. Tennis courts and a restaurant and bar are on the premises. The La Pinta chain of hotels has recently started offering nonsmoking rooms, and with advance notice, small pets are now allowed in some of the units. *$$; MC, V; traveler's checks OK; info@la pintahotels.com; www.lapintahotels.com; 8 miles south of San Quintín at km 11, then west at La Pinta sign for 2 miles.*

Motel María Celeste / ★

KM 193 MEXICO 1, SAN QUINTÍN; 616/165-3999, FAX 616/165-3699 The fairly new, two-story Motel María Celeste is comfortable and conveniently located. The 18 clean rooms have large showers, satellite TV, bottled water, and telephones. There is a rather narrow parking area in front, which is nice for security and keeps your vehicle out of the way of negligent drivers. Close to ATMs, drugstores, markets, bakeries, fuel, hardware, auto parts, a cyber cafe, and tourist assistance, the motel is a good stopover if you're in the area when you run out of daylight. *$; Cash only; on east side of highway in town.*

Old Mill Motel / ★★

OLD MILL RD, SAN QUINTÍN; 800/479-7962 US, FAX 616/165-3376 Originally built in the 1950s at the site of the area's old gristmill, the Old Mill is a favorite of many nostalgic old-timers, who wouldn't think of staying anywhere else. The central courtyard, with machinery from the former wheat grinder and a decrepit wagon, divides the older section of the hotel from the rows of newer rooms, some of which open up to the bay. With the public launch ramp nearby and several sportfishing operators in the immediate area, the Old Mill Motel is a favorite location for serious fishermen. Rooms are clean and comfortable, with simple decor; some have kitchens and ocean views. Older rooms have single or double beds, but the newer section has queen-size beds and larger bathrooms. A few of these upgraded rooms are fully wheelchair accessible, with wider doorways, more space in the bedroom, and rails in the bathrooms—the only such facilities found in this region of Baja. Purified water is provided in bottles, and nonpotable water is trucked in daily. There is ample parking nearby for any number of trailer boats. *$; No credit cards; traveler's checks OK; on Mexico 1 go 2.5 miles south from military base in Lázaro Cárdenas, then turn west at Old Mill sign and take rough dirt road 3.5 miles.* ♿

MULTISPORT PARADISE

Guarded for years by self-serving surfers and, later, windsurfers who tried desperately to deny or disguise its existence, the legendary **PUNTA SAN CARLOS** is no longer a secret. In fact, word's been out since the mid-1980s when rumors told of a remote, south-facing point in northern Baja where the wind and waves come together with such harmony you'd be singing for days. Located 240 miles south of the U.S. border, then 35 miles west on a rugged access road, Punta San Carlos has more secrets to reveal. Solo Sports, owned and operated by two ambitious Californians, has used the existing terrain and the availability of wind, water, and waves to develop this stretch of coastline into the ultimate adventure playground. Diversions include not only the world-class wavesailing and surfing that brought them here nearly eight years ago, but now incorporate a 26-mile network of single-track mountain biking trails that, coupled with the dramatic scenery, rivals anything north of the border. Instructional clinics, hiking, kayaking, and, more recently, kiteboarding have also joined the lineup at San Carlos.

Why is San Carlos so desirable? The region churns up a variety of wave-riding conditions: the beach break (Old Man's Beach Break) is mellow and mushy with a sandy bottom—perfect for beginners; the point break is faster and steeper—more powerful, for those with wave-riding experience; and the "Chile Bowl," a hollow reef where the waves break with a lot of force, is what pros dig—perfect for aerials and adrenaline-pumping off-the-lip maneuvers. Wherever you ride, side-offshore winds come from behind you and "down the line," as you work the waves. Ride the wave down the coast, ride the wind back up the coast, all day long. Typically the swells range from 2 to 10 feet, but early winter's slow-peeling storm sets have been known to rise with 20-foot faces. The best season for the wind and wave combination is March through October, but November through February brings in a more powerful wave with lighter winds—the surfer's preference.

To get to Punta San Carlos, from Mexico 1 near km 77, 13 miles south of El Rosario, head west on the rugged dirt road. This road is doable by most passenger cars, but it is not recommended for vehicles towing trailers. Allow about 1½–2 hours to cover the dusty 37 miles. The campground has no facilities—not even water; you must bring your own food and water, unless you are signed up with Solo Sports (see Guides and Outfitters in the El Rosario section).

—*Lori Makabe*

El Rosario

Situated in a verdant cultivated valley formed by Río de Rosario, this small town was once an important stopover on the hazardous trip down the peninsula back in the days when it took 2½ days to travel between El Rosario and Ensenada. Today, travelers still consider El Rosario (the Rosary) an important stop for refueling—for the body as well as the vehicle. A prepay, self-serve Pemex station (rare in Baja) is conveniently located near the town's other fuel stop—Mama Espinoza's Restaurant—the hangout for a diverse crowd and an icon of the early days of adventure and exploration. A checkpoint for the off-road Baja 1000, El Rosario was also the first Baja destination of the Flying Samaritans, an organization of American doctors who still fly into outlying areas to provide volunteer medical services.

Mexico 1 takes a 90-degree turn in town, and it is beyond this point that many travelers feel they are truly beginning their journey into Baja. In the fall and early winter, the surrounding hillsides turn vibrant red as villagers spread chiles to dry in the desert sun. A "No Tire Basura" (Do Not Throw Trash) sign stands adjacent to the city dump. Along the highway just outside of town are piles of magenta sea urchin shells. Harvested from the Pacific and plucked open, their mushy contents are exported to sushi markets abroad. As you head farther south, the desert makes a gradual transition. Low scrub bushes are joined by agaves (century plants), and soon the *cirio* or *boojum* trees (see sidebar "Curious About Cirios?") appear, curly and deformed, along with a variety of other cactus. It is essential to top off your fuel tanks in El Rosario before heading deeper into this desert, for the next supply could be as far away as Guerrero Negro, 220 miles south. **NOTE:** A band of petty thieves have been known to work the El Rosario area. Keep your valuables in sight and locked at all times.

EXPLORING

Don't miss **MAMA ESPINOZA'S** (Mexico 1; 616/165-8770), a reputable restaurant (see review) as well as the area's unofficial museum, with old photos, maps, posters, and stickers papering the walls, and huge fossilized ammonites on display. Wander the grounds surrounding this famous eatery to find the monument dedicated to members of the Mother Lode Chapter of the Flying Samaritans who perished in a plane crash while on a volunteer mission to Baja in 2000. Every Wednesday morning, local farmers and vendors set up a **MARKET** just east of Mama Espinoza's Restaurant.

The badly eroded remnants of the **MISIÓN NUESTRA SEÑORA DEL ROSARIO** are located on a rise about 100 yards off Mexico 1, just east (south on Mexico 1) of the village's 90-degree curve (look for the sign). Wooden walkways, fencing, and an entry gate have been added to this site lately, in an attempt to preserve what's left of the melted ruins. A nearby archeological dig yielded a duck-billed dinosaur fossil—the only such dinosaur site in Baja California.

To reach the area's popular **PACIFIC COAST** destinations, travel the dirt access roads leading west. Most are passable with passenger cars and RVs, but are not recommended for vehicles towing trailers. For more details on Punta Baja and Punta San Carlos, see the Adventures section.

ADVENTURES

FISHING / Ask around town for current road conditions, and if they sound good for what you're driving, head for the Pacific coast. From Mexico 1 at the 90-degree curve, continue straight onto the dirt road heading southwest. Cross the river (dry or shallow) and continue for 3 miles to the sign for **PUNTA BAJA**. Another 7 miles of rough road will put you at the Pacific on the northern end of **BAHÍA DEL ROSARIO**. There's a fish camp nearby, where you can buy fish, negotiate to rent a *panga*, or hire a local to take you out to fish for tuna, *bonito*, and yellowtail. Spearfishing is also good in the bay. There are no facilities here, so make sure you have enough drinking water and food to be self-sufficient if you plan to camp.

WINDSURFING, MOUNTAIN BIKING, SURFING, AND KITEBOARDING / Located about 51 miles from El Rosario, **PUNTA SAN CARLOS** is believed to be the best **WAVESAILING** spot on the west coast of North America. It's also becoming known as a world-class **MULTISPORT DESTINATION**, with miles of single-track mountain biking trails as well as hiking, surfing, kayaking, and kiteboarding opportunities. To get there, about 14 miles south of town near km 77, head west on the dirt road for 37 rugged miles to the coast. See "Multi-Sport Paradise" sidebar and the Guides and Outfitters section below for more information.

DIVING / If you have gear and feel adventurous, hire a *pangero* (skiff driver) to take you 10 miles south to **ISLA SAN GERÓNIMO** and the **SACRAMENTO REEF**. The turbulent waters of both have caused numerous shipwrecks, which make exciting dive sites for experienced divers. There are no facilities on the island or at the coast, and full wet suits are necessary in the cold Pacific year-round.

GUIDES AND OUTFITTERS

HORIZON CHARTERS (858/277-7823 US; divesd@aol.com; www.earthwindow.com/horizon), based in San Diego, offers dive trips to the Sacramento Reef as well as longer diving excursions aboard their fully equipped dive boats.

In 1996 Kevin Trejo and Ron Smith of **SOLO SPORTS** (Punta San Carlos; 949/453-1950 US, fax 949/453-8082 baja@solosports.net; www.solosports.net) signed a long-term lease for the use of 5 square miles of the desert surrounding Punta San Carlos. Since then, amid the grumblings of naysayers, they've established a reputable year-round "resort" for windsurfing, mountain biking, surfing, and kiteboarding. Guests sleep in two-person dome tents, use solar power and propane water heaters, and feast on all-you-can-eat meals three times a day. Shaded and carpeted wind shelters provide protection from the elements as clients dine, watch movies, play pool or foosball, and lounge about between sailing or surfing sessions. High-quality toys in the form of full-suspension K2 mountain bikes; Mistral, F2, and JP windsurf boards; Ezzy and Naish sails and trainer kites; and Terry Senate surfboards are rigged and readily available. All-inclusive eight-day packages (limited to 20 guests a week) run $1,350 US per person and include round-trip transportation from San Diego, housing, meals, and gear. Solo Sports also rents gear (when available) and sells dinner to those who prefer to drive in and camp on their own, but don't feel like cooking. From Mexico 1 south of El Rosario near km 77, head west on the dirt road for 37 miles.

RESTAURANTS

Mama Espinoza's Restaurant / ★★

MEXICO 1, EL ROSARIO; 616/165-8770 Mama Espinoza played a crucial role in promoting Baja travel back when El Rosario was considered the jumping-off place into the sparsely populated wilderness to the south. A kind and generous soul, her family's hospitality and lobster burritos are the second most important reason to stop in El Rosario (the last Pemex station for more than 200 miles is the first reason). The small establishment is a combination restaurant, family dining room, gift shop, and makeshift museum. Mama's daughter, Rolly Hale, and son-in-law, Oscar, are the proprietors today, carrying on the tradition of good food and friendly service. The specialty of the house is lobster burritos, but they'll also fix the crustaceans with butter and *limón* or, for breakfast, in a tasty omelet with shredded crabmeat. The menu also includes fresh fish, calamari, crab, carne asada, and steaks. A portion of your spending here goes to help the needy. *$$; No credit cards; traveler's checks OK; breakfast, lunch, dinner every day; full bar; no reservations; just south of Pemex station.*

LODGINGS

Motel La Cabaña / ★

MEXICO 1, EL ROSARIO; 616/165-8770 Part of the same complex as Mama Espinoza's Restaurant, and under the same family management team, this two-story motel has 12 well-kept rooms with different combinations of queen, full, and twin-size beds. The bathrooms are clean with tiled showers. Six of the rooms are fairly new and more modern. Due to its close proximity to the 24-hour Pemex station and highway, you might consider using earplugs here, but it's a pleasant place to stay if you've run out of daylight, have vehicular problems, or want to explore the area. *$; No credit cards; traveler's checks OK; just south of the Pemex station.*

CURIOUS ABOUT CIRIOS?

Lurching up from the desert floor to heights of 40 feet or more, the cactus known as **CIRIO**, or more whimsically, *boojum*, quickly captures the attention of passersby. With a thick base and a tapering top, the young plant has been likened to an upside-down carrot or candle, hence the name *cirio* (the tapered wax candles used in the mission churches). Some of these behemoths branch out at the top of their trunks like candelabrum, their skinny tips often drooping at odd angles. Cousins of the scraggly ocotillo, these Dr. Seussian cacti have been perfecting their lifestyle for millions of years. Within three days of rain, *cirio* get right to work. Little leaves pop out on the short twigs, which cover the trunk, cranking out chlorophyll as fast as they can. In July and August, white to yellow flowers attract insects and hummingbirds for pollination. When moisture disappears, the leaves fall off and the *cirios* become dormant. The thick outer layer of their tough trunk prevents dehydration. Growing approximately 1 foot every 10 years, these unique cacti can live to be more than 350 years old. With the exception of a colony in Sonora on mainland Mexico, *cirio* are unique to central Baja, and are found only between the northern edge of the Viscaíno Desert and El Rosario. Start looking for these distinctive plants about 10 miles south of El Rosario near km 71 on Mexico 1.

—*Fred Jones and Susan McCombs*

Cataviña

With Baja's most impressive desert scenery as its backdrop, the tiny outpost of Cataviña straddles Mexico 1 in the northern region of the Parque Natural de Desierto Central, amid the bizarre and beautiful Cataviña Boulder Field. The settlement marks the middle of the longest stretch of highway void of services, but local vendors sometimes peddle *magna sin* (unleaded gasoline) here from 5-gallon cans (about 25 percent higher than the going rate). Along with the Hotel La Pinta, the nicest of the La Pinta chain and the heart of this oasis, there are a few roadside cafes, but your focus will remain on the surrounding landscape. Giant *cardóns,* twisted *cirios,* elephant trees, century plants, and a variety of succulents and palms emerge from magnificent rock formations. Try to time your stop to experience either a sunrise or sunset in Cataviña, and walk among the simple beauty of this desert paradise.

EXPLORING

Between El Rosario and Cataviña, there are a few places worth exploring. Near km 114, a dirt road west (not suitable for large motor homes or trailers) leads 3 miles to the ruins of **MISIÓN SAN FERNANDO,** which was founded by Father Junípero Serra in 1769. Near km 149, a 9-mile gravel and dirt road (take the right fork at the windmill) leads to the onyx quarry known as **EL MÁRMOL** (the Marble). A crumbling **SCHOOLHOUSE**—built entirely of thick onyx blocks—

echoes childhood sounds near the former center of the quarry's operations, while foundations of homes and two cemeteries stand as testimony to the quarry's once-thriving economy.

The Cataviña area has a number of **CAVE PAINTINGS** with easy access if you know where to look. To reach what is believed by some to be a **SPIRITUAL SITE** for the indigenous tribes that once thrived in this oasis setting, park near km 171 when you see the small rancho on the east side of the highway. The resident (who also runs a small, primitive campground) will either guide you to the site or point you in the right direction for a small fee ($2 US). If no one is around, look high in the bluffs directly across the *arroyo* for a sheet of plywood that marks the entrance to this small cave. Inside the low-ceilinged shelter you'll see fine examples of geometric-abstract art, depicting celestial symbols with suns, spirals, and unidentifiable markings. These paintings are believed to be 500–1,000 years old. The surrounding *arroyos* make wonderful day hikes. Notice the large stand of **BLUE PALMS** in the *arroyo* near the cave paintings as well as those near the Hotel La Pinta.

RESTAURANTS

Las Cazuelas Restaurant / ★

MEXICO 1 (HOTEL LA PINTA), CATAVIÑA; 619/275-4500 US OR 800/800-9632 US A modest restaurant offering a modest menu of sandwiches, fish, beef, and chicken, Las Cazuelas is still the nicest place to eat in "town." Entrees are served with a side of vegetables and rice or potatoes; soup and salad are extra. Breakfast includes hearty servings of hotcakes, French toast, oatmeal, or, for those who woke up on the wrong side of the bed together, *huevos divorciados* (divorced eggs)—two eggs, one served with red sauce, the other with green, separated in the center by *chilaquiles*—crisp tortilla strips and salsa. Another house specialty is the *huevos motuleños*—two eggs served on beans and tortillas, topped with ranchero sauce, string beans, ham, and cheese. *$; MC, V; traveler's checks OK; breakfast, lunch, dinner every day; full bar; no reservations; info@lapintahotels.com; www.lapintahotels.com; located in Hotel La Pinta on the highway.*

LODGINGS

Hotel La Pinta / ★★

MEXICO 1, CATAVIÑA; 619/275-4500 US OR 800/800-9632 US The only hotel in town, La Pinta has an attractive exterior that lures weary travelers off the highway into a pleasant courtyard cooled by a large fountain and a swimming pool surrounded by lawn and palm trees. Patrons can stroll the hotel's private cactus garden out back or take photographs in the surrounding boulder field. The hotel also features a recreation room and children's playground. Recently remodeled rooms are decorated with Mexican handicrafts and boast designed floor tiles and tiled bathrooms. Each room comes with satellite TV, but no telephones. At night, the parking lot is well lit and has a security guard. The La Pinta chain of hotels has recently started offering nonsmoking rooms, and with advance notice, small pets are now allowed in some of the units. *$$; MC, V; traveler's checks OK; info@lapintahotels.com; www.lapinta hotels.com; west side of the highway.*

Santa Ynés Ranch Campground

CALLE RANCHO SANTA YNÉS, CATAVIÑA Founded by a Spanish mission soldier in the late 1700s, Santa Ynés Ranch has long served as a way station for travelers. Oscar Valdez, great-grandson of the mission soldier, is the proprietor today, and he'll make you feel right at home. For campers this is the best choice in the area, unless you choose to spend the night among the boulders. The large campground has a few mesquite trees for shade, hot showers, flush toilets, and a rustic restaurant. Campsites cost $3 US a night. It is also possible to arrange for a guide to some of the area's cave paintings. And if you have a day or two to burn, they can set you up with a guide to the adobe ruins of Misión Santa María, a 3- to 4-hour journey (one-way) by four-wheel-drive. *$; Cash only; 1 mile south of Cataviña, then follow signs ½ mile east.*

Bahía de los Ángeles

A favorite of John Steinbeck, Bahía de los Ángeles—more commonly called the "Bay of L.A.,"—is a large inlet with 10 miles of waterfront and more than a dozen offshore islands—all of them dwarfed by **ISLA ÁNGEL DE LA GUARDA** (Guardian Angel Island), the largest island in the Sea of Cortez. This island, along with a chain of others outside the bay, makes up what's referred to as the **MIDRIFF AREA**—the narrow waistline of the Sea of Cortez. Here the sea is forced between landmasses and offshore islands, generating strong currents and upwelling—the continuous stirring of the sea—churning nutrients from the depths close to the surface, which, in turn, supports an abundance of sea life.

Just a day's drive from the border, Bahía de los Ángeles is the most popular drive-to fishing spot in Baja. Summer water temperatures can lure *dorado*, yellowtail, and yellowfin tuna into the nutrient-rich waters of the bay. The islands inside the bay are great for snorkeling, diving, kayaking, and bird-watching. Dolphins and whales play in the deep channel known as **CANAL DE BALLENAS** (Whale Channel) that runs between Isla Ángel de la Guarda and the inner islands; in the winter, several species of migrating whales, including the world's largest animals—blue whales—feed inside the bay. Whale skeletons are a part of the eclectic collection inside the worthwhile Nature and Cultural Museum located near the center of town.

Plan your trip around your favorite activities, as winter temperatures hover in the mid-50s, while summers can scorch—frequently topping the century mark. Winters are also very windy, making boating and kayaking too dangerous, often for days at a time, while windsurfers and kiteboarders prefer such gales.

ACCESS AND INFORMATION

The road to Bahía de los Ángeles, near km 44 on Mexico 1, can be an adventure itself. As you leave Mexico 1, you'll pass through stands of *cirio, cardón,* and elephant trees, some hosting clumps of unusual ball moss—but keep at least one eye on the road.

The initial 5 miles of well-paved highway quickly deteriorates into a 36-mile obstacle course of deep, sometimes-unavoidable potholes. You can dodge some of them, but not all—drive slowly to save your shocks as well as your nerves. Allow at least 1½ hours for this gauntlet. Just about the time you think you can't take another jolt, you are rewarded with a panoramic view of the bay and your first glimpse of the Sea of Cortez. The small, unimpressive village of Bahía de los Ángeles comes into view to the right, and the road leads you to the center of town.

The remoteness of the settlement means that communications, groceries, electricity, and drinking water are limited, so come prepared. There are a handful of hotels, campgrounds, restaurants, a telephone office, and markets within the village, and an airstrip—but not much else outside of town. Gasoline is sometimes for sale here from 50-gallon drums for 25 percent more than you'll find on Mexico 1. **NOTE:** There is no commercial bus service to Bahía de los Ángeles.

EXPLORING

For a glimpse into the history and natural resources of the area, visit the **MUSEO DE NATURALEZA Y CULTURA** (Nature and Culture Museum) just behind the quiet central plaza. Learn about the many species of birds, whales, and other sea life that inhabit this island-laden bay, and see displays of the artifacts left behind by indigenous tribes as well as tools from the miners and missionaries. It's open daily (9am–noon and sometimes 2pm–4pm); donations are accepted. A few miles north of town on the waterfront, it may be possible to observe several species of endangered sea turtles at the **PROGRAMA TORTUGA MARINA** (on the waterfront north of town), where marine biologists and university students study, rescue, and track loggerhead turtles.

PUNTA LA GRINGA is a popular beach with splendid views of the bay, the islands, and the surrounding mountain and desert terrain. Beachcombing can be good here, and fishing from shore can yield spotted bay bass, triggerfish, and sometimes halibut. To reach this point, follow the dirt road north along the coast for about 5 miles. There are no facilities.

Since the wonders of this huge bay are best seen from the water, arrange a **NATURE TOUR** from **CAMP GECKO** (5 miles south of town; gecko@starband.net; www.campgecko.com) for an up-close look at these intriguing islands. Many species of whales, including blues, humpbacks, sperm, finbacks, and orcas, as well as dolphins, sea lions, and other marine life thrive among these islands along with an abundance of birds. In the summer and fall, whale sharks frequent these waters. **DAGGETT'S** (La Gringa Rd; 664/650-3207; see review) and **GUILLERMO'S** (Main St; 664/650-3209), both in town, also offer sightseeing boat rides and whale shark observation.

ADVENTURES

BIRD-WATCHING / The shoreline and guano-capped islands, where more than 50 species feed and nest, are great for bird-watching. Sightings include vultures, pelicans, herons, ospreys, frigate birds, cormorants, Heerman's gulls, royal and elegant terns, and blue-footed boobies. Isla Raza, south of the "Bay of L.A.," is the breeding and nesting ground for about 90 percent of the planet's population of elegant terns.

FISHING / Strong tidal currents in the waters of the Bay of L.A. supply nutrients that support an abundance of fish. In the summer months, when yellowtail, *dorado,* and yellowfin tuna are present, the fishing can be excellent. Many other species, such as *cabrilla,* barracuda, and grouper, are found throughout the year, but keep in mind that winters are cold and windy. The best times of year to fish these waters are summer (if you can stand the heat) and fall. Several guides know the waters well (see Guides and Outfitters). Do-it-yourselfers either launch from the remote beaches surrounding the village or use one of the boat ramps in town.

DIVING AND SNORKELING / The islands offer excellent diving and snorkeling opportunities with good visibility and an abundance of colorful sea life. The most popular and easily accessible sites surround **ISLA CORONADO,** just 2 miles east of **PUNTA LA GRINGA** (the bay's northernmost point). The trip takes about 25 minutes by boat from the town center, less if you launch or leave from a destination closer to the island. There are many other dive sites in the area, including two wrecks. Mornings are best for snorkeling, before the afternoon winds kick in. Colorful angelfish, damselfish, butterflyfish, a variety of rays and eels, nudibranches, and numerous spiny creatures such as urchins and lobsters inhabit these waters. Specimens of grouper and bass get very big—some larger than you!

Several places in town rent snorkeling gear. Divers are on their own as far as equipment; however, **CAMP GECKO** (5 miles south of town; gecko@starband. net; www.campgecko.com) has a compressor to fill your tanks. For transportation to the dive sites, contact **GUILLERMO'S** (Main St; 664/650-3209) or others listed in Guides and Outfitters.

KAYAKING / The Bay of L.A.'s many islands have become a haven for kayakers seeking day trips as well as longer excursions. Short and long itineraries can be created among the islands, many of which lie no farther than 4 miles off the coast. Sand and gravel landings are common; the waters are rich with marine life and the islands are home to a multitude of birds. It's no wonder that marine biologists are continually studying this protected sanctuary. One of the most popular day trips is from **PUNTA LA GRINGA** (the bay's northernmost point) out to **ISLA CORONADO,** a distance of about 2 miles each way. Itineraries popular among hard-core kayakers include a route around the 37-mile-long **ISLA ÁNGEL DE LA GUARDA** or heading south as far as San Francisquito, both major expeditions requiring more than 100 miles of paddling.

If you choose to go out paddling on your own, it is necessary to visit the **RESERVA** (reservations office; located next door to the museum) to file a float

THE PHANTOM ESCALERA NÁUTICA

Just about the time the Pacific Ocean disappears from view, giving way to cactus, rock, and mesa on Mexico 1 (heading south), Escalera Náutica signs appear along the highway. The signs, bearing both a logo of a boat on a launch ramp and an ever-decreasing number of kilometers, conjure visions of a large oasis in the center of the desert peninsula. Curious travelers, mesmerized by these shining lures, are led, instead, southeast for 42 miles across a minefield of alignment-tweaking potholes to the tiny town of Bahía de los Ángeles by the Sea of Cortez. Or, following the signs located farther south along Mexico 1, they encounter the best road in Baja—3 miles of sinfully wide, four-lane highway that abruptly change into an intense washboard road leading straight to the even tinier settlement of Santa Rosalillita on the Pacific. What travelers won't find, however, is the phantom **ESCALERA NÁUTICA**—at least not yet.

Envisioned decades ago by FONATUR, the Mexican government's tourism agency, and swiftly endorsed by President Vicente Fox within his first 100 days in office, the Escalera Náutica (Nautical Ladder) is a proposed network of 22 ports—none of them farther than 125 nautical miles apart—along Mexico's Pacific and Sea of Cortez coastlines, and includes the construction of a "Boat Highway" across the narrowest part of the Baja peninsula, terminating in the aforementioned Bahía de los Ángeles and Santa Rosalillita.

Under this $225 million plan, the five existing usable ports (in Baja: Ensenada, La Paz, and Cabo San Lucas; on the mainland: Guaymas and Mazatlan) will be modernized. Seven existing ports (in Baja on the Sea of Cortez: San Felipe, Santa Rosalía, Mulegé, and Loreto; in Baja on the Pacific: San Carlos; on the mainland: Punta Peñasco and Topolobampo) will be improved and deemed usable, and another 10 new seaports will

plan. They may ask you to register and make reservations for camping on the islands. Do not set out without thorough knowledge of the currents, tides, and distances within your float plan. Even experienced kayakers have gotten into trouble here. Winds can be brutal, conditions change rapidly, and the currents between islands are dangerously strong. It is highly recommended that someone else onshore knows your expected return time or date.

WINDSURFING AND KITEBOARDING / Although it can be on the chilly side, winter is the best season here for windsurfing and kiteboarding. The Bay of L.A. can howl for days upon end, frustrating the kayakers and fishermen, while wind junkies carry toothy smiles. Winds are fluky close to town, so the preferred launch is in the vicinity of the northern point, **PUNTA LA GRINGA**. Since the islands prevent any sizable shore break, smooth, fast speed-sailing (5.0–6.5 range sail sizes) is what you can expect with side-shore to side-offshore winds funneling in from the north and northwest. Kiters who can't yet stay upwind can enjoy miles of unobstructed beach downwind.

be constructed in low-income regions to jump-start tourism (in Baja on the Pacific: Cabo Colonet, Punta Canoa, Santa Rosalillita, Bahía Tortugas, Punta Abreojos, and San Juanico; in Baja on the Sea of Cortez: Bahía San Luis Gonzaga and Bahía de los Ángeles; on the mainland: Bahía Kino and Altata). In addition, 20 airports will be rebuilt. Roads will be constructed and improved, providing easier access for trailering boats from Arizona and California. Hotels and marinas are also on the drawing boards.

The proposed "Boat Highway" is actually part of a 30-year-old goal to bridge the peninsula's two coasts. Along this overland connection, "Boat Platforms" (flat-bed trucks) will haul yachts from the Pacific (where a breakwater is already under construction) to the Sea of Cortez or vice versa. The 80-mile shortcut is designed to bring greater recreational boating opportunities and much desired tourist dollars to the upper Sea of Cortez. Not everyone, however, is onboard with the plan.

Those opposed include local fishermen, environmental groups, and citizens concerned with overdevelopment and increased boating activity within the fragile marine environments. Since many of the ports scheduled for development lie within or near protected marine reserves, the project is incompatible with local and worldwide conservation efforts. Others fear the project will be started, only to fall into ruin through lack of funds, creating eyesores along otherwise pristine shorelines. (Though the entire project has not been fully funded, a breakwater has already been constructed in Santa Rosalillita.)

Phantom or reality? Only time, politics, tourism, and foreign investors will tell if the Escalera Náutica will ever materialize. Or will it remain, as it is today, just a few illusory signs along the desert highway, leading travelers astray?

—Susan McCombs

GUIDES AND OUTFITTERS
LARRY AND RAQUEL'S MOTEL (2 miles north of town on La Gringa Rd; bahia tours@yahoo.com) rents single kayaks as well as tandems for $15–$25 US a day, and offers day trips in 22-foot *pangas* for $120–$150 US. **COSTA DEL SOL** (Main St) and **DAGGETT'S** (La Gringa Rd; 664-650-3206) also have kayaks. **CAMP GECKO** (5 miles south of town; gecko@starband.net; www.campgecko. com) has kayaks for rent and is the home base of **DR. ABRAHAM VASQUEZ,** a local bilingual guide who has a 32-foot cruiser, is knowledgeable about the area, and is dedicated to low-impact eco-tourism.

Ken Streater of **DESTINATION WILDERNESS** (800/423-8868 US; info@ wildernesstrips.com; www.wildernesstrips.com) has been guiding adventure trips since 1985. In 1999, his company began offering multiday packages November through April involving two days of whale-watching at Scammon's Lagoon (see the South Central Baja chapter for details) followed by three days of kayaking in the Bay of L.A. Paddlers travel south from Camp Gecko and camp along the way, reaching Los Animas Bay before being transported by *panga* back (upwind) to their base camp. All-inclusive trips start at $2,250 US, which includes round-trip (drive/fly) transportation from San Diego.

RESTAURANTS

Costa del Sol / ★

MAIN ST, BAHÍA DE LOS ÁNGELES Small and tastefully decorated, this eatery has a good reputation among tourists and locals. A colorful tropical mural adorns the wall of the cozy indoor dining area, but the patio view is hard to beat. Sip a margarita while taking in the expansive view of the bay. The menu is simple but the food is tasty. For breakfast try the *chilaquiles con huevos*—eggs topped with crispy tortilla strips smothered with green chile sauce. The *sincronizados*—ham, cheese, and guacamole wrapped in a flour tortilla—is popular for lunch. Fish tacos, burritos, and enchiladas are also on the menu for lunch. For dinner, try the fresh scallops or shrimp *al mojo de ajo* (cooked with garlic). *$; No credit cards; traveler's checks OK; breakfast, lunch, dinner every day; full bar; no reservations; costadelsolhotel@hotmail.com; west side of main street.*

Guillermo's Restaurant / ★★

MAIN ST, BAHÍA DE LOS ÁNGELES; 664/650-3209 This beachfront restaurant has the best food in town and is quite popular among kayaking groups and local gringos. Mounted trophy fish, potted plants, and a stone-faced bar decorate the interior, but if the weather permits, dine under one of the two large *palapas* outside affording wonderful views of the islands. The breakfast menu offers lobster or shrimp omelets, or a tasty quesadilla with eggs, chorizo (spicy pork sausage), and potatoes. For dinner try their special scallops—wrapped in bacon and prepared with a sauce of butter, white wine, and garlic—served with rice and vegetables. If you're really hungry, order the seafood combo—fresh lobster, shrimp, scallops, and fish, all sautéed in butter and garlic, and served with soup or salad. *$$; No credit cards; traveler's checks OK; breakfast, lunch, dinner every day; full bar; no reservations; one block east of main street.*

Villa Vitta Restaurant / ✰

MAIN ST, BAHÍA DE LOS ÁNGELES; 664/650-3208 Established in 1977, Villa Vitta is the largest restaurant in town. The interior, though basic, is almost churchlike, with massive carved wooden doors, high windows, and round lights hanging from the low-pitched ceiling. There's a fireplace for cool evenings and a roofed poolside patio area for hot afternoons. The breakfast menu includes huevos rancheros and *huevos a la mexicana* as well as omelets, hotcakes, French toast, fresh-squeezed orange juice, and smoothies. Hamburgers, pasta, and fresh fish are available for lunch, served with fries. For dinner, choose from lobster, fish (whole or fillet), shrimp, scallops, carne asada, and beef fajitas, all served with salad, beans, rice, and tortillas. The adjoining hotel and RV park make up what is known as Villa Vitta Resort, which, over the past few years, has suffered from frequent changes in management, security problems, and unreliability, though you may find that this situation has improved. *$$; Cash only; breakfast, lunch, dinner every day; full bar; no reservations; west side of main street.*

LODGINGS

Costa del Sol Hotel / ★★☆

MAIN ST, BAHÍA DE LOS ÁNGELES Four years ago, Sandra López came to the Bay of L.A. from mainland Mexico and opened this very attractive seven-room hotel on the main drag. Immaculately clean, this is the only lodging in town with 24-hour electricity—a huge plus on hot summer nights. The wide, stone stairway welcomes visitors to what at first resembles a large, tastefully designed Mexican casa. Terra cotta in color, the two-toned, tile-roofed building blends well with its desert surroundings. The inside is equally appealing, with modern wood furnishings imported from the mainland. Colorful curtains and bedspreads liven the spacious rooms, which include air conditioning, satellite TV, separate sink and toilet areas, and firm, comfortable beds. The on-site restaurant (see review) serves three meals a day, and there's ample off-street parking. *$; No credit cards; traveler's checks OK; costadelsol hotel@hotmail.com; west side of main street.*

Daggett's Beach Camping

LA GRINGA RD, BAHÍA DE LOS ÁNGELES; 664-650-3207, FAX 664-650-3206 Offering 16 spaces with shade *palapas* and a large overflow camping area, Daggett's is the nicest campground in the area. Ruben Daggett runs the basic but tidy facility with clean bathrooms, hot water, and flush toilets. A launch ramp is suitable for small boats, and when you haul in your catch, make use of the fish-cleaning station and barbecue pits. Low tide creates tidal pools right in front of the campground—great for exploring. Beware of stingrays in the summer and fall. *$; Cash only; follow signs from north end of town 2 miles to beach.*

Guillermo's Motel / ★

MAIN ST, BAHÍA DE LOS ÁNGELES; 664/650-3209 Guillermo's knew what they were doing when they added a motel to their restaurant and RV park a few years ago. The simple one-story, flat-roofed building fills up fast when there's a group of kayakers in town, which is often. The motel's seven spacious rooms all front the beach, providing easy access to the bay. Each room has two to four queen-size beds and a large bathroom with a sink in a nearby alcove—a nice feature when you are sharing a room with several people.

A ceiling fan and central air conditioning cool your room, but only 7–11pm when the electricity is on. After dinner next door at Guillermo's Restaurant (see review), come back to the motel to relax on the porch in time to watch the play of light on the islands as the sun sets behind you. If you've arrived on the night of a full moon, linger a little longer to witness the glowing orb rise slowly from the sea. *$; No credit cards; traveler's checks OK; one block east of main street.*

Larry and Raquel's Motel / ★

LA GRINGA RD, BAHÍA DE LOS ÁNGELES; 619/422-3454 US This two-story beachfront motel has become a popular staging center for kayakers heading out or returning from multiday trips. The eight rooms on the ground floor are fairly basic, with tile floors, air conditioning, and modest furnishings. A plus for this establishment is their alternative energy sources—solar panels and a wind generator—that keep the power flowing most of the time. A small restaurant, bar, and kitchen are on the second floor, offering great views of the bay and islands. Tide pools out front can be explored at low tide, and bird-watching is good from the outdoor seating area. Larry and Raquel are friendly and helpful and will make you feel welcome. Arrive early to secure a room, since this place can fill up quickly, especially toward evening. *$; No credit cards; traveler's checks OK; bahiatours@yahoo. com; two miles north of town.*

Santa Rosalillita and Punta Rosarito

Twenty-two miles south of the junction to Bahía de los Ángeles, signs point to a broad, paved road luring travelers west toward the Pacific and the small fishing village of Santa Rosalillita. This superhighway is part of the proposed **ESCALERA NÁUTICA** (Nautical Ladder), part of a multimillion-dollar marina/airport/roadway development plan (involving four Mexican states) that will someday allow boaters to cheat their way across Baja using "boat platforms" rather than circumnavigating the peninsula by sea (see "The Phantom Escalera Náutica" sidebar). Just before press time, the first 3 miles of this road were the smoothest and the widest on the entire peninsula (more asphalt is expected in the next few years). The next 7 miles, however, will rattle the crowns right off your teeth. But if you're a die-hard surfer, windsurfer, or kiteboarder, the rewards are well worth the dental work.

The once-quiet fishing village of **SANTA ROSALILLITA** sits at the northern end of a 30-mile crescent bay with expansive, pristine beaches. Monster trucks, a large crane, and work crews have recently invaded the settlement, constructing a breakwater and marina—part of the Escalera Náutica. But away from this building project, the quiet coastline north and south offers spectacular scenery, endless waves, and miles of perfect Pacific sand. There are no services in town, with the exception of a small market, but sometimes *magna sin* is sold from jugs. Bring your own food and drinking water, and come prepared to camp.

ADVENTURES

WINDSURFERS and **KITEBOARDERS** have plenty of room to launch and play in the swells to the north of the new breakwater, where you'll find an expansive beach and a wave that won't quit. The closer you get to the northern point, the more defined the waves. Small breakers on the inside are gentle and perfect for novice wavesailors, while larger surf outside won't bore the pros. Side-onshore winds and smooth water between the waves almost assure you of a good session here—if the wind cooperates. **SURFERS** can sometimes work the waves near the point, but prefer the better-formed point break known as **ALEJANDRO'S** about 4 miles north. To get there, backtrack to the main dirt road, and then follow signs to San José.

South of Rosalillita, **PUNTA ROSARITO** has long been a favorite among **SURFERS** seeking the perfect wave. Nicknamed "the Wall," this break is characterized by its steep face and lengthy curl. Unless you have four-wheel-drive, you'll need to go back to Mexico 1 for access to Punta Rosarito. From Mexico 1 near km 62.5, head west on the dirt road about 3 miles through the wide *arroyo* and veer right at the fork. Look for remnants of an old adobe structure on the right, and turn left (west). This road leads to the beach just north of the point, where you can park on the bluffs. This access is passable by passenger cars, but not recommended for RVs or vehicles towing trailers. There are no services at Punta Rosarito.

State Line: Baja California and Baja California Sur

Eighty miles south of the junction to Bahía de los Ángeles is the state line separating the northern state of Baja California and the southern state, Baja California Sur. A 135-foot Mexican eagle—**MONUMENTO ÁGUILA**—marks this crossing along with a huge Mexican flag, both visible for miles. There's a large military installation here, as well as a **CHECKPOINT** and an **AGRICULTURAL PESTICIDE SPRAY STATION**. Vehicle searches are possible and officials will ask if you have any citrus fruits. They may or may not ask for your stamped tourist card. Usually you'll be waved through to the next stop, which is the pesticide spray station for Mediterranean fruitflies (aka med flies). A uniformed officer will approach your vehicle and ask for 10 pesos (about $1 US). He will then wave you over to the unfortunate soul in the white biochemical suit wearing a respirator and a backpack tank containing malathion. **WARNING:** Roll up your windows and close your vents. Watch as the car in front of you is sprayed. They spray the wheels, tires, and underneath your vehicle, and then you may proceed south, med fly–free. **NOTE:** Don't forget to set your watch ahead one hour, as you are crossing into the Mountain Time Zone.

ADVENTURES

The best **FISHING** in the state-line area is at Laguna Manuella. Access is near the village of Jesús María at around km 96 on Mexico 1, where an oiled road to the west leads to a wide gravel road and then 7½ miles of washboard to the fish camp near the mouth of the bay. Use caution when leaving this main road, as the sand is very soft. Shore fishing can yield sand bass, halibut, *corvina* (soft-mouthed, migratory croaker), and sometimes *sierra*. Hire a *pangero* to take you out farther for croaker, *corbina* (slender, dark grey surf croaker), white sea bass, grouper, and occasionally yellowtail.

RESTAURANTS

La Espinita Restaurant / ★

MEXICO 1, STATE LINE Guadalupe and Francisco Grado have operated La Espinita ("the Little Thorn") for eight years, serving fresh seafood and Mexican specialties. Located just north of the state line and almost directly across from the Pemex station, this is a convenient stop for travelers on the move who need refueling (food), but don't want to make the drive into Guerrero Negro (2 miles south and then 2.5 miles west). The clean interior, with its salmon-colored walls, bright fabrics, and large windows, is bathed in natural light. Breakfast is the usual array of egg dishes such as *chilaquiles* and huevos rancheros, and is highlighted with shrimp and crab omelets. Lunch and dinner options include chimichangas (deep-fried burritos), lobster, and fresh fish, shrimp, or scallops—either fried or served *al mojo de ajo* (cooked with garlic). Entrees come with rice, beans, and a small salad. There's a public telephone available inside the restaurant, and the Grados allow free overnight parking in their large off-highway lot. *$; Cash only; breakfast, lunch, dinner every day; full bar; no reservations; on west side of highway.*

SOUTH-CENTRAL BAJA

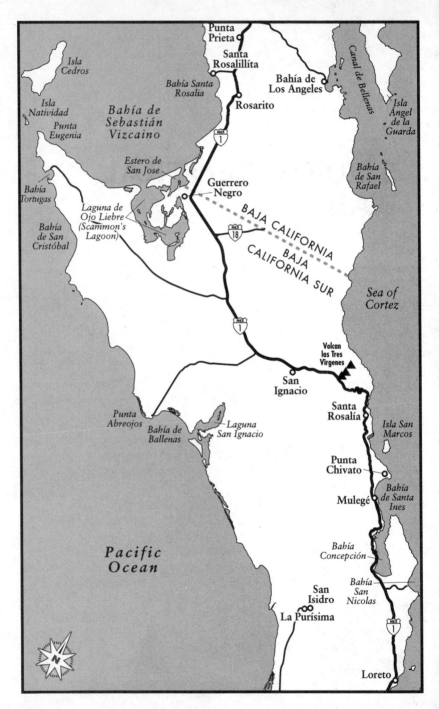

SOUTH-CENTRAL BAJA

Guerrero Negro to Bahía Concepción

If it's not spectacular scenery you're viewing in this section of Baja, it's the fascinating creatures that inhabit the surrounding water, desert, and mountain environments. Ospreys rule the skies in the northern region, building their huge nests on man-made platforms atop roadside power poles. Just a few miles south of Guerrero Negro, a signed spur road leads west through the world's largest salt operations (and a sanctuary for migratory birds) to Parque Natural de la Ballena Gris (Gray Whale Natural Park), the northernmost of several gray whale breeding grounds along Baja's Pacific coast. From December through early April this inlet, known as Scammon's Lagoon, is thick with these tremendous mammals and their calves. Spectators can view the whales from shore or get a closer look from permitted boats with certified guides.

Farther south is the parched Vizcaíno Desert, one of the only fog deserts in the world. This vast wilderness is part of an International Biosphere Reserve and home to a rare herd of pronghorn antelope. The isolated herd of about 120 animals lives 1,000 miles from others of its kind, surviving on water droplets deposited by fog on the scarce vegetation. Unlike other pronghorns, the Vizcaíno herd will not drink water from the few livestock tanks dotting their domain. Also inhabiting the desert here are burrowing owls and desert foxes, while the shoreline of this reserve harbors elephant seals, loggerhead, and leatherback turtles.

Southeast lies the Sierra de San Francisco, a mountain range where Paleolithic artists left hundreds of ritualistic cave murals and many mysteries surrounding their identity. Remote canyon walls, caves, and overhangs covered with larger-than-life, two-toned human figures are concentrated in this arid region, where visits require surefooted mules, permits, and authorized guides.

Gradually Mexico 1 descends into the date-palm oasis of San Ignacio, a charming Mexican village with its ornate and well-preserved mission church and access to Laguna San Ignacio, home of the friendliest whales in Baja. Southeast of San Ignacio, evidence of the region's volcanic past is evident along both sides of the highway, with heaping lava flows and the solitary and majestic *Volcan las Tres Vírgenes* (Three Virgins Volcano).

More visual stimulation is in store as you catch your first glimpse of the Sea of Cortez—only to see it disappear while you negotiate the devilish and dizzying *Cuesta de Infierno* (the Slope of Hell). Soon you reach the water's edge, near the French-inspired former mining town of Santa Rosalía, marking the transition from arid desert to the subtropical region of Baja that has entranced travelers for centuries.

From here the highway follows the coast to Mulegé, another palm-shaded oasis and popular tourist center with a salty estuary, a tropical feel, and numerous opportunities for adventure. This chapter ends just south of Mulegé at Bahía Concepción, a 25-mile bay where kayakers often begin their voyages and pristine beaches and spectacular vistas abound.

ACCESS AND INFORMATION

The primary access to this portion of the peninsula is Mexico 1, that reliable ribbon of asphalt stretching from Tijuana to Cabo San Lucas. Having just a single highway does have its benefits: it's very difficult to get lost. **NOTE:** Remember that in Baja California Sur, the km marker numbers decrease as you travel from north to south; see "Demystifying the Km Markers" in Planning a Trip.

BUS SERVICE is available through Autotransportes de Baja California (ABC; 664/686-9010, Tijuana; http://abc.com.mx), Autotransportes Águila, and Tres Estrellas de Oro (664/626-1701, Tijuana), with bus stations in most major towns and bus stops along the highway in the smaller villages. **FERRY SERVICE** across the Sea of Cortez to and from the port city of Guaymas on the mainland is available in Santa Rosalía (see Santa Rosalía's Access and Information section).

Some travelers access this section of Baja by landing **PRIVATE PLANES** on the small airstrips in San Ignacio, Santa Rosalía, Palo Verde, Punta Chivato, Mulegé, Posada Concepción, and San Nicholas. For more information on small airplane travel, contact the **BAJA BUSH PILOTS** (480/730-3250 US, fax 530/730-3251 US; www.bajabushpilots.com).

Guerrero Negro

The dusty, windblown town of Guerrero Negro sits just south of the state line separating Baja California from Baja California Sur. Named after the whaling ship *Black Warrior,* which sank in the harbor in the late 1850s, Guerrero Negro was once a whaling port, where whalers nearly annihilated the planet's gray whale population. Now the largest city between Ensenada and Ciudad Constitución, Guerrero Negro is home to the world's largest **SALT OPERATIONS,** Exportadora de Sal, S.A. (ESSA), which is the town's chief employer.

It's also home to Parque Natural de la Ballena Gris (Gray Whale Natural Park) and Scammon's Lagoon, the northernmost of several **GRAY WHALE BREEDING AND CALVING GROUNDS** along Baja's Pacific coast. Between January and March, tourists from all over the world come here to frolic with the gray whales that migrate to Guerrero Negro's warm-water lagoons. Although several whale-watching outfitters operate within the area, visitors can often see whales from shore, especially close to the end of the old salt-loading pier west of town, where fishing and bird-watching are also popular. While in the area, be on the lookout for **OSPREY,** (large seagoing birds of prey) and their huge nests. Keep a jacket handy, as this region is often foggy with chilly temperatures and brisk winds that blow in from the Pacific.

ACCESS AND INFORMATION

The town of Guerrero Negro, with a population of about 12,000, lies 2 miles south and 2.5 miles west of the **MONUMENTO ÁGUILA** (Eagle Monument, at the state line). Several convenient **SERVICES** are available here that can't be found in the smaller villages, such as auto mechanics, auto parts stores, and *ferreterías* (hardware stores), all located on the road leading into town, **BOULEVARD ZAPATA.** This main drag also has two Pemex stations, a hospital, a Banamex with an ATM (Blvd Zapata, about 3 miles from Mexico 1; 615/157-0555), a *tortillería,* a bakery, several sizable grocery stores, ice, hotels, a SuperPollo (Blvd Zapata, just past the hospital)—great for a quick meal of inexpensive grilled chicken—and other restaurants. The best source of **TOURIST INFORMATION** in the area is the small gift shop/eco-tour office at the Malarrimo Restaurant (Blvd Zapata; 615/157-0250).

Just past the Malarrimo on the left side of Boulevard Zapata is the small **BUS TERMINAL** (615/157-0611) where Autotransportes de Águila and Autotransportes de Baja California (ABC; http://abc.com.mx) arrive and depart. **TAXIS** are usually available as well for local transport. **NOTE:** Km markers decrease from Guerrero Negro whether you're heading north or south. Heading north, they reset at the junction to Bahía de los Ángeles; heading south, they reset at Santa Rosalía (see Demystifying the Km Markers in the Planning a Trip chapter).

EXPLORING

Prior to the realization that tourists had a love affair with whales, Guerrero Negro was basically a company town, devoted solely to salt production. ESSA operates some 70 square miles of evaporative salt ponds just south of town, an area teeming with bird life. The company relies on the area's hot desert sun and high winds, producing some 5 million tons of salt annually. After the evaporative process, the salt is harvested, loaded onto huge trucks, transported to the north end of the bay, off-loaded onto barges, towed to Isla Cedros and off-loaded again (whew!), where it is finally packed into freighters bound for destinations around the world. Watching the monster trucks in action as they move mountains of salt can be a fascinating experience, and bird-watchers will appreciate the great blue herons, snowy egrets, black-necked stilts, and ospreys. Tours of the salt works are available through **MALARRIMO ECO-TOURS** (Blvd Zapata; 615/157-0100; malarimo@telnor.net; www.malarimo.com/ingles.htm).

ADVENTURES

SURFING AND WINDSURFING / The coastline along the sparsely populated Vizcaíno Peninsula produces some of the best (but most difficult-to-reach) surf breaks in Baja. From Ejido Vizcaíno on Mexico 1, **PUNTA EUGENIA** is a 120-mile trek on a dirt road through the desert. Other surfing sites along the coast in this area include **PUNTA ASUNCIÓN,** 70 miles west of Vizcaíno, and a string of other points to the south including **PUNTA SAN HIPÓLITO, LA BOCANA,** and **PUNTA ABREOJOS,** which is also popular for windsurfing. A more direct spur road leads to Abreojos from Mexico 1, north of San Ignacio at km 98. Large

NESTING GROUNDS OF THE CALIFORNIA GRAY WHALES

Three warm-water lagoons on the Pacific coast of Baja provide a winter sanctuary where California gray whales come to mate, give birth, and nurture their calves before heading back to their summer feeding grounds in the cold Bering Sea. This annual reproduction ritual attracts thousands of whale-watching tourists and has come to symbolize Mexico's dedication to protect one of its most important natural resources.

Although it's possible to see a whale's "blow" (exhalation) and to catch fleeting glimpses of back and tail from shore, the best way to experience these magnificent creatures is up close—aboard a whale-watching *panga*. From a seat in these sturdy skiffs, you're right at water level and stand a good chance of looking a gray whale in the eye.

LAGUNA OJO DE LIEBRE (SCAMMON'S LAGOON), near Guerrero Negro, **LAGUNA SAN IGNACIO,** southwest of San Ignacio, and **LAGUNA MAGDALENA,** near Ciudad Constitución (see the Mid-South chapter), provide warm, protected waters—perfect conditions for whale nurseries. Lacking blubber, baby whales would freeze to death if born in the chilly waters farther north. For this reason, the gray whales swim 5,000 miles south every spring to Baja—the longest migration of any marine mammal. Since female whales usually get pregnant every other year, some of the females (and a majority of the males) come here to mate. When observing a sexually active pod, whale watchers are always on the lookout for the "pink floyd," the nickname given the enormous male penis that can sometimes be seen when the male rolls on his back at the surface.

motor homes, trailers, or low-clearance passenger cars should not attempt to drive out to the Vizcaíno Peninsula without a high-clearance or four-wheel-drive escort, and it is wise to carry extra gas. High-clearance trucks are best. For people who are not camping, there are limited rustic lodgings and cafes at Bahía Tortugas and Bahía Asunción.

WHALE-WATCHING / PARQUE NATURAL DE LA BALLENA GRIS (Gray Whale Natural Park) has the largest concentration of gray whales of all of the Pacific lagoons. The park is located in the large **LAGUNA OJO DE LIEBRE** (Eye of the Hare Lagoon), where the southernmost region was named **SCAMMON'S LAGOON** after an American whaler who found the breeding/birthing ground in the mid-1800s. Scammon and the whalers who followed nearly wiped out the gray whale population. Today the whales are protected and it's estimated that their numbers now exceed 20,000.

To reach the park and arrange your own whale-watching tour with the *pangeros* of the *ejido* (cooperative) based there, take Mexico 1 south about 8 miles to the small cement whale monument and hand-painted sign marked "Parque Natural de la Ballena Gris." The washboard dirt road (sometimes

While courting couples seem to congregate in the strong currents near the mouths of these bays, the inner lagoons are filled with mother–calf pairs. Baby whales spend much of their time nursing and the rest of the time building muscle and learning skills they'll need for their long journey north. Because the newborns can't hold their breath very long, they spend a good deal of time at the surface. With mother close by, the 15-foot-long calves often approach boats out of curiosity. Lunging out of the water, they expose a mouth full of baleen and a bumpy black head—delighting whale watchers.

Once in a while, whales approach the boats and roll onto their sides, close enough to allow passengers to reach out and stroke their rostrums (upper jaw), long baleen plates (filter-feeding system), or barnacle-encrusted bodies. Another interesting behavior is known as *spy hopping*: the animal slowly rises out of the water, snout first, often exposing its eye to the air. Some speculate that spy hopping allows the animal an above-water view of its surroundings. Without creating even a ripple, the whale then sinks back into the murky water. A few minutes later, it may surface on the other side of the boat, adding to the excitement and mystery that has made whale-watching so popular.

The most amazing part of the whale-watching experience comes not from close encounters, but from the realization that less than 100 years ago, in these same lagoons, these gentle giants were being slaughtered by whalers who would mercilessly harpoon the baby to get to its fiercely protective mother. Today, this tribe of migrating marine mammals that narrowly escaped a close brush with extinction bravely allow their new-born calves to swim over and open the door to understanding.

—*Carrie Robertson*

graded) gets smoother as you reach the bleached-white salt flats, about 17 miles from the highway. At the gated checkpoint, an attendant will let you in; proceed to the parking lot (fee $3 US) and arrange an excursion with the local *pangeros*. Such tours usually cost $25–$45 US per person ($15 for children), depending on the length of your trip. You can also walk around the area, toward the narrow opening of the salt-crusted inlet where females give birth (bring binoculars). Camping is allowed at this windy site ($4 US; no facilities), and the restaurant La Palapa serves decent meals.

Access to this natural park is only allowed December through March or April, when the whales are in. Boating in Scammon's Lagoon and all of the Pacific lagoons is tightly regulated during whale-watching season to protect the recovering species in their breeding grounds. Private boats, kayaks, and wind-surfers are not allowed in these waters from December through April. See the Guides and Outfitters section for information on booking a whale-watching tour with round-trip transportation.

GUIDES AND OUTFITTERS

Several operators in Guerrero Negro have permits allowing them to take groups on whale-watching tours. Such tours fill up during the whale season, and reservations are highly recommended to assure a seat; however, if you've failed to get reservations, last-minute vacancies are possible and worth looking into. Outfitters with permits include **MALARRIMO ECO-TOURS** (Blvd Zapata; 615/157-0100, fax 615/157-0100; malarimo@telnor.net; www.malarrimo.com/ingles. htm), **LAGUNA TOURS** (Blvd Zapata; 615/157-0050; lagtours@nextgeninter. net.mx), and **MARIO'S TOURS** (Mexico 1, just south of state line; 615/157-1940 or 615/159-4033). Prices range from $40 to $50 US per person for 4-hour tours, which include round-trip transportation to Scammon's Lagoon, a 2-hour *panga* tour among the whales, and lunch. These outfitters also guide other adventures, including bird-watching, cave painting trips, and desert tours.

FESTIVALS AND EVENTS

The **FESTIVAL DE LA BALLENA GRIS** (Festival of the Gray Whale) is a four-day event held each year in mid-February at the Scammon's Lagoon access area. Educational lectures, art exhibits, movies, live music, and food booths line the dirt parking lot near the loading pier.

RESTAURANTS

Las Cazuelas Restaurant / ★

BLVD EMILIANO ZAPATA, GUERRERO NEGRO; 615/159-1681 OR 615/159-4255 Shadowed by the large hotel Posada de Don Vicente, Las Cazuelas ("the Pots") is nothing fancy, but seems to be popular with locals—a pretty good sign. Murals and old photographs cover the walls while large windows reveal the goings-on in town. The breakfast menu offers hotcakes, eggs, and a fish omelet. Lunches are primarily fish tacos or *tortas* (Mexican sandwiches), both served with a large selection of toppings and salsas. For dinner, try the white seabass *a la veracruzana* (sautéed with a tomato sauce, onions, peppers, and olives) or the foil-wrapped fresh fish. Other dinner choices include fresh seafood, steaks, and Mexican entrees such as chicken mole and enchiladas. If you're traveling with a group, this restaurant can easily accommodate you with its banquet-style tables. *$$; No credit cards; traveler's checks OK; breakfast, lunch, dinner every day; full bar; no reservations; east end of town.*

Las Cazuelas Restaurant/Hotel La Pinta

MEXICO I (HOTEL LA PINTA), GUERRERO NEGRO; 615/157-1305 OR 800/800-9632 US Occupying a small area in the spacious Hotel La Pinta, Las Cazuelas is a somber restaurant with dark wood tables, chairs, and floors. A wall of windows opens onto the central courtyard, but overall, this place could use some color; the plain white tablecloths and white walls do little to brighten it up. The limited breakfast menu offers Mexican egg dishes, ham and eggs, and oatmeal. Lunch and dinner menus include chowder, seafood cocktails, fried or garlic shrimp, scallops, steak, or fish. Enchiladas, tacos, burritos, and hamburgers are also available. There's plenty of parking and this is a convenient stop with easy access back onto Mexico 1. *$; MC, V, traveler's checks OK; breakfast, lunch, dinner every day; full bar; reservations recommended; info@lapintahotels.com; www.lapintahotels.com; on the highway at the state line.*

Malarrimo Restaurant / ★★★

BLVD EMILIANO ZAPATA, GUERRERO NEGRO; 615/157-0250 Although a popular tourist stop for years, Malarrimo Restaurant, now under chef Enrique Achoy's trained expertise, has become a must stop for those in the know. Trained in international cuisine, Achoy personally selects his seafood and beef, preparing cuisine that can be ranked as the best in central Baja. Divided into several rooms, the restaurant carries a nautical theme decorated with maps, ship paintings, fishing floats, and whalebones, along with a great collection of gray whale photos. A good way to start the day is with a shrimp or crab omelet. Unusual for Mexico, the restaurant offers a low-fat omelet of egg whites, mushrooms, and *salsa ranchera*. Before dinner, sip a glass of Monte Xanic or another label from their wine list, which features a sampling of Baja California vintages. When you're ready, settle in and order the house specialty, *mano de léon* (lion's paw), a large scallop found only in nearby Laguna Ojo de Liebre that is served with a sauce of fresh herb butter, garlic, and secret ingredients. For dessert, have a slice of flan or a scoop of ice cream. *$–$$; No credit cards; traveler's checks OK; breakfast, lunch, dinner every day; full bar; no reservations; malarimo@ telnor.net; north side of the street at the east end of town.*

Mario's

MEXICO I, GUERRERO NEGRO; 615/157-1940 It's hard to miss this huge *palapa* restaurant on the highway that looks like it belongs in the South Pacific. When the cold air comes through in wintertime, however, some say it feels like the *North* Pacific. Inside, a central post, support beams, and woodwork rise to a high central crown. The decor is simple with plastic chairs and tables arranged around the dirt floor. Breakfast choices include French toast and omelets made with lobster or shrimp. An interesting choice on the dinner menu is *callo de hacha*—the adductor muscle of the hatchet shell—not noted for being tender. As it is, Mario's is one of the priciest places in town. Regardless, it's worth a try—but pick a warm night, something not too common in Guerrero Negro. Mario Maga, the owner, also holds a permit to give whale-watching tours that depart from this establishment. *$–$$; No credit cards; traveler's checks OK; breakfast, lunch, dinner every day; full bar; no reservations; west side of highway between state line and Blvd Emiliano Zapata.*

LODGINGS

Hotel La Pinta / ★

MEXICO 1, GUERRERO NEGRO; 615/157-1305 OR 800/800-9632 US The Hotel La Pinta is the most attractive hotel in this unexciting desert terrain and a convenient stop for travelers on the move. The 28 spacious rooms are comfortable, with satellite TV, clean bathrooms, tile floors, and Mexican handicrafts on the walls. By prior arrangement, local tour operators will pick you up in front of the hotel for your excursion, which makes it easy to quickly shower away the salt spray from a day with the gray whales or a tour of the salt flats. The La Pinta chain recently began offering nonsmoking rooms and, with advance notice, some will now allow pets into a few of their units. A large parking area in front of the hotel allows enough room for even large vehicles with something in tow. *$$; MC, V; traveler's checks OK; reservations@lapintahotels.com; www.lapintahotels.com; at the state line on the west side of the highway.*

Malarrimo Motel/Cabañas Don Miguelito / ★★☆

BLVD EMILIANO ZAPATA, GUERRERO NEGRO; 615/157-0250 Adjoining the Malarrimo Restaurant, this motel features 16 units arranged in a cluster with passageways between them. Ten of the rooms offer basic but clean lodging with a single and queen-size bed, hand-carved headboards imported from mainland Mexico, satellite TV, and small private bathrooms. The six larger cabañas are much nicer with two queen-size beds, tile floors and bathrooms, brightly colored walls and accessories, and lofts—perfect for kids. A spacious parking lot is conveniently adjacent. *$; No credit cards; traveler's checks OK; malarimo@telnor.net; north side of the street on the east side of town.*

Malarrimo RV Park

BLVD EMILIANO ZAPATA, GUERRERO NEGRO; 615/157-0250 The RV park is the best place in Guerrero Negro for those who are camping. Thirty-six campsites with full hookups lie behind the restaurant and motel, with 15 overflow campsites located across the street. Amenities include hot showers, bathrooms, and night security. A gift shop, a market, and an eco-tour center are also located on the premises. *$; No credit cards; traveler's checks OK; north side of the street on the east side of town.*

Motel Posada de Don Vicente / ★

BLVD EMILIANO ZAPATA, GUERRERO NEGRO; 615/157-0288 This large, two-story motel is designed in a U-shape with 28 rooms and a relatively good location set well back from the busy street, which minimizes disturbing road noises at night. A large sign and bright red and yellow walls make this motel easy to spot if you're coming in after the sun sets. The rooms are clean and simple, with two double beds, satellite TV, and ceiling fans. Its close proximity to the highway makes for easy entry and exit from Guerrero Negro, and the on-site restaurant offers a meal if you're too travel-weary to drive or walk somewhere else. Off-street parking is available, but is best for small vehicles. *$; No credit cards; traveler's checks OK; on east side of town.*

San Ignacio

A few hours' drive deeper into Baja California Sur brings you to the enchanting town of San Ignacio. A large gray whale skeleton marks the entrance to town, a reminder that these intriguing mammals are not too far away. The complete opposite of Guerrero Negro's industrialization, San Ignacio is a quiet village surrounded by flat mesas and a thriving colony of date palms fed by a year-round spring. Introduced by the Spanish *padres,* the Arabian date palms have multiplied to fill the valley. A kilo bag of San Ignacio dates is a great snack while driving down the highway. Dried figs are also a local delicacy.

ACCESS AND INFORMATION

San Ignacio is just off Mexico 1 near km 72. The **BUS STATION** is on the highway by the Pemex station. The compactness of San Ignacio is centered around the *zócalo* (public square). The streets are wide (small RVs only) and there's plenty of parking, so it's easy to drive in and explore on foot. You'll find a bank, a phone *caseta,* a pharmacy, and a post office nearby. The square is fringed with huge Indian laurel trees, providing shade and allowing tourists to savor the ambience of this peaceful village, particularly on hot summer days. This is the place where locals come to lounge on concrete benches for hours, quietly visiting, laughing, or playing checkers.

EXPLORING

Dominating the western side of the *zócalo* is the magnificent **MISIÓN SAN IGNACIO,** one of Baja's most impressive and ornate churches, founded by the Jesuits in 1786 and still functioning today. Its 4-foot-thick walls, built of volcanic rock, effectively insulate the interior from climatic changes. Examine the Moorish designs and elaborate stonework framing the windows and doors. Study the magnificent wooden doors carved on the Mexican mainland, and if they open, step inside to see the worn stone flooring, carved altars, and a statue of Saint Ignacio Loyola, the town's patron saint.

Adjacent to the church stands the delightful **SAN IGNACIO MUSEUM,** devoted to interpreting the stunning, larger-than-life cave paintings found nearby. Next to the museum is the small office of the **NATIONAL INSTITUTE OF ANTHROPOLOGY AND HISTORY** (INAH; 615/154-0222), where adventurers can register and obtain the required permits for visiting the mural caves—a mandatory first stop for those wishing to view these national wonders.

SAN IGNACIO'S ROCK ART

Little is known of the ancient artists whose murals and petroglyphs are hidden deep within the Sierra de San Francisco north of San Ignacio. Some of the compositions are so high off the ground they appear to have been created by a race of giants. Cochimí Indians encountered by the first explorers had no oral history of the painters. Jesuit missionaries were the first Europeans to see the murals, in the mid-1700s, but their meager accounts lay buried within their dusty archives for more than 200 years.

In December 1993 these archeological sites, believed to be thousands of years old, were named to UNESCO's World Heritage list. Many have studied these murals, including mystery writer Erle Stanley Gardner. **CUEVA PINTADA** (Painted Cave), also known as Gardner's Cave, contains the best-preserved murals in the region and quite possibly in North America. Situated within the sheer walls of the remote Arroyo de San Pablo, Cueva Pintada is nearly 500 feet long—a rock art gallery. Wall and ceiling paintings depicting oversize shamanistic human figures, a whale, bighorn sheep, deer, fish, and a multitude of birds are found here, amid the spectacular scenery of the narrow gorge. Photojournalist Harry W. Crosby created a photographic journal of his travels to well-known and previously undiscovered paintings. His book, *The Cave Paintings of Baja California*, is a "must read" for anyone interested in visiting these historic works of art.

It is possible to visit several of the murals with an authorized guide; however, a trip into the Sierra de San Francisco is not for everyone. Because of the rugged terrain, access to the grandest of these sites is limited to surefooted mules and burros—often stubborn, ornery, and uncomfortable to ride for long periods of time. Strenuous hiking is also required; participants need to be in good physical condition with no medical problems. Camping gear, supplies, and water are packed in and out. Guides are mandatory, and are appointed on a rotating schedule; some speak English, while many do not. You may need to hire a translator in addition to your guide. It is possible to arrange such trips from home using a reputable outfitter (see Guides and Outfitters), or, with some advanced planning and foresight, you can deal with authorized guides (and their mules) and purchase needed supplies upon arrival in San Ignacio. **NOTE:** Many of the remote mural sites require reservations and registration with the National Institute of Anthropology and History (INAH) as far as six months in advance.

—*Lori Makabe*

ADVENTURES

WHALE-WATCHING / An important source of income for local businesses is taking tourists to Laguna San Ignacio, 45 miles southwest of the village, to view the gray whales when they come to calve and mate between January and April. The whales in this lagoon have been nicknamed the "friendlies" because of their willingness to approach boats and eager whale-watchers. The washboard road is deeply rutted and hard on car suspensions—might as well hire a van rather than beating up your own vehicle. There are several tour guides in town. **ECO-TURISMO KUYIMA** (Morelos 23; 615/154-0070; kuyimasi@cybermex.net; www.kuyima.com/html) on the southeast corner of the *zócalo* offers van transportation, a restaurant, and primitive lodging on the shore of the lagoon. **EL PADRINO RV PARK** (just south of Hotel La Pinta; 615/154-0300) and **MOTEL LA POSADA** (2 blocks east of town past the mission; 615/154-0313) are other local outfitters with the required permits.

CAVE PAINTINGS / Although **CUEVA PINTADA** (see the "San Ignacio's Rock Art" sidebar) and many of the other cave mural sites lie in areas that require hiking or pack trips, one of them—**CUEVA DEL RATÓN**—can be reached by passenger car (high-clearance vehicles recommended) and is located next to the road. Before you begin this adventure, you must first visit the **INAH OFFICE** (just west of Misíon San Ignacio; 615/154-0222) on the *zócalo* to **REGISTER** and obtain the **REQUIRED PERMIT(S)**. They can give you current road conditions as well as a general map of the area. They will also arrange transportation if you'd rather not take your own vehicle. Such day trips usually leave around 7am and return by 6pm. If you plan to drive, allow a good part of the day (5–6 hours) for this trip.

From San Ignacio, drive 28 miles north on Mexico 1 to the dirt road near km 118 marked **RANCHO SAN FRANCISCO DE LA SIERRA** and a sign reading "Pinturas Rupestres." Follow this road for 21 miles. The drive passes through a few miles of desert before climbing a steep, rocky, narrow road with tight switchbacks and spectacular canyon vistas. Soon you'll drive right past **CUEVA DEL RATÓN** (mouse cave), enclosed in a chain-link fence (with a locked gate) on the south side of the road; it's necessary to continue another 2 miles to the village to see the *cordinador* (coordinator), who will assign you a guide for the day; guide fees currently run about $9 US per day. The 40-foot-wide mural features a tall, black-faced humanoid figure, bighorn sheep, deer, and a mountain lion among its figures and markings. Although smaller than the other murals that lie deeper within San Pablo Canyon, Cueva del Ratón is very worthwhile to visit—especially if you don't have the time, the energy, or the bottom design for a three-day mule trip. Other such sites that are well worth the effort include **CUEVA PALMARITO** and **CUEVA SERPIENTE** (serpent cave), both possible to visit in an 8-hour day trip from San Ignacio.

GUIDES AND OUTFITTERS

ECOTURISMO KUYIMA (Morelos 23; 615/154-0070; kuyimasi@cybermex.net; www.kuyima.com/html) offers day trips to Cueva del Ratón as well as 3- to 10-day excursions into the Sierras, taking in a large number of murals deep within the canyons. Day-trip prices start at about $35 US per person for groups of 10 (more for smaller groups) and include transportation, gate fees, park and camera permits, and a box lunch. They also offer whale-watching tours and ecology-based adventure camps for children.

The San Ignacio office of the **INAH** (National Institute of Anthropology and History; 615/154-0222) located on the square next to the museum can help arrange your trip to the rock art sites, assigns knowledgeable guides, and offers a wealth of information.

ABEL AGUILAR SESEÑA of **EL PADRINO ECO-TOURS** (just south of Hotel La Pinta; 615/154-0089) has been guiding mule-packing trips to Cueva Pintada as well as day trips to Cueva del Ratón, Cueva Palmarito, and Cueva Serpiente for 12 years; he speaks limited English. **MOTEL LA POSADA** (2 blocks east of town past the mission; 615/154-0313) can also arrange for guides, mules, and transportation for day trips and longer excursions.

FESTIVALS AND EVENTS

The last weekend in July each year marks the end of the date harvest as well as the celebration of San Ignacio's patron saint with the **FESTIVAL SAN IGNACIO LOYOLA**. This sleepy town comes to life as lights are strung along the plaza illuminating evening dances, live music, and food booths. Horse racing, cockfights, and fireworks round out the list of festivities before the town returns once again to its normal, peaceful setting.

RESTAURANTS

Flojo's / ★

ENTRANCE RD (EL PADRINO RV PARK), SAN IGNACIO; 615/154-0089

Plastic tables and chairs define this eatery's simplicity, but the menu has a few choices not common to Baja. *Almejas rancheros* (clams in a rich tomato-based sauce with onions and peppers) are a good choice on a cool night, while meat-eaters might enjoy their *Milanesa,* an Italian-style, thin-cut breaded veal. Other menu items include broiled lobster, sautéed shrimp, scallops, and fish, as well as steaks. Breakfasts are pretty quick here by Mexican standards, and include huevos any way you'd like them, along with fresh juice, breakfast quesadillas, and burritos. *$–$$; No credit cards; traveler's checks OK; breakfast, lunch, dinner every day; full bar; no reservations; elpadrino@prodigy.net. mx; just south of Hotel La Pinta.*

La Muralla Restaurant / ★

ENTRANCE RD, SAN IGNACIO Popular with locals yet undiscovered by tourists, La Muralla ("the Wall") features an eye-catching red exterior. In simple Mexican style, plastic tables and chairs are neatly arranged on the cement floor of the *palapa* dining room. For breakfast, try the *chilaquiles* and *nopales* (eggs with fried tortilla strips, green chile sauce, and cooked prickly pear cactus) or an egg burrito. The dinner menu offers seafood, including *mano de león* (lion's paw), a large scallop found only in Laguna Ojo de Liebre, as well as beef and Mexican combinations. On the porch there's a pool table and a small *tienda* (store) selling snacks and sodas. *$; Cash only; breakfast, lunch, dinner every day; full bar; no reservations; right side of entrance road into town, 100 yards south of highway.*

Las Cazuelas / ★

ENTRANCE RD (HOTEL LA PINTA), SAN IGNACIO; 619/275-4500 US OR 800/800-9632 US Similar to other Hotel La Pinta restaurants, this one is clean, comfortable, and overpriced. This location, however, features a local delight that's worth trying, even if it's the focus of your dining experience: date pie, made with local San Ignacio dates. Other menu selections include standard Mexican fare with enchiladas, *pescado al mojo de ajo* (fish cooked with garlic), broiled lobster, steaks, and a decent *pollo en mole* (chicken cooked until tender in a thick, chocolaty sauce). With the exception of the whale-watching season, this seems to be a very lonely restaurant, frequented mostly by hotel guests. *$; MC, V; traveler's checks OK; breakfast, lunch, dinner every day; full bar; reservations recommended; info@lapintahotels.com; www.lapintahotels. com; 1 mile from highway, on entrance road toward town.*

Restaurante Quichule / ★

KM 78 MEXICO I, SAN IGNACIO This roadside eatery is clean, colorful, and often filled with residents and Mexican travelers—usually a good sign. Seafood cocktails made with shrimp, clams, or scallops are very popular here. Other menu options include enchiladas, burritos, beefsteaks, and seafood choices including broiled lobster and sautéed or *ranchero* shrimp or fish. Abalone is offered, but it's not recommended. *$; No credit cards; traveler's checks OK; breakfast, lunch, dinner every day; beer only; no reservations; 2 miles north of San Ignacio turnoff, beside military checkpoint just north of town.*

Rice and Beans Oasis / ★

SAN LINO RD, SAN IGNACIO; 615/154-0283, FAX 615/154-0283 A recent addition to the scene near San Ignacio, Rice and Beans is owned and operated by the family of Ricardo Romo Cota, who runs the extremely popular waterfront eatery of the same name in San Felipe. Their signs and menus claim "Healthy Mexican Food," and from our observations it

SOUTH-CENTRAL BAJA THREE-DAY TOUR

DAY 1: After an evening at the Rice and Beans Oasis Hotel and breakfast at their restaurant, visit the quaint town of San Ignacio, surrounded by a dense orchard of date palms introduced by Spanish *padres* 250 years ago. Sit in the *zócalo* shaded by old Indian laurel trees, and absorb the grandeur of **MISIÓN SAN IGNACIO.** Visit the mission church and the town's small museum, devoted to the native people who once populated this region. When hunger strikes, head for lunch at **FLOJO'S** restaurant, located inside El Padrino RV Park. Afterward, head south on Mexico 1 for 45 miles. Pass jumbled lava flows studded with white-barked elephant trees, and behold the majestic 6,547-foot **VOLCAN LAS TRES VÍRGENES** just north of the highway. Arrive in the historic town of **SANTA ROSALÍA** alongside the sparkling Sea of Cortez. If you feel like it, stroll the rocky shoreline where the highway first meets the sea. Then treat yourself to a waterfront room at the Hotel **EL MORRO** with views of the sea and Isla San Marcos. Freshen up and then enjoy a relaxed dinner in the hotel's French-inspired **RESTAURANT.** After dinner, take an evening stroll to enjoy the night sky.

DAY 2: Head into the heart of Santa Rosalía and breakfast on the renowned pastries and authentic French bread at **PANADERÍA EL BOLEO.** Step inside **IGLESIA SANTA BÁRBARA**—the landmark church designed by French architect Alexandre Gustave Eiffel (of Eiffel Tower fame). Walk the intriguing streets of this thriving Mexican-French town. When it's time for lunch, order up the tastiest grilled chicken and seafood around at **TERCO'S POLLITO.** Drive up the hill north of town to the area known as **MESA FRANCESA.** Visit the **HOTEL FRANCES,** noticing the French architecture, steam locomotive, and old mining machinery in the neighborhood. Walk over to the **MUSEO**

appears that they do make an extra effort to reduce the amount of lard and butter in their recipes—a rare practice in Mexico. Portions are hefty, and include—you guessed it—rice and beans. Order your clams, fish, or shrimp as a ceviche, a soup, in tacos, *a la veracruzana,* breaded, or grilled—or spring for a *hamburguesa,* burrito, or fajita platter. The walls are plastered with photos, posters, and decals, mainly featuring off-road-racing events. Prices are reasonable and the staff accommodating. This is the only place in the region that has a realistically usable ramp for wheelchair access. *$; MC, V, traveler's checks OK; breakfast, lunch, dinner every day; full bar; no reservations; first hard right as you approach town, 1 mile north of Pemex station (look for signs), then take frontage road.* &

HISTÓRICO MINERO and learn about Compañía del Boleo, the mining company that built the town. After your museum visit, hit the road again, traveling 38 miles south to semitropical **MULEGÉ,** where you'll have dinner and spend the night. Check in at the **HOTEL SERENIDAD,** former stomping grounds of mystery writer Erle Stanley Gardner. Take a refreshing dip in the pool, then plan on dinner at the hotel. You might even be driven to change out of your grubby traveling clothes and spruce up a little for a special evening. Pick the magic time when the changing shades of light on the water follow the disappearance of the sun for the day. After a nightcap in the hotel's comfortable lounge, retire to your room.

DAY 3: Start the day with an early-morning visit to **MISIÓN SANTA ROSALÍA DE MULEGÉ.** Located across Río Mulegé (aka Río Santa Rosalía) from town, the church is one of only a handful of mission churches still usable today. Afterward, head to the town center and take a walk down Calle Madero to visit the 100-year-old **HOTEL HACIENDA.** Have breakfast at their small cafe and then zigzag your way up the stone stairway that leads to the **TERRITORIAL PRISON MUSEUM** for a bird's-eye view of the town. If it's open, tour the museum's displays. When you're ready for lunch, try **EL PATRÓN** for fresh seafood. After lunch, hit the road—your next hotel lies only 25 miles away on the aquamarine **BAHÍA CONCEPCIÓN,** but be sure to make it a leisurely drive to allow time for enjoying the beaches and views along the way. Do a little sunbathing or swimming to while away the afternoon. Check in at the **HOTEL SAN BUENAVENTURA** for a romantic night on the shores of this lovely bay. Relax and watch the sunset colors emerge. Dine in the hotel's restaurant, where the menu usually includes lobster, and then step outside to take in the night sky.

LODGINGS

El Padrino RV Park

ENTRANCE RD, SAN IGNACIO; 615/154-0089 Tucked among the thick date-palm forest, this RV park is the closest to town and offers the most amenities, as well as the date palm backdrop. Fifteen of the 40 campsites have full hookups and there's a shower house with hot water and *baños* (bathrooms) that are usually in working order—something not always easy to find in these parts. Flojo's is the on-site restaurant (see review), and there's a small pool and a dump station. Keep in mind that camping among the palm trees can be buggy—it's wise to keep the repellent handy. *$; No credit cards; traveler's checks OK; elpadrino@ prodigy.net.mx; 200 yards north of town near Hotel La Pinta.*

Hotel La Pinta / ★

ENTRANCE RD, SAN IGNACIO; 615/154-0300 OR 800/800-9632 US The contrast of white walls, red-tile roofing, and the encompassing greenery of the surrounding date palms make this La Pinta an inviting stop. The 28 rooms are clean and simple with two queen-size beds, tiled floors and bathrooms (some rooms have carpet), and Mexican handicrafts. Amenities include satellite TV, air conditioning, and heaters. There's a swimming pool, an on-site restaurant—Las Cazuelas (see review)—and a bar, and sometimes *magna sin* (unleaded gas) is available here for guests (but don't rely on it). The La Pinta chain of hotels has recently started offering nonsmoking rooms, and with advance notice, small pets are now allowed in some of the units. When the whales are in (Jan–Apr), this hotel is often packed, so don't expect to drop in for a room as you can at many of the La Pintas—reservations are a must. Parking is suitable for passenger cars, but not for larger vehicles. This hotel is close enough to town that a brisk walk through the palm groves is a pleasurable way to see the attractions of San Ignacio. *$–$$; MC, V; traveler's checks OK; info@lapintahotels.com; www.lapintahotels.com; 1 mile from highway.*

Rice and Beans Oasis Hotel and RV Park / ★★

SAN LINO RD, SAN IGNACIO; 615/154-0283, FAX 615/154-0283 The boxlike, plain white exterior of this two-story hotel may tempt you to make a quick judgment about the place; however, a closer look reveals some thoughtful details. Eleven spacious rooms—six just recently completed—include tiled floors and large showers, satellite TV, queen-size beds, remote-control air conditioning, and ceiling fans. Rooms are well kept and the grounds, although sparsely landscaped, are tidy. A night watchman guards the large parking lot. Although this establishment is not in town, the on-site restaurant, Rice and Beans Oasis (see review), warrants any inconvenience. *$; MC, V; traveler's checks OK; 1 mile west of Pemex station on frontage road.*

Santa Rosalía

From Mexico 1, Santa Rosalía looks like a grungy old town with barren hills and an uninviting waterfront. Turn off the highway and onto the orderly streets, however, and you'll be pleasantly surprised. This city of nearly 20,000 residents has a unique history and is a great place to find a good meal, spend a few days exploring, stock up on provisions, or seek auto parts that may have been unavailable since Guerrero Negro.

Oddly enough, the dominant culture of this port city in the early part of the 20th century was European. In 1885, the French mining company Compañía del Boleo (El Boleo) took over a copper mining operation begun by Germans after a local rancher discovered *boleos* (balls) of copper ore. El Boleo signed an agreement with the Mexican government granting them mineral rights to the hills surrounding Santa Rosalía. In exchange for these rights, the company agreed to build a town and a port and to provide jobs for the local people. They built a huge transporting and smeltering complex and eventually a narrow-gauge railroad, using six steam-powered locomotives. The waterfront buzzed with activity as large sailing vessels arrived from Europe hauling cargos of coal and lumber as well as equipment and supplies for the mines and mining officials. The town developed with a predominance of French-colonial style wooden homes and buildings, and was soon referred to as La Ciudad de Madera ("the City of Wood"). Nearly 375 miles of tunnels were honeycombed into the hills and nearby Arroyo del Boleo, yielding more than 10,000 tons of copper annually. Steady production continued until the 1950s, when the ore played out.

Left behind are the tidy rows of houses and businesses built of the imported wood and reflective of this French era, along with a thriving port city that is proud of its past. A simple metal church designed by Alexandre Eiffel sits on the main street, while El Boleo Panadería, the town's famous bakery, never fails to lure loyal customers as well as newcomers. Strategically placed mining equipment and steam locomotives are on display throughout the streets, and a drive up Mesa Francesa reveals the historic Hotel Frances, the Museum of Mining History, and the decaying remnants of the foundry below. Many of the old wooden buildings, with their wraparound verandas and high-pitched roofs, are being refurbished with assistance from the National Institute of Anthropology and History (INAH), and a recent ruling requires any new construction to follow a strict building code designed to maintain the French style.

Although Santa Rosalía holds the seat of government for the Mulegé district, the town still relies heavily on its natural resources. Fishing fleets provide low but steady incomes while gypsum and manganese are both mined in the area. Tourism tends to be seasonal, with slow summers and busy shoulder seasons. Sportfishing can be good here, especially around nearby San Marcos Island, but most of the charter fishing boats leave from points farther south, where a couple of RV parks are popular with campers and the tourist-oriented town of Mulegé lures anglers. The Santa Rosalía port houses a small marina with a community of live-aboards and the SEMATUR Ferry Terminal, providing ferry service to mainland Mexico's largest west coast port city, Guaymas, an 8-hour voyage across the Sea of Cortez.

ACCESS AND INFORMATION

BY CAR, Santa Rosalía lies 45 miles southeast of San Ignacio and 38 miles north of Mulegé on Mexico 1 along the Sea of Cortez. Most of the narrow city streets are one way, and it's not advisable to drive large RVs or trailers into town. Instead, park near the green and blue SEMATUR Ferry Terminal and walk. From Mexico 1, Avenida Alvaro Obregón leads away from the waterfront and Avenidas Constitución and Montoya take you back to the highway. NOTE: Try to fill your gas tanks elsewhere if possible—Santa Rosalía's Pemex station attendants are notorious for ripping off unwary tourists and locals alike.

BUS SERVICE is available at TERMINAL DE AUTOBUSES (bus terminal; Mexico 1; 615/152-0150) on the west side of the highway, south of the

SEMATUR Ferry Terminal. Autotransportes Águila and Autotransportes de Baja California (ABC; http://abc.com.mx) both stop here on their peninsular routes north and south.

For Baja visitors who wish to continue on to mainland Mexico, Santa Rosalía offers passenger and vehicular **FERRY SERVICE** across the Sea of Cortez. The voyage across to Guaymas cuts hundreds of miles off of a journey there by car. It is wise to arrive one or two days early to allow sufficient time to work out the reservation details and complete the necessary paperwork. You'll need your original vehicle title or registration and three copies, a major credit card, a driver's license, a passport, and a valid Mexican visa (tourist card). Tickets are available at the green and blue **SEMATUR FERRY TERMINAL** (Mexico 1; 615/152-0013 or 0014; www.ferrysematur.com.mx) on the Muelle Fiscal (public pier). Departures from Santa Rosalía are on Sunday and Wednesday (8am), arriving in Guaymas at approximately 3pm. From the mainland, ferries leave Guaymas on Tuesday and Friday (8am), arriving in Santa Rosalía about seven hours later. Current passenger fares are approximately $40 US for general "salon" tickets and $68 for "tourist class" with a cabin, bunk beds, and a washbasin. If you've brought your sleeping bag and insulated pad, the salon section is not a bad choice; sleeping out on the deck under the stars can be a wonderful experience—weather permitting. Vehicle prices depend on the size of your rig, starting at about $280 for a 15½-foot auto and increasing by footage. Passengers are not allowed on the vehicle deck—not even to attend to pets.

BANCOMER and **BANAMEX** (both with **ATMS**) are located on the corner of Avenida Obregón and Calle 5 and are open 8:30am–3pm. **INTERNET VISION** (Av Obregón), across from the bakery, is a good place to check your email as is **INTERNET CAFÉ** (Av Obregón and Calle Playa), located upstairs and next to Terco's Pollito.

EXPLORING

The best place to take in the peaceful but unappealing waterfront of this copper town is to walk south along the **MALECÓN** that starts near the entrance to the harbor. Shell collectors will find plenty to gather north of town, along the rocky beach where Mexico 1 heads inland. Turn off the highway onto Avenida Obregón and follow your nose a few blocks west to **PANADERÍA EL BOLEO** (Av Obregón 30; 615/152-0310), a traditional bakery founded in 1901 in the height of the mining boom. Note the well-worn path to the counter as you stand in line to order your Mexican pastries and French breads. Across the street at **LA MICHOACANA,** order a healthy shot of fresh-squeezed orange juice or *jugo de zanahoría* (carrot juice) to go with your bakery purchases. Or if you prefer ice cream, continue west past the banks at Calle 5 and look for **THRIFTY ICE CREAM** (Calle 5) on the north side of the street.

Santa Rosalía doesn't harbor many tourist-type stores, a trait that some travelers find appealing. Take some time to wander the narrow streets and observe where the locals shop. Head back toward the waterfront to Calle Plaza, where there's always something happening in the shady **PLAZA BENITO JUÁREZ** (Calles Plaza and Constitución). The plaza's decorative gazebo is often used for public announcements, special events, and performances by children from the nearby elementary school. Closer to the highway, study the nice collection of historic photographs taken during Santa Rosalía's mining and shipping era at **BIBLIOTECA MAHATMA GANDHI** (Calle Playa), the northernmost library in Baja California Sur; open Monday through Friday (10am–5pm).

A trip into Santa Rosalía wouldn't be complete without a visit to **IGLESIA SANTA BÁRBARA** (Av Obregón at Altamirano), the church designed by France's well-known architect **ALEXANDRE GUSTAVE EIFFEL** of Eiffel Tower fame. This simple steel structure was originally a prototype for France's missionary colonies, as the entire building was shippable and not likely to rust or be eaten by termites in tropical locations. The portable church got rave reviews at the Paris World Exposition in 1889, but then wound up in a warehouse in Brussels, where it was later purchased and shipped by the French mining company El Boleo to the heart of Santa Rosalía, where it is was assembled and is still in use today. Step inside to get a closer look at the drab, prefab iron panels that contrast with radiant colors from the stained-glass windows.

Mosey up the steep hill north of town, taking Calle Altamirano to the neighborhood known as **MESA FRANCESA**. Among the wood-framed buildings, a retired steam locomotive in the wide cobblestone street, and mining carts, you'll find the **HOTEL FRANCES** (Calle Jean M. Cousteau 15; 615/152-2052), a beautifully restored colonial-style hotel and **NATIONAL HISTORIC MONUMENT** founded in 1886 by El Boleo. For a small fee ($1 US), you can step inside to see the interior, with its alternating dark and light wooden floors, ceilings, and shiny, varnished paneling. Keeping with the upper-class French tradition, the walls are covered with *tissus muraux* (wall fabric)—in this case, Mexican bandanas—that look surprisingly tasteful bordered in wood. It's easy to drift back in time. Large reprints of old photographs show four-masted square-riggers anchored in the makeshift harbor. Mining tools and memorabilia are on display, and the high wooden ceilings hide stories of adventure and promise. A large wraparound veranda offers bird's-eye views of what's left of the copper foundry to the east. If you prefer not to go inside, visit the small exhibits of mining tools, photos, and equipment on display around the outdoor pool. The northern end of the hotel has a good view of the El Boleo complex, and if you look north, you'll see a long horizontal chute running from the foundry below to a smokestack up on the hill. This cement chute, reminiscent of China's Great Wall in miniature, was built to draw the foundry's thick smoke away from town.

Just south of the hotel on the other side of the cobbled street is **MUSEO HISTÓRICO MINERO DE SANTA ROSALÍA** (Museum of Mining History; Calle Jean M. Cousteau). Housed in a former schoolhouse, this museum was the headquarters of El Boleo, the company that built the town. The interior was left intact with original furnishings, typewriters, electric ceiling fans, and a telephone system. Exhibits include mining tools, lanterns, volt and watt meters, scales, and mineral samples, along with maps, ship's logs, payroll records, an old oxcart, and a bicycle. The museum is worth a visit, and has an impressive view of the area. Open Monday through Saturday (9am–6pm).

ADVENTURES

FISHING / For sportfishing, charter a *panga* at **SAN LUCAS RV PARK** (km 182), 9 miles south of Santa Rosalía on Mexico 1. The local *pangeros* are commercial fishermen who can lead you to excellent fishing for *dorado,* yellowtail, yellowfin tuna, and grouper around Isla San Marcos. Rates are negotiable, but usually run about $125 US per day.

WINDSURFING AND KITEBOARDING / If it's windy, the rocky beach just north of town where Mexico 1 first arrives at sea level is a great place to throw off the road dust and hit the water for some high-energy windsurfing or kiteboarding. The north winds are side-onshore and the beach, although rocky, is user friendly (watch for glass). A small point to the north knocks down some of the chop, allowing for smooth show-off jibes on the inside, while nice ramps can sometimes build on the outside.

RESTAURANTS

Ángel Café / ★

AV OBREGÓN 34, SANTA ROSALÍA; 615/152-1292 Conveniently located near the banks, this colorful cafe is a good place to buzz into your day with a cappuccino or latte on their street-side patio. Their breakfast menu is stacked with the usual Mexican egg specialties such as huevos rancheros and *chiliquiles,* but also offers specials including the belt-busting *carne asada con huevos y papas* (shredded beef with eggs and potatoes) and omelets stuffed with shrimp, cheese, or vegetables. Light eaters may prefer the yogurt and fruit plate. For lunch try the sizable grilled chicken breast sandwich, served on a sesame seed bun—a filling meal. Dinner options include fresh seafood served either breaded, with garlic, or *a la plancha* (cooked on the grill). Finish off your meal with a slice of cheesecake or their caramelized flan. *$; Cash only; breakfast, lunch, dinner daily; beer and tequila; no reservations; Obregón at Calle 5.*

El Morro Restaurant / ★★

KM 194 MEXICO 1, SANTA ROSALÍA; 615/152-0414 Genteel decor, including tile floors, comfortable chairs, cloth napkins, and soft lighting, is complemented by a romantic view of the Sea of Cortez in this quaint restaurant. Crab Thermidor, chicken in almond sauce, and the house specialty—coquilles St. Jacques (fish fillet in peanut sauce or cilantro cream)—reflect the French influence evident throughout Santa Rosalía. Dinners are served with soup, salad, and vegetables. *$$; Cash only; breakfast, lunch, dinner every day; full bar; no reservations; east side of highway at south end of town.*

Hotel Frances Restaurant / ★★

CALLE JEAN M. COUSTEAU 15, MESA FRANCESA, SANTA ROSALÍA; 615/152-2052 OR FAX 615/152-2052 A restored remnant of the glory and panache of the French occupation, the Hotel Frances is a delightful place to savor a leisurely meal. Polished wood floors and finely turned wood furniture give the feeling of luxury. The tables are nicely set with linen tablecloths and colorful napkins that complement the deep magenta fabric walls. The breakfast menu includes fresh carrot juice, eggs with beef *machaca* (shredded dried meat), hotcakes, and specialties such as *omelet minero*—an omelet stuffed with beef fajitas and fresh tomato. Lunch choices include fish fillets, sandwiches, and *chilaquiles* with beef. For dinner, try their *Camarónes Azteca*—a layered dish with shrimp, vegetables, tortillas, cheese, and *crema* in a hearty red *ranchero* sauce. For dessert, order Kahlúa over ice cream, or their wonderful Mexican hot chocolate. *$; No credit cards; traveler's checks OK; breakfast, lunch Mon–Sat; full bar; reservations required (winter); take Altamirano uphill, turn right, and follow signs.*

Restaurant-Bar El Muelle / ★★

AV CONSTITUCIÓN AT CALLE PLAZA, SANTA ROSALÍA; 615/152-0931 Ask the locals in town where they go for seafood and they'll recommend El Muelle ("the Pier"). This indoor/outdoor eatery has an expansive menu with a focus on fresh local ingredients. A blue awning surrounds the enclosed patio, which tends to fill up, especially on weekends. Order a bowl of their rich and filling *sopa de mariscos* (seafood soup) or a heaping plate of sautéed scallops. If you're really hungry, try their Marinera Combo—shrimp, scallops, and a lobster tail. Other options include steaks from Sonora, pizzas, tostadas, enchiladas, and carne asada. The breakfast menu has scores of choices, from fresh fruit plates and hotcakes to *huevos con chorizo* (eggs with spicy pork sausage). Parking is tight, so you might be better off finding this place on foot. *$–$$; No credit cards; traveler's checks OK; breakfast, lunch, dinner every day; full bar; no reservations; kitty-corner from Plaza Juárez.*

Terco's Pollito / ★★

AV OBREGÓN AT CALLE PLAYA 1, SANTA ROSALÍA; 615/152-0075 Popular with locals and savvy gringos, Terco's Pollito has been serving their family's special recipe chicken since 1962. The modern interior is tastefully decorated, with Saltillo tile floors and sponge-painted walls bearing human figures and animals reflective of Baja's ancient rock art. The house specialty is their moist and juicy rotisserie chicken, served by the *cuarto* (quarter), *medio* (half), or *entero* (whole). Order your chicken for the road, enjoy it on their shaded patio, or inside the air-conditioned dining room. Dinners include a shredded cabbage salad, mashed potatoes, and bread. Other popular specialties include their lobster salad, *pescado a la veracruzana,* skewered seafood, and a wonderful onion cream soup with Parmesan cheese and croutons. For a caffeine fix, or to finish off your meal, try one of their Frapuchinos, Frapemokas, or Vanilla Francesa drinks. *$–$$; MC, V; no traveler's checks; breakfast, lunch, dinner every day; full bar; no reservations; first establishment as you enter town, past school on the right.*

LODGINGS

Camacho RV Park

KM 182 MEXICO 1, SANTA ROSALÍA Located on San Lucas Cove, this simple RV park has 10 campsites (no hookups) right on the beach. Facilities include shade *palapas,* rest rooms with flush toilets, and hot showers. Palm and mesquite trees provide some shade and privacy. A security guard patrols the park at night. Fishing trips can be arranged here with the local *pangeros.* The sunrises can be spectacular, with a view looking directly at Isla San Marcos, 5 miles east. Park your folding chairs in front of your rig inches from the water with your morning coffee in hand and watch the birds come to life as the dawn evolves. *$; Cash only; 9 miles south of town, then ½ mile east at sign on highway.*

Hotel El Morro / ★★

KM 194 MEXICO 1, SANTA ROSALÍA; 615/152-0414 Hidden from the highway, Hotel El Morro sits on a cliff overlooking the Sea of Cortez. The Spanish-colonial complex, with its white stucco walls, arches, and red-tile roofing, stands among mature palms and flowering bougainvillea, creating a tropical feel. The 40 spacious rooms are arranged in a large U-shape around the parking area. Choice rooms face the sea and feature an interior rock wall, carpet, queen-size beds, easy chairs, satellite TV, air conditioning, and terraces overlooking the water. Follow the concrete walkway through the attractive gardens to the swimming pool, aviary, and on-site restaurant (see review). *$; No credit cards; traveler's checks OK; look for sign 1 mile south of town, east side of highway.*

Hotel Frances / ★★

CALLE JEAN M. COUSTEAU 15, MESA FRANCESA, SANTA ROSALÍA; 615/152-2052, FAX 615/152-2052 Established in 1886 and recently reincarnated, Hotel Frances sits on a hilltop overlooking the sparkling Sea of Cortez. Strolling through the palatial lobby and sitting rooms of this French-inspired antique building, it's easy see why this landmark hotel was named a National Historic Monument. Walls are wainscoted and finely finished; the dark wooden floors are continually dry-mopped to keep them glossy; expect a frown from the attendant if you forget to wipe your feet. The two-story hotel has 17 very clean rooms finished in three different color themes (the yellow room is *really* yellow), with lofty ceilings, large tiled bathrooms, color TV, and air conditioning. There's a restaurant (see review), off-street parking, a swimming pool, and a small on-site museum (see Exploring). *$; Cash only; salomon@ lapaz.cromwell.com.mx; take Altamirano uphill, turn right, and follow signs.*

Punta Chivato

Located 35 miles south of Santa Rosalía, 26 miles north of Mulegé, 113 miles north of Loreto, and just far enough off the highway to be out of the mainstream tourist flow, Punta Chivato was once a favorite purlieu of John Wayne, who would fly in whenever he got the urge for some serious fishing. Considered by many to be one of Baja's prime destinations, this remote point offers a wide range of activities, from beachcombing to scuba diving, snorkeling, kayaking, windsurfing, and fishing. Quality seaside dining and splendid accommodations are other options, since the Hotel Punta Chivato has once again changed ownership, this time falling into the hands of Giusseppe Marcelletti, an imaginative Italian who reopened the hotel as Posada de las Flores Punta Chivato (see review), and is also responsible for the posh Posada de las Flores Loreto (see the Mid-South chapter). Expansive beaches, sheltered coves, rugged volcanic outcroppings, and offshore islands can almost assure you of an adventure at Punta Chivato, if you choose to make the effort to get here.

ACCESS AND INFORMATION

To get to Punta Chivato **BY CAR,** from Mexico 1, turn east on the dirt road (signed) just south of km 155. The 11-mile washboard access road deters many travelers who don't feel the need to rattle their screws any looser—but it is perfectly passable by any passenger car, and if you're lucky, you could find the road freshly graded and smooth. Near the 2-mile mark, a new road to the right (signed) shortcuts the old one, offering access to the southern **SHELL BEACH** area and the hotel, 8 miles ahead.

There's an **AIRSTRIP** (dirt) for private planes. Services are minimal; there's a **BOAT RAMP** near the hotel, and a **PRIMITIVE WATERFRONT CAMPGROUND** (no hookups, primitive facilities; $5 US a night) a bit farther east.

EXPLORING AND ADVENTURES

For beachcombing, **SHELL BEACH** is one of the best places in the region, if not the entire peninsula. This stretch of sand southwest of the hotel is a magnet for nice specimens of pen shells, colorful scallops, murex, bonnets, and occasionally cowries and worm shells. Even the bluffs 50 feet away from the beach are loaded with shells as well as fossils.

SNORKELING AND DIVING are good in front of the hotel and around the volcanic outcroppings that separate the numerous small coves in the area. More adventurous souls will want to hire a *pangero* or take a private boat to dive the **SANTA INÉS ISLANDS** 2 miles east of the campground. **CORTEZ EXPLORERS** (75A Moctezuma, Mulegé; 615/153-0500, fax 615/153-0500; www.cortez-explorer.com), based in Mulegé, offers dive trips to these islands. Visibility is best in the late summer and early fall. This is also a great area to explore by **KAYAK.** Paddle around to find the coves and isolated beaches north of the campground, or visit the Santa Inés Islands.

FISHING can also be excellent in the summer and fall, with the offshore islands yielding grouper, yellowtail, and *sierra*, while farther out there's a good chance for *dorado*, yellowfin tuna, and sometimes billfish. Small boats can usually be launched regardless of the wind direction, due to the number of protected coves that face opposing directions.

Speaking of wind, the winters here are plenty windy, with side-shore and off-shore conditions for **WINDSURFING** from the campground. Inexperienced sailors and those with equipment failure run the risk of not being able to return to the point, necessitating either a boat rescue or a very long swim. The launch is also tricky, as you'll need to negotiate a rocky reef just offshore before you hit the wind line, but once out you'll find nice rollers and you'll most likely have the place to yourself.

RESTAURANTS

Hacienda Chivato / ★★

DOMICILIO CONOCIDO (HOTEL POSADA DE LAS FLORES), PUNTA CHI-VATO; 615/153-0188 OR TOLL-FREE 877/245-2860 US, FAX 615/155-5600
Located within the remote and recently renovated Hotel Posada de Las Flores, Hacienda Chivato is a great place to watch the sunset colors fade into night. Since view tables are limited, order a glass of Baja California wine and drink in the scenery from the patio before your seating. Start off with a lobster salad, or share an order of tangy *ceviche de pescado*—sure to ease your hunger after a day at play. Choose from five pasta selections, which rotate monthly; garlic prawns or grilled New York steaks should satisfy any appetite; the sizzling fajita platters, though generous, are heavy on the oil. For dessert try the chocolate mousse or their decadent and wonderfully textured *flan de la casa. $$; MC, V, traveler's checks OK; breakfast, lunch, dinner every day; full bar; reservations recommended; hotel@posadadelasflores.com; www.posadadelas flores.com; follow smaller signs to "Playa" or "Hotel."*

LODGINGS

Hotel Posada de las Flores Punta Chivato / ★★★

DOMICILIO CONOCIDO, PUNTA CHIVATO; 615/153-0188 OR TOLL-FREE 877/245-2860 US, FAX 615/155-5600 Sitting squarely on a bluff overlooking the expansive Bahía Santa Inés, this out-of-the-way luxury resort targets a refined, exclusive clientele, many of whom arrive via private plane. Posada de las Flores is the updated version of the former Hotel Punta Chivato, a legendary fly-in fishing resort once popular among Hollywood celebrities. The original structure remains the same, with its hacienda-style tile roof, stone arches, and flagstone walkways, while the interior and the surrounding property have been tastefully renovated. The color-washed walls are complemented by tile and slate flooring, rustic wooden doors and window frames, and handcrafted furniture brought over from mainland Mexico. A large *palapa* bar and dining terrace—only a stone's throw from the water—are open when the weather is conducive. Room sizes vary from small and standard with no view to luxurious junior suites with sitting rooms, interior rock walls, king-size beds, fireplaces, and umbrella-shaded view terraces. Each of the 20 units is air-conditioned and designated nonsmoking; breakfast is included with your stay. Children under 12 are not accepted, and ice chests with fish are not allowed in the rooms (the hotel provides cold storage). An in-house tour company offers packages and multiday excursions within the surrounding area; there's also a swimming pool on-site for leisurely days in the sun. In August, this resort is packed with Italian tourists. *$$$; MC, V, traveler's checks OK; hotel@posadadelasflores.com; www.posadadelas flores.com; follow smaller signs to "Playa" or "Hotel."*

Mulegé

First impressions of Mulegé invariably focus on the vast forest of date palms growing throughout the village. Like San Ignacio with its freshwater spring to the north, Mulegé is built around the Río Mulegé (aka Río Santa Rosalía) estuary, which creates the very image of a tropical paradise. The town's friendly residents and peaceful ambience are two good reasons why many gringos choose Mulegé for their winter hideaways or permanent residences.

Mulegé's population has steadily grown to nearly 5,000 residents. With a wealth of area activities, tourism forms the base of the town's economy. Climate is another draw for this region of the peninsula. Just a day's drive north of the Tropic of Cancer, the weather here is pleasant most of the year with winter temperatures averaging 67°F with little rainfall. Late summer and early fall can be unpleasant, however, with high humidity, *chubascos* (rainstorms), and daytime temperatures in the 90°F range.

ACCESS AND INFORMATION

BY CAR, Mulegé sits to the north of Mexico 1 near km 134. In old Baja fashion, the town's narrow streets were squeezed between hills on both sides of the river, which worked fine for pre-automobile transportation, but they're totally unsuited for larger RVs or trailers. A pickup truck or van is the most one can expect to get around in without being hopelessly hung up on a corner. Leave the big rig at the RV park and walk or bike into town. There's also an **AIRSTRIP** (at Hotel Serenidad) for private planes, and a **BUS STOP.**

With the exception of a bank, the town offers a number of **SERVICES** useful to travelers. Auto and tire repair, welding and auto parts, numerous restaurants, hotels, RV parks, and markets are found in town, as well as a dive shop, ice creamery, Laundromat, and Pemex station. (A larger, more convenient Pemex is located just 12 miles south.) To keep in touch with the folks back home, check your email at the **HOTEL HACIENDA** (Calle Madero 3; 615/153-0021) where they have six computers on-line. The cost is 1 peso per minute or 40 pesos per hour.

EXPLORING

With its characteristic L-shape and simplistic design, **MISIÓN SANTA ROSALÍA DE MULEGÉ** (Calle Zaragoza, then west) was built in the mid-1700s and, after several restorations, continues to serve the community. If you have the chance to enter, you'll see the old mission bell and a statue of the town's patron saint. Located on a small rise overlooking the river, the mission offers a nice perspective of the palm-forested town. If you're up for a hike, climb the hill behind the mission.

Another hilltop viewpoint is **MUSEO MULEGÉ** (Calle Cananea, top of the hill), also referred to as the **OLD PRISON MUSEUM**, with a vantage point on the north side of town. The fortress is a former prison, once known as the "prison without locks," as the inmates had liberty to hold jobs and come and go as they pleased during daylight hours, as long as they returned to their cells by 6pm. Inside you can view the prison's cells and a nice collection of miscellaneous items including fossils and marine specimens, old diving equipment, Indian artifacts, and tools from the mission. Inconsistently open Monday through Saturday (9am–1pm); donations are requested.

At the mouth of the river estuary, there's yet another view of the area. Climb up **EL SOMBRERITO** (the Little Hat) for great views of the coastline and the *arroyo* filled with palms. A great way to explore Mulegé is by bicycle. If you don't have your own, several places in town have **MOUNTAIN BIKE RENTALS** by the hour, day, or week including **CORTEZ EXPLORERS** (75A Moctezuma; 615/153-0500) and the **HOTEL HACIENDA** (Calle Madero 3; 615/153-0021).

The shady **PLAZA CORONA** (at Calle Zaragoza) is a central square close to many of the restaurants and services in town. Along the north end of Zaragoza toward Moctezuma, there are a few curio shops, a phone *caseta,* and Laundromat; if you're in the mood for ice cream, you'll want to hit **BLANCA'S** (Calle Zaragoza at Moctezuma). For gift selections and nice imported furniture, **CASA BONITA** (Calle Madero next to Mesquite Bar; 615/153-0166) and **REGALOS NANCY** (Calle Madero across from church; 615/153-0111) offer some of the best choices in town. And if it's pastries or fresh bread you're craving, pedal that bike along the river to the **BAKERY** at **VILLA MARÍA ISABEL RV PARK** (km 134 Mexico 1, past Orchard RV Park; 615/153-0246; open Nov–May).

Mulegé is home to a number of **TACO STANDS,** perfect for a quick lunch or midmorning snack. The best and most consistent in town is **TAQUERÍA DONEY** (Calle Moctezuma near Mexico 1), serving mouth-watering carne asada (grilled beef) and pollo (chicken) tacos, as well as fried *camarónes* (shrimp) and *pescado* (fish) tacos with a nice array of toppings; **ASADERO RAMÓN** (Calle Madero at Romero Rubio) also serves up a good carne asada and occasionally *carnitas* and fish.

STREET EATS

Stacked inside a glass box on an apparatus that's part display case and part bicycle are mountains of sliced cucumbers, papaya, jicama, cantaloupe, and watermelon, making a beautiful tableau. Should you just photograph the scene, or plunk down your pesos and purchase a plastic cup stuffed with vitamin-packed, fat-free fruits and vegetables? Or you see the locals wolfing down delicious-smelling tacos at a tiny street-corner stand. Should you eat on the street? Such a dilemma!

If you can't decide whether it's safe and wise to buy a fish taco from the lady presiding over a vat of hot oil in the middle of the urban jungle, you're not alone. Even seasoned roadies weigh the options and consider the consequences of an unwise decision. But no matter how small and primitive these street-side stands may be, they are also virtual exhibition kitchens, with the cooks and their chopping boards right there for your inspection. How often do you check out the kitchen of a restaurant while on the road, searching for clues to cleanliness? The good news is that at an alfresco taco or fruit stand, you can see the cook up close. Here are a few common-sense tips for surviving—and even thriving!—on street eats.

Obviously, vendors rely on repeat customers, so look for places that are crowded with locals. You might have to wait a bit longer, but in the meantime, you can practice your Spanish. It's also a good idea to eat *when* the locals do, so the food is fresh. *Desayuno* is the early breakfast (6–8am), *almuerzo* is the popular late breakfast (10–11am), *la comida* is the main meal of the day (usually eaten between 2–5pm), while *la cena* is the lighter evening meal enjoyed after 7pm. Make sure there's a washing-up area, and that the cook wipes up spills regularly. If you prefer to watch your fish being fried or meat being grilled, ask the vendor to do so, and wait for it. That way you know it hasn't been sitting out. Stands may be battered and not particularly picturesque, but look beyond that, judging the cleanliness of the kitchen and the cook's hygiene. Dishes of condiments may sit open during peak business hours, but should be covered when things quiet down. Trust your nose (old oil smells bad) and your instincts! *¡Buen provecho!*

—*Jane Onstott*

ADVENTURES

CAVE PAINTINGS / There are two highly recommended day trips to Indian rock art sites in the Mulegé area: Cañón La Trinidad, southwest of town, and San Borjitas, in the mountains west of Punta Chivato. **CAÑÓN LA TRINIDAD** is a scenic canyon located within Rancho La Trinidad, 18 miles from Mexico 1. The area was named for the triple peaks rising above the private ranch. The rocky, narrow canyon has numerous painted caves within a relatively short distance of each other. The Trinidad Deer, believed to be one of the finest of the known deer paintings on the peninsula, is surrounded by fawns; nearby are six-fingered humanoid figures. Access to these paintings a few years ago required swimming several sections of the canyon, but a recent storm caused an upstream dam to break, rearranging the boulders and filling the large pools with rock. The hiking is still somewhat rugged with several stream crossings, but if you're in fairly good condition, this adventure should be *no problema*. **SAN BORJITAS**, 18 miles west of Palo Verde, near the turnoff to Punta Chivato, is home to a sizable grotto with close to 60 human figures—well worth enduring the drive to get there. The ceiling of this deep cave is covered with human figures—many more than 8 feet tall—painted in red, black, gray, and yellow. Some of the figures are impaled with arrows, while others show genitalia. The hike to the grotto is only about ½ mile. Both of these sites are well preserved and protected by the Mexican government, so registration with the National Institute of Anthropology and History (INAH) and the presence of an authorized guide are both necessary; see the Guides and Outfitters section for local guide services.

DIVING AND SNORKELING / The Mulegé area offers several opportunities for diving and snorkeling. **ISLA SAN MARCOS**, the site of a large gypsum mine, is 4 miles off the coast equidistant between Mulegé and Santa Rosalía. The southeastern and northwestern ends of this island offer shallow reefs good for snorkeling and diving. The **ISLAS SANTA INÉZ**, a tiny group of islands near Punta Chivato, also make an excellent snorkeling and diving destination. Sightings include the common yet colorful parrotfish and wrasse, coral hawkfish, barracuda, green moray eels, and nudibranches, while many other species are found along the rocky bottom and ledges; see Guides and Outfitters section for transportation.

KAYAKING / Mulegé makes an excellent home base for kayakers interested in paddling nearby or those seeking multiday adventures. It's a 15-mile trip north to **PUNTA CHIVATO**, while about the same distance south will put you well inside **BAHÍA CONCEPCIÓN**, one of the most popular kayaking destinations on the peninsula; see the Bahía Concepción section. Guided trips and rentals are available through **ECOMUNDO** (km 111 Mexico 1; 615/153-0320; ecomundo@aol.com; http://home.earthlink.net/~rcmathews/), an ecology-conscious recreational center located 14 miles south of Mulegé on Bahía Concepción. Those not comfortable with the open sea or long excursions may prefer a mellow trip up the brackish estuary known as **RÍO MULEGÉ** or Río Santa Rosalía (best at high tide). The waterway is just short of 2 miles long, stretching from the lighthouse at the mouth of the river to the highway bridge, and is home to many species of wading birds including egrets and great blue herons.

FISHING / Fishing the waters around Mulegé can be rewarding, with probable catches of grouper and *cabrilla* close to shore. Migratory game fish species include *dorado*, yellowtail, yellowfin tuna, *sierra,* roosterfish, and often marlin. Do-it-yourselfers can launch their small boats at the **RAMP** on the east side of the airstrip at the **HOTEL SERENIDAD** (Hotel Serenidad Rd; 615/153-0530) and from many of the campgrounds along the river (if you're camped there). See Guides and Outfitters if you're interested in charters.

GUIDES AND OUTFITTERS

Mulegé's **SALVADOR CASTRO DREW** (phone/fax 615/153-0232), who may also be reached at Hotel Las Casitas (615/153-0019), and **CIRO CUESTA ROMERO** (Baja Adventure Tours; Calle Madero across from church; 615/153-0481; cirocuesta@yahoo.com.mx) are both authorized by the INAH to guide trips to see the nearby **CAVE PAINTINGS** at Cañón La Trinidad and San Borjitas (see Adventures). They both speak excellent English and are knowledgeable of the area's history as well as the surrounding plant and animal species. Tours include transportation, registration with the INAH office (expect to pay a small camera fee and a hefty video camera fee), ranch admission, and lunch. Some tours visit ranches to watch villagers make goat cheese or tan hides. Both guides also offer educational tours of Mulegé, and trips to the petroglyphs at Bahía Concepción as well as whale-watching excursions to Laguna San Ignacio (winter only).

CORTEZ EXPLORERS (75A Moctezuma; 615/153-0500, fax 615/153-0500; info@cortez-explorer.com; www.cortez-explorer.com), owned and operated by Bea and Andy Sidler, has a fine reputation for quality service and knowledgeable divemasters. Their dive shop offers rental equipment, air fills, and introductory dive courses (beginners and refreshers). Diving and snorkeling excursions use their custom dive boat with certified local guides. Snorkeling excursions cost $30 US per person; guided dives with your own equipment run $50; and two-tank dives with all rental equipment, transportation, and a guide cost $80.

ECOMUNDO/BAJA TROPICALES/MULEGÉ KAYAKS (Km 111 Mexico 1, 14 miles south of Mulegé; 615/153-0320; ecomundo@ aol.com; http://home.earth-link.net/~rcmathews/), located at the environmentally friendly EcoMundo Outdoor Education and Recreation Center (see Bahía Concepción section), offers paddling and snorkeling lessons and leads combination snorkeling/kayaking excursions in Bahía Concepción. Trips range from half-day to multidays with custom-designed itineraries. EcoMundo also provides transportation at the end of your excursion, and can outfit your group with rental kayaks, life jackets, VHF radios, maps, and camping gear. Rental rates are $25 US a day for open-top single sea kayaks and $35 US a day for doubles (discounts for multiday rentals). Guided trips cost about $50 US per person per day.

HOTEL SERENIDAD (Hotel Serenidad Rd; 615/153-0530, fax 615/153-0111) has a *panga* fleet with experienced local captains such as Alejandro, the hotel's friendly bartender. Their 23-foot *pangas* can hold up to four fishermen. Boats leave from the hotel at 6:30am and return about 1pm. Rates are $140 US per day. Other experienced fishing guides are **CAPTAIN ABEL HIGUERA** (615/153-0653), whose English is limited; rates start at $130 US a day including bait, lures, and fillet service; and **ANTONIO ROMERO** (615/153-0029) with similar English ability and rates, and with boats available for charter through Orchard RV Park (see Lodgings).

NIGHTLIFE

The sidewalks don't roll up after dark in Mulegé the way they do in some small towns on the peninsula, but that doesn't mean there are many places to choose from for nightlife. The **MESQUITE BAR AND GRILL** (Calle Zaragoza at Calle Madero) has live music Thursday through Sunday nights. The **HOOK-UP BAR** at Hotel Hacienda (Calle Madero 3; 615/153-0021 or 800/346-3942 US) is a popular sports bar; **EL PATRÓN** (Calle Madero at waterfront; 615/153-0028; see review) restaurant often has live music on Friday and Saturday nights.

FESTIVALS AND EVENTS

September 3–5 brings **MULEGÉ DAYS,** a celebration of the founding of this sub-tropical town. Festivities include competitive games, food booths, an arts and crafts fair, boxing, a parade, and horse races. Call (615/153-0049) for more information.

The **HEROICO MULEGÉ** celebration, held on October 3, commemorates this date in 1847 when Captain Manuel Piñeda and his band of local ranchers defeated a group of North American invaders sent to locations throughout Mexico in an attempt to strong-arm a peace agreement between the two countries. This is a large celebration often attended by the governor of Baja California Sur, who declares Mulegé the state capital and seat of government for the day. There's a parade, speeches, dancing, and a genuinely festive atmosphere. Call (615/153-0049) for more information.

RESTAURANTS

El Patrón / ★

CALLE MADERO AT WATERFRONT, MULEGÉ; 615/153-0028 Formerly known as Café La Almeja (Clam Café), El Patrón is a delightful sand-floored *palapa* eatery on Mulegé's waterfront. Lilly Acosta Corrella renamed this reputable restaurant after the death of her husband, Roman, since he often referred to those around him as *patrón* (boss or chief). Order a cold beer and enjoy the relaxed atmosphere and hospitable service. Nothing quite beats their house specialty—*sopa de siete mares* (seven seas soup), a rich and filling stew brimming with clams, fish, octopus, shrimp, and scallops in a tangy broth. Or choose from chocolate clams, fish tacos or fillets, and shrimp entrees. El Patrón often has live music on Friday and Saturday nights. *$; Cash only; lunch, dinner every day; full bar; no reservations; north side of river.*

Hotel Serenidad Restaurant / ★★

HOTEL SERENIDAD RD, MULEGÉ; 615/153-0530, FAX 615/153-0111 An institution in Mulegé, the Hotel Serenidad is an American-owned hotel and restaurant famous for its all-you-can-eat Saturday night pig roasts—complete with live mariachi music. Folks come from miles away, and pilots often fly their private planes down just for the occasion. The high ceilings allow a feeling of openness, while brick-lined arches and colorful fringed tablecloths give this restaurant a warm, hacienda-style environment. Enjoy a glass of Chilean wine on their poolside terrace or, if it's a cool evening, dine inside. For breakfast, try the *huevos a caballo* (eggs over a corn tortilla, with avocado and cheese). For dinner, don't miss the house specialty: grilled kebabs—your choice of chicken, shrimp, or scallops in a savory marinade, served with soup, baked potato, and vegetables. A secluded banquet room here can accommodate large groups (up to 200 people). *$; MC, V; traveler's checks OK; breakfast, lunch, dinner every day (closed Sept); full bar; reservations recommended; south of town, 2½ miles from Mulegé bridge, then left ½ mile on dirt road.*

Los Equipales Restaurant / ★★

CALLE MOCTEZUMA, MULEGÉ; 615/153-0330 OR 615/153-0083 Proprietor Francisco Marron has nurtured this centrally located restaurant for more than 12 years and established quite a following of tourists as well as locals. Dine on the second-story veranda for a bird's-eye view of the town and a cooling breeze. The cavernous interior is busy with waiters hustling beneath beamed ceilings, around the fireplace, and below the ball game most likely featured on the satellite TV—a big draw at the bar, which is open to the dining room. Get here early at dinnertime, or expect to wait for a table. The menu is unimaginative, but entrees come with chips and salsa and a hearty potato soup. Dinner choices include *sopa de mariscos* (seafood soup); a lobster salad; breaded or garlicked shrimp, fish, or scallops; grilled quail; pork ribs; *langosta asar con ajo* (broiled lobster seasoned with garlic). Poached eggs are offered on the breakfast menu—something you don't find too often in Baja—along with the usual egg dishes. Service is friendly and attentive, and the wine list offers a nice selection of Baja California wines. *$–$$; No credit cards; traveler's checks OK; breakfast, lunch, dinner every day; full bar; reservations recommended; 2 blocks north of town square and ½ block west.*

Restaurante Las Casitas / ★

CALLE MADERO 50, MULEGÉ; 615/153-0019, FAX 615/153-0190 The small patio dining area at Las Casitas is filled with lush vegetation, creating a cozy breakfast spot. Inside, the windowless dining room has a beamed ceiling and wooden tables, brightened up a bit by colorful tablecloths and flower centerpieces. Breakfasts include fresh fruit and fruit juices, hotcakes, huevos rancheros, and *molletes con chorizo* (thick French bread smothered with beans, pork sausage, grated cheese, and salsa). Lunch specials include vegetarian enchiladas and fish fillets, fixed your favorite style (*a la veracruzana, al mojo de ajo,* or fried). For dinner, try their abalone-style squid—sautéed and tender—or the charbroiled baby-back ribs. If you're up for it, their specialty drink is the Patty Loca—brandy, soda, and cola. The Friday night Mexican buffet and Saturday night pork roast, both with live mariachi music, are popular and festive. *$; MC, V, traveler's checks OK; breakfast, lunch, dinner every day; full bar; reservations recommended; www.bajaquest.com/mulege/casitas.com; 1 block east of town square on right.*

LODGINGS

Hotel Hacienda / ★

CALLE MADERO 3, MULEGÉ; 615/153-0021 OR 800/346-3942 US More than a century old, Hotel Hacienda is steeped in history. From the narrow street, enter through the large doorway to be immersed in a Spanish courtyard from ages gone by. The two-story hotel frames the far sides of the yard, beyond numerous palm trees and a pool. A small on-site cafe and sports bar offer meals, drinks, and occasional live music. The 21 clean but plain rooms include air conditioning, tile floors, showers, and queen-size beds; some rooms have satellite TV. The hotel's central location puts all of Mulegé within easy walking distance. The only parking is a small lot behind the hotel or outside on the narrow street—get right up against the curb. *$; No credit cards; traveler's checks OK; haciendahotel_mulege@hotmail.com; east side of town square.*

Hotel Serenidad / ★★

HOTEL SERENIDAD RD, MULEGÉ; 615/153-0530, FAX 615/153-0111 American Don Johnson, who served as U.S. consular representative for several years, has owned and managed this resort with his wife, Nancy, and two daughters for about 35 years. The elaborate hotel grounds feature palms, flowering plants, and patios, while several separate buildings house a total of 47 units, ranging from basic rooms to three-bedroom riverfront villas. All have air conditioning and tile floors; some have fireplaces. A large pool with swim-up bar lies next to the river. There's also a boat ramp here, handy for easy in and out at high tide. The Serenidad's well-maintained, 4,000-foot airstrip makes this resort popular among small-plane owners, and the on-site restaurant is well known for its Saturday night pig roasts. To work off that pork dinner, there's a tennis court, or the hotel staff can arrange for activities in the area, including snorkeling and diving, sportfishing, and kayaking. The Serenidad complex uses a reverse osmosis system for purified drinking water, and has plenty of secure parking and two gift stores. *$; MC, V; traveler's checks OK; www.serenidad.com; south of town, 2½ miles from Mulegé bridge, then left ½ mile on dirt road.*

Orchard RV Park

MEXICO 1, MULEGÉ; 615/153-0300 One of Baja California's most pleasant and spacious RV parks, Orchard offers 43 campsites (25 pull-through) tucked between towering trees and flowering shrubs, right on the river. Bird-watchers will appreciate the variety of colorful species on site. More prosaically, its bathrooms are equipped with hot showers and clean toilets. Take a walk down the road to the river's mouth with your binoculars, or walk upstream and visit the town or the mission on foot. The popularity of Orchard and the increasing number of permanent residences in the park mean that it's only a matter of time before this campground runs out of space and is closed to the public. Enjoy it while it's available. *$; Cash only; orchardvvv@prodigy.net.mx; http://orchard. mulege.com.mx; south of town, 1 mile from bridge.*

Bahía Concepción

The turquoise bays and sandy crescent beaches of Bahía Concepción are almost too much to handle while attempting to concentrate on this meandering stretch of Mexico 1. If the views don't tempt you off the highway, maybe the adventure possibilities will, with offshore islands, abundant marine and bird life, isolated coves, Indian rock art, and hot springs available within this stunning stretch of undeveloped coastline. This 27-mile-long marine preserve sits between the southern end of the Sierra de Guadalupe and the rugged Peninsula Concepción. Less than 8 miles across at its widest and 2 miles at its narrowest, Bahía Concepción is a haven for kayakers, who come here for multiday trips between the bay's inner islands and the coast. Other water lovers play here as well, and each year the area campgrounds become a little bit more impacted with sunbathers, snorkelers, bird-watchers, and fishermen.

The bay has limited facilities, so it's good to be self-sufficient, at least regarding food and water. There are a few lodgings available if you don't have an RV or camping gear, and car-campers will find plenty of places to pitch a tent. Most of the access roads are passable without four-wheel drive. The best seasons to visit Bahía Concepción are the crowd-free shoulder seasons—just after Easter and before Thanksgiving—offering perfect weather and bathwater-warm waters. Winters can be windy and cool, while summers are hot and balmy but rarely break the century mark.

ACCESS AND INFORMATION

Most visitors to Bahía Concepción drive in via Mexico 1. Remember: The km markers in this region decrease as you head south; they zero-out in Loreto. Some visitors choose to fly—the closest international airport is in Loreto, roughly 75 miles south (see the Mid-South chapter). Autotransportes de Baja California (ABC; http://abc.com.mx) and Autotransportes de Águila provide **BUS SERVICE AT PLAYA CONCEPCIÓN** (near km 111 on Mexico 1) as they pass through the area, but you'll need to request this stop, and a small tip will be appreciated.

GUIDES AND OUTFITTERS

Bahía Concepción offers paddlers a chance to cruise silently along inaccessible shorelines, studying rock formations, beaches, and wildlife amid spectacular desert surroundings. While many choose to stay in the protected bay, some adventurers embark upon multiday excursions, traveling 80 miles south to Loreto. **ECOMUNDO/BAJA TROPICALES** (km 111 Mexico 1, 14 miles south of Mulegé; 615/153-0320; ecomundo@aol.com; http://home.earthlink.net/~rc mathews/) rents kayaks and leads short kayaking and snorkeling excursions to nearby islands, as well as longer excursions to Isla San Marcos. **NATIONAL OUTDOOR LEADERSHIP SCHOOL** (NOLS; 307/332-5300 US; www.nols.edu), a leader in outdoor education since 1965, offers college credit courses from their ocean-based program in Coyote Bay, 18 miles south of Mulegé. Courses include a 25-day backpacking course in the Sierra de Guadalupe and 21-day sea kayaking and sailing courses in Bahía Concepción. The school does not take drop-ins.

LODGINGS

EcoMundo/Baja Tropicales

KM 111 MEXICO 1, BAHÍA CONCEPCIÓN; 615/153-0320 Setting the precedent for eco-tourism and environmental awareness in the area, EcoMundo offers a low-impact alternative to the usual beachfront resorts in this region of Baja. Envisioned by Roy Mahoff and Becky Aparicio more than 10 years ago, and created in 1997, this resort/recreational center uses solar power, composting toilets, and gray-water irrigation systems. The resort was built using energy-efficient hay bale and adobe construction with *palapa* roofing—a perfect combination in this subtropical climate. Lodging is available in the form of campsites ($6 US a day), "Tropical Igloos" (open-air *palapas* with hammocks or cots and solar lighting; $12 US a day), or "Tropical Cabañas"(enclosed *palapas* with hammocks or cots and solar lighting; $20 US a day). RVs and generators are not allowed. The on-site juice bar/cafe serves coffee, beer, and healthy sandwiches, and there's a bookstore with a nice selection of Baja books. Tidal hot springs are also located on the property, and kayaking and snorkeling tours and rentals are available. For your southerly expedition, if you choose not to paddle back against the wind, EcoMundo will even arrange pickups. *$; Cash only; ecomundo@aol.com; http://home.earthlink.net/~rcmathews/; 14 miles south of Mulegé, look for large signs.*

Hotel San Buenaventura / ★★

KM 94 MEXICO 1, BAHÍA CONCEPCIÓN; 613/104-4064 OR 615/153-0408, FAX 615/153-0408 A seashell driveway leads to this small hotel, campground, and restaurant—one of the only "resorts" in the area. Built in the bottom of an *arroyo*, Buenaventura has its own private beach between two hilly points, and is a relaxing place to spend some time away from the towns. Each of the 20 rooms is air-conditioned, with your choice of double or queen-size beds, ceiling fans, and private patios. Bird-watching fans will love the multitude of wading birds and pelicans in the area. The on-site restaurant specializes in seafood. A boat ramp and rental kayaks are available; across the highway, a small store sells staple goods and rents snorkeling gear. The location's downside is that trucks brake noisily at night as they come downhill on the highway. *$; Cash only; www.hotelsanbuenaventura.com; 25 miles south of Mulegé.*

Playa El Requesón

KM 92 MEXICO 1, BAHÍA CONCEPCIÓN Playa El Requesón is located on a sandbar connecting the shoreline with a small island. Camping on the spit, you're surrounded by water. Avoid the narrowest section of the beach, as it sometimes disappears at high tide. Some folks spend their entire winter here; Others spend a night or two at El Requesón to break up their journey. Large chocolate clams can be dug in the shallows along the spit at low tide. Around the point of land on the northwest corner of the beach is a portion of the old Baja highway. Facilities are limited to trash barrels and pit toilets, so come prepared; fees ($3–$4 US) are usually collected in the morning. To the south on a rocky mountainside, you'll notice a large painted floral design—a strange diversion done by unknown, industrious people who lugged gallons and gallons of paint up the steep, crumbly hillside. *$; Cash only; 26 miles south of Mulege.*

Playa Santispac

KM 114 MEXICO 1, BAHÍA CONCEPCIÓN You can't miss the large white-rock letters on the hill above Mexico 1 as it winds around the curve to Santispac—the largest campground on Bahía Concepción and one of the most scenic beaches accessible from the highway. Numerous offshore islands dot the azure and aqua bay. Isla Pelicano is only ½ mile from shore—a great place to snorkel and explore. If you're lucky enough to find a vacancy on the waterfront, you can sleep to the sounds of tiny waves lapping at the sand. The beach is well protected by the islands, making this a great place for swimming, snorkeling, and launching kayaks. Two small restaurants are located here: Anna's serves fresh-baked breads and goodies as well as meals and beer; Ray's is more of a seafood place. The campground has cold showers, pit toilets, trash barrels, and a dump station. A remnant of the old highway winds around the bottom of the ridge to the north, leading to Campo Playa Punta Arena, a mile or so away. To the south there are a couple of hot spring soaking-tubs constructed by the locals. In the summer, remember to shuffle your feet to scare away the stingrays. *$; Cash only; 13 miles south of Mulege.*

THE MID-SOUTH

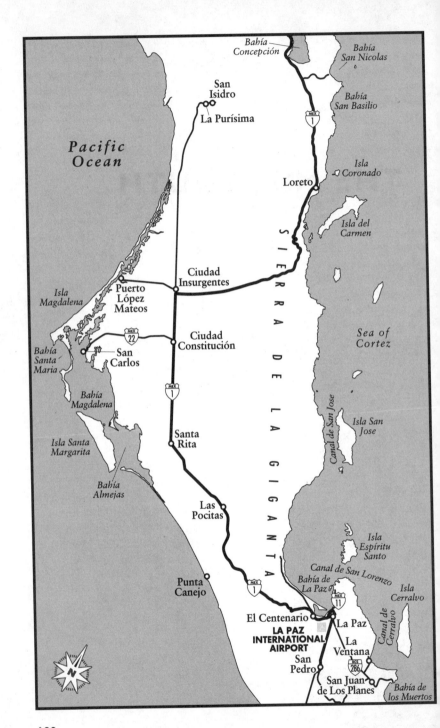

THE MID-SOUTH

Loreto to La Paz

Crisscrossing the peninsula on this 223-mile journey, start by immersing yourself in the history of Loreto, a quaint seaside village and site of the first Spanish mission in all of Baja California. With the azure waters of the Sea of Cortez at your back, gaze upward at the towering jagged peaks of the Sierra de la Giganta mountain range. Loreto is headquarters for another of Baja's four national parks, Parque Nacional Bahía de Loreto, where sea-based adventures abound. Then head southwest and experience the immensity of Magdalena Bay, a winter breeding grounds for several thousand California gray whales. Explore the rugged Pacific coast by venturing off the highway to watch the waves crash on the cliffs below a remote fishing village.

At journey's end, explore the subtle sophistication of La Paz and check into a classy hotel. As evening falls, relax with a margarita and watch the sun paint the Bay of Peace with colors of fire.

Loreto

In the 1700s, Loreto thrived as a political and religious capital. Its mission, founded in 1697, was the first in all of the Californias. More than two centuries later, in the 1950s, sportfishermen heard tales of the abundance of fish in the Sea of Cortez, and made Loreto their private-plane getaway. By the early 1970s, when the Transpeninsular Highway (Mexico 1) was complete, the Mexican department for tourism development (FONATUR) funded an international airport and a few small resort-style hotels in Loreto. Since then, development has slowed down and Loreto remains a quaint Mexican village.

This settlement of almost 10,000 inhabitants still has a traditional, small-town atmosphere. Every month folks gather for **BOHEMIAN NIGHTS** in the town plaza, where schoolchildren present folk dances and local musicians strum classic ballads (see Festivals and Events). The music reverberates off the old stone walls of **MISIÓN NUESTRA SEÑORA DE LORETO**, which has stood for more than 300 years in the town center (see Exploring). Loreto's warm sea temperatures and nutrient-rich waters attract game fish and the folks who chase them. Whereas sportfishing is popular during the hot summer months, sea kayaking, diving, and pleasant weather draw tourists to Loreto throughout the year. Recently the Mexican government formed Parque Nacional Bahía de Loreto, preserving the water, islands, and shoreline near Loreto.

ACCESS AND INFORMATION
Loreto lies on the Sea of Cortez, 84 miles south of Mulegé and roughly 225 miles north of La Paz. The town sits just east of Mexico 1, and with the exception of a few one-way streets, is very easy to get around in **BY CAR**.

LORETO THREE-DAY TOUR

DAY ONE: Wake up at the **HOTEL OASIS** with its palm-lined view of Isla del Carmen. Walk north along the *malecón* to the town center for a healthy stack of pancakes with fresh juice at **CAFÉ OLÉ**. For a taste of history, check out the old photographs in the entrance of the Loreto municipal building at **PLAZA JUÁREZ**. Wander westward up the cobbled street through Loreto's *Centro Histórico* to browse the souvenir shops. Inside the **MISIÓN NUESTRA SEÑORA DE LORETO**, visit the Virgin of Loreto statue, then take the self-guided tour at the **MUSEO DE LAS MISIONES** next door. Stop for lunch at **EL REY DEL TACO**, the popular taco stand located one block northwest of the mission grounds. Loop back toward the plaza for a scoop of mango ice cream at **LA MICHOACANA** (Madero and Juárez). Back at Hotel Oasis, take a refreshing dip and relax poolside. Around 4pm, when Loreto's shops reopen after siesta, head to **ARTURO'S SPORTS FISHING** to book Day Three's snorkel tour. At nearby **LAS PARRAS TOURS**, schedule a tour of Misión San Javier for mañana (Day Two). Before sunset, head back to the *malecón* for a well-deserved *cerveza* and dinner at **CHILE WILLIE RESTAURANT BAR** on the waterfront. After dinner, meander back to the plaza and the classy **POSADA DE LAS FLORES** hotel. Enter the elegant courtyard and wind up the spiral staircase for a nightcap on the rooftop.

DAY TWO: Rise early for a quick breakfast on the patio at Hotel Oasis. When your guide arrives from **LAS PARRAS TOURS**, you're off by taxi van for your tour of

---

Flight arrivals to Loreto are limited and generally more expensive than those into La Paz. Receiving seven flights a week to and from Los Angeles, the **LORETO INTERNATIONAL AIRPORT** (3 miles south of town; 613/135-0499) is serviced by Aerocalifornia (613/135-0555 or 800/237-6225 US, fax 613/135-0566) and Aerolitoral, a subsidiary of Aero Mexico (613/135-0999; www.aeromexico.com). Some visitors prefer to fly into La Paz, rent a car, and then travel north to Loreto exploring along the way (see the La Paz section in this chapter).

The only **RENTAL CAR COMPANY** in Loreto is Budget (Av Hidalgo; 613/135-1149, fax 613/135-1090; budgetloreto@yahoo.com.mx). They offer VW bugs, compact cars, Jeeps, vans, and ATVs.

Águila (Calle Salvatierra; 613/135-0767) provides **BUS TRANSPORTATION** on Mexico 1 both north and south with three to five buses departing and arriving daily in each direction. Modern, comfortable coaches make the 4-hour drive to La Paz and the 2-hour drive north to Mulegé.

There are many useful **SERVICES** in town, including two Pemex stations (Calles Salvaterria and Juárez), a Bancomer with ATM (Madero), auto parts and repair, Internet cafes, a clinic, a phone *caseta*, a Laundromat, a *tortillería*, and numerous hotels and restaurants. Tucked away in the southeast corner of

MISIÓN SAN JAVIER. The tour snakes through a beautiful canyon on the old road once used by natives and *padres*. Continue on to the quaint mountain **VILLAGE OF SAN JAVIER** for a tour of the mission and gardens. Lunch, provided by Las Parras, includes burritos and quesadillas made with fresh local cheese. Back in Loreto, take a quick dip in the pool or relax with a margarita at the Hotel Oasis bar and watch the sea change hues at sunset. Stroll into town, wandering up Boulevard Hidalgo to enjoy an authentic Mexican meal at **MÉXICO LINDO Y QUÉ RICO.** After dinner, treat yourself to a slice of fresh apple pie and an organic cafe mocha at **TIFFANY'S PIZZA PARLOR AND CAPPUCCINO BAR.**

DAY THREE: After your continental breakfast at Hotel Oasis, pack your swimsuit, hat, camera, and sunscreen for your half-day **SNORKEL TOUR** with Arturo's Sports Fishing to Isla Coronado, where you might see pods of dolphin or a solitary sea lion. Don't forget the binoculars for sighting other marine mammals and birds. While leaving the harbor on this 20-minute boat ride, capture the most picturesque view of Loreto— a morning shot from a quarter mile offshore. Then turn your focus to the island's red-rock hillsides dotted with tall green cactus, white sand beaches, and aqua bays. After snorkeling and lunch (included in your tour) on the beach, it's back to Loreto and a siesta in the hotel's hammocks. At dinnertime, wander over to **NUEVA PLAYA BLANCA** (Av Hidalgo and Madero; 613/135-1126) for a meal, where you can take in a nightcap and live music downstairs at **MIKE'S BAR**—the perfect end to a great day!

the municipal building on Loreto's main plaza, the **LORETO TOURIST CENTER** (Madero at Salvatierra; 613/135-0411; www.loreto.com) offers a variety of brochures describing some of the local attractions and hotels. Open weekdays (8am–3pm). The local hotel association (613/135-0133; www.gotoloreto.com) also has helpful information.

Need to check your email? **CASETA SOLEDAD** (Calle Salvatierra; 613/135-0351) has a faster connection rate than the popular **INTERNET CAFE** (Madero and Av Hidalgo; 613/135-0284), and Loreto's best deal on Internet service is **S@YEK INTERNET** (Héroes de la Independencia 11-B; 613/135-0392).

EXPLORING

To feel the pulse of Loreto, stand in **PLAZA JUÁREZ,** bordered by Calle Salvatierra and Avenida Hidalgo. Flowering plants, a bust of Benito Juárez (Mexico's Abe Lincoln), and the commemorative mission bell add charm and history to this site. Loreto's historic **MISIÓN NUESTRA SEÑORA DE LORETO** (on the plaza) was founded in 1697 by Jesuit priests and was the first mission in all of the Californias. The church, rebuilt after an earthquake in the late 1800s, gradually fell to ruins, and was reconstructed again in 1955. The bell tower, located on Calle Salvatierra, was a later addition to the original mission design and stands as a landmark for Loreto's historic town center. Extending off the west side of Misión Loreto is **MUSEO DE LAS MISIONES** (next to the mission; 613/135-0441), featuring displays ranging from pre-colonization indigenous times through the mission period.

Loreto's **MALECÓN** offers views of Isla del Carmen to the east and the craggy Sierra de la Giganta mountain range to the west. The milelong sidewalk starts at Hotel Oasis at Calle Baja California and López Mateos, runs past the marina, and ends at Hotel La Pinta to the north at Calle Davis.

MCLULU'S TACOS (Av Hidalgo and Colegio) serves shrimp, fish, and beef tacos and is popular with tourists due to its central location near the cobblestoned historic center. For a more authentic taco dining experience, head a couple of blocks north to **EL TACO DEL REY** (Juárez and Misionero), a white cement structure run by the Garcia family since 1983. Built under the sweeping branches of an old *tamarindo* tree, this lunch spot serves excellent fish tacos and is only open 9am–2pm. **HINT:** This place is very popular with locals and travelers in the know. In the center of town, you'll find **RIGO'S TACOS** (Blvd Hidalgo 25; 613/135-0360), a classic late-night carne asada (grilled beef) taco stand, complete with Mexican soap operas and bright fluorescent lights.

SHOPPING

For regional folk art, check out the collection of pottery, woodcarvings, leather goods, and palm baskets at **LAS PARRAS TOURS** (Madero and Av Hidalgo; 613/135-1010). For folk art from mainland Mexico, try **EL ALACRÁN** (Calle Salvatierra #47; 613/135-0029) and **LA CASA DE LA ABUELA** (across the street).

ADVENTURES

BAY OF LORETO NATIONAL PARK / In 1997, due to the depletion in the area's fishery, Mexico's President Zedillo created a national marine park, deeming nearly half a million acres of water, islands, and shoreline near Loreto a natural protected area, and naming it **PARQUE NACIONAL BAHÍA DE LORETO**. The park encompass much of the shoreline and the five offshore islands—Coronado, Carmen, Danzante, Monserrat, and Santa Catalán. Industrial fishing is now illegal within these boundaries. Drawing a line on a map is one thing, but actually changing local fishing practices and enforcing new laws has been a challenge for the branch of the federal government called SEMARNAP. The new rules affect tourists as well, stating that any person using the park for snorkeling, scuba diving, water skiing, touring in motor boats, sailing, or kayaking is required to pay a fee of $5 a day to the SEMARNAP office in Loreto (López Mateos y Carrillo; 613/135-0477; parquenacional@prodigy.net.mx). No official web site or printed regulations exist in English, but information about the park can be found by logging onto www.bigfishloreto.com and selecting the link "Marine Park."

FISHING / Pelagic fish put Loreto on the map in the 1950s. Today, mostly due to commercial fishing, the local fish populations seem to be dwindling. Nevertheless, several sportfishing tournaments are held each year, and in the end, anglers usually fly home with coolers full of *dorado,* yellowtail, and tuna. See Guides and Outfitters for details.

SEA KAYAKING / An intimate way to discover the treasures of Baja's marine wilderness is to quietly paddle along its shores in a sea kayak. From your small craft, observe as ospreys whistle overhead, schools of baitfish boil around you, and occasional pods of dolphins cruise by. Guided sea kayaking tours are often booked in advance as weeklong vacation packages, or experienced paddlers can rent sea kayaks and arrange shuttles. Loreto-based kayaking companies employ Mexican guides with local knowledge, which gives them an advantage over U.S.-based kayak companies that operate only seasonally in Baja, usually during the winter months. See Guides and Outfitters for details.

SNORKELING AND DIVING / One of the most popular tours from Loreto is a half-day snorkeling trip to Isla Coronados, the northernmost island visible from town. The 20-minute *panga* ride takes you to the island's rocky eastern shoreline, offering good snorkeling and diving. The other two islands that dot the horizon, Carmen and Danzante, are also options. A wide variety of colorful tropical fish and schools of snapper and mullet are commonly seen among sea fans and corals. Occasionally divers encounter a sea turtle, sea lion, or manta ray. Boat trips usually include lunch, cold drinks, and snorkel equipment; see Guides and Outfitters for details. For a low-budget approach, bring your own snorkel gear and refreshments and negotiate directly with the *pangeros* at the marina for a shuttle to the island.

WHALE-WATCHING / The blue whale, which can reach 100 feet in length, is the largest animal to ever inhabit the earth, and can be seen in the waters off Loreto. March is the month you're most likely to spot a blue whale, and you might even encounter researchers tracking the leviathan's migration patterns. Boaters might also encounter fin, Bryde's, gray, humpback, pilot, or sperm whales in area waters. Gray whales abound in the Pacific lagoons from January to March. Loreto outfitters can book your day trip to Puerto López Mateos, a two-hour drive across the peninsula. See Guides and Outfitters for details.

MOUNTAIN BIKING / Rugged roads and trails in the Sierra de la Giganta surrounding Loreto are great adventures for intermediate to advanced mountain bikers. A favorite route is the 25-mile haul up to San Javier (see below). Easier routes around Loreto take you through desert scenery or out to rocky coastal points. See Guides and Outfitters for details.

MULE PACK TRIPS / If you enjoy camping out, thrive on learning natural history and culture, and yearn to experience the cowboy life of a century past, consider joining a mule pack trip through the central mountains of Baja. Mule riders visit cave paintings, tour old missions in the mountains, and clop down trails along the gulf coast. Multiday trips visit area ranches, where riders sample local cuisine and see real *rancheros* at work. See Guides and Outfitters for more details.

MEXICAN STREET NAMES—MEXICAN HEROES

Like many countries around the globe, Mexico honors the achievements of its founders and illustrious citizens with streets named in their memory. In Baja, it matters not whether you are in Tijuana, San Ignacio, or San José del Cabo, for there will invariably be an Avenida Benito Juárez, a Calle Miguel Hidalgo, and a Boulevard Lázaro Cárdenas. Yet the traveler, while struggling to pronounce these names, knows little about them. Here's a rundown on a few of Mexico's most popular heroes:

PADRE MIGUEL HIDALGO Y COSTILLA 1753–1811 Padre Hidalgo was ordained as a priest in 1778 and appointed to Dolores in the state of Guanajuato, now called Dolores Hidalgo in his honor. He was a well-educated, unconventional intellectual who questioned authority and encouraged the arts and the cultivation of wine grapes, olives, and silkworms—all banned by the highly autocratic Spanish colonial regime. When his trees and vines were destroyed, he replanted in defiance. In 1810, the first revolutionary movement was fomenting, with Hidalgo a key figure. Betrayed by one of his own, he made the famous cry for independence known as "El Grito" in the first hours of September 16, 1810, eventually leading to Mexican independence. Although it would take more than a decade and considerable violence and bloodshed before Mexico achieved autonomy, Miguel Hidalgo was the impetus for ending Spain's subjugation of the country. In 1811, he was captured, taken to Chihuahua with revolutionary heroes Allende, Aldama, and Jimenez, and executed. For 10 years, their heads were displayed publicly in steel cages in Guanajuato as a deterrent against revolt, which failed to dissuade the fight for freedom. September 16 is widely celebrated as Mexican Independence Day.

BENITO JUÁREZ 1806–1872 Regarded as one of the greatest heroes in Mexican history, Benito Juárez was president of Mexico from 1861 to 1863 and again from 1867 to 1872. He was a full-blooded Zapotec Indian, born near the town of Oaxaca and educated as a lawyer. While governing Oaxaca, he was jailed in 1853 when General Santa

GUIDES AND OUTFITTERS

ARTURO'S SPORTS FISHING (Av Hidalgo and Pipila; 613/135-0766, fax 613/135-0022; arturosport@loretoweb.com.mx; www.arturosport.com) has been a leading sportfishing business in town since 1984. In recent years, owner Arturo Susarrey has branched out to also offer scuba diving, snorkeling, whale-watching, and tours to Misíon San Javier. Multiday packages with lodging are available. Owned by Pam Bolles and Francisco "Cuervo" Muñoz, **BAJA BIG FISH COMPANY** (Calle Salvatierra; 613/135-1603, cell 613/104-0109, or 888/533-2252 US; bolles@bajabigfish.com; www.bajabigfish.com) offers trips with bilingual guides who are experienced in standard sportfishing as well as fly-

Anna seized power. Juárez escaped to New Orleans, and returned to take part in Santa Anna's downfall. Under the new government, Juárez became Minister of Justice, implementing reforms that would become part of the Constitution of 1857. During his first presidential period, facing a bankrupt treasury, Juárez suspended payments to France, Spain, and Great Britain. France used the issue as an excuse to invade, landing troops at Veracruz and eventually taking Mexico City. When the French were finally overthrown and Archduke Maximilian executed, Juárez returned to Mexico City and was reelected president. He died of a heart attack while at his desk on July 18, 1872.

IGNACIO ZARAGOZA 1829–1862 Born in Texas to parents from Veracruz, General Ignacio Zaragoza was the Mexican commander of the battle of Puebla, fought on the morning of May 5, 1862, against invading French armies marching from Veracruz to Mexico City. The French greatly outnumbered the ragtag Mexicans, but Zaragoza and his men prevailed. Sadly, Zaragoza died from typhus at the age of 33, only four months after the victory at Puebla. Buried in Mexico City, he was finally interred at Puebla on May 5, 1962, 100 years after the famous battle we celebrate as Cinco de Mayo, which commemorates the cause of freedom against tyranny.

LÁZARO CÁRDENAS 1895–1970 A man who apparently could not be corrupted, Lázaro Cárdenas, beloved president of Mexico from 1934 to 1940, was known for his honesty. He implemented the *ejido* (cooperative property) land reform system, trade unions, secular schools, and—his most famous and daring act—the nationalization of Mexico's oil industry in 1938. This resulted in the boycotting of Mexican oil by world powers, a serious blow to the economy, which was saved only by World War II. Refusing to reside in Chapultepec Castle, his style was modest and unassuming; he cut his salary in half and attended his inauguration in a business suit rather than his general's uniform. He was embraced by the populace as a true man of the people and today holds an untouchable, saintly status among the working class throughout Mexico.

—*Sabrina Lear*

fishing techniques. The shop sells colorful fishing flies, hand-tied by Pam and designed for landing *dorado,* yellowtail, and other game fish in the Sea of Cortez.

Specializing in scuba diving and snorkeling trips, **BAJA OUTPOST** (López Mateos and Calle Jordan; 613/135-1134 or 888/649-5951 US; outpost@baja outpost.com; www.bajaoutpost.com) is a rustic B&B near the south end of the *malecón* that also offers whale-watching, kayaking, and mission tours. SSI (Scuba Schools International) certification classes are also available. **DOLPHIN DIVE CENTER** (Antonio Mijares and Playa in Colonia Zaragoza; 626/447-5536 or 800/298-9009 US, fax 626/447-8685; loreto@dolphindivebaja.com; www. dolphindivebaja.com) is a PADI (Professional Association of Diving Instructors) international dive resort next door to Villas de Loreto Hotel that offers dive services for hotel guests and walk-in clients. Owned by Bruce Williams and Susan Speck, author of *Diving Baja California,* the center has *pangas* right on the hotel beach and a secure area specially designed for dive gear. Local manager and dive master Raphael has fished and dived the waters off Loreto all his life. Multiday packages, equipment rentals, certifications, and air fills are available.

GEA ECO CENTER (Av Hidalgo and Colegio; phone and fax 613/135-0086; antaresgea@prodigy.net.mx; www.ravenadventures.com/gea.html) is a nonprofit center in downtown Loreto open to the public that features displays and educational materials. Headquarters for a Loreto-based environmental organization, Grupo Ecologista Antares, the center brings together specialists, conservationists, fishermen, and local citizens to discuss issues threatening sea turtles, sharks, and other at-risk marine animals. In winter months, the center runs **WHALE-WATCH OUTINGS** to the islands near Loreto, searching for a variety of marine mammals, including the 100-foot blue whale.

PADDLING SOUTH (PO Box 827, Calistoga, CA 94515; 800/398-6200 US; info@tourbaja.com; www.tourbaja.com), Loreto's original sea kayaking company, has been running multiday expeditions since the early '80s. Paddling South's owner, Trudi Angell, an American and 20-year Loreto resident, organizes guided kayaking tours along the islands and coastlines of the Bay of Loreto National Park. Her outfitting company specializes in self-support trips, with participants and their trained guides carrying camping supplies and provisions with them inside the kayaks. In cooperation with **REI ADVENTURES**, they also offer multiactivity combo trips, which include kayaking, mountain biking, and whale-watching. Trudi also runs multiday mule-packing trips under a sister company, **SADDLING SOUTH**, and mountain biking treks into the sierras under **PEDALING SOUTH**. Her husband, Douglas Knapp, runs **SAIL BAJA**, which focuses on small sailboat instructional courses on the Sea of Cortez.

LAS PARRAS TOURS (Madero and Av Hidalgo; 613/135-1010; lasparras@loretoweb.com.mx; www.lasparrastours.com) is a multisport company right in the heart of town that specializes in diving, natural history, and cultural tours. They offer guided local tours, dive and snorkel trips, whale-watching excursions, and mountain bike tours. Las Parras, named for a prominent mountain peak west of Loreto, also offers SSI dive certifications, mountain bike rentals, and sea kayak rentals.

FESTIVALS AND EVENTS

The first Friday of every month, *Loretanos* gather at the central plaza at about 9pm to enjoy a social event called **NOCHE BOHEMIA** (Bohemian Night), when musicians accompany amateur singers and speakers present local poetry and historical anecdotes. Even non–Spanish speakers will enjoy the music and community spirit.

In one of the hottest months of the year, Loreto celebrates **NUESTRA SEÑORA DE LORETO FESTIVAL,** honoring its patron saint with special masses at the mission church, a carnival, and nightly musical shows, September 6–8 (www.loreto. com). A theater stage and children's fair rides are also set up on the *malecón* to take advantage of the cooler evenings after sunset.

During **FOUNDING OF LORETO CULTURAL WEEK,** October 19–25, the city of Loreto and the Casa de Cultura organize art displays and various local artist presentations to celebrate the founding of Loreto more than 300 years ago (www.loreto.com). The cultural museum plans special historical exhibits, and the church presents classical music in the evenings. A reenactment of the arrival of Loreto's founder, Padre Salvatierra, and his planting of the flag of Spain, takes place at the edge of the sea.

RESTAURANTS

Café Olé / ★★

MADERO 14, LORETO; 613/135-0496 Café Olé is perhaps the most popular eating establishment in town. One group of older expatriates sit at the same table for hours every morning, drinking coffee out of personalized cups they keep in the cafe's kitchen. Its location on a quaint cobblestone street near the plaza is part of the establishment's recipe for success. Other ingredients are generous portions, affordable prices, and quick service. For breakfast try the *huevos con nopalitos* (scrambled eggs with chopped prickly pear cactus) and fresh-squeezed orange juice. For lunch, the hamburgers and fries are some of the best in town. Fresh fish specials round out the dinner menu. *$; Cash only; breakfast, lunch every day, dinner Mon–Sat; beer only; no reservations; just north of traffic light at Blvd Hidalgo.*

Chile Willie Restaurant Bar / ★★☆

LÓPEZ MATEOS AND PADRE KINO, LORETO; 613/135-0677, FAX 613/135-0712 Offering Loreto's only waterfront tables, Chile Willie is the perfect place to take in the colors of sunset, catch a moonrise over the water, gaze up at the stars glittering above, or, on chilly nights, dine under the *palapa* roof. Start with their steamed chocolate clams drizzled with melted butter and garlic, then dive into the seafood combo or the Mediterranean mixed grill—a lamb skewer served with smoked pork and Italian sausage. Stay to watch the moon rise as you linger over Mexican coffee for dessert. *$; MC, V; traveler's checks OK; breakfast every day Apr–Oct, lunch, dinner every day; full bar; no reservations; lastrojes@prodigy.net.mx; north end of malecón.*

El Nido / ★★

CALLE SALVATIERRA 154, LORETO; 613/135-0027 El Nido's sturdy brick walls accented with dark wooden beams give this popular steak house a masculine, ranch-style atmosphere. El Nido ("the Nest") is a friendly place known for its excellent grilled beef, seafood, and wine selection, including several labels produced in Baja California. Watch the chef prepare tender cuts, shipped from the beef-producing state of Sonora, over a mesquite-fired grill right in the dining room. Besides beef, popular choices are the seafood combo and shrimp kebab. All dinners come with bean soup, salad, and baked potato. Don't skip the flan for dessert. Waiters in traditional white *guayabera* shirts are attentive, while the Mexican trio, strumming and singing traditional songs, will make you feel like your evening at El Nido is a special occasion. *$; No credit cards; traveler's checks OK; lunch, dinner every day; full bar; reservations recommended; elnidolto@loretoweb.com.mx; www.loreto.com/elnido; at beginning of town.*

La Palapa / ★★

AV HIDALGO AND PIPILA, LORETO; 613/135-1101 La Palapa is a favorite "end-of-the-trip" dinner spot for groups returning from a week of sea kayaking or mountain biking. Sportfishermen also frequent the eatery, whose kitchen will prepare their catch for $3 US per person. La Palapa features long tables arranged on a painted red cement floor. Soft light seeps through red lampshades. At the entryway, the smell of *huachinango* (whole red snapper), chicken, and beef sizzling over mesquite coals entices those walking by to come in and take a seat. Other popular dishes include the seafood combo (fish, shrimp, and scallops) and clams grilled in the shell with butter and garlic. Waiters here prepare your gourmet caesar salad dressing fresh at the table. *$; No credit cards; traveler's checks OK; lunch, dinner Mon–Sat; full bar; no reservations; half block from malecón.*

México Lindo y Qué Rico / ★★

AV HIDALGO AND COLEGIO, LORETO Translating to "Beautiful Mexico and How Tasty," this family-run restaurant offers both atmosphere and economic fare. Traditional woven Mexican blankets add a splash of color to the wall decorations. The breakfast menu features hefty portions of classic choices such as spicy huevos rancheros and *huevos a la mexicana* (eggs scrambled with salsa). The lunch and dinner menus include *queso fundido con chorizo* (melted cheese with sausage); a flavorful tortilla soup served with avocado slices and laced with juicy bacon drippings; fish in chipotle sauce; and chiles rellenos stuffed with shrimp and topped with cream and cheese. Try them with a cold Bohemia beer. *$; No credit cards; traveler's checks OK; breakfast, lunch, dinner every day; full bar; no reservations; about 2 blocks west of Madero.*

Pachamamá Restaurante / ★★

EAST SIDE OF PLAZA, LORETO; 613/135-1655, FAX 613/135-1655 Pachamamá ("Mother Earth") is the name of an Argentinean mythical divinity that gives fertility to the fields. Combining their talents as chefs and hosts, with their Argentinean and Mexican backgrounds, Ale (Alejandra) Gutierrez and León Castellanos have created a homey yet elegant cafe in the heart of downtown Loreto. Along with a menu that includes empanadas and Spanish-style tortillas, diners may find cannelloni—spinach and ricotta crepes with *bolognesa; fugazzeta*—a double-layer pizza filled with ham, cheese, and onions; imported cheeses and Mediterranean salads; and grilled sandwiches with homemade bread. Their *chimichurri,* a thick sauce made from olive oil, garlic, parsley, and herbs, is so popular that the owners can hardly keep it in stock. Desserts may include *panqueques* (Argentina's caramel crepes), or a flan that melts in your mouth. Dine within the traditional-style wood and adobe structure, or outside beneath a covered patio facing the tranquil cobbled plaza. *$; Cash only; lunch, dinner Wed–Mon; full bar; reservations recommended; pachamama@prodigy.net.mx; center of town.*

The Roof Garden / ★★★

POSADA DE LAS FLORES HOTEL, MADERO 78, LORETO; 613/135-1165 OR 877/245-2860 US Thick wooden doors, classy antiques and pottery, and bold yet muted colors draw you through arches, past pillars, and under the glass-bottomed swimming pool to the spiral stairway leading to this romantic dining terrace. Order a glass of wine or a margarita and take in the bird's eye view of Loreto. The menu features Mexican specialties such as chicken or fresh fish fajitas served on a sizzling platter; seafood-, meat-, and vegetable-based pastas; or seafood entrees such as *camarónes ajillo* served with vegetables. For dessert, you can't go wrong with their chocolate offerings, or, if you like sharing, split the *Babarese,* a rich and creamy flan presented with gelatin leaf cutouts. The wine list is well chosen and the wait staff is professional and unobtrusive. *$$; MC, V; traveler's checks OK; breakfast, lunch, dinner every day; full bar; reservations recommended; hotel@posadadelasflores.com; www.posadadelasflores.com; 3rd floor of hotel, on the main plaza at Madero and Salvatierra.*

Tiffany's Pizza Parlor and Cappuccino Bar / ★★

AV HIDALGO, LORETO; 613/135-5004 PHONE AND FAX Drawing from her Greek-Italian heritage, Denise Sferas brings pizza, cappuccino, and a little bit of Italy to Loreto. Dining in this small, home-style restaurant feels like eating at home as Denise cooks your hamburger or rolls out your pizza dough. A large Tiffany's Special pizza is made with Italian sausage, ham, mushrooms, and black olives. The closest thing to Starbucks this side of La Paz, Tiffany's serves cappuccino, espresso, latte, and cafe mocha made with organic coffee grown in Chiapas, Mexico. A baker at heart, Denise always keeps a fresh apple pie or tray of cinnamon rolls out on the counter to accompany the coffee drinks. The family restaurant is named for the owner's daughter, Tiffany. *$; Cash only; lunch, dinner Wed–Mon; full bar; no reservations; denise@loretoweb.com.mx; halfway between Independencia and Pino Suárez.*

LODGINGS

Hotel La Pinta Loreto / ★★

CALLE DAVIS, LORETO; 613/135-0025 OR 800/800-9632 US, FAX 613/135-0026 Hotel La Pinta Loreto is at the north end of the *malecón*, fronting a sandy beach. At the entrance, guests drive through a grandiose archway and down a long cobblestone boulevard that leads to the 48-room hotel. The cement brick buildings are painted a mixture of bright purple, mustard yellow, electric orange, pink, and blue—gaudy to many tastes but attractively modern to others. The large, air-conditioned rooms are comfortable and clean, and include a private patio and TV. Toned down for a more relaxing atmosphere, the room interiors are white-on-white with colorful accessories. Landscaping includes leafy ficus trees trimmed into cylindrical shapes, towering *cardón* cactus, and flowering bougainvillea. The sunny hotel pool and shady *palapa* bar face the wide beach that leads to the shoreline about 50 yards away. The La Pinta chain of hotels has recently started offering nonsmoking rooms, and with advance notice, small pets are now allowed in some of the units. *$$; AE, MC, V; traveler's checks OK; nhblto@loretoweb.com.mx; www.lapintahotels.com; at north end of malecón.*

Hotel Oasis / ★★

CALLE BAJA CALIFORNIA AND LÓPEZ MATEOS, LORETO; 613/135-0211 OR 800/497-3923 US, FAX 613/135-0795 The Oasis is easily recognized by the brightly colored mural on its wall, prominently displayed at the south end of the *malecón*. In operation since 1960, this hotel offers 40 air-conditioned rooms and a traditional, ranch-style atmosphere. The clean, spacious rooms feature two double beds and have no TVs or phones. Oceanfront units offer great views with private balconies or patios and hammocks. Dine at the terrace restaurant that looks past palm trees and across the sea toward Isla del Carmen. Near the back of the property is a peaceful pool surrounded by palms and flowering bougainvillea. A chain-linked fence cuts off the hotel property from the beach in front, although guests may access the beach through a small gate. Full meal packages, bed-and-breakfast packages, and fishing charters are also available. *$; MC, V; traveler's checks OK; loreto.oasis@loretoweb.com.mx; www.hoteloasis.com; south end of malecón.*

Loreto Desert Sun / ★★

KM 112 MEXICO 1, NOPOLÓ; 613/133-0612 OR 800/578-4487 US, FAX 613/133-0377 Loreto Desert Sun, located 5 miles south of Loreto, is an adults-only, all-inclusive, 236-room hotel funded in part by the Mexican tourism department, FONATUR. Loreto Desert Sun, and a new hotel under construction to the south, make up the area known as Nopoló (www.puntano polo.com). If you're shy, beware: Desert Sun features Baja's only "clothing-optional" beach; guests enjoy the freedom of au naturel sunbathing and even play volleyball in the buff. Swimsuits are also optional in the resort's 35-seat hot tub. Rooms feature air conditioning, telephone, TV, and a choice of balcony or patio. Room prices include all meals, alcoholic beverages, snacks, room service, and nightly entertainment. Whale-watching, deep-sea fishing, scuba diving, windsurfing, sailing, and kayaking are all available in a variety of packages. *$$; AE, MC, V; traveler's checks OK; solare@loretodesertsun.com.mx; www.solare resorts.com/loreto; on highway 5 miles south of Loreto.*

Plaza Loreto / ★★

AV HIDALGO 2, LORETO; 613/135-0280, FAX 613/135-0855 A little more upscale than the Hotel Junípero across the street, Plaza Loreto has 32 rooms, each with two double beds, TV, and air conditioning. This neo-colonial hotel is centrally located, one block from Misión Loreto. The "plaza" to which the name refers is an inner courtyard built around a large coconut palm tree. Furnished with four umbrella-covered tables and potted plants lining the walls, the courtyard is a nice place to relax. Built in 1990, the resort mimics old-style architecture with archways, wooden trim, and a Spanish-tiled roof. Rooms surround the courtyard on three floors. *$; AE, MC, V; traveler's checks OK; hotelplazaloreto@prodigy.net.mx; www.hotelplazaloreto.com; at corner of Pino Suarez.*

Posada de Las Flores / ★★★☆

MADERO 78, LORETO; 613/135-1165 OR 877/245-2860 US, FAX 613/135-1099 Loreto's most expensive and elegant hotel features tasteful interior designs and colonial style architecture that, despite being built in 1998, blends perfectly with the adobe-colored buildings, cobble-stone streets, and historic mission nearby. A thick wooden doorway at the entrance opens to an indoor courtyard and fountain surrounded by pillars and the hotel's 15 rooms. Inlaid stone-tile floors, antique wooden armoires, Talavera pottery, and a brass chandelier define the Old World decor. The most striking feature is the glass ceiling, which is actually the bottom of the swimming pool on the upper deck. All rooms are nonsmoking and air-conditioned and are com-plete with satellite TV, VCR, safe, and phone. Enjoy breakfast (included) at the Roof Garden, the hotel's charming rooftop terrace restaurant (see review). Exclusive in nature, this posh hotel allows no children under 12 and screens curious visitors who come to look around. The owner, Giusseppe Marcelletti, also owns the chic Posada de Las Flores Punta Chivato, 26 miles north of Mulegé. *$$; MC, V; traveler's checks OK; hotel@posadadelasflores.com; www. posadadelasflores.com; on main plaza at Calle Salvatierra.*

Villas de Loreto / ★★

ANTONIO MIJARES AND IGNACIO ZARAGOZA, LORETO; 613/135-0586 PHONE AND FAX Located on the water in south Loreto, this 11-room hotel offers smoke-free, beachfront rooms with air conditioning and refrigerator. The price of a room includes continental breakfast and free use of bicycles—downtown Loreto is a five-minute bike ride on a dirt road. A good place for families, the peaceful hotel grounds are filled with tall, swaying palm trees and a well-maintained pool. A white-roped hammock is strung between two palms—the perfect place to relax in the shade. The hotel's outdoor Restaurant Amore is set under the shady canopy of an olive tree and serves basic Mexican fare for breakfast, lunch, and dinner. A variety of multiday guided tours including kayaking, mountain biking, and snorkeling are available. For do-it-yourselfers, the resort rents sea kayaks and offers dropoff and pickup services for multiday trips. Snorkeling and diving trips are available through the onsite Dolphin Dive Center (see Guides and Outfitters). *$–$$; MC, V; traveler's checks OK; info@villasde-loreto.com; www.villasdeloreto.com; take Madero south across dry riverbed and one block past stop sign, turn left on Antonio Mijares, and go 1 block.*

San Javier Mission and Village

Just beyond the volcanic ridges west of Loreto, the historic mountain village of San Javier is a quiet farming community that lies 25 miles west of Loreto on a graded dirt road, tucked away deep within the Sierra de la Giganta. With only 100 residents, San Javier sits in a quiet oasis flanked by high basalt mountains. Built in the mid-1700s, the stone church at San Javier is the most well-preserved of all the missions in Baja California.

This mountainous country was untouched and wild when the missionaries first traveled west from Loreto into the water-rich sites frequented by the indigenous Guaycura and Cochimí tribes. The impressive Misión San Francisco Javier was built of stone taken from the nearby mountainsides and worked by the indigenous converts under supervision of masons and architects brought from the Mexican mainland three centuries ago. The tireless Jesuit missionary Juan de Ugarte taught agriculture to his neophytes and planted fruit trees in the fertile soil, creating the orchards that still produce olives and other fruits today. The priest also planted the peninsula's first vineyard at San Javier, producing the very first California wine. In the orchards behind the mission, visitors can view one of the original olive trees, now gnarled and old, planted by the *padres* more than 200 years ago. Both the mission and the ancient tree stand as testimony to the strength and endurance of Catholicism on the peninsula.

ACCESS AND INFORMATION

From Mexico 1 at km 117, the San Javier turnoff is 1 mile south of Loreto. The 25-mile-long graded road takes about an hour to drive and is usually in good shape. Guided tours including transportation are available in Loreto (see Guides and Outfitters in that section for details).

EXPLORING

At the town's entrance, the narrow dirt road turns to a cobbled boulevard that leads the way to **MISIÓN SAN JAVIER,** now a national treasure of Mexico. The old mission's original stone masonry, tall bell towers, and cemetery stand among palms and original olive orchards.

To make your trip an overnight excursion, reserve a room in advance at **CASA DE ANA** (613/135-1552), quaint bungalows at the entrance to the village with a view up the wide brick boulevard toward Misíon San Javier. The Bastida family runs **LA PALAPA RESTAURANT** (across from mission), serving *machaca* (dried, shredded meat) burritos and quesadillas made with beans and fresh goat cheese. Memo Bastida tells of his grandmother, who lived to be more than 100 years old, recalling masses at the mission given by Dominican priests.

FESTIVALS AND EVENTS

For a few days each year, the sleepy town of San Javier is transformed into a bustling hive of activity during the **SAN JAVIER SAINT DAY FESTIVAL**, which has been celebrated December 1–3 for more than 200 years. Just 50 years ago, prior to road access into the rugged canyons, families would travel for many days to the festival, riding mules along trails through the mountains. Today many people from Loreto make a pilgrimage for the event, hiking the 25 miles to pay their respects to the statue of San Francisco Javier, the patron saint who lived in the 16th century, and was known for his healing miracles.

Inside the church, the statue of San Javier is brought down from its spectacular gold-leafed altar and set within reach of faithful pilgrims, that they might touch the idol and receive spiritual consolation and healing. Many come to the festival to pay their *mandas* (personal promises) to San Javier in return for his answered prayers. Other people attend the three-day event on a more social level, to dance and to reunite with family and friends. Street vendors hawking wares and local villagers selling food create a festival atmosphere at the event.

Puerto Escondido

Driving south from Loreto, Mexico 1 follows the Sea of Cortez for about 35 miles before heading west toward the Pacific. If you like to explore, this is a good place to spend some time. This stretch of highway can get you close to isolated, alternative resorts, spectacular island vistas, and secluded beaches as it climbs through the mountains and drops back down to the sea.

At km 94 on Mexico 1, 16 miles south of Loreto, is the road to Puerto Escondido (Hidden Port). A popular anchorage for sailboats and other cruising vessels, Puerto Escondido is dotted with masts year-round. A **LARGE PUBLIC BOAT RAMP** offers one of Baja's best launches. Other than that, the port has few facilities—only remnants of an abandoned development project (see "The Phantom Escalera Náutica" sidebar).

ADVENTURES

HIKING / Take a strenuous hike through **TABOR CANYON**, a narrow *arroyo*, up and over boulders, and, in rainy season, through pools, deep into the Sierra de la Giganta. The unmarked trailhead is accessible from a dirt road that runs west off Mexico 1 at km 94, directly across from the Puerto Escondido turnoff. Drive about 200 yards up the dirt road and park near the red building at the power station. Crawl through the fence and follow the riverbed to the right. After about an hour of boulder hopping and creek wading, you'll find one pool after another, surrounded by palm trees and tall canyon walls. Tabor Canyon is one of several nearby *arroyos* in the steep, jagged mountains worth exploring.

SNORKELING / Local *pangeros* will take you out snorkeling to **HONEYMOON COVE** on Isla Danzante or to other sites where sheltered coves harbor colorful reef fish, eels, and invertebrates; inquire at Puerto Escondido, Ensenada Blanca, or Tripui RV Park (see below) for more details.

LODGINGS

Tripui RV Park and Hotel

KM 94 MEXICO 1, PUERTO ESCONDIDO; 613/133-0814, FAX 613/133-0828 Set about 500 yards from a scenic bay filled with luxury yachts and sailboats, this expansive RV park and small hotel offer a large swimming pool, grassy lawns, palm trees, a laundry, and a grocery store. In 1987 Alma Aguilar and Francisco Rivas started the RV park, which features 133 permanent spaces and 31 overnight spaces. The hotel, added in 1990, has six air-conditioned rooms that include TV and coffeemaker. Other services include camper storage, Internet service, and a restaurant-bar open for lunch and dinner. *$; No credit cards; traveler's checks OK; tripuivacation@hotmail.com; www.truipui.com; 16 miles south of Loreto.*

Ensenada Blanca

About 28 miles south of Loreto, at the village of Ligui (km 83) on Mexico 1, a dirt road leads east less than a mile to Ensenada Blanca, a fish camp. There are no services, but a couple of resorts provide access to many adventures.

LODGINGS

Danzante Resort / ★★

ENSENADA BLANCA, 31 MILES SOUTH OF LORETO; 408/354-0042 US, FAX 408/354-3268 US Perched like an eagle's nest atop a hill, this 10-acre resort offers a bird's-eye view of red-hued mountains, a white sandy beach, and desert islands floating on a blue sea. The predominant island is Isla Danzante (Dancer Island), from which the resort gained its name. Although the beach below is farther than just a casual stroll away, you can't beat the view. Each of the nine suites feature hand-painted tiles, wooden beams, and French doors. Behind each room is a *palapa*-covered terrace with a hammock—the perfect place to relax in the heat of the day. A small pool, picnic tables, and a dining room make up the common area where guests enjoy happy hour, snacks, and three meals a day. Room prices include free kayaking, snorkeling, and horseback riding. For an additional fee, go scuba diving, boat touring, or sportfishing. Mike and Lauren Farley, who own and operate the resort, are authors of three books, including *Baja California Diver's Guide*. An off-the-grid establishment, Danzante relies on solar power and trucked-in water. *$$; No credit cards; traveler's checks OK; info@danzante.com; www.danzante.com; continue 2 miles on a bumpy dirt road.*

El Santuario Eco Retreat / ★★☆

ENSENADA BLANCA, 30 MILES SOUTH OF LORETO; 613/104-4254 OR 805/541-7921 US Hidden away on a white sandy beach in a quiet bay south of Loreto, El Santuario (the Sanctuary) is a casual place to commune with nature, yourself, and others. An intimate eco-retreat owned and operated by Bill Paff and Denise Jones, El Santuario is a cluster of yurts and beachfront *casitas* that operate on solar power and trucked-in water. Their motto, "Be still and dance," is designed to attract an alternative clientele seeking isolation and a peaceful setting surrounded by wilderness. Guests are welcome to use the communal kitchen, although Bill and Denise prepare most meals. The center's two yurts are made of wood and white canvas and have windows to let in light and a top vent to regulate temperature. Guests stay in stucco *casitas* that are tucked between the vegetated dunes. Water-based activities include kayaking and beachcombing, and are included in the price. *$; No credit cards; traveler's checks OK; 3-night minimum; closed Aug–Sept; baja@el-santuario.com; www. el-santuario.com; from Ensenada Blanca fish camp, go 1 more mile on bumpy dirt road to sign for El Santuario.*

Agua Verde

About 35 miles south of Loreto, a rough dirt road branches off of Mexico 1, leading to the small fishing village of Agua Verde (Green Water). This road is the last drivable access to the Sea of Cortez for many miles, leaving a long stretch of pristine shoreline to the south accessible only by boaters and kayakers. Agua Verde sits on the small, scenic Bahía Agua Verde.

ACCESS AND INFORMATION

To reach this peaceful settlement, on Mexico 1 between km 63 and km 64, just before the highway veers westward toward the Pacific, turn left on the dirt road. The rough, 25-mile drive takes about 90 minutes, and should not be attempted without a high-clearance vehicle.

Villagers are friendly, but the area is not geared for tourism. Water comes from a communal garden hose and the local store is bare bones—bring your own food and water. The village's boat launch is badly littered, but a sandy beach about 200 yards to the north is cleaner and available for **PRIMITIVE CAMPING**.

EXPLORING

The most pristine area at Bahía Agua Verde is accessible by a dirt road that forks to the west about a mile north of town. This road leads to a sandy spit on the north end of the bay, where two cement structures have been erected. Park where the road deteriorates and walk down to the beach. The steep rock walls that drop into the sea offer good snorkeling.

ADVENTURES

RANCHO SAN COSME (Agua Verde Rd), an off-the-beaten-track, seaside goat ranch, offers mule rides, boat trips, primitive campsites, and meals. Rancho San Cosme, named for a small island off the coast, remains a working ranch as it has been for generations, raising free-range pigs, chickens, and goats. Operated by Guadalupe and Alejo Romero and their five children, the ranch trucks in its own water and relies on solar power. For visiting tourists, the women dish up home-cooked meals prepared over a wood-fired stove in the small kitchen. Rancho San Cosme is a good taking-off point for a hike to the hot springs that are about an hour's walk north along the beach. The ranch can provide directions, a guide, and mules for the trip, but has no phone, so arrangements must be made on-site. To reach the ranch from Mexico 1, head east on the dirt road to Agua Verde. After about 15 miles, look for the ranch on the left.

The Pacific

South of Loreto, Mexico 1 swings westward toward the Pacific, leaving the towering mountains behind for the flat land known as Llano de Magdalena (Magdalena Plain). Though not on the ocean, the twin agricultural communities of Ciudad Insurgentes and Ciudad Constitución are gateway cities to the Pacific, as well as the region's main population centers and handy places to stock up on supplies. Profitable crops of cotton, wheat, beans, garbanzos, corn, oranges, limes, and mangos grow in the fertile plains. Many of these crops are exported to other countries from the deepwater port of San Carlos, 34 miles west of Constitución.

Both Puerto San Carlos and nearby Puerto López Mateos are launch points for whale-watching, sportfishing, and other outdoor adventures in Bahía Magdalena. To the north lie the traditional mountain villages of La Purísima, San Isidro, and Comondú. A long dirt road leads to the small fishing village of San Juanico, nicknamed "Scorpion Bay" by American surfers who travel long distances to ride its famous point breaks. This section ends with another popular Pacific surf spot, Punta Conejo, and finally La Paz, the capital of Baja California Sur.

Since no airports or ferries service this area, the only way to get here is **BY CAR OR BUS.** No rental car companies operate here; however, buses travel to every town in this region except San Juanico. Many of the secondary roads are paved, although sometimes riddled with potholes, and even the dirt roads are usually passable by car because of the generally flat topography. More than rocks or steep inclines, the greatest hazard to motorists is loose sand. The district's official **TOURISM OFFICE** (Calle Matamoros; 613/132-4843) is located in Ciudad Constitución.

Ciudad Insurgentes

Roughly 70 miles southwest of Loreto is Ciudad Insurgentes. A paved road leads from Mexico 1 to this simple farming community (population 11,500), built around the highway and offering few attractions to the passing tourist other than grocery stores, taco stands, and a Pemex station. The local bakery, **PANIFI-CADORA LA CASA DEL PAN** (Juárez; 613/131-0030) is packed with pan dulce (sweet breads) and other goodies. Just north of the Pemex is another necessity, **EL SACRIFICIO** (Juárez), the town's ice cream and juice bar. The best **FISH TACO STAND** for miles closes around 2pm; it's located next door to **MERCADITO JUÁREZ** (Juárez and Serapio Rendon). At this time, no lodging is available in Insurgentes.

La Purísima, San Isidro, and Comondú

Head north from Ciudad Insurgentes on the unnamed paved road, and you'll find the essence of old Mexico. The attraction of the remote mountain villages of La Purísima, San Isidro, and the twin villages of San José de Comondú and San Miguel de Comondú is simply that there's nothing "to do"—no fancy restaurants, no souvenir shops, and no tour operators. Separated from Mexico 1 by desert, mountains, and valleys, these villages offer a glimpse into Baja's past.

ACCESS AND INFORMATION

You can reach these traditional villages by taking the **BUS** (one daily) to La Purísima or San Isidro from Ciudad Insurgentes. From either village, you might be able to catch a ride the last 20 miles up to the twin villages of San José de Comondú and San Miguel de Comondú. Or better yet, **DRIVE** the easier of two routes—it's longer, but paved most of the way from Ciudad Insurgentes. Head north on the paved secondary road (marked but unnamed) off of Mexico 1. (The alternative route requires careful navigation along the rough, 37-mile dirt road at the San Isidro turnoff that cuts west from Mexico 1 at km 60, about 45 miles south of Mulegé; high-clearance vehicles are recommended.) It is also possible to reach these villages via San Juanico (Scorpion Bay).

Water is available in all of the towns (often from garden hoses), and there are small eateries sprinkled near La Purísima, with primitive lodging at **MOTEL NELVA**, located behind the church in San Isidro.

EXPLORING

La Purísima lies on the old California mission trail, **EL CAMINO REAL**. The crumbling foundation of **MISIÓN LA PURÍSIMA CONCEPCIÓN**, built in 1717, can be found several miles north of the village.

Sandwiched between arid mountains, the Comondú valley is lush with shimmering date palms, sugarcane fields, fruit trees, and old mission vineyards that produce the grapes for local wine. Flowering bougainvillea trail over ancient adobe houses roofed with cane and sod. During harvest time, donkey power is harnessed to mill sugarcane grown in the valley. In San José, a box-shaped **MISSION HOUSE** from the 1700s has been converted into a church, and a mission bell stands outside to beckon the faithful.

San Juanico (Scorpion Bay)

Far from paradise, the town of San Juanico is a simple village with dirt roads, an on-and-off water supply, and electricity produced by a diesel generator. Fish and lobster are the main source of income for the 500 inhabitants, but lately tourism has funneled additional money into town as a growing number of surfers discover the point break at nearby Punta Pequeña. Americans have built vacation homes in a settlement just outside the village toward the lighthouse and the famous breaks. In a town still unspoiled by tourism, the local people are genuinely helpful and gracious to visitors. However, things could change rapidly, as San Juanico is slated for development as part of the Mexican government's proposed **ESCALERA NÁUTICA** (see sidebar).

Although it's a three-day drive from San Diego, San Juanico gets so crowded that as many as 60 vehicles line the cliffs near the lighthouse, and competition for waves is fierce as surfers jockey for position. Nobody knows exactly why surfers nicknamed the place "Scorpion Bay." Perhaps it was named for desert scorpions known to hide under sleeping bags and surfboards, or maybe it refers to the "stinging" fights that sometimes break out in the lineup.

ACCESS AND INFORMATION

To reach Scorpion Bay, take the unnamed paved road north of Ciudad Insurgentes toward La Purísima; then take the dirt road leading northwest about 30 miles to San Juanico.

EXPLORING

SCORPION BAY CANTINA (Scorpion Bay) sits right over the best breaks and offers rustic lodging and camping, meals, and the town's only bar. A long, sandy beach on the south end of town is great for taking long walks and collecting shells. When the swell is down, rent a sit-on-top **KAYAK** from Scorpion Bay Cantina and paddle out into the bay to look for pods of dolphins or observe frigate birds and pelicans.

ADVENTURES

SURFING / When a southwest swell rolls in, as many as eight different point breaks form near the lighthouse at **PUNTA PEQUEÑA** and make for some of the best surfing in all of Baja. **FIRST POINT,** sometimes called **UNO,** only breaks in a significant south swell. **SECOND POINT (DOS)** is a small right break with a sandy bottom, ridable at 1 foot or less and great for novices. The other surf points tend to be more advanced, usually with rocky bottoms. The middle breaks can be good for **WAVESAILING.** Expect the largest crowds and the most consistent swells July through October.

Puerto Adolfo López Mateos

This dusty little town on the Pacific, with a population of only 2,300, earns its living from Bahía Magdalena (Magdalena Bay). Besides whale-watching, other sources of income for López Mateos come from sportfishing, commercial fishing, and the Maredén packing plant where workers can tuna, sardines, beans, and tomato sauce.

Accessible by Puerto López Mateos as well as Puerto San Carlos, "Mag Bay" stretches for 200 miles along the Pacific coast, a very popular area for whale-watching, fishing, and sea kayaking. Local *pangeros* take visitors out into the bay or out to the nearby barrier islands that separate the bay from the ocean. Formed by sand dunes, the islands are inhabited by seabirds and covered with flowering verbena. Coyotes swim from island to island, living off fish and mice. To get fresh water, they lick morning dew off plants.

The animals that have put Magdalena Bay on the map, however, are the gray whales that migrate here every winter to breed. Nobody knows the exact number of gray whales in Magdalena Bay, but estimates are from 1,000 to 3,000. The population rises every year as the species, which experienced a close brush with extinction some 50 years ago, makes a recovery. Even though their numbers are still much lower than before the days of whaling, the gray whale is back, and has become the lifeblood of both ports on the bay.

ACCESS AND INFORMATION

Puerto López Mateos is located 21 miles west of Ciudad Insurgentes. Head north on the unnamed paved road for 1¼ miles. Look for signs and turn west on the next unnamed paved road. There is daily **BUS SERVICE** between Ciudad Constitución and López Mateos. Although most whale-watchers arrive by road, small planes land daily at the local **AIRSTRIP**.

The port town is built around a cement plaza, a police station, and a small church. It offers only a few small grocery stores, a hotel, two restaurants, and a few taco stands. Many of the eateries are only open January through March, when the gray whales are in the bay.

EXPLORING

López Mateo's handful of grocery stores all carry basic staples and are on the main dirt roads in town. **ABARROTES LUPITA** (613/131-5116) and **TIENDA SINDICÁL** (613/131-5159) both offer a good selection. The open-air restaurant **TACOS CACTUS** (across from Centro Cívico Social y Cultural) is a step up from the street taco stands in the plaza. One of the better restaurants in town is **RESTAURANT CABAÑA BRISA** (Calle Rodríguez). Marked by a large white whale skull, this family-run restaurant is open January through March. Serving fish, shrimp, lobster, chicken, and beef, owners Mirella and Federico Albarez operate the restaurant on the front patio of their home.

HOTEL POSADA TORNAVUELTA (Calle Rodríguez; 613/131-5106) is a good value, offering eight rooms; it is bare-bones but clean and comfortable, with hot water and double beds. Primitive **CAMPING** is available just to the north of the Embarcadero, although beaches are muddy, brown, and often littered with trash.

At the northwest end of town (the route from town is clearly marked with blue signs) is the **EMBARCADERO,** a simple wooden pier that is packed with *pangas* every morning during the whale-watching months. The scene there is lively when the whales are in, with vendors selling food, film, *artesanías,* and whale-watching excursions. Near the pier is a good place to launch **SEA KAYAKS** to paddle out to the pristine, sand-dune-covered islands that lie across the bay. Remember that during whale season, many areas are off-limits to kayakers.

ADVENTURES

WHALE-WATCHING / Magdalena attracts only an estimated 6 percent of all the gray whales that come to mate or give birth in Baja's lagoons (Scammon's Lagoon in Guerrero Negro attracts the most at about 50 percent). Nevertheless, the whales are in such tight concentrations here that the bay provides very favorable whale-watching. The season runs from mid-December to mid-April. A cooperative of *pangeros* operates out of both López Mateos and San Carlos, offering whale-watching tours that run about $56 US an hour per boat (for up to six people). Sign up in town when you arrive, or let an outfitter from La Paz or Loreto make all the arrangements.

Two cooperatives in López Mateos, **UNION DE LANCHEROS TURÍSTICOS** (613/131-5114) and **COOPERATIVA DE SERVICIOS TURÍSTICOS AQUENDI** (613/131-5105), organize local *pangeros* to set prices and equally divvy out the whale-watching business. Whale watchers can simply show up at the Embarcadero and hire a *panga,* or prearrange a guided tour with an English-speaking naturalist through one of the many companies that deliver groups from Loreto or La Paz.

FISHING AND BEACHCOMBING / If you like beachcombing, privacy, and long walks, hire a local *pangero* to take you out to the barrier islands of Magdalena Bay and pick you up a few hours later. Hike across the dunes for a mile or so to reach the Pacific side of the islands, which have long, flat beaches that face breaking waves. In low season, May through November, prices can be as low as $30 US for a dropoff and pickup, especially at López Mateos, where the islands are closer to the boat launch than at San Carlos.

Local *pangeros* will take visitors out to the islands, through the mangroves, or sportfishing in the bay. The price of a *panga* trip in the winter is set at $56 US per hour, but in low season it's negotiable. Two well-established *pangeros* in town are **MARIO CASTRO** (613/131-5115) and **RIGOBERTO ARAGÓN** (613/131-5032).

BIRD-WATCHING / The uninhabited barrier islands and mangroves in Mag Bay are filled with a variety of seabirds. *Pangeros* will take bird-watchers through the narrow canals that cut through the green mangroves, looking for egrets, cormorants, and kingfishers. On the sandbars and banks of the islands, look for great blue herons, flocks of white pelicans, godwits, reddish egrets, and pairs of American oystercatchers. Whale-watching rates of $56 US per hour also apply to bird-watching, but can be much less during low season, May through November.

SEA KAYAKING / Kayaking is the best way to access the natural canals that course through Magdalena Bay. The canals twist and turn for miles, creating a maze of mangroves, so don't go in too deep. Kayaking is restricted in parts of the bay during whale-watching season, December through March, and no kayaks are available for rent in either López Mateos or San Carlos. Bring your own kayak, or rent them in La Paz or Loreto.

FESTIVALS AND EVENTS
The largest annual event around Magdalena Bay, **FESTIVAL DE LA BALLENA GRIS (GRAY WHALE FESTIVAL)**, is celebrated in early February with live music, *artesanías*, and food booths. During this time, both López Mateos and San Carlos pay homage to the marine mammals that, despite their short stay every winter, boost the local economies like no other industry.

Puerto San Carlos
Built in the 1960s to support a commercial port and the Conservera San Carlos cannery, the town of San Carlos sits on a hooked peninsula, which is almost an island, separated from land by a bridged causeway. Most of the streets in town are named after Mexican ports. San Carlos is one of only two deepwater ports on Baja's Pacific side (the other is at Ensenada) where fish, seafood, and agricultural products are exported worldwide. Tourist-oriented activities include whale-watching, bird-watching, clamming, sportfishing, and kayaking. Along the drive into town, count how many osprey nests you see, built on top of the power poles paralleling the road. Both female and male ospreys—a type of sea eagle with white markings on the underside—help guard their large nests made of sticks and debris.

ACCESS AND INFORMATION
From Ciudad Constitución on Mexico 1, take Mexico 22 toward Puerto San Carlos. The 35-mile **DRIVE** takes less than an hour on a well-maintained, paved road. The **BUS STATION** (Puerto Morelos, 1 block from plaza), operate buses to and from Ciudad Constitución.

Compared to Puerto López Mateos, Puerto San Carlos (population 3,600) offers much more for tourists—restaurants, hotels, an RV park, and a new Pemex gas station. The town's Internet cafe, **COMPUTIME** (Paseo Costero 22; 613/136-0002), located on the north side of town, offers four computers, a printer, and a copier.

EXPLORING
The paved road leading into San Carlos skirts downtown, passes the Mexican Navy base, then swings left and turns to dirt as it heads south toward the fish cannery. Most of the businesses in town are on the dirt roads east of the paved road. The police station, the telephone office, and a taco stand surround the

THE VIRGIN OF GUADALUPE

At **KM 140** on Mexico 1, just north of the turnoff to Loma Amarilla, stands an ornate shrine honoring Mexico's patron saint, the Virgin of Guadalupe. Housed in a bright orange cement-block structure and decorated with artificial flowers, the ceramic-tiled, mosaic image of Mary is a regular stop for many Catholics driving past. Paying homage to the mother of Jesus, they duck inside to light a candle, say a prayer, and drop a few coins in the box. Another ceramic-tiled Virgin of Guadalupe shrine is embedded within the side of a boulder at the south end of **PLAYA LIGUI** south of Loreto, encouraging seaside supplications.

According to legend, in 1531 an apparition of the Virgin Mary appeared to Juan Diego in Guadalupe, near Mexico City. This miraculous event facilitated the conversion of the native Indian tribes to Catholicism. To this day, her image, dressed in a green cape and emanating golden rays, is the most popular religious icon in all of Mexico, surpassing even that of her son, Jesus Christ. Many other shrines to the Virgin of Guadalupe, although usually less ornate than these, can be seen up and down Mexico 1 and throughout the republic.

—Carrie Robertson

MAIN PLAZA (Puerto La Paz and Juárez). A new Pemex station (Puerto La Paz and Loreto) is located a half block north of Hotel Alcatraz. The largest grocery store is **FALAYMA MINI SUPER** (La Paz and Juárez; 613/136-0102).

Lodging alternatives include the Irish-themed **HOTEL BRENNAN** (Acapulco and Pichilingue; 613/136-0288) with secure parking, clean rooms, direct TV, and queen-size beds, and the **HOTEL BAJA MAR** (Topolobampo and Progreso; 613/136-0005), offering basic, clean rooms for $24 US for two people, which makes it the best deal in town. Under new ownership and newly renovated, **RV PARK NANCY** (613/136-0195) is located kitty-corner from Hotel Brennan. A nice area for **FREE CAMPING** is near the School for Field Studies on the east end of town. You'll find a clean beach and small sand dunes. In the winter, this beach is often lined with RVs.

ADVENTURES

WHALE-WATCHING / Puerto San Carlos owes much of its prosperity to the gray whale and its ability to attract tourists to this small town on a dead-end road. Business in San Carlos is so prosperous during January through March that some shops close for the rest of the year; see Guides and Outfitters for details.

FISHING / When the whales and the whale-watching tourists leave the area, local *pangeros* are available the rest of the year to take tourists out fishing, bird-watching, or sightseeing. Clamming is also popular at several spots in Magdalena Bay. In the mangrove-lined bay, fish for halibut or red bass; outside the bay try for marlin, *dorado,* and *wahoo.* Some fishermen trailer their own boats to San Carlos and launch on the concrete **BOAT RAMP.** All boaters should register with the **CAPITANA DEL PUERTO** (Port Captain; 613/136-0133). Remember that boating is restricted in many areas during whale-watching season.

GUIDES AND OUTFITTERS

Bryan Freitas of **MAG BAY TOURS** (800/599-8676 US; booking@magbaytours.com; www.magbaytours.com) has been leading surfers to the uncrowded waves of Bahía Santa María for more than 12 years. The perfect C-shaped bay lies on the outer edge of Bahía Magdalena and has three right-hand point breaks (summer) and a pristine setting well worth the trip. Eight-day packages run $970 US plus airfare, and include transfers, meals, and lodging. June through October, trips book up, so reservations are recommended well in advance. Mag Bay Tours can also arrange **SPORTFISHING** trips.

Local whale-watching tour companies in San Carlos include **VIAJES MAR Y ARENA** (Yelapa and Tampico; 613/136-0076; fito_gonzalez@latinmail.com), **UNIÓN DE LANCHEROS Y SERVICIOS TURÍSTICOS** (López Mateos; 613/136-0026), **ULISTURS** (Moreles; 613/136-0250), and **SOTO'S TOURS** (Mazatlán and Acapulco; 613/136-0030). All offer similar trips that start at about $56 US an hour for a skiff that holds up to six people. Three La Paz outfitters offer multiday whale-watching excursions from base camps near San Carlos: **BAJA EXPEDITIONS** (612/125-3828; 800/843-6967 US; www.bajaex.com), **BAJA QUEST** (612/123-5320; www.bajaquest.com.mx), and **MAR Y AVENTURAS** (800/355-7140 US; www.kayakbaja.com). For more detailed information on these outfitters, see the La Paz Guides and Outfitters section.

RESTAURANTS

Restaurant Gran Bahía / ★

MEXICO 22, PUERTO SAN CARLOS; 613/136-0466 Perched on a small hill right at the entrance to town is this pleasant *palapa*-roofed restaurant serving seafood specialties. Look out onto the bay from an outdoor table under coconut palm trees (keep your eyes peeled for whale spouts out on the bay) and try their famous *puro marisco* (pure seafood)—a whole fish grilled over ironwood coals, topped with cooked chiles, tomatoes, and onions. Because the dish takes time to prepare, call first or come with time to kill. The dish requires a minimum party of four. *$; No credit cards; travelers checks OK; breakfast, lunch, dinner every day Jan–Mar (Tues–Sun only, Apr–Dec); full bar; no reservations; near entrance to town on the right.*

Restaurant Los Arcos / ★

170 PUERTO LA PAZ, PUERTO SAN CARLOS; 613/136-0347 This mom-and-pop patio restaurant has a cozy feel with brick arched doorways, colorful tablecloths, and a carefully manicured cactus garden lined with clamshells. A whale mural decorates one of the walls. Located next door to the owners' home on the only paved street in the middle of town, Los Arcos is easy to find. Try the delicious *sopa de mariscos* (seafood soup) or the seafood combo. *$; Cash only; breakfast, lunch, dinner every day; beer only; no reservations; middle of town.*

LODGINGS

Hotel Alcatraz / ★★

SAN JOSE DEL CABO AND PICHILINGUE, PUERTO SAN CARLOS; 613/136-0017, FAX 613/136-0086 Owner María Eugenia Infante's red-brick house sits in front of this peaceful hotel. To reach the 23 rooms that are set well off the street, walk down the driveway lined with flowering pink bougainvillea. Sheltered by ivy-covered walls and towering coconut palm trees, the two-story hotel in the back features classical Mexican architecture, a Spanish-tiled roof, and red doors that add a splash of color to the decor. Rooms include a minifridge, TV, air conditioning, and two beds. The rooms face the hotel's outdoor restaurant/bar, El Patio, which serves basic Mexican fare and seafood. Even if you're not staying for the night, stop by to have a drink and listen to the birds chirping in the trees above. *$; No credit cards; traveler's checks OK; near center of town.*

Ciudad Constitución

More than 52,000 residents make up this agricultural market hub, the second largest population center in the state. A monument to General Agustín Olachea Aviles, one of Baja California Sur's former governors, was erected at the northern entrance to town for his dedication to the promotion of Ciudad Constitución as an agriculturally suitable region. Wonderful fruits and vegetables can be found at the town's market, along with fresh shellfish and other seafood.

ACCESS AND INFORMATION

On the **DRIVE** from Loreto to La Paz, Ciudad Constitución is the perfect place to replenish supplies. Mexico 1 becomes the poorly designed main street through town—Boulevard Agustín Olachea. Flanked by one-way streets on either side for local traffic, palm-lined cement islands separate the three busy roadways, creating an often-dangerous traffic pattern. Adding to the confusion, many of the traffic lights don't work and street signs are frequently twisted to read incorrectly. The central **BUS STATION** is located west of Mexico 1 on Avenida Rosaura Zapata.

Ciudad Constitución has plenty of opportunities to shop for groceries, fill up with gas, fix a leaky radiator, find an ATM, or check your email. Along Boulevard Olachea you'll find two Pemex stations and three banks—Bancomer, Banamex, and Banca Serfin. Across from Banamex, **CAFE INTERNET** (Blvd Olachea and Mina; 613/132-3620) offers several computers in a quiet, cool office. There are also several lodging and restaurant options in town.

EXPLORING

SUPERMERCADO PERALTA (Hermengildo and Galeana; 613/132-0224) is well stocked and offers a dropoff laundry service; or try the large American-style grocery store on the east end of town, **SUPERMARKET EL CRUCERO** (Francisco Villa and Calle del Rio; 613/132-2212). The traditional market, **MERCADO CENTRAL** (Juárez between Hidalgo and Bravo), is where six *cocinas* (kitchens) offer tasty Mexican breakfasts and lunches. **SUPER AMERICANA** (Bravo 161, half block east of Blvd Olachea; 613/132-0439) carries Mexican products such as *huaraches* (leather sandals with rubber soles), cowboy hats, guitars, terra-cotta pottery, and 4-foot-tall statues of the Virgin of Guadalupe. **LA MICHOACANA** (Blvd Olachea and Obregón) sells fresh-fruit popsicles, ice cream, and juices. Nearby is **TACOS ARANDA** (Bravo and Blvd Olachea), a wooden shack that is closed and deserted all day, but full of action at night—a very popular roadside stand.

RESTAURANTS

Nuevo Dragón Restaurant / ★

BLVD AGUSTÍN OLACHEA 1134, CIUDAD CONSTITUCIÓN; 613/132-2922
Who'd have thought you could find a Cantonese restaurant in the middle of Baja? Painted red and white on the outside, and offering something different from basic Mexican fare, this place is hard to miss. Inside, the white walls are decorated with framed Chinese silk tapestries. The Huang family, originally from China, started Nuevo Dragón in 1985 using traditional recipes with a few Mexican twists. For example, the delicious egg rolls served with authentic Chinese mustard are wrapped in a flour tortilla and deep-fried to perfection. The menu also features items such as chow mein, soups, chop suey, and fried rice. *$; Cash only; lunch, dinner every day; full bar; no reservations; Olachea at Corregidora, 1 block south of the Olachea statue.*

Restaurant Estrella del Mar / ★

BLVD OLACHEA AND CARR A SAN CARLOS, CIUDAD CONSTITUCIÓN; 613/132-0955 One of Constitución's longest-running restaurants, Estrella del Mar (Sea Star) specializes in seafood. A tall *palapa* roof and rows of windows that surround the room give the spacious dining area an open feel. Menu specialties include fried *huachinango* (red snapper) and a rich and wonderful *sopa de mariscos* (seafood soup). Other favorites are *filete de pescado* (fish fillet) prepared *al vapor,* wrapped in foil and steamed over the grill in garlic and butter; and tortilla soup. *$; MC, V; traveler's checks OK; breakfast, lunch, dinner every day Dec–Mar, lunch, dinner every day Apr–Nov; full bar; no reservations; 2 buildings north of San Carlos turnoff.*

LODGINGS

Hotel Oasis / ★

VICENTE GUERRERO 284, CIUDAD CONSTITUCIÓN; 613/132-4458
Though there are a few places in town to stay (and camping options, too), our favorite is the butterscotch yellow Hotel Oasis. This hotel is hard to miss, despite its obscure location three blocks off the main street. The rooms face a center courtyard that offers secure parking near your room. Well maintained, with firm beds and clean tile floors, the 14 rooms built in 1995 are comfortable and come with a phone and a color TV, including one movie channel in English. *$; Cash only; 3 blocks west of main street.*

Manfred's RV Park

KM 213, MEXICO I, CIUDAD CONSTITUCIÓN; 613/132-1103 Under new management, this 85-space, pull-through RV park set on 15,000 square meters of palm-shaded grounds is a popular stop for RV groups caravanning down the peninsula. Use of clean rest rooms, showers, and a large swimming pool is included in the $14–16 US nightly fee. Car or tent camping costs $12–15 US; an on-site apartment rents for $35 US per night. *$; Cash only; closed June–Aug; ½ mile north of town.*

Punta Conejo

A little-known **SURF SPOT** on the Pacific, Punta Conejo (Rabbit Point) is a left point break during both northwest and southwest swells. Local surfers from La Paz sometimes choose Punta Conejo over popular sites near Todos Santos to avoid the crowds. A graded dirt road leaves Mexico 1 at km 80, about 50 miles north of La Paz. The turnoff is marked by an old wrecked pickup truck. Budget 30–45 minutes to navigate the 12-mile washboard road. A few small fishing shacks are clustered around the point, but no water or facilities are available.

RESTAURANTS

Restaurant San Agustín / ★★☆

KM 77 MEXICO I, SAN AGUSTÍN; 613/133-1101 This roadside restaurant, about 48 miles north of La Paz, has been serving home-cooked regional food to travelers since 1951. Recognizable by its unique pink exterior, the small restaurant specializes in *machaca* (dried, shredded meat) burritos and *quesito de corazón* (heart-shaped cheese), both made from locally raised cattle. While most customers dine in, some just stop by to pick up a round of the regional cheese. Diners can usually watch one of the women of the Landa Flores family making cheese—an all-day process. During your meal, don't be surprised to see real Mexican *vaqueros* tie their mules to the fence and come inside for burritos and cold beer. *$; Cash only; breakfast, lunch, dinner every day; beer only; no reservations; north of La Paz.*

La Paz

Since 1535, when Hernán Cortez established Baja's first European settlement along the bay that we now call La Paz, the area has endured aggressive conquerors, raiding pirates, crusading missionaries, and exploitation of its once famous pearl beds. Years later, Spanish explorer Sebastian Vizcaino established a base here, naming it La Paz (Peace). Living up to its name, La Paz today is a peaceful city where its formula of magical ingredients creates an atmosphere that is purely *tranquilo*.

Natural beauty surrounds the city, from the sandy beaches and green mangroves north of town to the cactus-covered Sierra de La Laguna, the mountains that stand out along its southern horizon. Península Mogote is just across Bahía de La Paz, and several uninhabited islands lie within a short boat trip of the city, making La Paz a popular base camp for fishing, kayaking, snorkeling, and diving excursions.

Established as the capital of Baja California Sur in 1892, La Paz still thrives as a center for politics, culture, academics, and science. Three universities and several trade and language schools are scattered throughout town, resulting in a progressive mentality and a high level of education among the population, now just over 180,000.

Unlike Cabo San Lucas, which was built around tourism, La Paz was already a thriving community long before the first tourists arrived. And unlike Tijuana and Ensenada, which are heavily influenced by their close proximity to the U.S. border, La Paz maintains its authenticity as a charming Mexican town, rich with history and culture. However, some real threats do exist for La Paz. Tourism brings development. Rising real estate prices, increased traffic, and infiltration of fast-food chains threaten the quaintness and true essence of the town. La Paz will continue to face these challenges, but by preserving its past and adding the benefits of a modern community this city of peace seems to keep getting better.

ACCESS AND INFORMATION

LA PAZ INTERNATIONAL AIRPORT (km 9 Mexico 1; 612/124-6336) and its principal carrier, Aerocalifornia (612/125-1023 or 800/237-6225 US, fax 612/122-0794), offer daily flights from Los Angeles, Tucson, and Tijuana. Aero Mexico (612/122-0091 or 800/237-6639 US; www.aeromexico.com) also services La Paz from Los Angeles, San Diego, and various airports in mainland Mexico.

DRIVING Baja's Mexico 1 between Loreto and La Paz requires four hours and covers 223 miles of pavement. La Paz **RENTAL CAR** companies, most with offices on the *malecón* and at the airport, include Alamo (612/122-6262, fax 612/122-4601), Avis (612/122-2651 phone and fax or airport 612/124-6312), Budget (612/122-7655, fax 612/125-6686), Dollar (612/122-6060 or airport 612/124-6282, fax 612/122-6040), and National (612/125-4747, fax 612/125-6595).

BUS SERVICE is available the entire length of the peninsula from Tijuana to Cabo with Autotransportes Águila (612/122-4270) and ABC (612/122-3063). La Paz has two terminals, one on the *malecón* (Paseo Obregón 125; 612/122-

DIVE IN!

Although Los Cabos might be Baja California's most popular scuba destination, the islands and nearby seamounts around La Paz offer some of the most populated dive sites in the Sea of Cortez. About 800 species of fish exist here, some reef dwellers and some pelagic, including whale sharks and giant manta rays. Summer and fall are the best seasons for diving in the Sea of Cortez, when visibility clears to around 100 feet and water temperatures reach about 80° F. Here are some of our favorite dive sites:

ISLA ESPÍRITU SANTO, located about 5 miles north of Península Pichilingue, offers several sites popular with La Paz dive companies. Near the south end of this 15-mile-long island is a popular and easy dive called **SWANEE REEF,** which lies in 30–50 feet of water. This dive features rock formations covered with coral heads and sandy areas where fields of garden eels wave in the surge like prairie grass.

On the leeward side of Espíritu Santo lie two shipwrecks. The wreck of the **SALVATIERRA** is a 300-foot-long ferry that sunk in 1976. Lying in 60 feet of water and encrusted with lime-green branching corals, it's home to Cortez angelfish, green moray eels, large groupers, and schooling snappers. Divers can penetrate some of the openings and swim beside the 5-foot-wide propellers at the stern. The **FANG MING** is a large Chinese ship that was caught passing illegally through Mexican waters in the mid-1990s. It was confiscated and sunk intentionally by the government to take the pressure off existing reefs. The top of the ship lies in about 35 feet of water, while the bottom sits

7898) and another uptown (Jalisco and Independencia; 612/122-4270, fax 612/125-9422 ext 104), with buses departing and arriving every few hours.

Care to cruise over to mainland Mexico? **HIGH-SPEED FERRY** service (passenger only) is now available from La Paz to Topolobambo. French-owned **BAJA SPEED** (5 de Mayo at Obregón; 624/123-1313) offers daily service aboard the 400-passenger trimaran *Cortez* from Pichilingue (10 miles northeast of La Paz on the La Paz-Pichilingue Road, aka Mexico 11). This vessel slices previous voyage times in half, reaching the mainland in four hours. The *Cortez* leaves promptly at 8:30am, arriving at 12:30pm; it returns to La Paz at 7pm. First-class seats (recommended) come with a box lunch and cost 550 pesos (roughly $57 US); tourist-class seats are 100 pesos less. For a small fee, a shuttle bus will transport you from La Paz to the terminal.

If you'd like to take your vehicle over to the mainland, SEMATUR (612/125-4440, fax 612/122-2221 or in downtown La Paz at 5 de Mayo and Prieto; 612/125-2366; www.ferrysematur.com) runs **VEHICLE AND PASSENGER FERRIES** to Mazatlán (18 hours; salon class $40 US) and Topolobampo–Los Mochis (only vehicles at press time) twice a week. If you've brought your sleeping bag and insulated pad, the salon section is not a bad choice; sleeping out on the deck at about 70 feet. Despite its recent arrival, the wreck has begun to attract interesting and rare fish, including sea horses and brightly colored juvenile Cortez angelfish.

La Paz's most popular dive and snorkel site, **LOS ISLOTES**, is known for its resident sea lions. Located just north of Espíritu Santo, it is a 1- to 2-hour boat trip from La Paz. Many of the sea lions lounge on the rocks, barking loudly, while others drop into the shallow waters to check out divers.

One of the area's most advanced dive sites is a seamount that lies about 35 miles northeast of La Paz, known as **EL BAJO**. Although the top of El Bajo lies in about 60 feet of water, most dives here are done in the 100-foot range where divers are more likely to encounter schooling hammerhead sharks. No one can guarantee shark sightings, however, since the animals move in and out of the area at will. Strong currents and deep water make this a technical dive that can be difficult for beginners.

LA REINA (the Queen) is an outcropping of exposed rocks that lies about a mile off the northern tip of Isla Cerralvo, roughly 2 hours from La Paz. Offering good diving for all levels, La Reina has large coral-covered mounds creating interesting topography, and a maximum depth of 70 feet. Sea lions, orange cup coral, and an occasional sea turtle are some of the highlights. The biggest draw to this site, however, is the presence of manta rays.

—*Carrie Robertson*

under the stars can be a wonderful experience—weather permitting; however, larger, private rooms are also available. Vehicle prices depend on the size of your car or rig, starting at about $220 for a 15½-foot auto and increasing by footage. Passengers are not allowed on the vehicle deck—not even to attend to pets.

Special vehicle permits are required for vehicles traveling across to the mainland. Get them at the U.S.–Mexico border or purchase them in La Paz from **ADUANA MARITIMA** (north end of ferry terminal; 612/125-4440 ext 108). You'll need your original vehicle title or registration and three copies, a major credit card, a driver's license, a passport, and a valid Mexican visa.

The **LA PAZ TOURIST CENTER** (Paseo Obregón and 16 de Septiembre; 612/122-5939 or 866/733-5272 US) is a small government office officially known as **CORDINACIÓN ESTATAL DE PROMOCIÓN AL TURÍSMO**, on the water side of the *malecón*. Open Monday through Friday (8am–10pm) and Saturday and Sunday (12pm–10pm), the office provides a colorful packet of free information, brochures, and maps of La Paz and several other Baja locations. The main **OFFICE OF TOURISM** is in the yellow Fidepaz building (Mexico 1 and Av del Tiburon; 612/124-0100; turismo@gbcs.gob.mx). For more information log onto www.vivalapaz.com.

CAFE INTERNET (Jalisco and Albañez), in southwest La Paz, has several computers, air-conditioning, and a $2 US-per-hour rate to go on-line, which makes it popular with students of the tech school across the street. Downtown is **CAFECITO NET** (Francisco Madero 1520; 612/123-2617; lsclpz@prodigy.net. mx), which charges about $2 US per hour as well. A little more expensive but right on the *malecón* is **SERVICIO TURÍSTICO BRIONES** (Paseo Obregón and Muelle; 612/122-6837).

It's easy to lose your bearings in La Paz. Because the peninsula of Pichilingue separates Bahía de La Paz (the bay) from the Sea of Cortez, visitors tend to get turned around. To orient yourself, look out at the bay from the *malecón*—you're facing northwest—the Sea of Cortez lies over the mountains behind you and to your right.

The weather in La Paz is pleasant most of the year. The hottest months are usually May through October. Starting in July, there's the possibility of *chubascos* (violent thunderstorms) and even hurricanes. La Paz almost always enjoys a pleasant breeze from the north (in winter) or the south (in summer).

NOTE: A common scam on the roadways outside of La Paz involves an increase in the number of real or imagined traffic citations after 4pm, when the *policía* delegation offices are closed for the day. Officers may take your license, explaining that it's necessary for you to pick it up the following day at the police station in La Paz. Travelers who are just passing through will not want to be bothered with such a hassle, and most likely will be willing to pay a bribe to get out of the situation. If you feel that you've been wrongfully cited by the police, contact the **OFFICE OF TOURISM** (612/124-0424 or 612/124-0100).

EXPLORING

Restaurants, bars, hotels, and gift shops line the *malecón* street, **PASEO ALVARO OBREGÓN**. Understanding the true essence of La Paz starts with a walk along this picturesque waterfront. Communing with the bay is a daily ritual for many La Paz residents and visitors. Early morning and late evening, people run, walk, and bicycle along this 3-mile sidewalk. Join them! While getting your heart rate up, you can spot great blue herons, watch sailboats gracefully cruise the bay, or cheer on local teenagers playing soccer in the sand. At night, when the city lights reflect streaks of vibrating color onto the mirrorlike Bahía de La Paz, the *malecón* moves into full swing.

MUSEO DE ANTROPOLOGÍA (Anthropology Museum; Altamirano and 5 de Mayo; 612/125-6424) is tucked away uptown without a visible sign, and takes a bit of investigating to discover. All signs are in Spanish but even the non-Spanish speaker can easily trace the history of Baja California through viewing the various displays. A large mural depicts when near-naked natives, living on clams and cactus fruit, met the well-armed Spanish conquistadors in the 1500s. Ancient fossils, a 10-foot-long topographical map of the peninsula, and native artifacts are also on display. Open Monday through Saturday 9am–5pm; with no entrance fee and several interesting exhibits, it's definitely worth a visit.

At **PLAZA CONSTITUCIÓN**, you can find people promenading in the evenings, attending events, playing bingo, and visiting with friends. This concrete park is filled with trees, shoeshine stands, a fountain, and a gazebo. Relax on a park bench and enjoy the tranquil atmosphere of this traditional core of the city. The plaza is bordered by four streets: Independencia, Revolución, Francisco Madero, and 5 de Mayo. Across the street, tour the oldest church in La Paz, **CATEDRAL DE NUESTRA SEÑORA DE LA PAZ.** This large stone church, built in 1861, features twin bell towers and plum-colored stone bricks. It replaced La Paz's original mission from 1720, which stood a couple of blocks away.

One of La Paz's newest attractions is **EL SERPENTARIO** (Brecha California and Av Nueva Reforma; 612/122-5611), an outdoor educational zoo filled with fascinating reptiles from all over the world. About 30 percent of the live snakes, iguanas, lizards, geckos, turtles, and alligators on display are from Baja. There is also a large cactus garden exhibiting some of Baja's most beautiful desert flora. Founded in 2000, this reptilian zoo is run by CEMA de La Paz, a non-profit organization. Located about 15 minutes from downtown; from Abasolo, go north on Avenida Nueva Reforma and southwest on Brecha California half a block. Open Monday through Saturday 10am–6pm. The entry fee is $10 US.

La Paz has several **LANGUAGE SCHOOLS,** one of the newer ones being **SE HABLA LA PAZ** (Francisco Madero 540; 612/122-7763; www.sehablalapaz. com). This American-owned school offers instructional courses for all levels, and specializes in medical and dental programs for health-care professionals. They also set up home stays wherein students live with local families. **CENTRO DE IDIOMAS, CULTURAS Y COMUNICACIÓN** (Francisco Madero 2460; 612/ 125-7554; www.cicclapaz.com) offers everything from daily basic Spanish lessons to total-immersion programs.

Ten **BEACHES** stretch north of La Paz on the dead-end continuation of the *malecón,* most commonly known as the La Paz–Pichilingue Road (Mexico 11). Along the 17-mile paved drive, you'll pass several beautiful bays and coves, and wind your way through a vast forest of tall *cardón* cactus, some more than 400 years old. About 3 miles after the Pichilingue ferry terminal, the road forks. The left fork leads to **PLAYA BALANDRA,** a mangrove-filled lagoon great for kayaking, swimming, or bird-watching. Walk out through the shallow water to find the Balancing Rock, a La Paz icon that makes its way onto postcards and T-shirts. The right fork leads to **PLAYA TECOLOTE,** a wide-open beach great for long walks, volleyball, or relaxing. Playa Tecolote is home to a few low-key eating establishments, the best of which is **PALAPA AZUL** (blue *palapa*). Despite the natural beauty of both beaches, midweek visitors practically have the place to themselves.

La Paz's two indoor municipal markets are packed with vendors selling traditional foods, such as fruit, meat, fish, cheese, clothing, and shoes. In traditional, old-world fashion, you'll find no cash registers, linoleum flooring, or fluorescent lighting here. Near the main local bus stop downtown lies **MERCADO**

LA PAZ THREE-DAY TOUR

DAY ONE: Enjoy breakfast at your bed-and-breakfast, **EL ÁNGEL AZUL,** where you'll rest your head and rejuvenate between activities during your stay. Before heading out for the day, schedule tomorrow's snorkel tour with **BAJA EXPEDITIONS.** Then strap on your tennis shoes and join the parade of morning exercisers walking, running, and biking along La Paz's *malecón*. Explore Baja California's cultural history at **MUSEO DE ANTROPOLOGÍA,** and then head over to **PLAZA CONSTITUCIÓN** to people-watch and absorb the tranquil atmosphere. Tour **CATEDRAL DE NUESTRA SEÑORA DE LA PAZ,** located just across the street. Before leaving this part of town, stop in at **IBARRA'S POTTERY** to see their hand-painted, lead-free dinnerware. Hungry yet? Join the standing-room-only crowd waiting for fish tacos at **SUPER TACOS DE BAJA CALIFORNIA HERMANOS GONZÁLEZ.** Next door, at **LA PERLA DE LA PAZ** (Esquerro and Arreloa; 612/125-1113), stock up on drinking water and a bottle of fine wine because your next stop is the beach. Grab your sunscreen and hat and leave La Paz with at least four hours of daylight ahead of you. Head north on the *malecón* to cruise the scenic, 17-mile drive to beautiful **PLAYA TECOLOTE** and enjoy the view of Isla Espíritu Santo. Afterward, return to El Ángel Azul and rejuvenate in your room for an hour or two before a late dinner of gourmet lasagne at **LA PAZTA TRATTORÍA.** Finish your evening to the beat of live Latin American folk music at **PEÑA LA PITAHAYA DE JANICUA.** Don't get there too early—the music doesn't start until 10pm.

DAY TWO: Rise early and pack your swimsuit, sunscreen, hat, and binoculars for today's snorkel or dive trip with **BAJA EXPEDITIONS.** You'll munch on a light break-

MUNICIPAL FRANCISCO E. MADERO (Revolución and Degollado). **MERCADO NICOLÁS BRAVO** (Bravo and G. Prieto) is a little farther uptown. Adjacent to both markets are clusters of small *cocinas* (kitchens) that sell economical Mexican breakfasts and lunches. **PANIFICADORA KARLA** (Ortega and Legapsy; 612/122-6063), La Paz's most well stocked bakery, specializes in fresh Mexican pastries, doughnuts, breads, and cookies. An evening stroll on the *malecón* should always include a stop at **LA FUENTE** (Paseo Obregón and Muelle), a small ice cream shop that sells cones, juices, and *paletas* (fruit popsicles).

Although just about everything you need can be found in the mom-and-pop stores downtown, La Paz has several large **SUPERMARKET** chains. Look for **CCC, ARÁMBURO,** and **CASA LEY** with branches throughout the city. The government-subsidized **TIENDA ISSSTE** (Revolución and Bravo) offers the best prices for nonperishables, but selection varies from week to week.

fast courtesy of Baja Expeditions before the well-trained crew leads you on an underwater adventure near **ISLA ESPÍRITU SANTO** to swim with sea lions, angelfish, and, if you're lucky, a giant manta ray. The cruise includes lunch and snorkeling gear and returns to Marina de La Paz at 4pm. Freshen up at your bed-and-breakfast, but be sure to arrive at **BOUGAINVILLEA RESTAURANTE** in time to savor the sunset from the outdoor tables. After dinner, stroll along the *malecón* and stop for an ice cream at the popular **LA FUENTE**. Party animals can dance the night away at **LAS VARITAS**. Remember—in Mexico, the later it is, the livelier it gets.

DAY THREE: For breakfast, forego the fare at your bed-and-breakfast and order some fruit-filled crepes at **CAFÉ CAPRI** (Vista Coral 4; 612/123-3737), then drive a few miles southwest on the *malecón* to **ARTESANÍA CUAUHTÉMOC** to watch weavers make traditional Mexican blankets. Next, visit **EL SERPENTARIO**, the educational reptile zoo. Enjoy a lunch of delicately sautéed parrotfish while overlooking the bay at **LA POSADA DE ENGELBERT** (Av Nuevo Reforma and Playa Sur; 612/122-4011), just a block down the street from the zoo. After lunch, head northwest on the *malecón* and rent a kayak from **SCUBA BAJA JOE**. Paddle across La Paz Bay, through a sea of anchored sailboats, to **PENÍNSULA MOGOTE**. Explore the remote beaches, watch the birds, and keep an eye out for pods of dolphins. After turning in your kayak, catch happy hour at **PARADISE FOUND** (Paseo Obregón and Allende; 612/125-7340). Order an ice-cold *cerveza* and enjoy a free round of pool. Then head to **RANCHO VIEJO**, the best all-night taco stand in town. (The *tacos del pastor* are our favorites.) Stroll the *malecón*, take in the star-filled sky, and enjoy your last night in the city of peace.

SHOPPING

Visit **ARTESANÍAS** (Calle Artesanos and Arreola), the outdoor market featuring works by local artisans. For Mexican pottery, silver, and glassware, head to **ARTESANÍAS LA ANTIGUA CALIFORNIA** (Paseo Obregón 220; 612/125-5230) on the *malecón*. **UGUET'S TILES** (Mutualismo and Ocampo; 612/122-4623) sells Mexican ceramic tiles with fun designs including iguanas and turtles. Family-owned **IBARRA'S POTTERY** (G. Prieto 625; 612/122-0404) has been creating hand-painted ceramic kitchenware since 1950. Order a personalized plaque or design your own dinnerware. For traditional Mexican weavings, visit **ARTESANÍA CUAUHTÉMOC** (Abasolo 3315; 612/122-4575), where owner Fortunato Silva Moreno, 75, is teaching the weaving tradition to his grandsons. Watch them weave hand-spun cotton and wool on the assortment of wooden looms at this small, unassuming factory.

ADVENTURES

SNORKELING, DIVING, AND KAYAKING / La Paz is the gateway to the wild islands of the Sea of Cortez, the closest one being **ISLA ESPÍRITU SANTO** (Island of the Holy Spirit), which lies north of Península Pichilingue. When touring the islands, watch frigate birds soar over sculpted rock formations, picnic on sandy beaches, snorkel in emerald-colored lagoons, and visit a colony of barking sea lions. Diving, kayaking, and camping are activities that bring people out to this uninhabited island year-round. See Guides and Outfitters for more information.

Looking out across the bay from the *malecón,* through the fleet of anchored sailboats, you can see **PENÍNSULA MOGOTE,** a 7-mile-long thumb of land that forms the north side of Bahía de La Paz. Because the roads to Mogote are difficult to reach and limited to off-road vehicles, the peninsula remains undeveloped and is a great getaway from the city. The easiest access is via kayak from the *malecón,* which takes about an hour of paddling. **SCUBA BAJA JOE** (Ocampo 460; 612/122-4006) and a few other outfitters rent kayaks, and will deliver and pick them up from your launch on the *malecón.* Be sure to ask about currents, which, at certain tide levels, can make paddling more difficult.

FISHING / The best sportfishing grounds near La Paz are accessed by boat, between the islands and the city. Fish for *cabrilla, bonito,* roosterfish, yellowtail, *dorado,* marlin, tuna, and sailfish. Most fishing trips leave from the lighthouse at Punta Las Arenas, a 45-minute van ride from La Paz, to access the waters off **ISLA CERRALVO.** The best fishing is April through November, although people fish year-round. Book your trip at one of the major hotels in La Paz (see Lodgings).

WHALE-WATCHING / Most La Paz whale-watching tour companies take visitors by taxivan across the Baja peninsula to **MAGDALENA BAY.** Located about 160 miles north of La Paz on the Pacific, this is the breeding ground of the gray whale. Although humpback, fin, blue, pilot, and Bryde's whales are among the species that reside in the Sea of Cortez, they are more spread out and harder to locate than those in the Pacific. However, a few live-aboard vessels based in La Paz operate multiday trips that cover great distances, and these give passengers a very good chance of seeing whales and other marine life while underway. They include the highly recommended La Paz–based **BAJA EXPEDITIONS** (Paseo Obregón and Bravo; 612/125-3828 or 800/843-6967 US; www.bajaex.com), with their professionally staffed, 80-foot, 14-passenger *Don José;* **LINDBLAD EXPEDITIONS** (800/397-3348 US; www.expeditions.com), offering numerous guided voyages on their 70-guest, 152-foot vessels *Sea Bird* and *Sea Lion;* and **CRUISEWEST** (800/888-9378 US; www.cruisewest.com), featuring trips on their 212-foot, 102-guest *Spirit of Endeavor.* All three companies have excellent reputations and staff marine biologists and naturalists who give lectures and guide the educational expeditions.

GUIDES AND OUTFITTERS

A true pioneer in the adventure travel field, **BAJA EXPEDITIONS** (Paseo Obregón and Bravo; 612/125-3828 or 800/843-6967 US; www.bajaex.com) founder Tim Means was one of the first outdoor explorers to trek down the Baja peninsula. With no support boat or backing, his scouting expeditions would test kayaking, diving, and whale-watching routes, preparing the way for commercial trips. Today, Baja Expeditions employs experienced guides and naturalists to run their high-quality dive, kayak, and whale-watching excursions. In the summer months, they run daily and live-aboard dive and snorkel charters. In the winter, the focus changes to multiday kayaking trips to Espíritu Santo, or along the string of islands running from La Paz to Loreto. In January and February, they operate a whale-watching camp at Magdalena Bay.

With guides who speak Japanese, Spanish, and English, **BAJA QUEST** (Rangel 10; 612/123-5320, fax 612/123-5321; www.bajaquest.com.mx) caters to international adventure travelers. Owned by Adria Rocio Lozano, a Mexican national, and Gen Ito of Japan, Baja Quest operates dive excursions, dive-camping trips, environmental programs, dive certification courses, whale-watching, and kayaking journeys.

Under the direction of **BAJA DIVING SERVICE, CLUB CANTAMAR RESORT** (Km 17 La Paz–Pichilingue Rd; 612/122-7010, fax 612/122-8644; www.club cantamar.com) is based in a new hotel 10 miles north of town at Pichilingue. The advantage of staying at Cantamar is that you're closer to Espíritu Santo and other popular dive sites. On the flip side, you're also farther from restaurants and other city attractions. To solve the dilemma, the resort provides transit to La Paz upon request. Cantamar features diving, snorkeling, kayaking, sportfishing, whale-watching, a marina, and a live-aboard boat. Cantamar has the only on-site decompression chamber in Baja dedicated to sport divers. A week at the resort with five days of diving costs about $600 US. Standard rooms and suites are air conditioned, roomy, and nicely decorated with Mexican tile and rustic furniture.

At **LA CONCHA BEACH RESORT** (Km 5 La Paz–Pichilingue Rd; 612/121-6120, fax 612/121-6123; www.cortezclub.com), a beachfront luxury hotel 3 miles north of La Paz, the **CORTEZ CLUB** offers diving, snorkeling, and sportfishing trips aboard one of their 12 boats. A PADI dive training facility, the Cortez Club offers classes at all levels, from beginning open water all the way up to instructor, available in five languages. La Concha also rents kayaks and windsurfers on the beach.

FUN BAJA ADVENTURES (Km 2.5 La Paz–Pichilingue Rd; 612/121-5884, fax 612/121-5592; www.funbaja.com), located at Marina Palmira, features certified guides who are fluent in English, Japanese, and Spanish. Owner Enrique Castillo Rodríguez opened the business in 2000 offering diving, snorkeling, kayaking, camping, whale-watching, dive certifications, rental equipment, and tank fills. Their snorkel and dive boats are a common sight at Los Islotes, the sea lion colony north of Espíritu Santo.

BUCEO CAREY (Topete 3040; 612/123-2333 phone and fax; www.buceo carey.com), located at Marina de La Paz, specializes in dive instruction, diving and snorkeling tours, and dive equipment rentals and sales. Owner Gabrielle Vazquez, an SSI instructor certifier, started Buceo Carey in 1996 when he came to La Paz from Los Mochis on the Mexican mainland. Buceo Carey offers a wide range of SSI courses, from a one-day introduction to scuba all the way up to a multiday instructor course.

Just off the *malecón*, **SCUBA BAJA JOE** (Ocampo 460; 612/122-4006; www. scubabajajoe.com) offers snorkel and dive trips to Espíritu Santo, kayak rentals, and dive certification courses. Word of mouth has made this six-year-old business a success with owner Jose Antonio Aguilar at the helm. Born in Acapulco, Jose moved to La Paz 19 years ago to work as a dive guide in what he calls "world-class diving conditions" in the Sea of Cortez. He also rents kayaks by the day to paddle to Península Mogote. For do-it-yourself trips to Espíritu Santo, Scuba Baja Joe will arrange a shuttle to the islands.

David Jones, an American who moved to La Paz in 1995 to pursue a new way of life, owns **FISHERMEN'S FLEET** (670 Paseo Obregón; 612/122-1313; david@fishermensfleet.com; www.fishermensfleet.com), a sportfishing company. His captains will take you trolling for *dorado,* marlin, and roosterfish or drifting for *pargo,* tuna, and amber jack in some of the most productive waters in the Sea of Cortez. Early in the morning, customers are taken in a van about 50 minutes southeast to the lighthouse at Punta Las Arenas where they board one of the 20 *pangas* (skiffs) in the fleet. Fishermen's Fleet operates in an office next door to Hotel Los Arcos and offers packages including lodging and meals.

BAJA OUTDOOR ADVENTURES (BOA; Paseo Obregón and 16 de Septiembre; 612/125-5636 phone and fax; www.kayactivities.com) runs four-day and seven-day kayaking trips to Isla Espíritu Santo. Choose between a comfortable skiff-support trip and a more challenging self-supported trip wherein the paddlers carry everything they need inside the kayaks. For a do-it-yourself adventure, BOA will shuttle experienced kayakers with gear to the island, send them off with food and water, and pick them up at the end of the trip. BOA will also bring out fresh supplies midweek and take away your trash. Closed July through September.

MAR Y AVENTURAS (Sea and Adventures; 564 Topete; 612/123-0559 phone and fax or 800/355-7140 US; www.kayakbaja.com) is a Mexican outdoor company offering sea kayaking and whale-watching expeditions from La Paz and Loreto, focusing on natural history, wildlife encounters, and Baja culture. Owned and operated by Mary Harter and Ricardo Amador, a husband-and-wife team and former Baja Expeditions guides, Mar y Aventuras has been in business since 1993. They cover a broad range of services, including multiday kayak trips, snorkel and kayak day trips to Espíritu Santo, day kayak trips to El Mogote and Playa Tecolote, sportfishing excursions, and whale-watching tours. Experienced kayakers may organize a "do-it-yourself" expedition by renting kayaks and camping equipment and arranging for an island shuttle.

Rent a bike for the day, sign up for a day bike tour, or join a multiday mountain biking trek through the *sierras* of Baja. Owned by La Paz native Hiram Gastelum, **KATÚN TOURS** (16 de Septiembre 15; 612/123-3009; www.katuntours.com) offers weeklong expeditions along the old back roads of Baja, touring ranchos and old Spanish missions. Trips include camping gear, meals, bilingual guides, support vehicles, airport transfers, and hotel lodgings on the first and last nights. Besides cycling in Baja, Katún also runs bike tours in Copper Canyon in the state of Sinaloa, across the Sea of Cortez.

NIGHTLIFE

CINEMAS VERSALES PLUS (Revolución 1910 at Independencia; 612/122-9555), a downtown movie theater half a block southwest of Plaza Constitución, shows American films in English with Spanish subtitles. Although the four screens are in good condition, the volume is sometimes muddled and hard to hear—not a problem for the mostly Spanish-speaking audience reading subtitles. Be prepared for intermission, when the screen suddenly goes black at the climax of a love scene while the audience goes for more popcorn.

PEÑA LA PITAHAYA DE JANICUA (Paseo Obregón and Independencia; 612/125-5768; quitapenas81@hotmail.com) is a bohemian music bar and restaurant that attracts a mellow crowd of cultured, hip locals who gather to hear live Latin American and Mexican folk music performed on a small outdoor stage surrounded by thick stucco walls. "Pitahaya" is a Baja cactus that produces an edible fruit; "Peña" is a traditional meeting place for artists, an idea that began in Spain in the 1800s and is still alive in La Paz today. The Perez family, originally from Guadalajara, owns the establishment, which has its own six-piece band, Janicua. Using guitars, vocals, and percussion, Janicua performs *música folklórico* on Friday and Saturday, followed by visiting groups of musicians. Various solo artists perform Monday through Thursday. Music starts around 10pm and continues until 3am. The bar and restaurant open at 8pm. La Pitahaya is tucked behind La Fabula pizza restaurant on the *malecón*.

A local band, La Chuquez de la Cachana, plays live dance music at **LAS VARITAS** (Independencia and Dominguez; 612/125-2025) for the regular patrons who are there every weekend to shake it up. This late-night spot just starts to get going around midnight. By 2am, the place is packed with gyrating bodies dancing hip-to-hip, even on tabletops and benches. If you need some space, try the upstairs balconies that look down onto the dance floor, or arrive when they open at 10:30pm before it starts to cook. On Friday and Saturday there's a $3 US cover; closed Monday.

FESTIVALS AND EVENTS

For more information or schedules regarding these or any other festivals and events in La Paz, contact the Tourist Office (Paseo Obregón and 16 de Septiembre; 612/122-5939 or 866/733-5272 US; www.vivalapaz.com/festival).

Nine days before Ash Wednesday (usually around mid-February), **CARNAVAL** takes place in the port cities throughout Mexico as the precursor to the Lenten season. The La Paz version grows larger each year. Festivities include parades, music, performing arts, food booths, costumed dancing, and a wealth of activities and contests for children (even infants!).

Easter week in Mexico, **SEMANA SANTA (HOLY WEEK),** is as important as Christmas, in Baja as throughout the country. Religious processions and celebrations take place throughout the week. Easter is also time for Mexican and U.S. family vacations, so many Baja beaches can be extremely crowded.

RACE WEEK, La Paz's annual sailboat regatta (612/125-9605), usually falls during the last week in April and often attracts more than a hundred boaters. Activities include small regattas and the big race from Pichilingue to Isla La Partida, where beach activities, competitions, and games take place.

September 16 is **FIESTA PATRIA DE LA INDEPENDENCIA** (Mexican Independence Day), the most celebrated secular holiday, observing Mexico's independence from Spain in 1821. Street vendors sell Mexican flags, traditional foods, and *cerveza,* and the city shoots off fireworks at night.

The age-old, traditional **DÍA DE LOS MUERTOS** (Day of the Dead) falls November 1–2, when families celebrate the lives of their deceased relatives with all night devotions at area cemeteries, elaborate shrines, and fancy papier-mâché and candy skeletons.

RESTAURANTS

Bougainvillea Restaurante / ★★

MALECÓN DE VISTA CORAL, LA PAZ; 612/122-7744 PHONE AND FAX Offering the best dining view in all of La Paz, Bougainvillea Restaurante is perched on the end of the Vista Coral wharf. Get there before sunset to enjoy the view of the *malecón* and sailboats in the bay. From the outdoor tables, watch acrobatic pelicans dive-bomb unsuspecting fish in the shallow waters surrounding the wharf. The straightforward menu offers burgers, steaks, and pasta, as well as gourmet seafood dishes such as red snapper baked in a garlic, tomato, and basil salsa. For a more casual meal, share a pesto pizza baked in the restaurant's wood-fired ovens. The atmosphere at this American-owned establishment is tranquil with soft music, but service can be a little slow, so be ready for a leisurely meal. *$$–$$$; MC, V; traveler's checks OK; lunch, dinner every day; full bar; reservations recommended; southwest end of malecón.*

The Dock Café / ★★

TOPETE AND LEGASPY 3040, LA PAZ; 612/125-6626 With a full wall of windows overlooking Marina de La Paz, the Dock Cafe offers diners a glimpse into the life of the vagabonds who navigate the Sea of Cortez. The restaurant/bar is perched so close to the boat slips that diners watch the daily goings-on of the salty dogs and sailboat cruisers as they tend their vessels, take on water, and chat with fellow boaters. Sample the extra-large Dock burger and fries if you've worked up a sailor's appetite, or munch on lighter fare such as grilled fish, fajitas, soups, and salads. Happy hour, 4–7pm, features two-for-one drinks, and sometimes there is live music 7–10pm. *$$; MC, V; traveler's checks OK; breakfast, lunch, dinner every day; full bar; no reservations; at Marina de La Paz, southwest end of malecón.*

La Baguette Francesa / ★★

MARINA PALMIRA, HIGHWAY 11, LA PAZ; 612/127-9463 This petite French bakery/cafe offers a panoramic view of luxury sailboats at the upscale Marina Palmira, located in the northeast end of La Paz. Pick an outdoor table and gaze out at white masts, polished wooden decks, and shiny brass hardware. Often patronized by boat passengers and crew, La Baguette is the perfect spot to rub elbows with yachties while sipping coffee and munching on flaky French pastries. Try the cinnamon rolls or apple strudel. Menu items include sandwiches prepared on freshly baked French bread, goat-cheese bread with salad, and homemade beef pâté. Owners Jean Paul and Guadalupe Fleuret brought their style of baking from Southern France to La Paz in 1998. *$–$$; No credit cards; traveler's checks OK; breakfast, lunch Mon–Sat (closed in Sept); full bar; no reservations; labagett@hotmail.com; northeast on La Paz–Pichilingue Rd to km 2.5 and at Marina Palmira, walk to boats and turn left, about halfway down the walkway.*

La Pasta Trattoría / ★★★

ALLENDE 36, LA PAZ; 612/125-1195 PHONE AND FAX Freshly made pasta, crisp salads, and exquisitely prepared sauces have made this restaurant one of La Paz's most popular dining spots. Through a large window into the sparkling kitchen, diners can watch as the pasta is created from scratch. Although it maintains a casual atmosphere, La Pazta oozes refinement and attention to detail. The decor follows an old Mediterranean theme with stucco, exposed brick, and abstract paintings by local artists. Sip a glass of Baja California wine and order their tangy bruschetta with fresh tomatoes, garlic, and basil. Try a wood-fired pizza, savory lasagne, or spinach ravioli with cream sauce. La Pazta serves the freshest salads in town with a choice of three house-made dressings. The dessert menu features several frozen treats, including hot berries over ice cream topped with fresh whipped cream. Service is prompt and professional. *$–$$; AE, MC, V; traveler's checks OK; breakfast, lunch every day, dinner Wed–Mon; full bar; reservations recommended; mail@hotelmed.com; www.hotelmed.com; 1 block off the malecón.*

La Terraza Restaurant and Bar / ★★

PASEO OBREGÓN 1570, LA PAZ; 612/122-0777, 800/716-8799 OR 888/242-3757 US, FAX 612/125-5363 An established and reliable La Paz eatery, La Terraza is a great place to people-watch. Located just below Hotel Perla (see review) and under the same ownership, most of the restaurant is open air and offers terrific views of the waterfront and bay, especially at sunrise and sunset. Surrounded by tiled floors and walls, enjoy a hamburger or chiles rellenos while a flood of pedestrians and cars streams by outside the pillar-supported walls. In the evenings, Mexican trios wander in, peddling classical Spanish songs. The reliable menu offers fresh-squeezed juices and yummy huevos rancheros for breakfast and a tasty *pescado al mojo de ajo* (garlic fish) for dinner. *$$; AE, MC, V; traveler's checks OK; breakfast, lunch, dinner every day; full bar; no reservations; perla@lapaz.cromwell.com.mx; www.cromwell. com.mx/hperla/hperla.html; below Hotel Perla on malecón at Calle La Paz.*

Le Bistrot Francais Cafe Restaurant / ★★

CALLE ESQUERRO 10, LA PAZ; 612/125-6080 Shoppers will find this casual French hideaway a haven from the midday heat and traffic of downtown La Paz. Thick adobe walls and high ceilings, the trickling sound of the garden fountain, and an old European-style charm create a comfortable dining atmosphere. The menu offers a variety of French dishes priced affordably. Start off with the Bistrot salad of avocado, palm hearts, artichokes, and asparagus, followed by a chicken crepe made with mushrooms, cream cheese, and onions. Other menu specialties include lamb chops and grilled lobster. *$$; MC, V; traveler's checks OK; breakfast, lunch, dinner every day; full bar; no reservations; bistrot@prodigy.net.mx; www.prodigyweb.net. mx/bistrot; 1 block southwest of 16 de Septiembre.*

Rancho Viejo / ★★

DOMINGUEZ AND MARQUEZ DE LEÓN, LA PAZ; 612/128-4647 Rancho Viejo (Old Ranch) is an upscale and popular taco restaurant near the southwest end of the *malecón*. Sit outdoors at a wooden picnic table and watch the *taquero* prepare traditional Mexican *tacos de carne asada* (grilled, chopped beef) and *tacos del pastor* (flame-roasted pork). The fragrant smoke of juicy meat on the grill mixes with colorful light to create a warm and friendly atmosphere. Garnish your taco with sliced cucumber, radishes, shredded cabbage, and fresh salsas. On the back patio of the old stucco building, tables and wooden chairs create a more intimate dining area under a *palapa* roof. Breakfasts include omelets and hotcakes, while the lunch and dinner menu includes T-bone steak, grilled chicken, and fish. Although tacos are available only at night, regular menu items are available 24 hours a day, making

Rancho Viejo one of La Paz's only restaurants that never closes. *$; Cash only; breakfast, lunch, dinner every day; full bar; no reservations; uphill 1 block from Vista Coral on malecón.*

Señor Sushi / ★★

 FRANCISCO MADERO 1715, LA PAZ; 612/122-3425 Surrounded by red walls and Japanese paper lampshades, it's hard to remember you're in Baja while dining in this trendy sushi bar. Sushi in Baja? You betcha— many La Paz business types stop here to unwind after work with a light and healthy meal. Mexican or Japanese owners? Guess again—owner/operator Pernille Jorgenson of Denmark has lived in La Paz for more than a decade and brought Señor Sushi to life just over five years ago. Try the *masago especial* (cream cheese, fish eggs, salmon, crab, avocado, mushroom, green onion, and nori) followed by *kaory*, cubes of custard, topped with sliced fresh kiwi fruit. *$; Cash only; lunch, dinner every day; beer and sake; no reservations; contacto@ senorsushi.com.mx; www.senorsushi.com.mx; at Degollado near MAS department store.*

Super Tacos de Baja California Hermanos González

 MUTUALISMO BETWEEN ARIOLA AND IGNACIO BAÑUELOS CABEZUD, LA PAZ When you have a hankering for fish tacos, head to the corner of Mutualismo and Ariola and look for the crowd. Super Tacos González is arguably the most popular fish taco stand in town. A trip downtown isn't complete without one of their tasty tacos filled with your choice of fish, squid, octopus, clams, shrimp, scallops, lobster, or oysters. Everything is breaded, fried (or you can order *a la plancha*—grilled), and served in corn or flour tortillas. Dress your own taco from the salsa bar that includes nearly 20 toppings, including green peppers in cream, guacamole, shredded cabbage, and sliced cucumber. The González family owns two other taco stands in town under the same name with the same wonderful tacos (Degollado and Francisco Madero; and Isabelle Católica and Juárez). *$; Cash only; breakfast, lunch every day (until 5pm); no alcohol; no reservations; 1 block off malecón.*

LODGINGS

Cabañas de los Arcos and Hotel los Arcos / ★★★

 PASEO OBREGÓN 498, LA PAZ; 612/122-2744 OR 800/347-2252 US, FAX 612/125-4313 Traditionally a sportfishing hotel, the old Cabañas de los Arcos has been a stomping ground for Baja tourists since 1954. The original cabanas are intimate and comfortable with thatched roofs and winding cobblestone walkways shaded by huge laurel trees, palms, and flowering plants. Hotel los Arcos, adjacent to the cabanas, is the establishment's newer addition, a 130-room multistory building offering bay views from the upper floors and more luxurious interiors. Together, they make up some of La Paz's most upscale lodgings. Both sections offer swimming pools, double beds, air-conditioning, and satellite TV, while some have two queen-size beds and refrigerators. The newer section has a cafeteria, restaurant, bar, gift shop, sauna, and massage service. Sipping a piña colada in a lounge chair at the pool, you feel so secluded it's easy to forget that you're in the middle of a busy city. *$$; AE, MC, V; traveler's checks OK; www.losarcos.com; on southwest end of malecón at Rosales.*

Club El Moro / ★★⯪

KM 2 LA PAZ–PICHILINGUE RD, LA PAZ; 612/122-4084, FAX 612/125-2828 This classy 23-room hotel borders the busy *malecón* on the northeast end. Despite traffic just outside, it maintains a cozy, private feel due to clever landscaping and Moorish-inspired architectural design. Special touches such as the swinging bridge over the pool and a swim-up bar give this affordable hotel a boost toward luxury. Even the most basic rooms include two queen-size beds, clay-tile floors, and thick wooden furniture. The upstairs rooms have their own balcony with a table and chairs. The price of a room includes a continental breakfast in the hotel's restaurant, Cafe Gourmet, which features the best French rolls in town, served with real butter and good coffee. *$; MC, V; traveler's checks OK; elmoro@prodigy.net.mx; www.clubelmoro.com; near northeast end of malecón, where road becomes a divided highway.*

El Ángel Azul B&B / ★★★

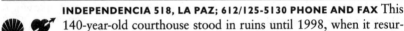

INDEPENDENCIA 518, LA PAZ; 612/125-5130 PHONE AND FAX This 140-year-old courthouse stood in ruins until 1998, when it resurfaced as one of La Paz's best-kept secrets. Renovated under the creative direction of Swiss owner Ester Ammann, this jewel of a bed-and-breakfast lies hidden away on a quiet corner uptown. Maintaining its original hacienda-style architecture with brick and adobe walls, El Ángel Azul is inconspicuous on the exterior, revealing only thick white stucco walls accented with cobalt blue trim. The front reception area opens to tables where guests have breakfast or relax with afternoon tea. Soft light streams in through French doors that connect the breakfast room to a grassy central courtyard filled with flowering bougainvillea and palms. The 10 air-conditioned, nonsmoking rooms surround the courtyard, each featuring built-in benches, single or queen-size beds, folk art, and cement-tile floors. Throughout the establishment, Mexican architecture mixes with European charm to create a simple yet elegant atmosphere. Breakfast is included with your stay, and bar service is available in the evening. To ensure that hotel guests have privacy and quiet, the bed-and-breakfast keeps its doors closed, so walk-ins need to ring the doorbell. *$$; MC, V; traveler's checks OK; hotel@elangelazul.com; www.elangelazul.com; at G. Prieto, 5 blocks up from malecón.*

Hotel Mediterrane / ★★★

ALLENDE 36, LA PAZ; 612/125-1195 PHONE AND FAX Once an abandoned house, this Greek-style, seven-room hotel offers sunlit studio suites that surround a palm-fringed courtyard. Whitewashed walls, arched doorways, and blue trim create a Mediterranean theme, while Mexican fabrics and wooden furniture bring you back to Baja. The Swiss and Mexican partners who brought it to life, Norbert and Saul, also own the famously popular La Pazta restaurant next door (see Restaurants). Guests of the hotel receive free use of the hotel's bicycles and kayaks. In the evenings, guests gather at the hotel's rooftop terrace to watch the amazing show of colors that takes place on the bay at sunset. *$; AE, MC, V; traveler's checks OK; mail@hotelmed.com; www.hotelmed.com; ½ block from malecón.*

Hotel Perla / ★★

PASEO OBREGÓN 1570, LA PAZ; 612/122-0777, FAX 612/125-5363 One of La Paz's most historic and well-known hotels, Hotel Perla was named after the once-famous pearl beds in La Paz Bay. Since its construction in 1940, this 110-room hotel overlooking the bay has been a reliable and safe place for tourists to stay. In the lobby, a photo gallery exhibits old photos of the hotel in its various incarnations. Hotel Perla's rooms are basic, clean, and comfortable, with king-size beds. The higher floors command a good view of the bay. The hotel is centrally located on the *malecón* and features an attractive outdoor pool on the second floor. Hotel Perla's ground-floor restaurant, La Terraza (see Restaurants), is a popular people-watching hangout, and its nightclub, La Cabaña, is popular with folks who like '70s music and flashing disco lights. *$$; AE, MC, V; traveler's checks OK; perla@lapaz.cromwell.com. mx; at Calle de La Paz.*

La Casa Triskel B&B

ALLENDE 305, LA PAZ; 612/123-0501 This small, offbeat bed-and-breakfast is set in a restored home built in 1915 and offers three rooms in a peaceful atmosphere. Inside the old one-story brick building surrounded by a yard and small garden are clean rooms that feature high ceilings, large windows, tile floors, and a mixture of twin and double beds. La Paz's most attractive budget option for the backpacking crowd, La Casa Triskel's affordable price includes breakfast and use of a communal kitchen and sunny patio area. The bathroom is shared with other guests but is spacious, with a large Mexican-tiled shower. The owners, Carina le Vaillant and Vladimin Rodríguez, are both teachers in La Paz. *$; No credit cards; traveler's checks OK; zoozoo@latinmail. com; at Serdan.*

La Concha Beach Resort / ★★

KM 5 LA PAZ–PICHILINGUE RD, LA PAZ; 612/121-6161 OR 800/999-2252 US, FAX 612/122-6123 OR 619/294-7366 US La Concha (the Shell) is unlike any other hotel in La Paz. While all the in-town hotels are separated from the water by the *malecón,* this 112-room multistory hotel is one of the only hotels in the area that is literally on the beach. It is located on Playa Caimancito, the first beach north of La Paz (toward Pichilingue). La Concha's fanfare of swimming pools, tennis courts, restaurant, bar, and gift shop fit the bill for vacationers who are looking for an all-inclusive place to stay. Those who want a less commercial yet more authentically Mexican experience will want to choose a hotel in town, however. La Concha recently added a captive dolphin center, housing wild bottlenose dolphins taken from a resident pod in Magdalena Bay—a very controversial project within the community. *$$; AE, MC, V; traveler's checks OK; laconcha@juno.com; www.laconcha.com; 5 km out of town toward Pichilingue.*

Oasis de Aripez RV Park

KM 15 MEXICO 1, EL CENTENARIO; 612/124-6090 This bayside RV park lies in the small town of El Centenario, just north of the La Paz airport. The park sits on a brown sandy beach and offers full hookups, showers, toilets, laundry, and boat access for about $10 US per night. *$; No credit cards; traveler's checks OK; about 4 miles north of airport turnoff.*

La Ventana

Geographically, Bahía de la Ventana (or simply La Ventana, "the Window") sits in a valley between two mountain ranges and faces the sea toward the majestic Isla Cerralvo, the southernmost island in the Sea of Cortez. The combination of steep mountains behind the bay and the island in front creates a natural wind tunnel in the region, and great bump-and-jump conditions for windsports. In fact, this windy little village lying 35 miles south of La Paz has grown into one the most popular windsurfing and kiteboarding resort areas on the Baja peninsula. Ten years ago, the only tourism-related business was an *ejido* (community-run) campground. The arrival of windsurfers, and more recently kiteboarders, has virtually blown money into town, resulting in the opening of services and windsurfing resorts.

ACCESS AND INFORMATION

To reach La Ventana by **CAR,** from La Paz take Mexico 286 toward San Juan de Los Planes. The turnoff to La Ventana is paved and well marked. Beyond La Ventana, the road continues for a couple of miles to the more substantial town of El Sargento (population 500), which has a small police station, a medical clinic, a taco stand, several small grocery stores, and a pharmacy that also sells gasoline. Beyond El Sargento, the pavement ends and turns to dirt, finally dissolving a few miles past town.

KITE CENTRAL

You may have seen them from a distance—acrobatic, colorful, bonnetlike objects—dancing in the air. Take a closer look. What appears to be elegant choreography is actually the world's fastest-growing extreme water sport: Kiteboarding has come to Baja. This electrifying and entertaining crossbreed of a sport involves four equipment elements: a kite, a line system, a control bar, and a board. Towed by the powerful kite and holding the control bar, the kiteboarder rides what is similar to a wakeboard or small surfboard. Wind is the natural element necessary for kiteboarding, and it's possible to kite in very light winds. When the water is frothy with whitecaps, however, kiters can launch spectacular 20- to 40-foot jumps and throw amazing spins, twists, and loops. Envisioned in the '70s, kiteboarding has recently developed into a full-blown industry, with rapidly evolving equipment designs and spiffy contests. At the same time, southern Baja (most notably La Ventana) is evolving into a prime winter kiteboarding destination. Warm, steady sideshore winds and miles of open beach attract kiters from all over North America. If kiteboarding looks like something you'd like to try, lessons from an experienced instructor are highly recommended. See the Guides and Outfitters section for recommendations.

—Lori Makabe

La Ventana has small grocery stores, restaurants, and two RV parks. The original campground is still in operation, a strip of oceanfront land sprinkled with mesquite trees and offering showers and flush toilets for $3 US per night. La Ventana's main season runs November through March. In summer the restaurants close and the town moves into slow motion, as the only tourists who venture down the dead-end road are an occasional fisherman or scuba diver in search of a boat ride to Isla Cerralvo.

EXPLORING

Besides wind, La Ventana offers a white sandy beach that curves 15 miles away to the east, great for long walks and **BEACHCOMBING**. In the mountains outside of town, **HIKERS** can find waterfalls in shady *arroyos* and thick *cardonals* (stands of *cardón* cactus). **SPORTFISHING** is also popular in the area. Deepwater channels on both sides of Isla Cerralvo are fish highways for schools of marlin, sailfish, tuna, wahoo, *dorado,* and roosterfish as they migrate north in the spring and south in the fall.

WARNING: Although the waters are inviting, beware of the thick colonies of sea urchins living among the rocks in this huge bay. In the warmer months, stingrays bury themselves in shallow, sandy areas. Be sure to ask a local gringo where to enter the water; shuffling your feet usually scares away the stingrays.

GUIDES AND OUTFITTERS

NEW WIND KITEBOARDING SCHOOL (PO Box 917, Hood River, OR 97031; 541/387-2440 US; newwind@gorge.net; www.newwindkiteboarding.com) in La Ventana specializes in kiteboarding, where the price of a lesson includes all the necessary equipment. Based in the Columbia River Gorge May through August, the school's instructors spend November through March in Baja. Located on the beach at Captain Bob's, about five lots north of Baja Joe's (see Lodgings).

At **SHELDON SAILS** (707/374-3053 US; sheldon_sails@yahoo.com; www.sheldonsails.com), sail designer Bruce Spradley teaches kiteboarding lessons and repairs sails and kites near his compound, located one lot off the beach behind Baja Joe's. Open November through March.

It is possible to arrange a day of fishing with the *pangeros* at the fish camps located in La Ventana and El Sargento during spring, summer, and fall. Look for the *pangas* on the beach and book a day trip with them. The closest charter boats that you can prebook depart from the lighthouse at **HOTEL LAS ARENAS** (Punta Arena; 888/644-7376 US; www.lasarenas.com) to the south. This 40-room sportfishing resort is so far off the grid that few people know about it. Diesel generators provide power, rooms have fans instead of air conditioning, fresh water is trucked in, and the on-site restaurant serves three meals a day. To find Hotel Las Arenas, located between the Punta Las Arenas lighthouse and Ensenada de Los Muertos, follow the small "Hotel" signs posted along the dirt road.

RESTAURANTS

El Rincón de la Bahía / ★

CALLE DE LA PLAYA, LA VENTANA; 612/126-5455, 044-612-6-5455 LOCAL CALLS A glassed-in *palapa* restaurant with a nice view of La Ventana Bay, El Rincón is a popular windsurfer hangout that specializes in reasonably priced seafood. Owner María de Jesús Burgoin León, with a soft smile and gentle composure, serves up specials such as *chiles relleno de camarón* (roasted green pepper stuffed with shrimp), stuffed clams, fish tacos, or grilled *tampiqueña* beef. Entrees are large and come with a side of beans, so share a plate or ask for a doggie bag. El Rincón is tucked away behind the family's grocery store, Mini Super Don Ruben. *$; No credit cards; traveler's checks OK; breakfast, lunch, dinner every day Nov–Mar, Mon–Fri only Apr–Oct; beer, wine, and tequila; no reservations; halfway between Baja Joe's and campground on dirt road that parallels paved road.*

Tacos León

PAVED ROAD, EL SARGENTO; 612/127-9165 This restaurant is a step up from your basic taco stand, offering tables and chairs in a walled-in structure complete with tablecloths. In addition to tacos, owner Alicia prepares seafood any style, hamburgers, *tortas*, breakfasts, and orders to go. *$; Cash only; breakfast, lunch every day, dinner Fri–Wed; beer only; no reservations; on the left (west) as you enter El Sargento.*

LODGINGS

Baja Adventures / ★★

DIRT ROAD, EL SARGENTO; 612/128-4333 PHONE AND FAX OR 800/533-8452 US After running Mr. Bill's windsurf resort in Buena Vista for more than 15 years, Bill Edsell opened Baja Adventures in 2001. This windsurf and kite bed-and-breakfast features six domed bungalows, each with an ocean view and your choice of twin or queen-size beds. Mexican tiles splash color among the rustic furnishings and quality fixtures, while solar panels provide electricity. Rigged gear is kept under a *palapa,* and the resort keeps a sandy launch cleared to facilitate launching. Packages include breakfast and lunch as well as use of windsurf and kiteboard gear, kayaks, mountain bikes, a Hobie catamaran, and snorkeling equipment. Diving and fishing trips can also be arranged. Lodging is surrounded by adobe-style concrete walls and located about 100 yards from the beach. *$$; MC, V; traveler's checks OK; mrbill@ ventanabay.com; www.ventanabay.com; ½ mile north of town—look for signs.*

Baja Joe's / ★★★

KM 5 LA VENTANA HWY, LA VENTANA; 612/126-2322, FAX 612/126-9226 Owners Joe and Angie Cheek started Baja Joe's in 1995, building it from the ground up. Seven stucco cabanas surround a palm-filled, brick courtyard at this dog-friendly windsurfing, kiteboarding, and fishing resort on the beach. Sail all day, then shower off and dine at the patio picnic table that faces the ocean and Isla Cerralvo. A common kitchen area is available to guests for preparing meals and storing food. Baja Joe's has a camp atmosphere and an island decor. The air-conditioned cabanas offer small refrigerators and a choice of twin, queen-, or king-size beds, as well as private or shared bathroom facilities. Toward the back of the property are six RVs, complete with kitchens and bathrooms, that have been cleverly disguised with bamboo to look like beach huts. Guests can rent gear or bring their own. Packages include free access to mountain bikes, kayaks, and snorkeling gear. Windsurfing or kiteboarding lessons and scuba diving trips can be arranged for an extra charge. The resort is open year-round, and summer activities focus on sportfishing, diving, and snorkeling. The buildings at Baja Joe's are washed with faded red, making it hard to miss from the paved road near the entrance to town. Just look for the resort's flags that are flapping in the strong winds that put this small town on the map. *$; MC, V; traveler's checks OK; bajajoe@ yahoo.com; www.bajajoe.com; near entrance to town, 5 miles from junction with Mexico 286.*

Captain's Cove / ★★

KM 9 LA VENTANA HWY, LA VENTANA; 310/833-3397 US, FAX 310/833-3781 US The large *palapa*-covered deck at Captain's Cove overlooks the beach and a sea full of colorful windsurf sails and kites. Run by Kitty and Kirk Robinson, owners of a Southern California windsurf shop, this 3-acre resort offers lodging with use of windsurfing and kiteboarding gear. Choose between camping, fully equipped trailers, or one of the four nicely furnished units (with double beds and refrigerators) known as Pelican Reef. Guests also have free use of kayaks, mountain bikes, snorkel gear, and surfboards during their stay. Lessons, sportfishing, and Hobie catamaran tours are available for an extra fee. If the on-site restaurant, Luz de Luna, is not open, you may want transportation into town for meals or groceries. *$$; AE, MC, V; traveler's checks OK; closed May–Oct; ckirks@pacbell.net; www.captainkirks.com; just past La Ventana campground, look for white windsurf board sign by road.*

Ventana Windsurf / ★★★

CALLE DE LA PLAYA, LA VENTANA; 612/163-4632 OR 707/738-1813 US Owner Steve Winiarski spent several winters windsurfing in Baja before starting construction on this small, intimate resort in 1995. Ventana Windsurf is an upscale but cozy place to stay, and the location—on the beach *and* in the heart of the action—makes it a popular destination for wind seekers. The tastefully designed bed-and-breakfast features plenty of windows, exposed wood, and artistic *palapa* roofs, and includes a main lodge where meals are served, three cabanas, and a two-bedroom beach house. Thick, queen-size futons are covered with feather mattresses. Outdoor redwood decks provide space for relaxing in or out of the sun, and an outdoor hot tub beckons after an afternoon of windsurfing. Packages include a healthy breakfast and lunch daily, five dinners a week, and use of windsurf gear. *$$; MC, V; traveler's checks OK; closed July 15–Oct 15; stephen@cask23.com; www.ventana-windsurf.com; look for signs near entrance to town.*

San Juan de Los Planes

Continuing south on Mexico 286 past the turnoff to La Ventana, in 3½ miles you'll reach this small agricultural community, which has one paved road, several *topes* (speed bumps), and a long row of bright streetlights recently installed by the government. The only pay phone in town can be found at **ABARROTES EL CAMINANTE** (612/125-3730), which also carries dried goods, meat, cheese, milk, bakery goods, and fresh produce. Gas is available at the north end of town inside **MISCELÁNEO ALONSO**, where you can buy *magna sin* out of a plastic barrel.

Mexico 286 south of Los Planes is a dirt road that continues another 10 miles to **BAHÍA DE LOS MUERTOS** (Bay of the Dead). To help market a large resort complex/housing development, the historic name was officially changed to **BAHÍA DE LOS SUEÑOS** (Bay of Dreams). The bay is a popular boat launch and snorkeling site, although snorkeling is better a few miles back at **HOTEL LAS ARENAS** (Punta Arena; 888/644-7376; www.lasarenas.com). Go for a day of snorkeling and then stop by the hotel's upstairs bar for a margarita.

THE CAPE REGION

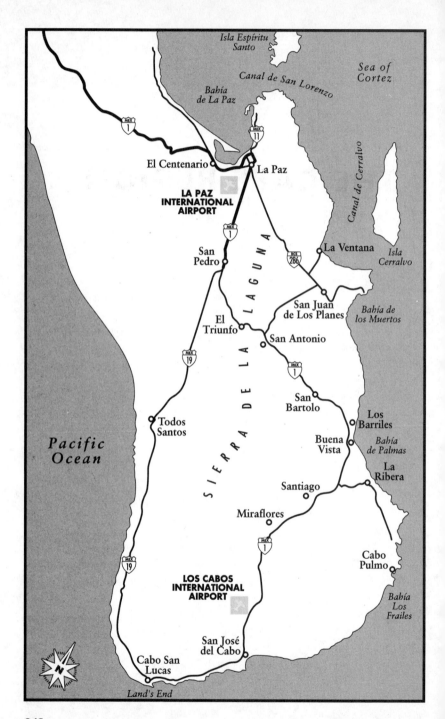

Isla Espíritu
Santo

Sea of
Cortez

Canal de San Lorenzo

Bahía
de La Paz

MEX 1

MEX 11

El Centenario

La Paz

**LA PAZ
INTERNATIONAL
AIRPORT**

Canal de Cerralvo

MEX 1

San
Pedro

La Ventana

BCS 286

Isla
Cerralvo

San Juan
de Los Planes

Bahía de
los Muertos

El
Triunfo

San Antonio

MEX 19

MEX 1

San
Bartolo

Los
Barriles

Todos
Santos

Buena
Vista

Bahía
de Palmas

Pacific
Ocean

La
Ribera

Santiago

Miraflores

MEX 1

MEX 19

Cabo
Pulmo

**LOS CABOS
INTERNATIONAL
AIRPORT**

Bahía
Los
Frailes

San José
del Cabo

Cabo San
Lucas

Land's End

N

THE CAPE REGION

Once remote and relatively inaccessible, Baja's southern tip was long known as Mexico's frontier—attracting only the most rugged outdoor enthusiasts, adventurous off-roaders, and affluent travelers. After John Steinbeck extolled its beauties and bountiful fishing in the '40s, Baja became a magnet for private aircraft travelers seeking the thrill of big game fishing—marlin, sailfish, *dorado, wahoo,* and tuna. Private fishing resorts with adjacent airfields sprang up along the Sea of Cortez to accommodate the sporty Hollywood set—among them, John Wayne, Desi Arnez, and Bing Crosby. In recent years change has been rapid. With increased access by the Carretera Transpeninsular (Mexico 1) and two international airports, droves of newcomers now visit the Cape, where, overall, prices tend to be higher than those found anywhere else on the peninsula.

Dramatically varied terrain, thick vegetation, and the warmest winter climate in Baja distinguish the Cape from regions north. The pine-crested mountains of the Sierra de la Laguna, with their sheer granite escarpments, create the spine of the Cape Region. At higher altitudes, rainfall—up to 40 inches a year—funnels into underground streams, which descend to fertile coastal plains, creating flowering desert valleys. Straddling the Tropic of Cancer, the Cape desert is less arid, supporting tropical plants among its succulents. Couple this with azure seas bordered by sun-drenched beaches, and you have an idyllic setting for resort development, retirement living, and outdoor recreational pursuits.

Today the Cape Region is comprised of several decidedly different areas. Relics of once-booming mining towns litter the northern mountain terrain. On the Sea of Cortez, the East Cape—Los Barriles, Buena Vista, La Ribera, and Cabo Pulmo—possesses rural charm, pristine beaches, and aquatic wonders. Farther south, the Los Cabos area—San José del Cabo, the Corridor, Cabo San Lucas—is a trinity of resorts characterized by upscale development but divided by their individual personalities: colonial San José, alluring with a quiet sophistication; the Corridor, a work-in-progress sprouting one posh resort and golf course after another, each trying to outdo the other in opulence; and Cabo San Lucas, a brash and flashy tourist center, attracting partiers, fishermen, and sunbathers.

On the Pacific side, life remains simple and relatively unchanged for the dozens of small Mexican villages scattered throughout the area. Todos Santos—a gem nestled between the Pacific and the rolling hills of the Sierra de la Lagunas—is an emerging art colony retaining much of its Mexican heritage. The dramatic mountain scenery and long, sandy beaches along the Pacific attract campers and surfers to this peaceful region of the Cape.

ACCESS AND INFORMATION

The **LOS CABOS INTERNATIONAL AIRPORT** is located just 8 miles north of San José del Cabo and 27 miles north of Cabo San Lucas. Eight major airlines currently serve this airport, providing international flights from the United States, as well as service between major Mexican cities. Carriers include Aero California (624/143-3700 or 800/237-6225 US), AeroMéxico (624/146-5089 or 800/237-6639 US), Alaska Airlines (624/146-5106 or 800/426-0333 US), American Airlines (624/146-5304 or 800/433-7300 US), America West (800/235-9292 US), Continental (624/146-5040 or 800/784-4444 US), Delta (800/241-4141 US), and Mexicana (624/142-0230 or 800/531-7921 US).

If transportation has not be prearranged with your hotel, consider taking one of the **COLECTIVOS** (shared vans) operating between the airport, San José del Cabo, and Cabo San Lucas. Drivers for these collective vans are as prevalent as the time-share solicitors lining the airport exit.

Auto Transportes Águila (624/142-1100 San José del Cabo or 624/143-7880 Cabo San Lucas) provides economical, reliable **BUS TRANSPORTATION** the length of the peninsula, or for getting to and from destinations in the greater Cape Region. **SUBUR CABOS** (Mexico 1; 624/146-0883) is a frequent shuttle service operating between a terminal 2 miles north of the airport and Cabo San Lucas, and is your best bet for **LOCAL BUS SERVICE** in this area.

RENTAL CAR agencies operating desks within the airport terminal include: Alamo (624/146-5026), Avis (624/146-0201), Budget (624/146-5333), Dollar (624/146-5060), Hertz (624/146-5988), National (624/146-5022), Payless (624/146-5290), and Thrifty (624/146-5240).

Although most travelers arrive by air, a considerable number choose to **DRIVE** Mexico 1 from the international border to Cabo San Lucas (1,059 miles). Two major highways thread their way through the Cape Region: Mexico 1 and Mexico 19. Mexico 1 traverses the peninsula south of La Paz, paving 134 miles through mountains and along the seacoast to Cabo San Lucas. Mexico 19 covers 78 miles, from its junction with Mexico 1 just 15 miles south of La Paz to Todos Santos, then turning southwest to skirt the Pacific before rejoining Mexico 1 at Cabo San Lucas. These paved conduits form a circuit and put visitors in touch with many of the major attractions. For those seeking the untouched beauty of desert, mountain, and shoreline, there is a network of dirt roads whose conditions vary considerably. Some are graded and easily traveled by a standard car; others can be rugged, deeply rutted, and/or extremely sandy. Keep in mind that the conditions of these roads can change drastically after heavy rains and from year to year.

Don't expect an inexpensive visit to the Cape. Prices tend to run the same or even higher here than prices you'd pay north of the border. On top of that, there's the Mexican government tax of 10 percent (12 percent for lodging; shown as IVA on your bill), plus many establishments add an additional "service tax" or service charge, ranging from 10 to 18 percent. And if that's not enough to squeeze the pesos out of your pocketbook, many establishments also charge 5–6 percent if you use your credit card! A little research will help you determine actual costs as well as prepare you in advance for these soaring charges. And fortunately there are still some bargains to be found, even in Cabo.

There are no government-operated tourist information centers south of La Paz at this time. Concierge services, local shopkeepers, and the free tourist publications—available at area hotels, restaurants, and shops—can provide helpful information. The **U.S. CONSULAR AGENT** in Cabo San Lucas (marina side of Marina Blvd, next to Bital Bank; 624/143-3536) is available to assist U.S. citizens with lost or stolen passports or other emergency situations.

The Cape Region is almost always drenched in sunshine. As a rule, it is generally warmer on the Sea of Cortez side and cooler on the Pacific side. During the winter months, the East Cape, aided by *El Norte* (the north wind), is somewhat cooler than Los Cabos. The most comfortable weather comes between November and May, with highs in the 70s or 80s, dipping into the 50s–60s at night. It's advisable to have a sweater or sweatshirt on hand for the cool winter evenings. Summers heat up considerably and the hurricane season, late July to late October, brings with it high humidity. Rarely over 100°F, the muggy weather can be uncomfortable. During this period the west side, cooled by Pacific breezes, runs 5–10 degrees cooler. The heaviest rains usually fall in September.

El Triunfo, San Antonio, and San Bartolo

Traversing the spine of the Sierra de la Lagunas south of La Paz, Mexico 1 rambles in a series of sharp curves and steep grades as it descends toward the sea. Often, following the late-summer rainy season, this route is reminiscent of Hawaii, as ferns, radiant floral displays, and lush greenery spring up among the rocky cliffs and carpet the valley floors. Fleeting views, captured between the rise and fall of the mountain terrain, expose the distant Sea of Cortez and Isla Cerralvo, one of the largest islands in the gulf. Although the road in this northern sector of the Cape is well traveled, the villages of El Triunfo, San Antonio, and San Bartolo remain relatively untouched by the continuous flow of vacationers on their way to and from more popular seaside resorts.

The area, however, has not always been known for its simplicity and solitude. Silver was unearthed in San Antonio in the mid-1700s, and in the late 1800s gold and silver were unearthed near El Triunfo (the Triumph). A gold rush of sorts occurred, drawing prospectors from as far away as Europe. A network of gold and silver mines tunneled the surrounding mountains, while adobe houses accommodated the growing population. The booming economy lasted until the end of the 19th century, when the ore played out. Both towns were abandoned by 1925, although a few ranchers remain.

Today, remains of a bygone era are found in El Triunfo's crumbling adobe buildings. On Mexico 1 at km 164, pass the pastel-colored **IGLESIA SANTA CRUZ** with its twin bell towers; cross **PUENTE EL TRIUNFO** (a bridge) and take an immediate right (west). This short dirt road leads to the **MINING RUINS** (straight ahead) and the elegant **CASA MUNICIPAL;** its clock tower still is an accurate monitor of time. Inside the courtyard, the deteriorating grand theater stage echoes the magnificence of another period. Community amenities included a post office. Beyond these municipal buildings are remains of the early-day **SMELTERY**. The giant brick chimney and maze of brick channels, where ore was separated from gold by intense heat, were engineering wonders of the time. The smeltering system was of European design, attributed to a group of Scottish technicians who supervised its construction. During your explorations, you will likely run across Mexican children peddling locally **WOVEN REED BASKETS,** and occasionally some of the adobe buildings along the highway are open, displaying handmade products from local *artesanos.*

South of El Truinfo, at km 156 on Mexico 1, San Antonio is now a farming community situated around a lush, fertile valley that drains into the Sea of Cortez. Here, a washboard road connects Mexico 1 with the coast 14 miles east. This dirt road intersects State Highway 286, a paved highway leading to La Paz (15 miles north) and San Juan de los Planes (3½ miles south). This is also the closest route to **BAHÍA DE LOS MUERTOS** (recently renamed Bahía de los Sueños—Bay of Dreams) and **BAHÍA DE LA VENTANA**—popular fishing, camping, and windsurfing destinations (see La Paz in the Mid-South chapter).

Continuing south, Mexico 1 begins its final descent through the mountains toward the Sea of Cortez. Explorers will enjoy **RANCHO VERDE RV HAVEN** (near km 141 Mexico 1; 612/126-9103 or 888/516-9462 US), which offers more than 3,000 acres of secluded wilderness, great for horseback riding and hiking. The next village, **SAN BARTOLO,** is home to a spring-fed water source supporting bountiful crops of citrus, avocados, mangos, papayas, and guavas. Local road-side stands sell fresh fruits and vegetables, along with mango chutney and *dulces* (candy) made from crystallized fruits. Three **SMALL ROADSIDE CAFES** offer Mexican specialties, including empanadas, quesadillas, and tamales. Visit the middle one, **ULT DOÑA TERE** (km 127 Mexico 1), where the pork and beef tamales come highly recommended. San Bartolo is the last mountain village north of the coastal plain at Bahía de Palmas.

Los Barriles and Buena Vista

Ending its mountainous, serpentine journey from the north, Mexico 1 again embraces the seashore midway between La Paz and Cabo San Lucas. Exposed are the turquoise waters of Bahía de Palmas, bordered by Punta Pescadero to the north and Punta Colorada to the south, edged by 20 miles of almost uninterrupted white sand beach. The area is the beginning of the East Cape, known for its fabulous fishing, diving, snorkeling, windsurfing, kayaking, and postcard-perfect beaches.

The twin communities of Los Barriles (the Barrels) and Buena Vista (Good View) are the northern anchors of the East Cape. Here you can still savor the laid-back ambience of a Mexican fishing village, awakening to crowing roosters calling up the sun. Unfenced cows are prone to wander village streets. Mexican children, laughing and joking, parade by on their way to and from school. Several days a week, locals gather around itinerant produce vendors who operate from small stalls or out of their trucks. But the region is rapidly developing. Americans and Canadians are buying land and building homes for vacation, retirement, and exile. This influx of newcomers has brought change and the expansion of local services.

ACCESS AND INFORMATION

Los Barriles is the center of area services, accessed by an unnamed, paved road from Mexico 1 at km 110. Several notable hotels, restaurants, grocery stores—and more recently gift shops, cyber cafes, and a beauty salon—have all taken up residence within the community. Need to check your email? Tap away at **CABONET** (Plaza del Pueblo; 624/141-0387) or **THE OFFICE** (20th de Noviembre; 624/141-0035).

Home of **VISTA SEA SPORT** (see Guides and Outfitters), an ATM (at the Pemex station; km 107, Mexico 1), and several resort hotels (see Lodgings), Buena Vista is the laid-back southern extension of Los Barriles, with boundaries straddling the highway near the Pemex station.

EXPLORING

Just off the highway is the modern **PLAZA DEL PUEBLO,** home to numerous businesses including **THE BAKERY** (624/141-0381), a cafe where locals gather to exchange stories over coffee, breakfast, or lunch (and a great place to order a box lunch for your day at play). **BUZZARD'S BAY SPORTS CANTINA** (624/141-0223) on the plaza's corner is a popular spot for satellite TV, a good hamburger, and karaoke. Also within the plaza are **BAJA BEACH COMPANY** (624/141-0266), with a nice selection of books about Baja, interior accessories, jewelry, T-shirts, and clothing; **A PLACE IN THE SUN** (624/141-0293), featuring home decorating accessories and furniture; and **EAST CAPE TACKLE** (624/141-0366), which caters to the needs of anglers and carries snorkeling gear. Plaza del Pueblo also houses a fitness center and property management office; check the community bulletin board for happenings around town.

Past **SUPER MERCADO CHAPITOS** (624/141-0202) and less than a mile from the highway, the road dead-ends at the paved, white-curbed thoroughfare of this village (20th de Noviembre) and the entrance to **HOTEL PALMAS DE CORTEZ** (see Lodgings), a landmark of the East Cape. Clustered at this intersection are the community health clinic, library, elementary school, and **LA CONCHA**—a small bleachered arena and the scene of celebrations, dances, and soccer games.

The town has many useful services, most located within a mile of Palmas de Cortez. Several eateries, Super Mercado Fayla, Thrifty ice cream, a money exchange, several gift shops, the East Cape Smoke House, an auto parts store, a mechanic, and an Internet cafe occupy the west side of the main drag, while the local *tortillería* and laundromat are found on the east side.

The Sea of Cortez is just one block east of this main road (20th de Noviembre). Arrive on the sandy shores early enough to watch the sun rise and behold the flurry of activity as fishermen congregate to launch their own vessels or catch charter boats from portable docks. If you're not an early riser, get in on the afternoon action (2–3 pm) as the returning boats parade home, colorful flags signaling the species and number of fish in the day's catch. Witness weigh-ins from *palapa* bars at **MARTÍN VERDUGO'S TRAILER PARK** (see below), **HOTEL PLAYA DEL SOL** (Domocilio Conocido; 624/141-0018 or 800/368-4334 US),

HOTEL PALMAS DE CORTEZ (see Lodgings), or **HOTEL RANCHO BUENA VISTA RESORT** (see Restaurants). Due to heavy vehicle traffic during the fishing season (May through October), the central beach lacks the serenity that swimmers and sunbathers seek; look for that in the miles of beach stretching north and south.

The unspoiled beaches in the East Cape attract visiting **CAMPERS AND RV-ERS** seeking shoreline nesting locations—difficult to find elsewhere in the Cape Region because of burgeoning resort development. Such facilities are becoming scarce even here, as many established parks convert to permanent lease agreements. Ever popular **MARTÍN VERDUGO'S TRAILER PARK** (20th de Noviembre, Los Barriles; 624/141-0054) caters to repeat customers, and each year, migrating campers pack in here like sardines. Full hookups, tent sites, a laundry, hot showers, a restaurant, and a *palapa* bar, as well as the recent addition of motel units, are found on the centrally located beachfront grounds. In contrast, **PLAYA NORTE CAMP GROUND** (2 miles north of Los Barriles) offers wide-open spaces and a bit more privacy. Suitable for self-contained units and camping only; there are no hookups, with minimal facilities at this time.

ADVENTURES

ATV ADVENTURES / Pack a cooler, binoculars, snorkeling gear, camera, and plenty of drinking water and rent an ATV from Amigo's Moto Rent (see Guides and Outfitters) for a **POPULAR RIDE** that takes you along the scenic coastline to Punta Pescadero, 9 miles north of Los Barriles. To get there, head left (north) on 20th de Noviembre. Stay on the dirt road hugging the shoreline (Carretera Los Barriles–El Cardonal) rather than veering left onto the paved route climbing into the mountains (a few miles from town). Refrain from speeding through residential areas and stay alert to oncoming traffic, especially on blind curves. This road is also a popular ride among **MOUNTAIN BIKERS** and, although rugged, is doable by passenger cars. This coastal drive offers numerous coves and beaches perfect for **SNORKELING**. Hotel Punta Pescadero (see Lodgings) sits on a rocky promontory overlooking waves crashing against rocks below in a photogenic protected cove—a perfect spot for a picnic lunch and refreshing ocean dip. The rocky shoreline is good for **SNORKELING, DIVING,** and **SPEARFISHING.** When the water is calm, you can **SWIM** through sea caves among colorful fish.

FISHING / From May through October, the East Cape is a **SPORTFISHING** Shangri-la (see the "Baja Hookup" sidebar). There are more boats anchored offshore here than perhaps anywhere in Baja. Charters are readily available through area hotels. Besides the offshore big ones—sailfish, marlin, *wahoo, dorado,* and tuna—casting from shore can be productive for *pargo,* parrotfish, *cabrilla,* grouper, and *sierra* throughout the year. The best source for current fishing action is the **EAST CAPE FISHING REPORT** (www.bajasmokedfish.com. mx), which has details regarding species and number caught, water conditions, and water temperatures. These reports are issued by **THE EAST CAPE SMOKE HOUSE** (20th de Noviembre; 624/141-0294; smokey@balandra.uabcs.mx), located in the heart of Los Barriles. The Smokehouse also does an excellent job

BAJA HOOKUP

The waters around the Cape Region are among the best in the world for fishing. The International Game Fish Association, an organization that tracks world-record catches, reports more deep-sea angling records from this area than any other in the world. Rookies as well as seasoned anglers stand a good chance of hooking a sizable billfish. The most common of these catches is the **STRIPED MARLIN.** Ranging from 125 to 200 pounds, stripers are exciting surface fighters, leaping and tail-walking across the water as they attempt to throw the hook. The less abundant **PACIFIC BLUE MARLIN** is on every angler's wish list. Powerful fighters, blues can top 1,000 pounds.

Although billfish are the most sought after, they aren't in great demand as table fare, and you don't need a huge marlin on the line to put you in the fighting chair. The giant-size **TUNA** found in these waters can be the most difficult to catch. Those over 100 pounds, referred to as *gorillas*, are known to bring many an angler to his knees by sounding to depths where they are hard to retrieve. **DORADO** (also known as mahimahi or dolphin fish) are spectacular to observe and excellent on the grill. They attack your lure with lightning speed, flashing iridescent shades of blue, green, and gold—hence the name *dorado* (Spanish for "golden"). Since *dorado* travel in small pods, double hookups are quite common. Other popular catches include **SAILFISH, WAHOO, YELLOWTAIL, SKIPJACK,** and **ROOSTERFISH.**

Fishing conditions vary from month to month due to changing ocean currents, water temperature, and fish migrations. During winter months (December through April), the fishing is generally better off the Cape at Cabo San Lucas, where Pacific currents bring in warm water. Later in the year (June through October), as the Sea of Cortez heats up and fish migrate north, the East Cape is a more productive area for the big ones. **FLY-FISHING** has also become extremely popular in the Cape Region. Some outfitters cater exclusively to fly-fishermen, and you'll often spot these specialized anglers fishing the shoreline as well as deeper waters in the early morning hours.

For most visitors, booking a trip aboard a guided sportfishing **CHARTER** is the best way to pursue your Baja catch. These boats are adequately equipped with suitable tackle, and charter companies can issue your fishing licenses. Boat captains are locals who know the territory. Advance reservations are well advised during the height of the season, and these can be made directly with sportfishing companies or through most hotels. Fortunately, in recent years an increasing number of outfitters and anglers are dedicated to the **CATCH-AND-RELEASE** philosophy. These marvelous fish are carefully released after the battle, unless they have been badly injured in the fight. If you want a record of your trophy fish, be sure to bring a camera or videocamera.

—Gail MacLaughlin

handling an angler's catch—cleaning, smoking, or freezing, then vacuum packing the fillets and preparing them for air travel. Smoked fish can also be purchased here, and fresh fish is sometimes available.

Increasing in popularity all along the Sea of Cortez is the sport of FLY-FISHING—for the big ones. For information on special fly-fishing packages and local instructional clinics, contact BAJA FLYCASTERS (flystr@teleport.com), BAJA ON THE FLY (bajafly@usa.net), or EAST CAPE TACKLE (Plaza del Pueblo, Los Barriles; 624/141-0366; karen@eastcapetackle.com), which also rents surf rods and carries a large selection of tackle. This is a good place to talk fishing and learn about the best local sites for surfcasting.

HIKING AND MOUNTAIN BIKING / The East Cape is home to numerous trails with stunning panoramic views that explore the surrounding desert. The PEMEX TRAIL, maintained by the friendly folks from Vela Highwind Center (see Guides and Outfitters), is well used by mountain bikers, hikers, and goats in the area. The trail starts off steep and wide and then narrows, making this a challenging single-track ride for experienced mountain bikers. Hikers have more freedom to enjoy panoramic views of the coast and the village below. Either trek up and backtrack down or continue on the 5-mile jaunt, which follows the ridge before dropping back into the *arroyo.* To reach this trail, either park at the Pemex station (south on Mexico 1) or find the small pullout just north of the Pemex. Walk or bike (very loose sand) 5–10 minutes up the *arroyo,* looking north for the huge boulder that marks the trailhead.

Capture a bird's-eye view of Los Barriles and Buena Vista by taking the access road from Mexico 1 between km 105 and 106 to the hilltop MONUMENTO LA BANDERA (Flag Monument). The gigantic, billowing Mexican flag, which is often posted here for holidays and special seasons, can be seen for miles. The 2-km dirt road up to the monument can be traversed by car or mountain bike, and visitors are guaranteed spectacular views of the region. One of the most popular mountain bike rides in the area is the MONUMENT LOOP. At the top of the hill, instead of veering left toward the monument, take the hairpin right turn. This challenging single-track ride follows the ridge for a few miles and ends in a sandy wash, which connects with Mexico 1 again a few miles east.

WINDSURFING AND KITEBOARDING / Los Barriles is extremely popular with windsurfers and more recently kiteboarders, who blow into town each winter to take advantage of *El Norte* (the north wind) as it howls down the Sea of Cortez. Thanks to near perfect side-shore conditions, large rolling swells, and warm water, this town has grown so popular that many "boardheads" have built homes and now stay for the winter, helping fuel the local economy before the spring arrival of the fishing crowd. Winds are typically best November through February, but it's not uncommon to get great conditions in April—depending on the year. Due to the strong winds, shorebreak, and, some years, rocky launches, Los Barriles is recommended for sailors who can already water-start. Popular launches include Playa del Sol Hotel, home of Vela's Highwind Center (see Guides and Outfitters), and Martín Verdugo's Trailer Park (see Exploring) in Los

Barriles and Playa Norte Campground (see Exploring) just north of town. Kiteboarding is probably best north of town and away from the crowds of windsurfers sailing out of Vela; see Guides and Outfitters for more information.

GUIDES AND OUTFITTERS

For ATV touring or snorkeling, **AMIGO'S MOTO RENT** (just east of Plaza del Pueblo, Los Barriles; 624/141-0430) maintains a fleet of **ATVS** available by the hour for $20 US, 3 hours for $50 US, or 4 hours for $60 US. Sign up for their half-day guided **SNORKELING** or mountain tours ($65 US for a single rider; $80 US for doubles) or arrange for a private tour. Amigo's also rents Wave Runners by the half hour for $40 US and hour for $70 US.

Under the direction of Mark and Jennifer Rayor, the first-rate dive operation **VISTA SEA SPORT** (near km 107 Mexico 1, Buena Vista; 624/141-0031; vsea sport@aol.com; www.vistaseasport.com) offers **SCUBA AND SNORKEL TOURS**, equipment rentals, and certification courses. Scuba diving tours range in price from $110 to $140 US. Dive destinations feature the best in the region, including Cabo Pulmo National Marine Reserve, Cabo Los Frailes, Punta Pescadero, Punta Perico, Isla Cerralvo, and Gordo Banks. Their PADI instruction and certification courses meet U.S. standards. Snorkel tours vary in destination and length, with a two-hour tour for $35 US per person, half-day tour for $50 US per person, and three-quarter-day tour for $60 US per person. To find Vista Sea Sport, turn east off the highway directly across from Calafia Restaurant and follow signs.

HOTEL PALMAS DE CORTEZ (20th de Noviembre, Los Barriles; 624/141-0050) maintains the largest **FISHING FLEET** (80 vessels) in the region, operated from their portable seaside docks. A 31-foot cruiser can fish with up to six people and runs $350 US per day; 23- to 25-foot *superpangas* run $220 US a day and can fish with three people. **HOTEL BUENA VISTA BEACH RESORT** (near km 104 Mexico 1, Buena Vista; 624/141-0177) maintains a fleet of 22 boats (cruisers and *superpangas)* and prides itself in releasing more than 700 billfish in 2001. *Superpangas* run $240 US per day and 31-foot cruisers cost $470 US a day. **HOTEL LOS BARRILES** (20th de Noviembre, Los Barriles; 624/141-0024) can book spiffy turbo diesel cruisers, including the 30-foot *Topaz Tournament* cruiser ($450 US a day), 28-foot *California* ($380 US a day), and 23- to 26-foot *superpangas* ($250–$270 US a day). Prices do not include bait, gear, or snacks. Boats leave promptly at 7am and return around 3pm.

LOS BARRILES HIGHWIND CENTER (20th de Noviembre, Los Barriles; www. losbarrileshighwindcenter.com), a small operation owned and operated by Jay Valentine, offers new and used **WINDSURFING** rentals ranging from $40 to $60 US a day. Instruction is available at all levels. **KITEBOARDING** gear is also for rent to experienced kiters. Look for the sail shelter at the beach entrance to Martín Verdugo's Trailer Park.

VELA HIGHWIND CENTER (at Hotel Playa del Sol, Domocilio Conocido, Los Barriles; 800/223-5443 US; info@velawindsurf.com; www.velawindsurf.com)

has been the center of the **WINDSURFING** scene on the East Cape for more than a decade. Based in Northern California, with five resorts in the Caribbean and one in Maui, Vela (Spanish for "sail") offers seven-night packages, which include windsurfing equipment, accommodations, meals, and daily clinics. The hospitable, experienced staff and wide range of alternative activities make this Los Barriles center a great multisport destination. Guests also have free use of kayaks, top-of-the-line mountain bikes, and snorkeling gear; scuba and fishing trips can be arranged for an additional fee. Private windsurfing lessons are available and kiteboarding lessons can also be arranged. Families are encouraged to bring the kids, as reasonably priced child-care is available. Vela also has alternative housing at Hotel Palmas de Cortez (see Lodgings). From Mexico 1, drive into Los Barriles, turn left onto 20th de Noviembre, and follow signs to Vela.

NIGHTLIFE

Local gringos, many of whom rise with the sun, describe 9pm as "Baja Midnight." Accordingly, most of the restaurants and bars are closed by 10pm. An exception is **BUZZARD'S BAY CANTINA** (Plaza del Pueblo, Los Barriles; 624/142-0223), where locals—both Mexican and American—have a rollicking good time with karaoke on Wednesday and Friday. **OTRA VEZ RESTAURANT** (20th de Noviembre, Los Barriles; 624/141-0249) features occasional evenings with live music. If you're in Barriles during the winter season, try to catch an evening with the Needlefish or the Jumping Cholla, two local gringo bands that get together for performances around town. **LA CONCHA** (across from Hotel Palmas de Cortez, Los Barriles) is the site of many weekend Mexican dances with live bands. This entertainment usually gets underway around 10pm and continues into the wee hours of the morning. The crowd is mostly Mexican locals, but outsiders are welcome to join in.

FESTIVALS AND EVENTS

The **PLAYA NORTE BAJA KITEBOARDING CHALLENGE** (carsoncat@hotmail.com) takes place in Los Barriles in mid-January, with proceeds benefiting an eco-project (including garbage awareness and recycling) at the local elementary school. Male and female competitors launch massive jumps and perform extreme aerial maneuvers, thrilling spectators and judges alike.

Once a month February through May, the Asociación de los Artes del Mar de Cortez hosts the popular **LAS CASAS DE LOS ARTES**. These are fund-raising home tours, which showcase five or six different homes a month, afford visitors up-close viewing of area homes featuring interesting architecture, creative interior decor, and private art collections. Check the bulletin boards around Los Barriles for exact dates and where to purchase tickets.

In April, the **BAJA SHAKESPEARE COMPANY** performs four consecutive-night showings of their annual Shakespearean production. These performances are held at the Hotel Palmas de Cortez in Los Barriles, on their large open-air stage overlooking the sea. Most of the actors are East Cape residents. This production is associated with the **EAST CAPE FESTIVAL DE ARTES** (624/141-0381 or 624/141-0265), which attracts a number of local and regional artists and craftsmen, also held at Hotel Palmas de Cortez. For more information visit the East Cape Smoke House (20th de Noviembre; 624/141-0294).

CHUY'S CATCH AND RELEASE TOURNAMENT (800/752-3555; www.hotel buenavista.com) is a popular East Cape fishing contest held the second weekend in October each year, with parties, traditional Mexican dancing, and $10,000 in prizes.

On November 20, Los Barriles celebrates **DÍA DE LA REVOLUCIÓN** (Anniversary of the Mexican Revolution of 1910) with a grand fiesta staged at La Concha (next to Tío Pablo's) with live Mexican entertainment, dances, a children's parade, and a carnival with game booths, an array of food vendors, and rides. Horse races are usually featured during the event—more like sandlot baseball than the real thing—but entertaining to observe.

RESTAURANTS

Baja Cactus / ★

KM 111.5 MEXICO 1, LOS BARRILES; 044-624/147-1820 CELL This simple open-air *palapa* restaurant is a recent newcomer on the scene, making a hit with locals because of its fresh seafood offerings at reasonable prices. Owner/managers José Mayoral and Enedina Gonzalez turn out a tasty *sopa de mariscos*—a hearty seafood soup with clams, shrimp, scallops, fish, lobster, and octopus. Fresh fish, shrimp, and scallops are prepared with a garlic sauce, sautéed with or without garlic, or breaded. Chicken and steaks are available as well as enchiladas and tacos. Entrees come with rice and salad, but can use some accompaniment for a hungry diner. Breakfast includes Mexican omelets, huevos rancheros, hotcakes, and oatmeal. There's no bar, but you are welcome to bring your own beer or wine, and soft drinks are available. *$; Cash only; breakfast, lunch, dinner Tues–Sun (closed Dec); no alcohol; no reservations; east side of highway by large illuminated Pepsi-Cola sign.*

Hotel Rancho Buena Vista Resort / ★★

NEAR KM 5 MEXICO 1, BUENA VISTA; 624/141-0177 This rustic beachside hotel set amid subtropical plantings has been ill kept, but the restaurant still exudes charm. It's one of the area's great places to go for dinner. Reserve a table in advance and take part in the family-style dinners prepared for guests. The menu varies each night, but a favorite among locals is Thursday carne asada night featuring this popular Mexican grilled beef served with sides of enchiladas, refried beans, salad, guacamole, rice, and salsas. Meals are all-you-can-eat, served from banquet tables set either indoors or poolside during balmy weather. Other dinners to consider are the Wednesday and Saturday Mexican buffets; save Sunday for fried chicken, mashed potatoes, and gravy if you've got the craving. Enjoy wonderful views, great meals, and reasonable prices. *$$; Cash only; breakfast, dinner every day; full bar; reservations required; opposite turnoff to Monumento Bandera, look for sign indicating "Hotel."*

Lonchería Tía Licha / ★★

BETWEEN KM 104–105 MEXICO 1, BUENA VISTA This favorite Mexican kitchen offers foods prepared to order. Breakfasts feature huevos rancheros, *huevos mexicana,* or your favorite style eggs with crisp bacon, accompanied by potatoes or frijoles and fresh, sweet orange juice. You can even order biscuits and gravy with your bacon and eggs. For lunch try the excellent green chile enchiladas or the chiles rellenos—the best in town. Other Mexican specialties include burritos, tacos, and a delicious barbecue-beef *torta* (sandwich) with cheese and jalapeños. Watch Tía Licha prepare your order in the kitchen while you wait. Indoor and outdoor seating is available and the service is friendly. *$; Cash only; breakfast, lunch Tues–Sun; no alcohol; no reservations; take turnoff to Spa Buena Vista, marked by signs to Hotel Buena Vista Beach Resort; restaurant is on left side of dirt road just before topes (speed bumps).*

Otra Vez Restaurante / ★★★

20TH DE NOVIEMBRE, LOS BARRILES; 624/141-0249 A colorful entrance arch welcomes customers to this popular American-owned *palapa* restaurant. Patrick and Linda Lambrecht, originally from San Diego, opened the casual eatery in 1995. The menu here is eclectic, with an emphasis on Thai recipes and fresh seafood. Choose the shrimp in mango with a fresh ginger sauce served over jasmine rice, or Chicken Under the Influence—presented with fresh broccoli, garlic, and capers, flash grilled, then sautéed with a light tequila cilantro sauce. Vegetarians will find a number of pasta choices and salads, while meat-eaters can choose from barbecue baby-back ribs, steaks, hamburgers, or the prime rib special. Grilled tuna is cooked to order and all fish specials are served with hefty portions of steamed veggies and pasta. Order a glass of Baja California wine to accompany your garlic bread, which is served with a zingy tomato, basil, garlic, and balsamic salsa. Or, top off your meal with an espresso. Breakfasts feature eggs dishes, omelets, or fancier options such as Lobster New Orleans. Service is helpful and prompt and the overall atmosphere is lively and delightful. *$$; MC, V; traveler's checks OK; breakfast, lunch, dinner every day (closed Aug–Sept); full bar; no reservations; otravez2000@prodigy.net.mx; just north of central Los Barriles.*

Taquería La Palma

1 BLOCK WEST OF TÍO PABLO'S, LOS BARRILES Family operated, this Mexican eatery serves up *grande burros* (super-size burritos), meal-sized *papas rellenos* (stuffed potatoes), and traditional tacos, all cradling succulent shrimp, chicken, beef, or pork fillings. An array of fresh condiments—pickled and plain onion, shredded cabbage, tomato, avocado, chiles, and salsas—accompanies orders. Try their tomatillo salsa—green, not hot, but very flavorful. Soft drinks are the only beverages served, but you are welcome to bring your own beer or wine. *$; Cash only; dinner Thurs–Tues; no alcohol; no reservations; behind Tío Pablo's.*

Taquería Los Barriles

ROAD INTO TOWN, LOS BARRILES Locals call this Silvia's and it's *the* place to see who's in town. The attraction is great tacos—fish, shrimp, chicken, beef, and pork—with a nice selection of fresh condiments and salsas inviting you to build your own magnificent creation. Fish and shrimp tacos can be ordered *a la plancha* (grilled) if you don't want them deep-fried. Other rave items include Sylvia's famous breakfast burritos and her Mexican beans. The awning-covered sidewalk eatery is good, cheap, and extremely popular. *$; Cash only; breakfast, lunch, dinner Wed–Mon; no alcohol; no reservations; near end of entrance road leading into town, across from elementary school.*

Tío Pablo's Bar and Grill / ★★

20TH DE NOVIEMBRE, LOS BARRILES; 624/141-0330 Legendary in Los Barriles, Tío's came into being with the 1991 arrival of Paul Gilbert, a crazy American who established a small "hot dog" stand, which grew and grew and grew. Today Tío's is the mainstay of American dining in the area, occupying an entire corner in the heart of Los Barriles. The huge white stucco building, canopied with a soaring *palapa*, is home to the Scorpion Bar and indoor/outdoor dining areas. It's a busy place—sports bar, watering hole, and restaurant—with a broad menu. Here Norte Americanos can get a pizza fix, visit a salad bar, bite into a scrumptious hamburger, or enjoy heaping helpings of familiar (but Americanized) Mexican dishes. Big eaters will want to consider Tío's belt buster steak (16 ounces of T-bone), and the varied menu has something for everyone—including vegetarians. If you've got room, order a hot fudge sundae for dessert. *$$; MC, V; traveler's checks OK; lunch, dinner every day; full bar; no reservations; across from Baja Properties.*

LODGINGS

Hotel Buena Vista Beach Resort / ★★

BETWEEN KM 104–105 MEXICO 1, BUENA VISTA; 624/141-0033 OR 800/752-3555 US This spacious resort sits among landscaped terraces descending to an expansive white sand beach. Mediterranean-style bungalows, each with its own private patio, lie off winding pathways. The resort's 60 rooms are spacious and simple, with no phone or TV distractions and a choice of either one king or two queen-size beds. Subtropical plants, stone walls, and arched bridges complement the property. Facilities include two swimming pools and two hot tubs fed by mineral hot springs that flow beneath the grounds. The larger main pool features a swim-up bar, an adjoining children's pool, and a volleyball pool. A formal indoor restaurant and sea view terrace accommodate diners. Tennis courts are located on the grounds, and arrangements can be made for horseback riding, scuba diving, snorkeling, and fishing—the big attraction. A number of marlin tournaments are headquartered here, all stressing catch-and-release policies, and the hotel maintains its own fleet of fishing boats (see Guides and Outfitters). Guests can choose between standard room rates or the American plan, which includes all meals. *$$$; MC, V; traveler's checks OK; info@hotelbuena vista.com; www.hotelbuenavista.com; look for sign on highway.*

Hotel Los Barriles / ★★

20TH DE NOVIEMBRE, LOS BARRILES; 624/141-0024 This handsome, hospitable hotel is centrally located; just a short walk from restaurants and the beach. The two-story, tile-roofed building surrounds a free-form swimming pool in a landscaped inner court setting with an inviting *palapa* bar. Twenty modern guest rooms are well appointed with rustic Mexican wood furnishings and carved headboards over two queen-size beds. Each room has its own phone, a quiet, remote-controlled air-conditioning unit, and bathrooms with hand-painted sinks and Mexican tile. Immaculately clean and comfortable, rooms here have to be one of the best buys in the Cape Region. The hotel provides fishermen with charter arrangements on a fleet of turbo diesel boats, operated by experienced Mexican captains who know the area (see Guides and Outfitters). *$; MC, V; traveler's checks OK; relax@losbarrileshotel. com; www.losbarrileshotel.com; on west side of street in the heart of town.*

Hotel Palmas de Cortez / ★★

20TH DE NOVIEMBRE, LOS BARRILES; 624/141-0050 OR 800/368-4334 US The grande dame of resorts in the Los Barriles/Buena Vista area, Palmas de Cortez dates back to 1958. Major expansion and renovation have kept this resort at the head of the class. A variety of palms and other mature trees, an aviary, and subtropical gardens occupy several acres fronting the Sea of Cortez's wide, flat beach in the heart of Los Barriles. The two-story beachfront buildings, highlighted with native stone, house 50 rooms, all with balconies or terraces affording stunning views. The 118-foot seaside infinity-edged swimming pool, guarded by a King Neptune statue, is impressive, especially when illuminated at night. The expanded *palapa* bar now seats 150, and the terrace has a dramatic new stage as a focal point and venue for live stage productions and musicians. The resort also has two new pools, tennis courts, two restaurants, two bars, three computers with internet access, and a children's play area. Enjoying a long-standing reputation as an excellent fishing resort, Palmas boasts the largest fishing fleet in the area (see Guides and Outfitters). Meals are included in room rates. *$$$; MC, V; traveler's checks OK; eastcape@pacbell.net; www.bajaresorts.com; from Mexico l, turn off at km 110, Los Barriles, and drive straight ahead to hotel entrance.*

Hotel Punta Pescadero / ★★

CARR LOS BARRILES–EL CARDONAL, 9 MILES NORTH OF LOS BARRILES; 624/141-0101 OR 800/426-2252 US, FAX 612/126-1771 Perched on a 125-acre bluff overlooking the Sea of Cortez, Hotel Punta Pescadero is remote, secluded, and popular among honeymooners. The views of the southern mountains and craggy shoreline are hard to beat. A 3,500-foot paved airstrip accommodates pilots who've been escaping to this special hideaway for decades. A series of low-profile, sand-colored buildings house 21 rooms, each with its own private terrace. Amenities include air conditioning, satellite TV, refrigerators, and attractive Mexican furnishings—but no phone. The larger units, with a separate living area, feature stone fireplaces. The landscaped grounds host a view terrace with a small swimming pool, adjacent bar, restaurant, and lighted tennis courts. At the terrace bar, sip a cold *cerveza* with lime or order one of their bracing margaritas, accompanied by an order of guacamole, chips, and salsa. The friendly staff can easily arrange snorkeling, scuba diving, fishing excursions, and trips to nearby cave paintings. Room rates include set-menu meals. The washboard, dirt access road is rather tortuous— but fortunately the hotel arranges for land taxis to and from nearby airports at La Paz and Los Cabos. *$$$; MC, V; traveler's checks OK; puntapes@prodigy. net.mx; www.punta-pescadero.com; 9 miles north of town on dirt road following the coast.*

Rancho Leonero Resort / ★★

NEAR KM 102 MEXICO 1, RANCHO LEONERO; 624/141-0216 OR 800-646-2252 US, FAX 624/126-1771 Inviting flagstone bungalows with palm-thatched roofs overlook the Sea of Cortez and 2 miles of nearly unoccupied pristine beach. This small, intimate resort with 35 rooms, a pool, tennis court, gym, and spacious landscaped grounds can make for a charming, out-of-the-way vacation retreat. The rustic seaside dining room, bar, and terrace are warm and inviting. Dining here is family-style, with meals included in the rate. Relax poolside, enjoy the beach, or set to sea aboard one of the boats in the hotel's successful fishing fleet. The hotel staff will also arrange diving, snorkeling, windsurfing, kayaking, and hiking activities for guests. *$$$; AE, MC, V; traveler's checks OK; www.rancho leonero.com; 4 miles south of Los Barriles, from highway follow graded dirt road with directional signing 5 miles to hotel.*

VACATION RENTALS

Many part-time or full-time residents of the East Cape rent their beachfront or neighborhood homes when they are away. Custom built, these charming rentals are great for families or groups and usually come fully equipped. For information and bookings, contact **EAST CAPE PROPERTY MANAGEMENT** (Plaza del Pueblo 14, Los Barriles; 624/141-0381; julie@abajavacation.com) or **SUNSET VACATION RENTALS** (624/141-0416 or 800/790-4321 US; www.eastcape rentals.com). An affordable option for families are the tile-roofed, flagstone bungalows at **QUINTA MARÍA** (Carretera Los Barriles–El Cardonal, 3½ miles north of town; 612/126-0821), where there's no extra charge for children.

La Ribera, Cabo Pulmo, and Bahía de los Frailes

The small Mexican community of La Ribera is surrounded by rich farmland and spawning real estate developments. Hotel Punta Colorada, south of La Ribera, has an isolated shoreline and stunning views (see Lodgings). Cabo Pulmo National Marine Park, one of the most popular Cape destinations for underwater adventures, is just down the road, as is the wind-sheltered Bahía de los Frailes, where fishing, snorkeling, boating, and beachcombing opportunities abound.

Corral de los Frailes, the rocky point named for its resemblance to hooded friars, juts seaward, forming the southern boundary of Cabo Pulmo and the easternmost point on the Baja peninsula. Just south of this point lies Bahía de los Frailes, the wind-sheltered bay protected by the towering promontory. During the windy season (December through March), this bay is a haven for cruising boats awaiting a calm day to continue their voyage. It's also a favorite with beach campers. Nestled here is Hotel Bahía de los Frailes, and above the bay there's a growing community of resort homes, with bird's-eye views of the sea.

El Camino Rural Costero (the Rural Coastal Road) is the rough route that connects La Ribera with San José del Cabo. Continuing south from Bahía de los Frailes, the road deteriorates rapidly and is best left to adventurous travelers with high-clearance four-wheel-drive vehicles who want to experience the untouched drama of the Baja coastline. A few small ranchos, little-known surf breaks, and some remote homes are found along the way. La Ribera has a Pemex station, numerous markets, a *tortillería, ferretería* (hardware store), pharmacy, and a few small restaurants.

ACCESS AND INFORMATION

The best access to these beach communities is from Mexico 1 near km 93, on a partially paved road that heads east to reach La Ribera in 7 miles. The Rural Coastal Road begins south of town as a washboard secondary road and gradually deteriorates into a raw, gnarly track with sand pits, oil-pan-grabbing rocks, and washouts. Someday this coastal route, which hugs the shoreline for 49 miles, will be paved (the northern 11 miles have paved portions), but today the region is still somewhat remote. Connecting with Mexico 1 at both ends, this route forms what is known as the **EAST CAPE LOOP**. The entire loop is not recommended for two-wheel-drive vehicles, but the paved northern section near La Ribera and Cabo Pulmo is suitable for passenger cars, providing access to some of Baja's prime destinations. The southern access is either through San José del Cabo via the beach at La Playita or just north of San José via the road leading to the small settlement of Palo Escopeta.

In 2001, hurricane Juliette washed out portions of the pavement leading to Cabo Pulmo, but dirt road repairs remain suitable for passenger cars. Keep in mind that heavy rains can greatly alter roads and highways in Baja, particularly during hurricane season—late July through October. Always check road conditions with locals before setting out.

ADVENTURES

CABO PULMO NATIONAL MARINE PARK / Just 5 miles from the end of the paved portion of the coast road lies the popular and worthwhile destination Cabo Pulmo—a shallow bay, harboring 5 miles of secluded white-sand beaches. Fishing and anchoring are prohibited within the bay, which has been designated by the Mexican government as Cabo Pulmo National Marine Park to protect this delicate habitat from commercial intrusions and destruction. The bay is home to the Cabo Pulmo Reef, Baja's only full-scale coral reef. Eight hard coral fingers, varying widely in depth, comprise this sizable reef, teeming with sub-tropical sea life. Rent a **KAYAK** and paddle among leaping manta rays and playful dolphins. Arrange a **SIGHTSEEING** excursion, or take a trip to Corral de los Frailes, home to a colony of sea lions. Playa La Sirenta (Mermaid Beach) is one of the most picturesque beaches in the area. Its name is derived from the giant rock formation that protects the cove and resembles the head and bust of a female. This beach, with great **SNORKELING** among nearby rocky reefs, is best reached by boat. (See Guides and Outfitters for details.) In the summer and fall, underwater visibility often exceeds 100 feet, making Cabo Pulmo an under-water paradise for novice **DIVERS,** as well as divers with more experience under their weight-belts. The inner coral heads close to shore provide easy access to snorkeling.

FISHING / North of Cabo Pulmo, outside the protected reserve of the national park, giant sea bass, snapper, *pargo,* ladyfish, and roosterfish are just a few of the sporty catches that can be fished from the shoreline. Larger game fish, such as *dorado,* tuna, and marlin, are the target just offshore. Fishing expe-ditions are easily arranged through diving operations or local fishermen. (See Guides and Outfitters.)

WINDSURFING / La Ribera, Cabo Pulmo, and Punta Colorada can all offer some of the better wavesailing conditions on the Sea of Cortez. When the winds fill in and the swell is big (usually November through March), La Ribera has playable waves. The breaks at both Cabo Pulmo and Punta Colorada can reach the 10- to 12-foot range and are excellent for experienced wave sailors.

GUIDES AND OUTFITTERS

Cabo Pulmo is home to three dive operators: **PEPE'S DIVE CENTER** (El Camino Rural Costero; 624/141-0001 or 877/733-2252 US), **CABO PULMO DIVERS** (on the beach; cabopulmodivers@yahoo.com), and **CABO PULMO BEACH RESORT** (El Camino Rural Costero; 624/141-0244; www.caboworld.com). All offer complete diving services, including knowledgeable dive masters, equipment and wet suit rentals, dive *pangas,* tank refills, guided tours, night diving, and PADI-approved scuba certification courses. They also rent kayaks and snorkeling equipment, and can arrange for sightseeing excursions on the bay or fishing trips outside the marine reserve. Cabo Pulmo Beach Resort offers a snorkeling tour for $35 US, rents kayaks by the day or hour, and provides transportation for those who arrange to paddle down the coast.

RESTAURANTS

Nancy's Restaurant and Bar / ★★

I BLOCK EAST OF EL CAMINO RURAL COSTERO, CABO PULMO Nancy arrived in Cabo Pulmo in the early '90s for the birth of her first granddaughter, now 10 years old. Deciding to make this her permanent home, she opened a small eatery and began to share her culinary talents. Today her little place has evolved into an artistic creation. Thick rock walls and arches frame garden views. Filigree ironwork accents this open *palapa* with Saltillo tile flooring—charming but not fancy. Try the seared fresh tuna served with wasabi sauce or the melt-in-your mouth crab cakes. There are scallops in orange sauce, lobster enchiladas, and a variety of shrimp dishes—with pasta, in garlic sauce, or in tacos. Nancy constantly experiments, much to the delight of her customers. This quaint little restaurant is tucked away off the main road. *$; Cash only; lunch, dinner every day; full bar; no reservations; look for unassuming, hand-lettered sign "Nancy's Restaurant" with arrow.*

Vianey Restaurante Bar / ★★

EL CAMINO RURAL COSTERO, LA RIBERA; 044-624/140-5271 CELL This rustic and charming *palapa* restaurant, on the south edge of town near the water tower, is well known by locals for superbly prepared seafood, steaks, poultry dishes, and Mexican specialties. Silvestre and Martina, the proprietors, take special pride in preparing each dish to order, so don't be in a hurry. Salsa, salad, and vegetable fixings are fresh from the fields, and the bread is baked from scratch. For lunch, choose scrumptious fish or shrimp tacos served with a fresh, lightly dressed avocado and tomato salad. At dinner, the chef's fish specialty is hard to beat, featuring the catch-of-the-day, usually prepared with a hint of horseradish. The steaks here are superb, a rarity in smaller Mexican restaurants. Margaritas are Mexican, not gringo. Olé! *$; Cash only; lunch, dinner every day; full bar; no reservations; from La Ribera junction, take El Camino Rural Costero ¾ mile to dirt road turnoff at restaurant sign just before crest of hill, then travel toward water tower and look for restaurant on left.*

LODGINGS

Cabo Pulmo Beach Resort / ★★

EL CAMINO RURAL COSTERO, CABO PULMO; 624/141-0244 PHONE AND FAX A cluster of palm-roofed *casitas* amid subtropical plantings, and just steps away from the beach, are available to overnighters or for extended stays. Accommodations vary, with larger units providing full kitchens, living room setups with separate bedrooms, patios, and view terraces with barbecue facilities. Studiolike accommodations come with kitchenettes, living-sleeping quarters in one room, and smaller patios. Lush ficus trees, a colorful profusion of bougainvillea, and bird-of-paradise plants adorn interior walled gardens, assuring privacy from neighboring facilities. Units are handsomely decorated with Mexican wood furnishings and tiled floors and countertops, and have fully equipped kitchens. Extra beds for children can be arranged. The resort, a center for diving operations, also provides kayaking, tennis, fishing, hiking, and rock climbing excursions. *$–$$; AE, MC, V; traveler's checks OK; pulmo@caboworld.com; www.caboworld.com; look for signs on Rural Coastal Rd.*

Hotel Bahía Los Frailes / ★★

EL CAMINO RURAL COSTERO, BAHÍA DE LOS FRAILES; 624/141-0122 OR 800/934-0295 US, FAX 624/142-3578 This intimate, secluded resort has long been a popular stopover for small, private aircraft seeking the Baja experience of quiet seaside relaxation with close proximity to prime fishing. The hotel's graded runway is nearby, and private planes still land here. However, with today's access via the graded road, many guests now arrive by car. Each room, with its own terrace, is situated beachside near the crystal-clear waters of the bay. Rooms have their own artistic decor, with handsomely tiled floors and baths, high-vaulted *palapa* roofs, tasteful rattan furnishings, beautiful mahogany interior doors, and sliding French-style glass doors. There are eight units available, including standard rooms (with two queen beds) and suites (with an additional separate living area). All meals are provided, served in a small but comfortable dining room with an adjacent terrace overlooking the beach and landscaped grounds. Fishing trips can be arranged through the hotel staff. *$$$$; AE, DIS, MC, V; traveler's checks OK; losfrailes@compuserve.com; 5 miles beyond Cabo Pulmo.*

Hotel Punta Colorada / ★★

ACCESS RD, LA RIBERA; 624/121-0044, 800/368-4334, OR 818/222-5066 US Established in the '60s, Hotel Punta Colorada has a well-earned reputation among anglers—location, location, location! Occupying a solitary position, the resort rests on a sandy point just north of the Pulmo Shoals—possibly *the* best fishing in the Sea of Cortez. Harboring a fleet of 28- to 32-foot cruisers and *superpangas,* the Mexican captains know the territory—and the fish. Thrill to the hookup of *dorado,* tuna, roosterfish, *wahoo,* or marlin. Catch and release, or have the chef prepare your catch for dinner. The low-profile buildings, amid lush subtropical landscaping, are perched above a vast white sand beach ideal for swimming, snorkeling, or casting a line from shore. When it's windy, this can be an excellent wavesailing location. Enjoy the laid-back atmosphere, with simple but comfortable rooms, a seaside terrace, a bar, and a dining room. All meals are included in the room rate. A nearby 3,200-foot, hard-packed airstrip is maintained for fly-ins. *$$; No credit cards; traveler's checks OK; www.bajaresorts.com; from junction in La Ribera, go 5 miles south and look for signs, then take 3-mile access road.*

Santiago and Miraflores

South of the turnoff to La Ribera, Mexico 1 continues on an inland route south for nearly 30 miles through the Central Cape on its way to Los Cabos. This stretch of highway, hilly but not mountainous, traverses the desert plain, occasionally dipping into huge *arroyos*. Smaller, more remote Mexican communities dot the landscape.

Santiago, the first village south of Buena Vista, is the largest of these Central Cape towns. A paved road heading west from Mexico 1 connects Santiago and the surrounding agricultural area. Fruit trees—avocado, citrus, papaya, and mango—are abundant. Many of the Cape Region restaurants obtain their fresh vegetables and herbs from organic gardens located here. The main crop, however, is palm fronds, harvested from fan palms for use in the popular *palapa* roof construction.

Just 2 miles south of the Santiago turnoff from Mexico 1, you'll enter the tropics as you cross the Tropic of Cancer. The demarcation is identified by a large white ball placed precisely on the 23.27 North Latitude parallel. Six miles beyond this marker is Miraflores, another quiet Mexican village.

South of the Miraflores turnoff, it's less than 20 miles to the Los Cabos International Airport (see Access and Information at the beginning of this chapter), the gateway to Los Cabos. Quiet, rural countryside is suddenly transformed as the highway widens into a divided four-lane thoroughfare jammed with airport taxis, buses, and private vehicles racing to their destinations. Billboards in English tout Cabo nightclubs, resort hotels, time-share condos, tequila labels, and pari-mutuel betting at Caliente Race and Sports Book. San José del Cabo, the Corridor, and Cabo San Lucas lie ahead on this 25-mile stretch of road leading to Land's End, the tip of the Baja Peninsula.

ACCESS AND INFORMATION

Reach Santiago from Mexico 1 at km 85; as you turn west off the highway you'll cross Arroyo de Santiago, the huge *arroyo* that skirts the village. The road is then divided by a cement median and becomes a one-way route leading to the quiet town plaza. Several small **TIENDAS** (stores), a Pemex station, and the police station border the plaza as well as **TÍO'S** (plaza; 624/130-2100), a good place for a quick burger or taco.

Miraflores can be reached via paved road heading west from Mexico 1 near km 71 at the Pemex station. The small village is clustered around the plaza.

EXPLORING

From Santiago's plaza, keep to the right as the paved road heads down the hill, passing the Palomar Restaurant (see Restaurants) on the left and a series of schools, including the only high school between La Paz and San José del Cabo. The Catholic Church holds its position at the T intersection. Turn right and follow the paved road and the signs picturing an elephant. Still looking for that elephant, you will find **PARQUE ZOOLÓGICO**—one of only three zoos in Baja.

(The other zoos are in Mexicali and Tijuana.) The landscaped grounds house a small collection of animals in small cages, including Leo the lion, a tiger, a monkey, a bear, a fox, and several varieties of birds and reptiles—many indigenous. No—you won't find that elephant, but you're likely to encounter groups of uniformed schoolchildren on a field trip. Admission is free, but donations will help improve conditions here one day.

Visitors to Miraflores often stop by **CURTIDURÍA MIRAFLORES,** a tannery that produces handmade saddles, bridles, and other equestrian gear, leather purses, and belts. Don't expect a spiffy retail leather outlet. This is a working hide tannery, and often items are made to order rather than available on the spot. The tannery is located on the hill to the left just before entering the village; look for the small sign "Leather Shop."

ADVENTURES

HIKING / For an adventurous day-trip, explore the scenic canyon above the hot spring near the tiny settlement of **AGUA CALIENTE** (Hot Water), located on the maze of dirt roads between Santiago and Miraflores. The hot spring has been captured in a primitive concrete tub for bathers and is not very inviting, but the scramble up the canyon beyond the hot spring is a fun adventure. It eventually leads to sheer granite cliffs and a series of refreshing pools—some with waterfalls. Camping is allowed in the area, but there are no facilities. To get there from Santiago, continue past the zoo. Stay on the well-traveled dirt track, continuing for about 9 miles. If you think you're lost, ask a local resident "Agua Caliente?" They will usually point you in the right direction.

Access to the interior of the **SIERRA DE LA LAGUNA** allows for excellent backpacking opportunities in this region, but guides are necessary as the routes are easily confused with livestock trails; see Guides and Outfitters in the San José del Cabo section for more information.

FESTIVALS AND EVENTS

Observing the day of the town's patron saint, the **SANTIAGO FESTIVAL** is staged for several days around July 25. The entire area turns out for music, dancing, cockfights, and horse races. Typically the plaza is the scene of carnival games, food vendors, and thrill rides.

RESTAURANTS

Palomar Restaurant and Bar / ★★

CALZADA MISIONEROS, SANTIAGO; 624/130-2126 OR 624/130-2019 The Palomar is a longtime favorite, dating back to the '50s when the likes of John Wayne and Bing Crosby fished, explored, and (it's said) dined here often. Mexican charm is a tradition at the Palomar, with dining on two levels: the upper covered terrace and the tree-shaded garden courtyard below. The furnishings and environment remain simple. The food has quality. Seafood is a specialty—the freshest available from Cape Region fishermen. Their *filete de pescado al mojo de ajo* (fish cooked with garlic sauce) is a standout. Catch of

263

the day comes grilled, breaded, *a la veracruzana* (with onions, peppers, and olives in tomato sauce), sautéed with shrimp, and with garlic or cilantro sauce. Try the *camarónes* (shrimp) in a spicy *mexicana* sauce. Meal accompaniments include fresh vegetables al dente and a tasty soup of the day. Mexican specialties—enchiladas, tostadas, chiles rellenos, *carne asada*—are also available. A number of Americans come here for their excellent pork chops, not a standard on Mexican menus. For dessert, treat yourself to their superb *flan de la casa.* *$–$$; No credit cards; traveler's checks OK; lunch every day, dinner Mon–Sat; full bar; no reservations; palomarsergio66@hotmail.com; on one-way paved road circling plaza, continue downhill and look on the left for a sign.*

San José del Cabo

Although its history is fraught with strife—raiding pirates, Indians resisting missionaries, occupation by military garrisons—San José del Cabo has retained the safe harbor attractiveness of its youth. Spanish galleons first visited Estero San José at the mouth of Río San José in the late 17th and early 18th centuries. Near the end of their lengthy voyages, plying the seas from the Philippines to Acapulco, they sought refuge here to refresh themselves and take on a fresh water supply.

Circumstances in the late 1970s changed San José's fate. The government opened Mexico 1 traversing the peninsula and established an international airport 8 miles away, and the Mexican National Foundation for Tourist Development (FONATUR) assisted several tourist developmental projects along 4,000 acres of San José's shoreline. This Zona Hotelera is now home to five beachfront resorts, as well as condos, elaborate homes, and a golf course.

But the colonial core is still evident in the adobe and brick buildings surrounding Plaza Mijares and 18th-century Iglesia San José. Fortunately, local residents have taken great pride in restoring the 100-year-old colonial architecture and preserving the laid-back ambience of this stylish seaside resort. Today visitors still refresh themselves in San José del Cabo.

ACCESS AND INFORMATION

San José del Cabo is 8 miles south of **LOS CABOS INTERNATIONAL AIRPORT** (see Access and Information at the beginning of this chapter), 21 miles northeast of the southern terminus of Mexico 1 at Cabo San Lucas, 115 miles south of La Paz, and 1,038 miles south of the U.S. border by car.

Between the airport and town, there's a long string of stoplights, which test your nerves as drivers bend most of the traffic laws. From Mexico 1, to access the **CENTRAL PLAZA** and the heart of San José **FROM THE NORTH,** turn left on "the down street," the one-way Calle Zaragoza (at the Y-intersection just past the second Pemex station) and left on Calle Morelos; look for parking. **FROM THE SOUTH,** turn right on Paseo San José or Valerio González and then left on Boulevard Mijares. To get back to the highway, take "the up street," Manuel Dobado. One-way streets, stalled traffic, and tight parking spaces—usually filled—are almost the rule during the busy tourist season. Park where you can and explore on foot.

TAXIS congregate at the beach hotels along Zona Hotelera (Paseo San José), and along Boulevard Mijares in the central section. **AUTOTRANSPORTES ÁGUILA** offers daily service throughout the region from the central **BUS STATION** (Valerio González; 624/142-1100).

Other services in town include a plethora of eateries, a handful of backpacker hotels, numerous banks with ATMs, a hospital, dental clinics, welders, mechanics, hardware and grocery stores, and several Pemex stations. Although there is no longer a tourist office in town, the residents are friendly and helpful.

Need to check your email? **TRAZZO DIGITAL** (Calle Zaragoza 24; 624/142-1220) is conveniently located across from the church and charges 25 pesos for 30 minutes. Or try **@ÑUITI CLUB INTERNET** (Valerio Gonzáles; 624/142-6535); offering a variety of business services, they have eight computers and the best Internet rates in town (30 pesos an hour).

EXPLORING

San José up close is a walking expedition, and the best place to start is in the **OLD TOWN** district at **PLAZA MIJARES**. As is true with most colonial Mexican towns, the plaza is the staging area for fiestas and celebrations as well as a popular gathering site. This one is particularly charming with its fanciful gazebo, stone paving, and attractive benches, surrounded by tropical plants and shaded by a variety of mature native trees. The plaza is situated at the intersection of Old Town San José's two main streets, Boulevard Mijares and Calle Zaragoza, and flanked on the west side by **IGLESIA SAN JOSÉ**. Although built in 1940, the existing church is positioned on the 1730 site of Misión San José del Cabo. Above the main entrance of today's twin-tower structure is a mosaic-tile mural depicting the slaying of the parish priest during the 1734 Indian uprising. The town's **CULTURAL CENTER** fronts the plaza on the north edge. Just a block away is **PALACIO MUNICIPAL,** an impressive structure built in 1927, with its prominent clock tower and interior patio. Used today primarily as office space, occasionally the building houses exhibits featuring local artists.

From the town plaza, the fingers of narrow side streets fan out, bordered by a number of restored adobe brick structures, which date back to the 1800s. Arched building entrances, revealing tree-shrouded, interior courtyard restaurants or shops, are not unusual. San José's main street, **BOULEVARD MIJARES,** is a broad avenue canopied by a tree-shaded median. Take a break, sip an ice-cold *cerveza* or a refreshing margarita at Tropicana's popular shaded sidewalk cafe (see Restaurants), and observe the pedestrian parade.

Whether it's an afternoon pick-me-up or a dessert in its own right, be sure to try one of the tasty frozen fruit or ice cream *paletas* at **LA MICHOACANA PALETERÍA Y NEVERÍA** (Calle Morelos), or try **BING HELADOS** (Blvd Mijares 28; 624/142-1085). If you prefer baked goods, a fresh-baked cheese or almond pastry from **BAKERY PAN TRIUNFO** (Calle Morelos and Obregón; 624/142-5720) should hit the spot.

Within recent years, a cluster of commendable **ART GALLERIES** have emerged on side-street locations behind (north of) the town plaza and church. Along Calle Obregón, you'll find the **DENNIS WENTWORTH PORTER GALLERY** (Obregón 20; 624/142-3141), with displays of vibrant oils and intriguing pastels created by this celebrated American contemporary impressionist who relocated here from Sedona, Arizona, in the mid-1990s. **THE BARKING DOG GALERÍAS** (624/142-3141), in adjacent quarters, features both contemporary and abstract works of Colorado artist Victoria Davis, as well as other changing exhibits. **PEZ GORDO** (Obregón 19; 624/142-5788), owned and operated by artist Dana Lieb, has a reputation for innovative exhibits and eclectic shows of works by numerous local artists, as well as paintings that are distinctively Dana's, recognized by her stylish and expressive, large-eyed female figures. **GALERÍA DE KAKI BASSI** (Obregón 1-A; 624/142-5515) features realist paintings, Rupestre Art, prints, and quality framing.

If you like cactus, don't miss the botanical gardens at **CACTI MUNDO** (Cactus World; Blvd Mijares just south of Plaza La Misión) for a look into the world of exotic succulents. Renowned cacti expert Pablo Gonzalez recently established this botanical garden, featuring 5,000 plants in 850 varieties, many rare or endangered.

Though nearly wiped out during hurricane Juliette in September 2001, **ESTERO SAN JOSÉ** (San José Estuary) is gradually making a comeback. Fan palms, marsh grasses, river cane, and tule growth surround the scenic tidewater, where Río San José meets the Sea of Cortez. Easily accessible, this oasis in the midst of the city provides sanctuary to more than 200 species of birds. Wind your way along the **FOOTPATH,** Paseo del Estero, following the water through lush growth, and spot herons, frigate birds, and sparrow hawks; or rent a **CANOE OR KAYAK** for a tour afloat. The path begins just east of the seaside hotel, Presidente Inter-Continental Hotel Los Cabos (see Lodgings), and emerges on Boulevard Mijares just a few blocks from downtown San José.

Designed by FONATUR, **CAMPO DEL GOLF SAN JOSÉ**'s (Paseo Finisterra 1; 624/1142-0905) 9-hole **GOLF COURSE** has nice ocean vistas and offers an affordable alternative to neighboring Corridor links. It's also more casual—golfing attire is not required. Greens fees run $30 US for 9 holes and $55 US for 18 holes. Night golfing is available, and there are also lighted tennis courts.

SHOPPING

Pleasantly void of Cabo San Lucas's high-pressure salesmanship, shopping in San José del Cabo is low key, still featuring an array of interesting shops and high-quality crafts. While browsing these streets, you will want to visit a few of the upscale artisan shops, even if you are not in the purchasing mood.

VERYKA GALERÍA (Blvd Mijares 6-B; 624/142-0575) carries a variety of arts and crafts from all over Mexico, along with woven fabrics, and a selection of

Artes de Los Muertos, the unique Mexican skeleton art. The **DANIEL ESPINOSA STUDIO** (Blvd Mijares 2; 624/142-6053) features the work of this internationally recognized Mexican designer known for his elegantly designed silver jewelry, including stylish brushed silver creations. **LA MINA** (Blvd Mijares 33; 624/142-3747) has a fine selection of designer jewelry in silver, gold, and precious stones. **SOL DORADO** (Blvd Mijares 33; 624/142-1950) is an expansive artisan shop with paintings, metal and carved sculpture, clay pottery, elegant jewelry, glassware, and scores of collectibles.

Along Calle Zaragoza are numerous shops, including **ADD** (at Hidalgo; 624/142-2777), with its wonderful collection of Mexican pottery, pewter, hand-painted dishes, hand-woven baskets, lamps, and vases. Next door, **LA PALOMA BOUTIQUE** (Calle Zaragoza; 624/142-6255) carries a wide selection of colorful cotton casual wear. Farther up the street on the north side, visit **CASA PAULINE** (Calle Zaragoza; 624/142-3070), which has a fine selection of unique linens and drapery fabrics, as well as an assortment of Mexican-made accent items and custom-made furniture. **WALLS AND MORE** (Calle Zaragoza and Hidalgo; 624/1142-0970) is a combination art gallery, picture framing studio, and eclectic collection. Next door, **OFELIA'S FINE SILVER** (Hidalgo 8; 624/142-4717) features collectible silver "Los Castillo," pieces designed by the famous Antonio Castillo Terán of Taxco.

ADVENTURES

FISHING / Because San José lacks a harbor and marinas with dock space for boats, most of the fishing trips from the city are on Mexican *pangas* launched from the beach. You can barter with the fishermen at La Playita east of town, or make arrangements through La Playita Resort Hotel (see Lodgings). **VICTOR'S SPORTFISHING FLEET** (office located in Posada Real Los Cabos, Zona Hotelera, Paseo San José; 624/142-1092, fax 624/142-1093) operates both *superpangas* and cruisers out of Playa Palmilla, just north of the Palmilla resort hotel (see Lodgings in The Corridor section). A full day of fishing with a *panga* runs about $185 US for three people, while a cruiser with up to four people costs $450 US. Victor will also set you up with a *panga* for whale-watching excursions.

SURFING / This section of the Cape is known for great surfing in the summer and fall when the Southern Hemisphere swells roll in. **ZIPPERS** (km 28.5 Mexico 1) is a quick right-handed wave, bouncy on the inside and by far the most popular and competitive ride in the area. Nearby **OLD MAN'S** is a great spot for learning, with a slow-moving, consistent wave. **COSTA AZUL SURF SHOP** (km 28.5 Mexico 1; 624/147-0071) and the **KILLER HOOK SURF SHOP** (Hidalgo; 624/142-2430) are local retail shops with surfboard rentals; see also Guides and Outfitters.

GUIDES AND OUTFITTERS

LA PLAYITA TOURS (Calle Juárez; 044-624/140-6470 cell; www.laplayitatours. com), located within walking distance from town, operates from La Playita beach just east of San José. They offer a 2½-hour ATV tour up the East Cape Rural Coastal Road for $50 US per person; rugged, all-day snorkeling trips to Cabo Pulmo for $100 US per person; and surf fishing from ATVs for $25 US an hour. **TÍO SPORTS** (Paseo San José; 624/143-3399; www.tiosports.com) operates a booth just outside the entrance to the Presidente Inter-Continental Los Cabos hotel near the estuary. Guided ATV tours cost $35–$45 US, and include sand dune or desert scenery tours. Wave runners are available here at $45 US per half hour or $80 US per hour; kayaks rent for $35 US for 3 hours. **CALIFORNIA ATV'S** (Paseo San José; 624/1443-5464), a division of Cabo San Lucas's **RANCHO TOURS** (ranchotours@prodigy.net.mx), maintains a booth near town. ATV tours include excursions to the Old Lighthouse for $50 US per person or $70 US for two. ATVs are also available for $20 US for one hour, $60 US for four hours, and $100 US per day.

BAJA SALVAJE (Baja Wild; Obregón and Guerrero; 624/148-2222 or 624/142-5300; www.bajawild.com) is recommended for their ecologically committed hiking, rock climbing, and mountain biking excursions. Investigate area flora and fauna, then pitch camp near hot springs and waterfalls; or take one of their Cabo Pulmo scuba diving, snorkeling, or kayak expeditions. Baja Salvaje also gives surfing lessons and guides surfers to the best breaks. Tours start at $55 US.

Organizing a full range of guided eco-conscious expeditions throughout southern Baja, **NÓMADAS DE BAJA** (Calle Zaragoza, across from Conaco office; 624/142-4388, fax 624/142-4388; nomadas@prodigy.net.mx; www.nomadas-debaja.com) uses licensed, bilingual guides and offers a variety of tours for all age groups. Choose from bird-watching, mountain hiking and camping, kayak tours, snorkeling and diving at Cabo Pulmo National Marine Park, mountain bike tours, and jeep adventures. Transportation, related gear, lunch, and/or snacks and beverages are included in their fees.

An international tour company with an excellent reputation, **BACKROADS** (800/462-2848 US; www.backroads.com) offers a popular six-day multisport adventure tour in the Cape Region. Clients bike, hike, and kayak—departing from San José del Cabo—with overnights at Los Frailes, Los Barriles, and Punta Pescadero. Arrangements feature upscale accommodations, support van transport, excellent meals, equipment rentals, and guides.

NIGHTLIFE

Although you wouldn't say that San José is the place to party hearty—that's its neighbor, Cabo San Lucas—you can catch some excellent live musical groups, some of which combine dancing, at a number of area lounge-style bars. **TROPICANA** (Blvd Mijares 30; 624/142-1580), **SIMPECAO** (1 block west of Bancomer on Zaragoza), and the **IGUANA BAR** (Blvd Mijares 24; 624/142-0266), all situated downtown, are the most consistent purveyors of music and dance entertainment, where live bands present a varied mix of Latino and international pop. Several of the upscale restaurant/bars offer live music sporadically on weekends. In the off-season, live musical entertainment wanes with the crowds. If you're really in the mood to party all night long, **WILD COYOTE BAR** (Puerto Paraiso Macro Plaza on the Marina, Cabo San Lucas; 624/143-6969 or 624/143-6966; www.coyoteugly.com.mx) in Cabo operates a special party bus that will pick you up in San José and deliver you back safely in the wee hours of the morn.

FESTIVALS AND EVENTS

Beginning with the Christmas season and sometimes lasting as late as March, Saturday evenings bring the town to life with the **PLAZA MIJARES MINI-FES-TIVAL,** where folk dancers perform, food vendors and local artists set up shop, and musicians sing and play at the plaza. Inquire at your hotel, or ask any shopkeeper if this mini-festival will take place during your stay. Proceeds often go to local charities.

The largest and most festive of local celebrations is held around March 19— **SAN JOSÉ FIESTA,** the feast day of San José's patron saint. Retaining its Mexican charm, the San José Fiesta features parades, a carnival, vendors hawking their wares and food specialties, horse races, and *folklóric* dancing at Plaza Mijares. The festival culminates with spectacular fireworks on the final night. Known to last up to 12 days on either side of March 19, this celebration dominates the otherwise quiet town. Streets are closed and music blares, even after midnight. If you plan on staying anywhere near the plaza, consider catching this festival on either end, and be sure to pack some earplugs.

RESTAURANTS

Baan Thai / ★★★

CALLE MORALES, SAN JOSÉ DEL CABO; 624/142-3344 The transformation of Baan Thai has caught the attention of locals who now flock to this popular restaurant. Change came with Carl Marts, former executive chef at the Twin Dolphin Hotel, now *jefe* here since he purchased this establishment in November 2001. Marts describes his menu as contemporary Asian cuisine, influenced by Japanese, Thai, Chinese, and Laotian themes, blended with his own creative inventions. He does wonders with fresh seafood; clams, mussels, crab, and fresh fish simmer with his clever tact. For starters, try the crispy spring rolls, filled with glass noodles, shrimp, and pork, and accompanied by a hot, sweet dipping sauce and sautéed, seasoned cucumbers. Lamb shank is braised and smothered in a green coconut curry with bok choy, cilantro, and lemongrass. For dessert, the Thai coconut ice cream comes crunchy with toasted coconut, ginger, and a squeeze of lime. The wine list includes Baja California labels as well as imports from Chile, Australia, and the United States. Thanks to Carl's innovative bent, the menu is not static. You're sure to make new discoveries with every visit. *$$; MC, V; traveler's checks OK; lunch, dinner Mon–Sat; full bar; no reservations; cabocarl@hotmail.com; between Obregón and Comonfort.*

Damiana / ★★

BLVD MIJARES 8, SAN JOSÉ DEL CABO; 624/142-0499 OR 624/142-2899 An 18th-century hacienda tucked behind the town plaza is home to Damiana. The restaurant takes its name from the fabled aphrodisiac liqueur, Damiana, derived from an indigenous herbal shrub. Charming adobe-walled interior rooms and a bougainvillea-drenched outdoor patio define the interior of this popular downtown eatery. Wrought-iron tables are staged on stone floors and draped in colorful linens, repeating the vivid shades of the flowering plants. Authentic tastes of Mexico are featured here. Tortilla and cheese soups, chayote salads, and bay scallop ceviche are among first-course selections. Rancheros Shrimp come in a flavorful *nopalito* (cactus) sauce, and chiles rellenos are stuffed with shrimp or Mexican Chihuahua cheese. A rarity on restaurant menus today is the fresh abalone, served when available, at market price. Don't forget to ask for a sample of Damiana—complimentary servings of the liqueur are available on request. *$$; AE, MC, V; traveler's checks OK; lunch, dinner every day; full bar; reservations recommended; damiana@prodigy.net.mx; east side of town plaza, Centro San José.*

El Chilar / ★★★

JUÁREZ 1490, SAN JOSÉ DEL CABO; 624/142-2544 A fairly recent addition to the dining scene, El Chilar is a small but very popular eatery, with a talented and ambitious chef from Oaxaca. Armando Montaño formulates the menu, which changes monthly. Using full-flavored chiles as a focal point, he has captured the attention of the local gringo community, which packs a full house during peak dinner hours. The variety of starters might include a salad or fresh greens with an apricot chipotle vinaigrette, followed by entrees such as thinly sliced flank steak marinated with a nutty cascabel chile sauce, or a succulent chicken breast with almond and chile *guajillo* sauce. Paintings by local artist Dana Lieb of Pez Gordo (see Exploring) adorn the walls, and the cozy cement quarters can get a bit loud when large groups are present, but overall the food and atmosphere are worth experiencing. *$$; No credit cards; traveler's checks OK; dinner Mon–Sat; full bar; reservations recommended; chilemuypicante@depelicula.com; at Calle Morelos.*

Fandango / ★★★

OBREGÓN 19, SAN JOSÉ DEL CABO; 624/142-2226 Housed in a restored adobe building, this bistro-style *cocina* is a winner, with its funky decor, indoor/outdoor dining, colorful wall murals, and taste-tested cuisine. Choose from the eclectic menu selections with Greek and Asian influences. The Cuban coconut prawns served with an apricot-horseradish dipping sauce are an excellent starter. Continue with the Mezze Plate, which includes a small Greek salad, spanakopita triangles, dolmas (stuffed grape leaves), and toasted pita wedges served with tzatziki and hummus—enough for two if preceding an entree. The catch of the day is often fresh *dorado,* grilled and served with a delectable sauce—light and not overpowering. Entrees are served with rice pilaf and grilled vegetables. Save room for an excellent Mexican flan with Kahlúa for dessert. The bar is also popular and Fandango is a busy place, so reserve a table, kick back, and enjoy. *$$; MC, V; traveler's checks OK; lunch, dinner Mon–Sat; full bar; reservations recommended; Old Town.*

La Picazón / ★★

VALERIO GONZÁLEZ, SAN JOSÉ DEL CABO; 624/147-3857 This tidy *palapa* serves up the best values in town and offers some unique alternatives to the ubiquitous fish tacos. Imelda and Alejandro Igartua opened La Picazón five years ago and have recently opened a similar restaurant in Cabo San Lucas (La Golondria and Calle Pescadores; 624/142-3410) to offer the locals there a reasonably priced eatery. Their motto, "Eat Well and Pay Less," is posted on the wall. Try the *tacos del pulpo al mojo de ajo*—soft tacos with octopus cooked in garlic—or sink your teeth into *tacones,* one of the house specialties. Served with a side of refreshing jicama salad, *tacones* (similar to wraps) are usually stuffed with shrimp, fish, or beef, and can easily feed two people. (One of the Cape's notable chefs was recently seen here devouring a *tacone,* with juice running down his arms and a huge smile on his face!) With friendly service and a colorful Mexican atmosphere, this place is hard to beat for late lunch or a quick dinner. *$; No credit cards; traveler's checks OK; lunch, dinner Mon–Sat; beer only; no reservations; near Mexico 1.*

Local Eight / ★★★☆

BLVD MIJARES, SAN JOSÉ DEL CABO; 624/142-6655 An upper-level terrace, shaded from sun and street distractions with rustic bamboo screening and an array of ferns and palms, is home to this artsy bistro and bar. Chad Owens and Chris Slater, two young, talented chefs who have earned a reputation among locals for their catering feats, are responsible for the palate-pleasing cuisine presented here. Choose from their fairly extensive wine selection and order samplings from the tasty tapas menu. Several can share the Local Eight Antipasto—a combination of octopus salad, fried artichoke hearts, roasted peppers, salami, hummus, fresh tomatoes, olives, and cheese served with pita and crackers. Crispy calamari with a wasabi cocktail sauce and sashimi with pineapple salsa are among other favorites. Recent entrees featured succulent parrotfish, marinated and grilled, served over rice with a tangy ginger sauce and a wonderful array of stir-fried vegetables. The roasted rack of lamb was accompanied by au gratin potatoes, ratatouille, tomato chutney, and a rosemary-shallot Merlot sauce. Portions are ample and the service is charming and attentive. *$$–$$$; MC, V; traveler's checks OK; dinner Mon–Sat; full bar; reservations recommended; morrison@cabonet.netmx; in Plaza La Misión.*

Mi Cocina / ★★☆

BLVD MIJARES 4, SAN JOSÉ DEL CABO; 624/142-5100, FAX 624/142-5110
During evening hours, the interior courtyard of the Casa Natalia hotel takes on a special ambience. Background music mingles with the steady rhythm of fountains as they cascade into reflective waters. Large copper braziers are ablaze, their dancing flames playing light games among stately palms and elegant tables. Under the creative direction of chef Axkana Ruiz, a host of innovative dishes have won a loyal following among locals, and raves among epicurean experts. Begin your evening with a selection from their extensive international wine list or collection of fine tequilas. Starter specials can include Mexican bruschetta, smoked tuna tartare, or tequila-cured salmon with dill-caper aioli. For dinner, try the grilled rack of lamb, seasoned with *acini de pepe* and Spanish saffron; Axkana's special seafood soup; or calamari done to perfection. Presentation and service complement the menu. Save room for a delicious crème brûlée with vanilla ice cream for dessert. This interior courtyard restaurant is overlooked by a charming *palapa* bar—a great choice for drinks and appetizers, even if you don't plan on dinner. *$$$; AE, DIS, MC, V; traveler's checks OK; dinner every day; full bar; reservations recommended; casa. natalia@cabonet.com.mx; www.casanatalia.com; behind town plaza.*

Morgan's Restaurant and Cellar / ★★★

HIDALGO AND DOBLADO, SAN JOSÉ DEL CABO; 624/142-3825 OR 624/142-3644
Once inside the ornate iron-gated entrance at Morgan's, you'll find yourself in a Tuscan-inspired courtyard surrounded by a balconied, two-story adobe building that looks more like a home than a restaurant. Dramatic wall murals—brilliantly colored barnyard cocks, French countryside landscapes—and hanging cookware with the glint of copper adorn the walls. The aroma of foods on the flaming courtyard grill immediately captures the senses. Grilled meats and seafood are the entree features here. Start with a crisp, locally grown, organic salad, and when you're ready, try the seared loin of pork or the rack of lamb, served with organic rhubarb. Pepper-crusted *ahi* tuna steak, grilled medium-rare, is served with a wild blackberry and merlot sauce; thick, juicy steaks are cooked to order. Dining has an intimate feel, with tables staged in semiprivate rooms upstairs overlooking the courtyard. Open-air courtyard dining is also an option if you arrive early. *$$$–$$$$; AE, MC, V; traveler's checks OK; dinner every day; full bar; reservations recommended; morgans@ prodigy.net.mx; www. morgansloscabos.com; in the heart of central San José, 1 block off Blvd Mijares.*

The Rusty Putter / ★★

PASEO SAN JOSÉ, SAN JOSÉ DEL CABO; 624/142-4546, FAX 624/142-0513 This spacious *palapa* sports bar and restaurant is perched on the hillside with an open-air terrace overlooking Zona Hotelera and the Sea of Cortez. The eclectic menu features everything from Black Angus steaks, prime rib, and giant burgers to hero-size sandwiches, meal-size salads, Mexican specialties, and fresh seafood. A popular feature is the sushi bar, where you'll find your favorite sushi or sashimi. Their sumptuous breakfasts are a big draw, along with the showing of major sports on giant television screens. Servings are ample, often large enough for two. The restaurant is set amid the Caddy Shack Miniature Golf Course, a landscaped, 18-hole putting course. *$$; MC, V; traveler's checks OK; breakfast, lunch, dinner every day; full bar; no reservations; rustyputter@big foot.com; Zona Hotelera Plaza, ½ mile off Mexico 1.*

Tequila Restaurant and Agave Lounge / ★★★

MANUEL DOBLADO 1011, SAN JOSÉ DEL CABO; 624/142-1155, FAX 624/142-3753 Chef Alejandro Rodriguez bills his creations as "Mediterranean cuisine with Mexican and Asian influences." His dishes are superb, many featuring fresh seafood selections garnered personally during his daily visits with local fishermen. Dine in a romantic courtyard with a fountain and candlelit tables under a canopy of trees and open sky. The courtyard is a level down from the entrance bar and cigar room, with its chic lighting and desert landscape paintings. Choose a taste of tequila from an extensive offering, or select from the 75 listed wines. Try the tequila shrimp with plantains, black beans, and a to-die-for tequila sauce. Another popular dish is the Lobster Bomb in wonton skin, under a black bean–chipotle sauce. Rodriguez also has a deft touch with meats, pastas, and salads, and it's almost impossible to resist the warm bread presented with your meal. *$$$–$$$$; No credit cards; traveler's checks OK; dinner every day; full bar; reservations recommended; www.tequila restaurant.com; just off Blvd Mijares in central San José.*

Tropicana Inn Bar and Grill / ★★

BLVD MIJARES 30, SAN JOSÉ DEL CABO; 624/142-0907 OR 624/142-1580, FAX 624/142-1590 The Tropicana is friendly and fun, whether you enjoy sidewalk dining, the dark paneled bar with its entertaining nightlife, or the main restaurant, reached via a descending staircase from the street-level bar. Canopied in a Polynesian-style *palapa,* the open-air, lower-level restaurant is spacious and the menu extensive. For breakfast, start light with an English muffin and fresh orange juice, or go hearty by ordering the breakfast skillet creation: eggs scrambled in a zesty blend of peppers, onion, sausage, and special Mexican pesto, seasoned with cilantro and jalapeños, served over country potatoes and topped with cheddar cheese and salsa. Lunch and dinner menus include a wide selection of salads, hamburgers, and steaks, as well as Mexican specialties such as fajitas and enchiladas. Seafood lovers might try the sea bass with an organic basil sauce or sautéed with a cilantro-lemon butter. *$$; AE, MC, V; traveler's checks OK; breakfast, lunch, dinner every day; full bar; no reservations; tropicana@1cabo net.com.mx; central San José.*

LODGINGS

Casa Natalia / ★★★

BLVD MIJARES 4, SAN JOSÉ DEL CABO; 624/142-5100 OR 888/277-3814 US, FAX 624/142-5110 This charming European-style hotel, just off the town plaza, is the creation of Nathalie and Loic Tenoux, who manage and maintain excellence. They began with a lovely courtyard home and renovated the structure under the guidance of renowned architect Luis Barragan, known for his nouveau-Mexican style. Each of the 18 suites—with hand-hewn wooden beams and textured walls in hues of blues, yellows, and terra-cotta—is individually decorated in a regional Mexican motif. Sliding glass doors open onto private terraces where relaxing hammocks and comfortable outdoor furnishings are shaded by a canopy of bougainvillea and bamboo. Meticulous attention to detail is evident in features that include handcrafted wood furniture, artistic sconces and lamps, original artwork, and colorful woven and embroidered fabrics. Two suites feature private spas. Guest facilities include the intimate courtyard restaurant Mi Cocina (see Restaurants), in-room spa services, and a swimming pool. Convenient shops and sightseeing in this picturesque Mexican town are at your doorstep. *$$$$; AE, DIS, MC, V; traveler's checks OK; casa.natalia@cabonet.com.mx; www.casanatalia.com; behind town plaza, Centro San José.*

El Encanto Inn and Suites / ★★

CALLE MORELOS 133, SAN JOSÉ DEL CABO; 624/142-0388, FAX 624/142-4620 Conveniently situated in the heart of Old Town San José, El Encanto and its guests are just steps away from restaurants, lounge bars, shops, and art galleries. A green awning identifies the iron-gated entrance to this intimate courtyard inn, with its interior brick paving, tropical plantings, and colonial-style buildings. While the entrance is charming, the 19 modern rooms are somewhat austere but adequately appointed with tile bathrooms, tile flooring, satellite TV, phone service, and air conditioning. Across the street is the more upscale El Encanto Suites—recently opened as part of the same complex, with 13 garden suites. This two-story colonial structure surrounds an interior landscaped courtyard, free-form swimming pool, and *palapa* bar. Swimming pool access is available to guests at either location. At the inn, there's no charge for children under 10. *$–$$; AE, MC, V; traveler's checks OK; elencant@prodigy.net.mx; www.el encantoinn.com; Old Town.*

Fiesta Inn Los Cabos / ★

PASEO SAN JOSÉ, SAN JOSÉ DEL CABO; 624/142-0701 OR 800/343-7821 US, FAX 624/142-0480 The three-storied, 152-room Fiesta Inn is situated on an expansive white-sand beach in the hotel zone. Walkways on the property thread through subtropical plants, palms, and desert cacti to the oceanfront swimming pool with its swim-up bar. Mini *palapas* dot the beach to shade sunbathers as the surf parades ashore. Because of a strong undertow, these waters are not suitable for swimming. The simple but spacious rooms have tile flooring and private terraces with either full or partial views of the ocean. Amenities include TV, air conditioning, and phone service. Other facilities include a spa, a gym, shuffleboard courts, a terrace restaurant/bar, and a beachfront sports bar. This is an all-inclusive resort with rates ($258 US for two people a night) covering three meals, snacks, soft drinks, cocktails, taxes, and gratuities. *$$; AE, MC, V; traveler's checks OK; www.fiestainn.com; Zona Hotelera.*

La Playita Resort Hotel / ★

PUEBLO LA PLAYA BEACH, SAN JOSÉ DEL CABO; 624/142-4166, FAX 624/142-4166 A pleasant getaway directly fronting the beach on the north end of San José del Cabo, La Playita is just 2 miles from the central district. The three-story, hacienda-style building houses 27 units overlooking a spacious patio, a pool, and the beach beyond. The rooms are rather spartan but comfortable and immaculately kept. Tile floors and baths, air conditioning, and satellite TV are among the appointments. An outdoor restaurant/bar is located in an adjacent building—a favorite meeting, greeting, and eating place among locals as well as hotel guests. Much of the charm is the staff's commitment to serving the needs of guests. The waters here are suitable for swimming, and the beach is home to a large *panga* fleet, where guests can barter for fresh fish or a day of sportfishing. *$; MC, V; traveler's checks OK; laplayitahotel@prodigy. net.mx; www.laplayitahotel.com; from Blvd Mijares in central San José, take Pueblo La Playa Beach turnoff and follow graded dirt road 2 miles.*

Posada Real Los Cabos / ★★

PASEO SAN JOSÉ, SAN JOSÉ DEL CABO; 624/142-0155 OR 800/528-1234 US, FAX 624/142-0460 Situated on the expansive, sandy shores of Zona Hotelera in San José del Cabo, this 17-year-old Best Western hotel has been completely renovated and updated. The low-rise, earth-toned buildings surround subtropical landscaping punctuated with desert cacti and a flowing watercourse with splashing fountains. The 140 rooms and eight suites, each with a private patio, open to sea views (full or partial). Room appointments include tiled floors and baths, air conditioning, satellite TV, telephones, and your choice of one king or two double beds. Refrigerators are available upon request. A large swimming pool and a *palapa*-covered swim-up bar front the beach. Additional facilities include a full-service restaurant, a beach-side snack bar, a lobby bar with frequent entertainment, a seaside hot tub, laundry facilities, tennis and volleyball courts, a putting green, and access to nearby golf courses. They also accommodate up to two children under 12 for free. *$$$; AE, MC, V; traveler's checks OK; pr2cabos@prodigy.net.mx; www.posadareal.com; on the beach in Zona Hotelera.*

Presidente Inter-Continental Los Cabos / ★★

PASEO SAN JOSÉ, SAN JOSÉ DEL CABO; 624/142-0211 OR 800/327-0200 US, FAX 624/142-0232 Bounded by the salty Sea of Cortez and the freshwater Estero San José, the Inter-Continental was the forerunner of resorts in this area—an aged beauty before its recent face-lift. Occupying 16 acres, the sprawling development is a cluster of three-storied buildings housing 400 spacious rooms, most with ocean views from private terraces. Amenities include four sparkling pools: one designated for adults only, another for children, one for active sports, and the granddaddy of them all, open to everyone for just plain swimming and pool-side relaxation. Other features include five restaurants, six bars, a spa, hot tubs, lighted tennis courts, and golf at the nearby world-class courses. Mexican fiestas are staged weekly, with entertainment, fireworks, and a spectacular buffet. Landscaped grounds are home to an amazing array of desert cacti, displayed in manicured garden settings canopied by palms. The Chiqui Club is for kids only, ages 5–12, featuring a multitude of supervised activities, including Spanish language classes and sports. The rate here is all-inclusive ($400 US for two people per night). *$$$$; AE, MC, V; traveler's checks OK; loscabos@interconti.com; www.interconti.com; northeast end of Zona Hotelera.* &

Tropicana Inn / ★★

BLVD MIJARES 30, SAN JOSÉ DEL CABO; 624/142-0907 OR 624/142-1580, FAX 624/142-1590 Centrally located, the Tropicana Inn is a San José landmark. Its sidewalk bar/restaurant (see Restaurants) has long been a congregating place for locals as well as tourists, many sipping their farewell Mexican margarita here before catching a taxi to the airport. But the hustle and bustle belie the inner nature of Tropicana. From the street-side restaurant/bar, stairs descend into an expansive *palapa* restaurant and beyond. Down yet another level lies the tile-and-cobblestone garden courtyard of the inn. Shielded from street noises, the two-storied inn surrounds fountains and a free-form swimming pool nestled amid lush plants and mature shade trees. The 40 well-appointed units (36 standard rooms, several suites, and a cabana) are attractively decorated, featuring tile bathrooms and flooring, queen beds (two per room), telephones, satellite TV, coffeemakers, and minibars. A complimentary continental breakfast is served poolside every morning. The inn caters to families, accommodating two children under 12 at no extra charge. *$$; AE, MC, V; traveler's checks OK; tropicana@1cabonet.com.mx; central San José.*

The Corridor

Southwest of San José del Cabo, Mexico 1 becomes a four-lane divided highway known as the *Corredor Turístico* (Tourist Corridor), more commonly referred to as "the Corridor." Burgeoning tourism is rapidly changing this 18-mile coastal strip, famed for its panoramic vistas and austere desert beauty. World-class golf courses line the drive, as do time-share condos and megaresorts claiming prime beach spots. Hidden behind their guarded gates are crescent coves, seaside cliffs, and rocky shores that punctuate the Baja coast—while unobstructed glimpses from the highway reveal calm bays and vast, seductive stretches of flat, sandy shoreline.

Within the Corridor's colony of upscale hotels, you'll find elegant lounges and restaurants, opulent spas, and award-winning, infinity-edged pools with swim-up bars. Overnight stays usually run $250 US and upward; suites at $2,000 to $3,000 a night are not unheard of. **CABO DEL SOL** (km 10) and **CABO REAL** (km 19.5) are large resort complexes encompassing 4,800 acres of desert along the coast. They are home to numerous golf courses, luxury hotels, beach clubs, and planned residential communities.

Even if you don't schedule an overnight stay, plan a visit for a casual poolside lunch, a relaxing drink, or a sumptuous dining experience. You'll understand why this is the fastest-growing resort region in all of Mexico.

EXPLORING

Before heading off to your favorite beach, visit **LA EUROPEA** (between km 6–7 Mexico 1; 624/145-8760). This huge wine and liquor store/delicatessen holds the largest selection of wines on the peninsula, with many of your favorite Baja California labels as well as an extensive international collection. They also carry a nice selection of tequila and beer along with an assortment of deli foods sure to help with your afternoon picnic. Open every day (9am–8pm).

ADVENTURES

BEACHES / Stretches of wide, sandy beaches and intimate coves lie just off the highway, some visible from the road, others hidden from view by the coastline or sprawling, high-rise beach resorts. Although Mexican law requires that beaches are to remain open to the public, many of the spectacular beaches in this area are cordoned off by these resorts. The following beaches are treasured exceptions.

PLAYA COSTA AZUL (km 28.5 Mexico 1) is a beautiful, wide stretch of sand just south of the La Jolla and Mykonos beach resorts. The beach is probably best known for the surf break dubbed **"ZIPPERS"** that batters the shoreline during the summer and fall. When it's calm, this is a good swimming spot. Surfboard rentals, instruction, and snorkeling and fishing gear are available across the highway at **COSTA AZUL SURF SHOP** (Plaza Costa Azul, km 28 Mexico 1; 624/142-2771; info@costa-azul.com.mx). Zippers Bar and Grill (see review) on the shoreline is popular with the beach crowd.

PLAYA PALMILLA (km 27 Mexico 1) is a charming crescent-shaped cove tucked behind the bluff of the Palmilla resort's famed golf course, just north of the hotel (see Lodgings). Follow the resort's entrance road past rows of low bungalows to the beach access road, which is marked with a sign for Pepe's Restaurant. The northern sector of the beach is busy with fishing *pangas*—Victor's Sport Fishing—available for charter (see Guides and Outfitters in San José del Cabo section). To the immediate south lies the beach, protected by a rocky

CORRIDOR TEE-OFF

With seven great courses emerging in just 10 short years, Los Cabos has become Mexico's golfing magnet, attracting scratch golfers and high handicappers alike. Most courses, with the exception of **QUERENCIA**—an exclusive, private club—are semi-private and arrangements can be made for play, with discounts often available if you are staying at one of the area resorts that promote golfing for guests. Afternoon play in general costs less. As a rule, greens fees include tax, cart, bottled water, use of the driving range, and sometimes practice balls. **RENTAL EQUIPMENT AND INSTRUCTION** are available at most courses. Golfing attire is required. These courses, creatively carved out of this rugged desert terrain, are incredibly beautiful, with dramatic mountain and ocean vistas. Perhaps the most difficult part of the game, wherever you play, will be keeping your eye on the ball amid such spectacular scenery. From north to south, the Corridor courses include:

PALMILLA (km 27.5 Mexico 1; 624/148-0525 or 800/637-2226 US; www.kollresorts.com), located 4 miles southwest of San José del Cabo, is a 27-hole course with three choices of topography—mountain, *arroyo*, and coastal—that was Jack Nicklaus's first Signature Course in Mexico. The course is often the venue for major tournaments—1997 PGA Senior Slam, 1997 Taylor Made Pro-Am, 1998 World Pro-Am. Greens fees are $195 US for 18 holes.

Six miles south of San José, **EL DORADO GOLF CLUB** (km 20 Mexico 1; 624/144-5451 or 800/393-0400 US; www.caboreal.com) is one of two courses in the Cabo Real resort complex. The Jack Nicklaus–designed 18-hole course captures the magic of the property. Seven holes are oceanfront; the rest are carved out of two picturesque canyons, surrounded by trees, cacti, and rock formations. Six holes come into play by four lakes. Greens fees are $214 US for 18 holes.

promontory, which creates a calm swimming cove with excellent snorkeling near the rocks. The southern point is a popular surf break in the summer and fall. Nearby Pepe's Restaurant (see review) overlooks the area from its two-story terrace—providing a bird's-eye view of the fishing scene and sweeping coastline.

PLAYA BUENOS AIRES (km 21–22 Mexico 1), near the south end of the El Dorado Golf Club, is an isolated section of white sand beach stretching for miles along the shores of Bahía El Bledito. Riptides are prevalent here, so ask a local swimmer before entering the water. Obscure access roads change with construction activity, but the beach can be reached through the *arroyo*, weather conditions permitting, just north of the Cabo Real resort complex. Four-wheel drive is recommended.

LA CONCHA BEACH (km 20 Mexico 1) is one of the most picturesque beach settings on the Corridor. Access is through the arched entrance of the Cabo Real

CABO REAL (km 19.5 Mexico 1; 624/144-0040 or 800/393-0400 US; www.cabo-real.com), also within the Cabo Real complex, is a quality course designed by Robert Trent Jones Jr., blending the dramatic setting of mountain and shoreline terrain. The course plays up 6,900 yards with four other tee options. Rolling greens, well-placed traps, *arroyos*, narrow terrain, and tricky winds can challenge your game here. Greens fees are $180 US for 18 holes.

Just 5 miles north of Cabo San Lucas, **CABO DEL SOL** (km 10.3 Mexico 1; 624/143-3149 or 800/386-2465 US; www.cabodelsol.com) is the third Jack Nicklaus Signature Course in the area. Host of the 1998 PGA Tour Senior Slam, this challenging course features seven oceanfront holes and is sometimes referred to as the "Pebble Beach of Baja." Greens fees are $185 US for 18 holes Sun–Wed, $228 US Thurs–Sat.

THE DESERT COURSE OF CABO DEL SOL (km 10.3 Mexico 1; 624/143-3149 or 800/386-2465 US; www.cabodelsol.com) is the newest golfing entrant in the Corridor. Designed by Tom Weiskopf, this course features unique layouts taking advantage of natural river washes, elevation changes, and dramatic bunkering. Five different tee boxes make this a playable course for novice and pro alike. Greens fees are $198 US for 18 holes.

The **RAVEN AT CABO SAN LUCAS** (km 3.7 Mexico 1; 624/143-4653 or 888/328-8501 US; golfcabo@cabonet.net.mx), formerly known as the Cabo San Lucas Country Club, was recently purchased by Intrawest Corporation. Co-designed by Roy and Matt Dye, this is the only course in Los Cabos with stunning views of Land's End. The seventh hole is the longest in Mexico, running 620 yards with a par 5. Greens fees are $165 US for 18 holes.

—Gail MacLaughlin

resort complex; follow signs to a rotary traffic circle several hundred meters north. A palm-lined stone pathway leads to the beach area overlooked by La Concha Beach Club facilities. Three sandy coves are nestled between rock formations. Rocks at the center cove block the surging surf, creating a calm, natural pool—ideal for children. The beach is lined with shade umbrellas; rest rooms, showers, and a wading pool are available to patrons of the club's upscale restaurant/bar (see review). The beach is open every day (10am–10pm).

RIO CARACOL BEACH (km 17.5 Mexico 1) is well marked by entrance signs at the dirt road access only a short distance from the Rio Caracol Beach Club parking area. A palm-shaded walk leads to a grassy hill. At the top, discover this new-to-the-scene, casual and friendly beach club, restaurant (see review), and bar overlooking an expansive white sand beach, dotted with palapas and lounge chairs. Rest rooms and a seaside swimming pool are available to patrons. The beach is open every day (10am–8pm).

The beauty of this swimming beach and public facilities—free rest rooms and showers—make **CHILENO** (km 14 Mexico 1) one of the most popular family beaches on the Corridor. A blue and white universal symbol sign is located at the dirt road access. Park near the chain-link fence and walk through the thick grove of fan palms. A sweeping curve of sandy beach lies beneath the rocky promontory site of the Hotel Cabo San Lucas (see Lodgings). Day boats from Cabo bring tourists to the area. Water sports equipment rentals—snorkel gear, umbrellas, sea kayaks, sailboards, scuba diving excursions—are available from the **ACUADEPORTES** booth at the south end. There is good snorkeling along the rocky sections at each end of the sand beach. Open every day (7am–7pm).

PLAYA SANTA MARÍA (km 12 Mexico 1) is a sandy, crescent-shaped bowl offering excellent swimming as well as snorkeling along the rock outcroppings on both the north and south ends. A short dirt access road is graded to the parking area (take the left fork) surrounded by chain-link fence. A long, sandy pathway leads to the beach. Usually less crowded than neighboring Chileno, this beach also attracts tourists aboard boating excursions from Cabo. No facilities. Open every day (7am–7pm).

Prior to the building of the Hotel Twin Dolphin resort (see Lodgings), **TWIN DOLPHINS BEACH** (km 11 Mexico 1) was formerly known as Playa La Viudas (Widows Beach). The rugged, ungraded access road is immediately adjacent to the hotel entrance on the south side. A series of three individual coves, segregated by rock formations, provide protected waters for swimming. Because of tough access, poor signage, and no facilities, this beach is rarely crowded and often unpopulated. Open every day (6am–8pm).

NIGHTLIFE

HAVANA (km 28.5 Mexico 1; 044-624/140-6576 cell), a super club perched above Playa Costal Azul, features jazz, bossa nova, and live classical music. Owner-operator Sheila often entertains with exceptional jazz vocals. **ZIPPERS BAR AND GRILL** (km 28.5 Mexico 1), just across the highway, features live bands on the weekends. Many other Corridor resorts occasionally feature traveling musicians, piano bars, and traditional music. Ask your concierge about scheduled performances.

RESTAURANTS

La Concha Beach Club Restaurant / ★★★

KM 19.5 MEXICO 1, THE CORRIDOR; 624/144-0011, FAX 624/144-0011
Visitors look through a frame of palm trees onto three sandy coves while dining beneath a soaring Polynesian-style *palapa* at this upscale outdoor restaurant. The food, with a hint of Asian inspiration, is as exceptional as the setting. For a starter or light meal, try the Uprfruki Salad—palm hearts, artichokes, tender asparagus, and fresh shrimp on a bed of crisp greens with a blackberry vinaigrette dressing. The grilled fresh tuna medallions, lightly dressed with a wasabi-caper sauce, are a standout. A shrimp-calamari kebab

encrusted in a coating of Parmesan, bread crumbs, and parsley is accented with a ponzu sauce (blended sesame paste, soy sauce, and rice vinegar). Lemon pork scaloppine is presented on a cloud of mashed sweet potatoes. A savory mushroom–bell pepper sauce accompanies fork-tender veal chops. Julienne vegetables, sautéed in garlic butter, and rice accompany entrees along with fresh-baked herbed focaccia with a refreshing cucumber-yogurt-tahini spread. Portions are ample but not overpowering, and the service is both pleasant and efficient. *$$; AE, MC, V; traveler's checks OK; lunch, dinner every day; full bar; no reservations; laconcha@prodigy.net.mx; enter at Cabo Real resort's arched entrance and follow signs on frontage road going north.*

La Paloma / ★★★

KM 27.5 MEXICO I (PALMILLA), THE CORRIDOR; 624/144-5000, FAX 624/144-5100 Balconied within the stately Palmilla resort, La Paloma affords dazzling views of lush tropical gardens, a sparkling mosaic-tiled swimming pool, and the Sea of Cortez with waves crashing on the rocky shore. Chef Jorge Sanchez's continental menu features a selection of meats, seafood, and pastas. Start with creamy asparagus soup served with paprika octopus *brunoise*. Try the delicious potato-crusted sea bass with sautéed spinach and red bell pepper cream sauce, served with saffron rice. Fresh gulf lobster and tuna are grilled and glazed with rich, tangy sauces. Pasta specials are house-made, such as the tortellini *maison,* filled with scallops and mushrooms and sauced with niçoise pipérade. The resort stages a buffet-style Mexican fiesta on Friday night, complete with a mariachi band, lavish costumed dancers, and an exciting fireworks display just off the beach. Renowned among locals is their awesome Mediterranean-Pacific buffet-brunch every Sunday. *$$$–$$$$; AE, DIS, MC, V; traveler's checks OK; breakfast, lunch, dinner every day, brunch Sun; full bar; reservations recommended; www.palmillaresort.com; turn off highway at entrance marked "Palmilla Resort."*

Pepe's Restaurant / ★★★

KM 27.5 MEXICO I, THE CORRIDOR; 624/144-5040 A refreshing change from the posh, expensive offerings of surrounding hotel restaurants, Pepe's is casual and economical. Fresh, simply prepared seafood dishes have made this charming beachfront eatery (with paper napkins) a hot spot. The menu is in three sections—items for $5, $10, and $25 US. Complimentary appetizers can include fresh tuna escabeche with onion, garlic, and chiles in a vinegar marinade—a nice start to any meal. The melt-in-your-mouth fish tacos are usually fresh *dorado,* deep fried and served in tortillas with house-made salsa. On request, Pepe will prepare your own freshly caught fish. During the busy season, a mariachi band serenades evening guests. Ask for Pepe when you arrive, and he'll buy your first drink—if he's not there, the waiter will pay for your first two drinks. *$–$$; No credit cards; traveler's checks OK; lunch, dinner every day; full bar; no reservations; at entrance road to Palmilla resort, follow signs.*

Pitahayas / ★★★★

KM 10 MEXICO 1 (SHERATON HACIENDA DEL MAR RESORT), THE COR-RIDOR; 624/1145-8010 EXT 4225 Winner of the 1999 Five-Star Diamond Award of the American Academy of Hospitality Sciences, Pitahayas is considered by many to be one of the finest restaurants in all of Baja. The large, Tahitian-style *palapa* offers commanding views of the Sea of Cortez and the rocky coastline to the south. Executive chef Volker Romeicke has a fine reputation for journeying into Pacific Rim cuisine using red curry mélanges, ginger with lime, and glazes with wasabi and *lilikoi* (passion fruit). Arrive in time to watch the colors of sunset until candlelight beckons; for a choice vintage, choose from their 700-bottle wine cellar located beneath the circular bar. Recent appetizers included an example of blended culture—Kahlúa pot stickers stuffed with smoked pork; a thick and delightful sweet potato soup flavored with bacon and Thai spices. Order the grilled yellow-fin tuna with a soy mustard sauce, or the trilogy of fresh local seafood, which includes a half lobster tail with a vanilla bean sauce, blackened fish with mango relish, and succulent sautéed butterfly shrimp drizzled with wasabi butter. For dessert, try the macadamia and chocolate cake with ginger ice cream. Service is splendid and the waiters are knowledgeable. Formal resort attire is requested. *$$$$; AE, MC, V; traveler's checks OK; dinner every day; full bar; reservations required; enter Cabo del Sol resort complex and follow signs.* &

Rio Caracol Beach Club Restaurant / ★★

KM 17 MEXICO 1, THE CORRIDOR; 624/144-0653 OR 624/144-0654 This beachy, casual outdoor restaurant overlooks a vast stretch of white-sand beach and the azure waters of the Sea of Cortez. Bring your swimsuit and stay awhile, enjoying the beach or the seaside swimming pool. The beach club restaurant boasts a simple but tasty menu, served on an outdoor brick terrace shaded by an overhead bamboo lattice and surrounded by green grass, palms, and vivid bougainvillea. A variety of snacks include fresh guacamole and crisp tortilla chips, ceviche, and barbecue wings. Choose from pastas, seafood, steaks, chowders, or salads. Cheeseburgers come in two sizes—a smaller version with fries for kids. The beer is cold and the service is friendly and prompt. *$; MC, V; traveler's checks OK; lunch, dinner Wed–Sun; full bar; no reservations; hudson@prodigy.net.mx; www.riocaracol.com; follow signs at access road.*

The Restaurant / ★★★★

KM 19.5 MEXICO 1 (LAS VENTANAS AL PARAISO), THE CORRIDOR; 624/144-0300, FAX 624/144-0301 Located within the award-winning and sublime Las Ventanas al Paraiso resort, the Restaurant follows the same pattern of excellence. Arrive with enough daylight to appreciate the Mexican-Mediterranean architecture, infinity-edged swimming pools, and intricate stone masonry. The outdoor dining pavilion, terraced above the pool, offers stunning views of the coast and golf course. The menu reflects the creative touch of executive chef Marc Lippman, previously of New York City's

critically acclaimed Wild Blue and Miami's Raleigh Hotel. Lippman's philosophy of "less is more" allows subtle seasonings to enhance rather than mask natural flavors. Steamed mussels are seasoned with tree chiles, tequila, coconut, and cilantro. *Cabrilla* (sea bass) comes sautéed with fennel and tomato confit, dressed in a bouillabaisse sauce. Rack of pork from the Niman Ranch is braised with rosemary, and accompanied by sweet potato purée and roasted plums. Select a bottle of wine from the extensive international collection (250 labels), where 3,000 bottles are stored within the walls of La Cava, an exquisite temperature-controlled dining room available for private gatherings. The dessert list is just as ethereal, masterfully orchestrated by Steve Lindsey, the Restaurant's pastry chef. Choose from a rum-soaked sponge cake topped with fresh fruits and tropical sabayon, or his flourless Valrhona chocolate cake topped with crispy praline chocolate and alternating layers of dark and white chocolate mousse, and shingled with spears of chocolate-caramel "cellophane." Dining here is an event, with service dedicated to making customers feel like royalty. Formal resort attire is requested. *$$$$; AE, MC, V; traveler's checks OK; dinner every day; full bar; reservations required; reservations@lasventanas.com.mx; www.rosewoodhotels.com; at Cabo Real resort complex.* &

Villa Serena Restaurant/Bar / ★★

KM 7.5 MEXICO I, THE CORRIDOR; 624/145-8244 Perched on the top of the hill with a sweeping ocean view, this simple restaurant exudes charm. Open-air terraces are set with surprisingly comfortable handmade Mexican tables and chairs. Diners here are treated to great seafood at affordable prices. The lobster plate for just under $10 US is a house specialty. Combo plates—pairing steak, lobster, shrimp, or pork ribs—are pricier. Try the tender grilled steak shish kebab—skewered with vegetables and served over a bed of rice. Crisp, meal-size salads and sandwiches are on the menu. Service is friendly and accommodating. Guests are invited to relax and go for a dip in the adjacent pool, so if it's a hot summer day, bring your swimsuit. *$–$$; MC, V; traveler's checks OK; breakfast, lunch, dinner every day; full bar; no reservations; 5 miles north of Cabo San Lucas, look for signs.*

Zippers Bar and Grill / ★

KM 28.5 MEXICO I, SAN JOSÉ DEL CABO Zippers' outdoor patio is just a step from the broad, sandy beach of Playa Costa Azul. It's an eating, drinking, greeting place for the beach and surf crowd. Locals as well as tourists congregate here, and swimsuits are not uncommon attire. The *palapa*-shaded dining area provides onlookers an opportunity to enjoy seaside views and surfing action while sipping a cold beer, spicy Bloody Mary, or margarita. Menu offerings of burgers, deli sandwiches, barbecue hot wings, fish-and-chips, mesquite-grilled steaks, and prime rib (Saturdays) are typically American. The beach bar is a good place to catch live bands on weekends during the busy season or to watch your favorite sports via satellite TV. *$; Cash only; lunch, dinner every day; full bar; no reservations; on beach next to arroyo.*

LODGINGS

Cabo Surf Hotel / ★★

KM 28 MEXICO I, THE CORRIDOR; 624/142-2666, FAX 624/142-2676
🐚 Tucked away in the rocky cliffside overlooking Playa Acapulqito (near Playa Costa Azul), the Cabo Surf Hotel sits just outside San José del Cabo. Marking the beginning of the Corridor, this charming, affordable jewel is unlike its neighboring resorts that vie for attention to the south. Ten hotel rooms and suites are housed in a whitewashed, tile-roofed hacienda with *palapa*-covered patios and a terrace restaurant/bar. The sea is only a step away from your balconied room, which overlooks a sparkling, mosaic-tiled pool and hot tub. The relatively new rooms are spacious and pleasantly furnished, but not fancy. Amenities include cable TV, air-conditioning, fans, two double beds, and nicely tiled floors and bathrooms. Excellent surfing is nearby, and scuba diving, snorkeling, and sportfishing are also close at hand. The attractions of San José are within minutes. *$$$; AE, MC, V; traveler's checks OK; info@cabosurf hotel.com; www.cabosurfhotel.com; on the beach.*

Casa del Mar Golf Resort and Spa / ★★★☆

KM 19.5 MEXICO I, THE CORRIDOR; 624/144-0030 OR 800/712-2987,
🐚 ⚓ **FAX 624/144-0034** This intimate resort with its warm, colonial architecture is subtle elegance. An oasis of lush gardens and Mexican-style fountains, the hotel and spa occupy the very tip of the Cabo Real development's southern beach, with views of the azure seas and distant mountains unobstructed by neighboring resorts. The casual sophistication of this retreat is carried out in the relaxed Tapango Restaurant, where arched windows in natural wood frame reflective pools and an open-air dining terrace overlooking one of several free-form swimming pools. The 31 suites and 25 deluxe rooms with ocean views are attractively designed with comfortable furnishings, marble floors, private balconies or terraces, hot tubs, air-conditioning, satellite TV, and refreshment bars. Lighted tennis courts, access to two world-class golf courses, and swimming pools with swim-up bars await guests. Their fabulous Spa with sauna, steam room, fully equipped gym, and therapeutic hot tub is also available, and a professional staff is on hand for massage, facials, and indigenous herbal treatments. Pamper yourself and for a week or a weekend. *$$$$; AE, MC, V; traveler's checks OK; casamar@cabonet.net.mx; www.casamarresort.com; in Cabo Real resort complex.*

Hotel Cabo San Lucas / ★★★☆

NEAR KM 14 MEXICO I, THE CORRIDOR; 624/144-0014 OR 323/512-3799 US, FAX 624/144-0015 Hotel Cabo San Lucas is the vision of American transplant Bud Parr, who entered the resort scene in 1962 just after the debut of Palmilla (see review), 8 miles to the north. Parr emulated Hawaiian garden themes in this semitropical resort, which sits on Punta Chileno above Chileno Bay, one of the area's most popular and scenic coves. Thousands of palm trees and subtropical plants surround the resort and line the winding flagstone walkways. Impressive rock walls support multileveled terraces where hotel rooms and villas overlook the sea. Water falls from reflective pools set within solid rock down into the swimming pool, which lies beneath the upper-level dining terrace. Suites and split-level villas feature comfortable king-size beds and air conditioning. Although the hotel lacks some of the amenities of the more recent Corridor creations, it has been well maintained and the rooms and villas come at lower rates than its higher-priced neighbors. Conveniently located close to the attractions of Cabo San Lucas, the hotel has a mature elegance with views that are hard to match. Canine friendly, this is also one of the few resorts in the Corridor with wheelchair access. Activities include tennis, snorkeling, scuba diving, fishing, horseback riding, tide pool tours, and Ping-Pong. *$$$$; AE, MC, V; traveler's checks OK; hotelcabo@ earthlink.net; www.hotelcabo.com; between km 14–15.* &

Hotel Twin Dolphin / ★★☆

KM 12 MEXICO 1, THE CORRIDOR; 624/145-8190 OR 800/421-8925 US, FAX 624/145-8196 Created by the late David Halliburton Sr.—an ecologist and oil millionaire—the Twin Dolphin was built on the spot where he used to fish as a boy. Positioned on 135 acres of manicured desert landscape, the hotel overlooks the Sea of Cortez and offers 50 ocean-view rooms and suites, each with its own private terrace. Entering the open-air lobby, you are immediately greeted by giant boulders cradling a large fountain with its centerpiece sculpture of twin dolphins, while views of the open sea can be seen beyond. Emphasizing serenity in this natural setting, there are no clocks, phones, televisions, or radios in the spacious rooms. The swimming pool is set at the rim of the property, overlooking the sea and the pristine beach below, where three crescent coves offer excellent snorkeling and swimming. Facilities include lighted tennis courts, an 18-hole putting green, an indoor-outdoor gym and fitness center, as well as a view restaurant and *palapa* bar. Activities include fishing, snorkeling, scuba diving, horseback riding, and access to area golf courses. Free shuttle service is provided to and from nearby Cabo San Lucas. *$$$$; AE, DIS, MC, V; traveler's checks OK; www.twindolphin.com; just off the highway.*

Las Ventanas al Paraíso / ★★★★

KM 19.5 MEXICO 1, THE CORRIDOR; 624/144-0300 OR 888/525-0483 US, FAX 624/144-0301 Consistently ranked among the top resorts worldwide, Las Ventanas al Paraíso (the Windows to Paradise) reigns paramount among the luxury resorts in Los Cabos. Exemplary personalized service and meticulous attention to detail keep this facility filled near capacity despite the rates—the highest ever charged in this market. Managed by Rosewood Hotels & Resorts, Las Ventanas' stylishly understated Mediterranean-Mexican style adobe buildings offer dramatic views of the sea and surrounding landscape. The smallest of the 61 guest suites is a posh 960-square-foot suite featuring original artwork, hand-painted walls, and an inlaid

pebble headboard. Terraces, hand-carved cedar doors, whirlpool baths, and terracotta fireplaces are standard. Treat yourself to a rooftop terrace suite. Paintings by Rodrigo Pimental line the walls at reception, and a stroll amid the corridors reveals similar museum-quality art. Gently sloping stairways disclose a serpentine network of fountains, an infinity-edged swimming pool, Cabo Real's oceanside 15th hole, and The Restaurant (see review), arguably the finest dining experience in Baja. Flickering torches illuminate pathways and dining areas after dark. An underground system of tunnels enables fast, unobtrusive service by the staff. Pool butlers cater to your every need, including those occasional cravings for frozen bon-bons. Pamper yourself with a Holistic Crystal Healing Massage at the exceptional spa, known for over 70 innovative treatments provided by the professional staff. The resort's golf courses, fitness center, tennis courts, and private yachts are readily available. And from your private terrace, sip the select, complimentary tequila and observe the night sky through your own private telescope. *$$$$; AE, MC, V; traveler's checks OK; 3-night minimum (weekends); www.rosewoodhotels.com; at Cabo Real resort.*

Meliá Cabo Real / ★★★

KM 19.5 MEXICO 1, THE CORRIDOR; 624/144-0000 OR 800/336-3542 US, FAX 624/144-0101 One of the first resort hotels in the Cabo Real development, the Spanish-owned Meliá Cabo Real made its debut on the Los Cabos scene nearly 10 years ago. Long rated as "Gran Turismo," Mexico's highest resort acclamation, everything here is on a grand scale. The open-air lobby, capped by a towering pyramid skylight of glass and onyx, is a local landmark. Renovations have kept the resort as spiffy and smart on today's lavish and competitive scene as it was when it first opened. Every one of the 302 rooms and splendid suites boast views from a private terrace—some overlooking gardens and golf courses, but most opening onto the sea. Nearby Playa Bledito offers a man-made breakwater creating a calm, natural swimming pool within the sea. Rooms are spacious and equipped with modern amenities; a full-service spa was recently added. A huge free-form swimming pool, two restaurants and three bar/lounges are also on the grounds. Golf and watersports are close by and a complimentary shuttle service is provided for nightlife excursions into Cabo. The Meliá chain of resorts offers two other properties in the Cape: Meliá Los Cabos (km 18.5 Mexico 1, the Corridor; 624/144-0202 or 800/336-3542 US) and Meliá San Lucas (Calle Playa El Médano, Cabo San Lucas; 624/143-4444 or 800/336-3542 US). *$$$$; AE, DIS, MC, V; traveler's checks OK; melia.cabo.real@solmelia.com; www.sol melia.com; Cabo Real resort development.*

Palmilla / ★★★★

KM 27 MEXICO 1, THE CORRIDOR; 624/144-5000 OR 800/637-2226 US, FAX 624/144-5100 Founded in 1956 by the son of a former Mexican president, the Palmilla was the forerunner of resort development in the Cape Region. It soon became a favorite destination of the rich and famous, who arrived by small private aircraft. Hollywood celebs seeking retreat were also attracted by the fabulous sportfishing offshore. Noted regulars included the Duke, Desi Arnez, and Bing Crosby. Currently operated by the Pinehurst Company, which is renowned for its golf resort developments, the original resort has been expanded and improved. A major addition is the world-class golf course designed by Jack Nicklaus. Flagstone pathways thread the grounds, accented by flowering hibiscus, bougainvillea, bird-of-paradise, and fragrant vines. The resort maintains its own fishing fleet, as well as a 4,500-foot illuminated airstrip. Other amenities include an oceanfront pool with swim-up bar, fitness center, tennis and volleyball courts, a bar, and two restaurants, including La Paloma (see review). Accommodations (115 rooms) range from ocean-view units to deluxe beachfront suites. A three- or four-night minimum stay is required, depending on the season, and no Saturday arrivals or departures are accepted. *$$$$; AE, DIS, MC, V; traveler's checks OK; 3-night minimum; www.palmilla resort.com; turn off at signed entrance.*

Sheraton Hacienda del Mar Resort and Spa / ★★★⯪

KM 10 MEXICO 1, THE CORRIDOR; 624/145-8000 OR 888/672-7137 US, FAX 624/145-8002 Lush, landscaped grounds surround the modernized hacienda-style architecture of this sprawling resort complex. Stroll the walkways past bubbling fountains and rock-bottomed ponds hidden within the cluster of 11 earth-toned buildings. Tastefully decorated, the Sheraton Hacienda offers 171 luxury suites and rooms, each with private patios and views of the gardens or sea. Spacious rooms with stylish and comfortable sitting areas sport all the modern features and include a choice of either one king or two queen-size beds, plus whirlpool tubs. Beachside, three cascading swimming pools emerge from subtropical greenery. World-class golf is adjacent and a fabulous spa and fitness center are located on the premises. The hotel's elegant seaside restaurant Pitahayas (see review) attracts diners from throughout the Cape Region. *$$$$; AE, MC, V; traveler's checks OK; information@hacien- dadelmar.com; www.sheratonhaciendadelmar.com; within Cabo del Sol resort complex.* &

Westin Regina Resort Los Cabos / ★★★

KM 22.5 MEXICO 1, THE CORRIDOR; 624/142-9000 OR 800/937-8461 US, FAX 624/142-9010 Designed by renowned Mexican architect Javier Sordo Magdaleno, the multicolored Westin Regina Resort flows against the curve of the beach—a drama that's hidden from roadside spectators. At first glance, this industrial-like, monolithic structure is less than inviting. Once you are inside the entrance, however, the resort's bold design frames the azure sea, adding a striking contrast to the building's burnt-orange walls. Visitors either love the blaring accent colors—magenta, purple, and shades of yellow—or see them as a gaudy imperfection. Spilling bougainvillea, tropical plants, and stately palms seem to anchor the terraced, geometric complex to the coastline, while

THE CAPE REGION THREE-DAY TOUR

DAY ONE: After an evening in San José del Cabo at the centrally located **TROPICANA INN,** enjoy their complimentary breakfast by the pool. Then browse the intriguing shops and galleries of **OLD TOWN.** Take time for a short hike on the palm-studded, winding footpath of **ESTERO SAN JOSÉ.** If you like exotic cactus, don't miss the botanical gardens of **CACTI MUNDO.** As the morning wanes, head southwest on Mexico 1, known as the Corridor, for lunch at **LA CONCHA BEACH CLUB RESTAURANT,** with its beautiful waterfront setting. Don't forget your swimsuit for a dip in the sea or the club pool. By midafternoon get back on Mexico 1, skirting fashionable resorts and spectacular scenery as you reach Cabo San Lucas. Check into **CASA RAFAEL'S** or the **HOTEL HACIENDA BEACH RESORT.** Town, shops, nightlife, and the marina are within walking distance. See if the concierge can get you on tonight's 2-hour **SUNSET COCKTAIL CRUISE** aboard the 100-foot luxury yacht *Kaleidoscope* (see the "Seagoing Adventures" sidebar for details). Visit **SANCHO PANZA WINE BISTRO** for a superb dinner with fine wine accompanied by live jazz. Afterward, if you have the stamina, join the crowd at **CABO WABO CANTINA,** where you can shoot a game of pool or party all night.

    DAY TWO: Enjoy the stuffed French toast at **MAMA'S ROYAL CAFÉ,** then it's off to the **GLASS FACTORY–VITROFUSION** to observe young glass masters as they roll and shape the molten glass. Continue north on Mexico 19 to Todos Santos, where you can stroll the quaint streets investigating **ART GALLERIES** and shops.

    Enjoy a crisp organic salad and pasta for lunch at **CAFÉ SANTA FÉ.** With the sun still high in the sky, head north on Mexico 19 to its junction with Mexico 1. Turn right and

seven serpentine swimming pools culminate near the wave-battered beach below. All 243 rooms and suites come with sea views, large marble bathrooms, handcrafted furniture, and furnished balconies, along with modern amenities. Four restaurants, lighted tennis courts, a full spa and fitness center, and access to area golf courses are all available to guests. *$$$$; AE, MC, V; traveler's checks OK; relos@westin.com; www.westin.com; watch for signs on highway.*

Cabo San Lucas

Cabo San Lucas, or more commonly "Cabo," is the last stop on the 1,059-mile ribbon of asphalt that threads its way down the Baja California peninsula. Here desert meets sea and Pacific meets Gulf in a grand finale of spectacular rock formations known as Land's End, including the region's most widely photographed symbol—the famed El Arco (the Arch).

    With its scenic harbor, expansive white-sand beaches, dramatic cliffs, desert scenery, and ocean waters teeming with big game fish, it was only a matter of follow Mexico 1 on its twisting, mountainous journey toward the Sea of Cortez. Stop at El Triunfo to inspect the brick ruins of a fascinating **SMELTERY**. Continue south to Los Barriles, the seaside community and home of **HOTEL PALMAS DE CORTEZ**. Check into a beachfront room at this legendary cornerstone, or if you prefer less elaborate lodging, **HOTEL LOS BARRILES**. Contact **VISTA SEA SPORT** and book tomorrow's snorkeling tour and arrange for late checkout at your hotel. For dinner, walk north to **OTRA VEZ RESTAURANTE** for fresh seafood or creative pasta. On your way back, stop in at **TÍO PABLO'S BAR AND GRILL** to order a box lunch for tomorrow. While you're waiting, indulge in a hot fudge sundae or take in a nightcap at their Scorpion Bar. Retire early to rest up for tomorrow's adventure.

DAY THREE: Get up with the sun and catch breakfast at **MARTIN VERDUGO'S** third-story, beachfront *palapa* restaurant. Join **VISTA SEA SPORT** by 7:30am for your snorkeling tour. Don't forget your camera, sodas or beer, and box lunch. You'll cruise south along the Sea of Cortez coastline to **CABO PULMO NATIONAL MARINE PARK** and arrive at Iguana Beach, accessible only by boat. The surrounding rock formations are great for rock climbing and hiking. Snorkel among countless colorful fish and living coral heads in water shallow enough for standing; a sea lion colony thrives nearby.

You should be back in Los Barriles around 2pm. Enjoy the late afternoon colors as you head south on Mexico 1 again. If you can finish before dark, stop at the charming Mexican village of Santiago for an early dinner at the **PALOMAR RESTAURANT AND BAR**. Or head back to San José del Cabo in time for a scrumptious dinner at **FANDANGO**. Spend tonight at **CASA NATALIA**, surrounded by intimate luxury.

time before the once quaint fishing village of the '30s would one day emerge as a major tourist destination.

Explored in the '50s and '60s by adventurous fishermen and a few cruising yachties, talk of Cabo slowly began to spread. In the early '70s, the completion of Mexico 1 paved the way for streams of boat-towing fishermen and a flood of RV travelers. By the '80s Cabo's fate was sealed. The construction of the Los Cabos International Airport and the arrival of cruise ships opened the once sleepy town to a plethora of pleasure seekers.

Today's Cabo is a play-hard-all-day-party-all-night scene. When the sun goes down, neon demands your attention as nightclubs buzz till dawn. More than 4,000 hotel rooms compete for visitors. In addition, a booming number of timeshares, condos, and vacation villas have become seasonal homes for regulars. More than 400 restaurants light up the town, many coming and going with the tourist seasons. Prolific construction continues to change the skyline and dampen the tranquil scene, which was still evident less than 20 years ago.

Though the city can sometimes resemble a perpetual spring break, Cabo has managed to retain some if its small-town feel. A few blocks off the main drag, the dirt streets are quiet and time-share solicitors nonexistent. Throughout the city, crime is low—your dollars are more likely to be taken with a phony traffic violation than by a common pickpocket.

Although some people take one look at Cabo's touristy atmosphere and head back to a more tranquil setting, those who stay to get wet, soak up the sun, meet the people, and discover the fine cuisine are likely to find themselves planning a return trip.

ACCESS AND INFORMATION

Cabo can be reached by **CAR** at the southern terminus of Mexico 1, where it meets Mexico 19. For information regarding **LOS CABOS INTERNATIONAL AIRPORT**, see Access and Information at the beginning of this chapter. At the central **BUS STATION** (Zaragoza at 16 de Septiembre), Águila (624/143-7880) offers service between Cabo San Lucas and San José, Todos Santos, and La Paz, as well as destinations farther north.

Internet cafes are common in town, making it easy to keep in touch. Shop around; prices range from $4 US to $12 US per hour.

EXPLORING

Enjoy a stroll along the **MARINA** (behind Plaza Las Glorias), where million-dollar megayachts from around the world occupy expansive slips beside seagoing, high-tech sportfishing machines. Wander into the **FISH MUSEUM** (Blvd Marina), where a display of lifelike replicas depicts denizens of the deep. Bookworms will enjoy **LIBROS, LIBROS** (Books, Books; Marina Blvd next to Carlos 'n Charlies; 624/143-3172) for local and regional books, newspapers, magazines, and CDs in Spanish and English. If the availability of Cuban cigars has you craving a puff or just plain curious, stop in to see the specialists at **J&J HABANOS** (Madero between Blvd Marina and Guerrero; 624/143-6160). With a large selection of cigars from around the world, J&J's also boasts the largest humidor in Mexico. And if your vice is more about those "social lubricants" distilled only in Mexico, you'll definitely want to pay a visit to **TEQUILAS Y TEQUILAS** (Cárdenas in Plaza del Mar; 624/143-4966).

THE GOLDEN CACTUS GALLERY (Guerrero and Madero, upstairs; 624/143-6399) features original paintings and lithographs by nine local artists, including owner Chris MacClure, all reflecting the Mexican culture and environment through different styles and media. **GALERÍA DE KAKI BASSI** (two locations: Morelos and Alikan or Blvd Marina at Puerto de Las Paraiso Mall; 624/143-3510 or 624/143-9510) displays artist Bassi's colorful acrylics and watercolors, excellent prints, as well as work by well-known artists from mainland Mexico. At **SERGIO BUSTAMANTE** (Plaza Bonita, Cardenas and Blvd Marina; 624/143-

2798), the works of this internationally known Mexican artist are on display, including jewelry, paintings, and his peculiar ceramic sculptures.

SHOPPING

Downtown Cabo is one huge shopping arena, with a multitude of shops, small and large, competing for your attention and your dollars. Strolling the narrow streets packed with vendors, time-share hawkers, and visitors is part of the tourist scene. For a never-ending assortment of Mexican souvenirs, investigate the small sidewalk stalls and closetlike stores along **BOULEVARD MARINA** and the network of narrower lanes that intersect this main drag. There is also an **OPEN-AIR MARKET** by the municipal pier (Blvd Marina), just past the entrance to the Hotel Finisterra. Bargaining is a Mexican pastime; don't pay the first price quoted.

Sorting out establishments of better quality and value is the real challenge. Here are some of our finds: **NECRI** (Blvd Marina; 624/143-0283) is a small shop with a great selection of Talavera pottery, pewter, and other fine-quality arts and crafts from mainland Mexico. High-quality items, with higher prices, can be found at **MAMA ELI'S** (Av Cabo San Lucas and Serdan; 624/143-1616) and **EL CALLEJÓN** (Guerrero between Cárdenas and Madero; 624/143-3188). The **BAJA WILDERNESS COMPANY** (16 de Septiembre and Obregón) sells unique, etched items of glass, stone, and tile using ancient figures from various Baja cave paintings as their theme. For original designs by Cabo's most successful clothing designer, browse the racks at **MAGIC OF THE MOON** (69 steps up from Blvd Marina on Calle Hidalgo; 624/143-3161; www.magicofthemoon.com). **THE COTTON CLUB–CALYPSO** (Cárdenas and Ocampo; 624/143-2388) and **H20 SWIMWEAR** (Madero and Guerrero; 624/143-1219) have the best selection of swimwear. For duty-free imported perfumes, check out **NAVARRO'S** (Blvd Marina, Plaza del Sol; 624/143-5335) and investigate **GOLD-DUCK** (Blvd Marina, Plaza Nautica L 3-B; 624/143-2335) for leather handbags, belts, and accessories. For jewelry, try **JOYERÍA MEXICO LINDO** (Blvd Marina, Plaza del Sol; 624/143-3898) or **PACIFIC JEWELRY** (Blvd Marina at Madero; 624/143-4447).

For one-stop gift shopping, a visit to **ARTESANO'S** (near Enriques at km 4 Mexico 1 toward the Corridor; 624/143-3850) is mandatory. Abel Romero, a transplant from Guadalajara, has been dealing with artisans from his hometown and other well-known art centers of mainland Mexico for more than nine years. His huge warehouse packs an extensive selection of items, delivered by the truckload. Browse the aisles for rustic furniture, dinnerware, pottery, glassware, hand-painted decorative tiles and sinks, pewter, and funky doodads for your home or garden. Have cash in hand, as Abel does not bargain or accept traveler's checks or credit cards. Another must is a visit to the **GLASS FACTORY–VITROFUSION** (toward Todos Santos on Mexico 19, first left past hospital and follow signs; 624/143-0255). Watch a dozen masterful artists at work as they blow and roll rustic, one-of-a-kind pieces, including vases, pitchers, and the ever-so-popular cobalt-rimmed drinking glasses. Guided tours are available and it's best to visit before 2pm, while the workers are still handling the molten glass.

ADVENTURES

BEACHES / PLAYA EL MÉDANO stretches for 2 miles along Bahía San Lucas, virtually Cabo's front yard, and is easily accessible. During peak seasons, Médano is certain to be packed with swimmers, sunbathers, and beach vendors. This beach is teeming with activities such as parasailing, water skiing, and beach volleyball. Jet Skis, wave runners, and kayaks can be rented here, and when you work up a thirst or an appetite, there are plenty of beach bars and restaurants to choose from.

The popular **PLAYA DE AMOR** (Lover's Beach)—near Land's End and Cabo's famous arch—touches both the Pacific Ocean and the Sea of Cortez. Access is by water taxi or by glass-bottom boat tour; pack a cooler and arrange for a dropoff at the beach, returning with a later tour. These services are available from both the Marina and the Municipal Pier. Swimming is safe on the Cortez side, but currents are dangerously strong on the Pacific side. Remember—not all of Baja's beaches are safe for swimming, and lifeguards are nonexistent.

PLAYA SOLMAR is a beautiful stretch of white sand beach battered by the charging Pacific. Heavy undertows make the area unsuitable for swimming, but since Solmar is usually uncrowded, it's a great spot for quiet lounging, reading, and sunbathing. Access is via the road to Hotel Solmar Suites Resort (see Lodgings).

EL FARO VIEJO (the Old Lighthouse) is an interesting excursion not far from town. Nearby dunes are frequented by horseback riders and ATVs. Access by car is risky because of loose sand, but if you don't mind walking part of the way in, take Mexico 19 about 3 miles toward Todos Santos. Turn left at the Coca-Cola distribution center, and then right at the first T-junction; park at Smokey's Bar and walk up the hill. See Guides and Outfitters for information regarding tours in this area.

ATV TOURS / ATVs are a popular way to explore desert, beaches, and the Old Lighthouse; however, keep in mind that irresponsible riders may injure themselves or the fragile desert and coastal environments. Stay on roads or trails and avoid area beaches—known to harbor sea turtle nests. Ride with your group and always wear a helmet; unhelmeted riders are promptly ticketed by local *policía*.

DIVING AND SNORKELING / Cabo is known for easy access to great diving and snorkeling. Take a snorkeling cruise aboard one of the catamarans departing from the marina, or if you'd like to be more independent, rent some snorkeling gear and hire one of the glass-bottom boat captains to take you and your buddy to the bay side of **PLAYA DE AMOR** (Lover's Beach), where a series of coral-encrusted rocks provides a haven for colorful fish. The brave can frolic with the nearby sea lion colony at **LAND'S END**. Certified divers may want to check out the famous **SANDFALL**, once documented by Jacques Cousteau, where a sometimes-steady stream of sand drops into a 6,000-foot submarine canyon only 30 yards from shore. And if it's large marine life you desire, take a boat trip to **BANCO GORDA**—by far the best chance to encounter whale sharks, striped marlin, manta rays, or, in winter—if you're lucky—gray whales. For the latest visibility, conditions, and costs, contact **AMIGOS DEL MAR** (Blvd Marina at Zona Naval; 624/443-0505; sealion@cabotel.com.mx; www.amigosdel mar.com), **CABO ACUADEPORTES** (Playa Médano at Hotel Hacienda Beach Resort; 624/143-0117), **LAND'S END DIVERS** (Plaza Las Glorias A-5; 624/143-2200; www.mexonline.com/landsend.htm), or **PROFESSIONAL DIVING SER-VICES** (Plaza Las Glorias H-6; 624/143-8972; caboprodive@yahoo.com; www.mexonline.com/caboprodive.htm).

FISHING / In the '50s and '60s, the waters of the Cape were referred to as "Marlin Alley." Sportfishing enthusiasts from around the world were drawn to this tiny fishing village. Cabo still attracts an international fishing clientele, as the largest jackpots in the fishing world are offered each October at the **BISBEE BLACK AND BLUE MARLIN TOURNAMENTS.** The best way for visitors to enjoy a day of fishing is to book a reservation aboard one of the many charter boats operated by experienced captains who know where and how to hook up with the big ones. Reservations are required a few days to a month in advance (depending on the season). For an idea of what such an excursion will cost, or to make advanced reservations, contact the **PISCES FLEET** (Blvd Marina and Madero; 624/143-1288; www.mexonline.com/pfleet1.htm), the **SOLMAR FLEET** (Av Solmar 1; 624/143-3535 or 800/344-3349 US; www.solmar.com), or **PICANTE SPORTFISHING** (Marina Fiesta Resort and Hotel; 624/143-2474, fax 624/143-5969; www.picantesporfishing.com). When it comes to marlin fishing, remember this important Cabo motto: catch and release!

HORSEBACK RIDING / Experience the beauty of Pacific beaches or the arid desert landscape on horseback. **RANCHO COLLINS** (entrance to Meliá San Lucas; 624/143-3652), just off Playa El Médano, offers guided tours to the Old Lighthouse and a 3½-hour ride through desertscape to the Pacific for $60 US per person (minimum of two riders). Guided rides along the beach are also available for about $20 US per person. **ESTABLOS LA ROSA** (km 4 Mexico 1; 624/143-4826) features private rides for all levels of horsemanship using either Western or English styles. Guided tours are available with mountain and beach trail rides. Reservations are recommended and rates start at $25 US an hour.

GUIDES AND OUTFITTERS

Operating from several area hotels, **BAJA'S ATV'S & WATERSPORTS** (16 de Sep-tiembre and Mendoza; 624/143-2050; bajasmotorent@prodigy.net.mx) offers banana boat tours, snorkeling, parasailing, wave runners, and a variety of ATV tours including desert, beach, the Old Lighthouse, and trips to the Sierra de La Lagunas.

Providing a wide selection of water activities, **CABO ACUADEPORTES** (by Hotel Hacienda Beach Resort; 624/143-0117) is located on Médano Beach. Walk up and rent a kayak or try parasailing. They also offer water skiing, scuba certification classes, snorkeling, and boat tours.

CABO SAFARIS (headquartered at the Hacienda Beach Hotel; 624/143-0663 or 888/411-2252 US; www.cabosafari.com) offers eco-tours to hot springs and waterfalls, natural history tours to area fossil beds, and their popular sea turtle experience, where clients observe sea turtles as they come ashore to deposit their eggs. Bilingual guides are medically trained safety specialists, and transport is in four-wheel drive suburbans. Day trips start as low as $45 US.

In addition to parasailing and scenic boat tours of Land's End, **JT WATER SPORTS** (on Playa El Médano; 044-624-147-8613 or 044-624-147-5543) rents kayaks, snorkeling gear, and wave runners.

Besides parasailing, **JUANCHO'S PARA-SAIL** (Activity Center, Médano Beach, next to Las Palmas Restaurant; 624/143-3093) also handles glass-bottom boat trips, water taxis, and mountain bike tours, as well equipment rentals including wave runners, snorkel gear, water skiing, banana boat rides, kayaks, windsurfing, and scooter rentals.

PANCHITO TOURS (Cerro los Venados M 1 lot 19; 624/143-8532; panchito tours@prodigy.net.mx) offers several area tours, including a snorkeling trip to Santa María Bay, a trip to San José del Cabo with a stop at the Glass Factory, and several sightseeing excursions complete with glass-bottom boat rides. All tours are given in air-conditioned vehicles and have bilingual guides. Sodas, beer, and water are provided, as well as beach gear for the snorkeling tour. Pickups can be arranged for passengers in the Corridor and in San José del Cabo.

PISCES WATER SPORTS (Médano Beach next to Cascadas Beach Club; 044-624-148-7530; pbauche@prodigy.net.mx) rents wave runners, catamarans, kayaks, boogie boards, skimboards, and snorkel gear. If you need more excitement, they take you parasailing or on a banana boat ride. They also provide glass-bottom boat tours and water taxis.

Besides offering scuba certification courses and guided diving and snorkeling tours, **TÍO SPORTS** (Médano Beach by Meliá San Lucas; 624/143-2986 or 624/143-3399; www.tiosports.com) also rents wave runners, ocean kayaks, catamarans, ATVs, and mountain bikes.

Specializing in ATV rentals and tours, **CABO'S MOTO RENT** (Cárdenas near Puerto Paraiso Macro Plaza; 624/143-0808) leads ATV excursions into the desert, to the beach, to the Old Lighthouse, and on a six-hour round-trip tour to Candelaria, a mountain village known for its rustic clay pottery and medicinal healers. Tours vary in price, with lower rates for those who ride double.

Sightseeing trips with **RANCHO TOURS** (Calle de Pescador at El Médano beach; 624/143-5464 or 624/143-9344; ranchotours@prodigy.net.mx) are given by professional bilingual guides from air-conditioned vans. Most tours vary in length from 3 to 10 hours, some combining land and sea excursions. Regional tours investigate the entire Cape Region including San José del Cabo, the East Cape, Todos Santos, and even La Paz. Snacks, beverages, and meals are included. This tour company will pick up passengers along the Corridor and in San José del Cabo.

SEAGOING ADVENTURES

Ahoy, mate! There's no need to be a drifter in the doldrums in Cabo. Whether you'd like to dine on the deck of a pirate ship, tour Land's End from a glass-bottom skiff, snorkel among colorful fish, or spot migrating whales from a romantic sunset cruise, there's a cargo of seagoing expeditions awaiting visitors of all ages. Reservations are almost always recommended, so come about at any hotel or contact the following helmsmen and they'll rig you right up. Aye—be sure to ask if your dinner cruise is the quiet and romantic type, or if the mates are prone to rocking the boat!

Operating 24-foot Zodiac inflatables, **CABO EXPEDITIONS** (Plaza Las Glorias dock; 624/143-2700; caboexp@cabonet.net.mx; www.caboexpeditions.com) provides exciting, intimate on-the-water experiences. Inflatable boats, the same type used by U.S. Navy SEALS, are very versatile and easy to launch and land in sandy, secluded coves. Snorkeling tours are offered daily. Guides, trained by the Sea World Education Center, provide commentary on marine ecology and local landmarks. Tours range from 2 to 4 hours at $35 to $40 US per person.

The recently launched, 144-foot dinner cruiser **CABO REY** (624/143-8260; www.caborey.com; caborey@hotmail.com) is a 600-passenger luxury catamaran with an emphasis on family-oriented day trips which include snorkeling, whale-watching, and sightseeing voyages around Los Cabos. Gourmet dining, a jewelry store, fine art gallery, hot tub, and cabaret-style shows round out the list of on-board possibilities. Prices start at $69 US.

ENCORE SAILING CHARTERS (Cabo Isla Marina, dock G; 044-624-147-5328 or 044-624-143-5543; www.jtwatersports.com) offers snorkeling trips and sunset sails aboard *Encore*, a sleek 60-foot racing yacht. The snorkeling cruise costs $50 US per person and includes lunch and beverages; the Sunset Sail is $35 US per person, including margaritas, beer, and sodas.

The **FONDO DE CRISTALES** (glass-bottom boats) leave from Plaza Las Glorias dock frequently for a 45-minute, round-trip tour of the craggy rock formations and El Arco—the famous arch at Land's End. Other sights include a sea lion colony, pelican rookery, and colorful tropical fish. This tour is great for young kids, and is best when the sun is still high in the sky. The cost is $10 US for adults; children under 12 are $5. You can also arrange for a dropoff at Lover's Beach and schedule a pickup with a later boat from the fleet.

Take to sea in style when you board **KALEIDOSCOPE CRUISES'** (Marina Fiesta Hotel, Dock A; 044-624-1148-7318) sleek, luxurious, 100-foot power catamaran for a 7-mile coastal cruise. Daytime and sunset cruises are available. Tequila, beer, sodas, and snacks are included. Cruises cost $39 US per person; children under 12 are free.

OCEANUS DOUBLE-DECKER CATAMARAN (Blvd Marina; 624/143-3929 or 624/143-1059) operates two trips daily: a four-hour snorkeling and beach trip and a sunset cruise. Both feature an open bar, snacks, and live music. Cost is $30–$35 US per person; children under 12 half price.

PEZ GATO CATAMARANS (Plaza Las Glorias dock; 624/143-3797; pezgato@cabotel.com.mx) has two 42-foot Hawaiian-style beach catamarans that provide for snorkeling tours and sunset cruises with all-you-can-drink margaritas, beer, sodas, and snacks. The snorkeling cruise runs $50 US; sunset cruise, $30; children under 12 are half price.

PIRATE SHIP CRUISES (Marina Dock; 624/143-2714; www.pirateshipcabo.com.mx) take you back in time as you board the 105-foot, 186-ton sailing ship *Sunderland*, an original tall ship built in 1885. Excursions are conducted under full sail and include snorkeling trips and sunset cruises. An open bar, beer, soda, snacks, and the ship's own "Pirate Punch" are included. The cost is $37 US per person.

SUNRIDER CRUISES (Plaza Las Glorias dock; 624/143-2252; fun@sun-rider.com; www.sun-rider.com) offer a snorkel/lunch cruise or a sunset dinner cruise aboard the 60-foot M.V. *Sunrider*. A Mexican buffet and open bar are featured for $40 US per person; children under 10 are free during daytime cruises, half price for dinner cruises.

—*Gail MacLaughlin*

NIGHTLIFE

Many folks travel to Cabo San Lucas just for the nightlife. Others strive to avoid it. In many places, drinks are cheaper than bottled water, and the waiters will gladly pour it down your throat if you'll let them. There's a "ladies night" somewhere in Cabo almost every night of the week, offering free drinks to ladies for a few hours, and usually denoting standing room only.

Some of the most popular after-dark hangouts include one of Cabo's legendary drinking establishments, **EL SQUID ROE** (Blvd Marina across from Plaza Bonita; 624/143-0655), built to handle even the rowdiest of crowds, and the **GIGGLING MARLIN** (Blvd Marina and Matamoros; 624/143-4144), another watering hole with a reputation for strong drinks and anesthetized patrons. The **NOWHERE BAR** (L-12 Plaza Bonita, next to Margaritavilla; 624/143-4493) packs a crowd on Tuesday evenings and weekends, and you can get as wild as you wish at the **WILD COYOTE BAR** (Puerto Paraiso Macro Plaza on the marina; 624/143-6969 or 624/143-6966; www.coyoteugly.com.mx), where sexy Coyote Girls not only tend bar but perform regularly with creative top-of-the-bar dance routines. **THE HARD ROCK CAFÉ** (Cárdenas, Plaza Bonita Mall; 624/143-3370) has live rock and roll six nights a week, and Sammy Hagar's **CABO WABO CANTINA** (Cárdenas and Guerrero; 624/143-1188; www.cabowabo.com), advertising "where the land ends is where the party begins," stages live bands with occasional appearances by the owner himself. Ride the **WAVE** (Morelos and Cárdenas; 624/143-0010; wave@cabotel.com.mx) for live music and disco, or **LAS VARITAS** (Valentine Gomex F. and Camino a San José; 624/143-9999; www.lasvaritas.com), another party-all-night site. With the alcohol flowing like water and limited parking at most locations, consider hiring a taxi—the drivers know all the hot spots.

FESTIVALS AND EVENTS

SPLASH ART AND CRAFT FESTIVALS feature quality local and regional artisans exhibiting at biannual events staged each April and November in front of the marina. For more information contact Galería de Kaki Bassi (624/143-3510).

Cabo's patron saint is celebrated at the **FESTIVAL OF SAN LUCAS** with Mexican music, dancing, a carnival, and feasting held for a week around October 18.

Baja's largest sailboat race, **BAJA HA-HA** (www.baja-haha.com), is a long-distance competition from San Diego to Cabo that is organized every fall (weather permitting) as a kickoff to the sailing season.

October is also the month of numerous fishing tournaments, including the **BISBEE BLACK AND BLUE MARLIN JACKPOT TOURNAMENT** (949/650-8006 US; www.bajatournaments.com), in which the winning team of anglers cashes in some big bucks. Weigh-ins are held each afternoon at the municipal pier.

RESTAURANTS

Café Canela / ★★

MARINA AT PLAZA LAS GLORIAS, CABO SAN LUCAS; 624/143-3435 This dockside, open-air cafe with a bistro flair is situated under a shady ramada on the marina side of Plaza Las Glorias. A table here gives you a bird's-eye view of daily marina activity: million-dollar yachts at berth, deckhands taking on water and loading *cerveza*, and the constant parade of rapt tourists. Start your day with a European pastry and fresh-fruit smoothie or espresso, or try their delicious cinnamon waffles. For lunch, order a pita bread sandwich stuffed with chicken, beef, or veggies and served with a creamy garlic dressing. Seafood specialties change regularly, and the salads are fresh and creative. Finish your meal with one of their excellent desserts. Service is friendly, but don't be in a hurry. *$; AE, MC, V; traveler's checks OK; breakfast, lunch, dinner every day; full bar, no reservations; waterfront, central Cabo.*

Carnitas El Michoacano

LEONA VICARIO, CABO SAN LUCAS This outdoor, street-side *taquería* serves a variety of delicious pork selections. Choose from the posted menu of ribs, *gorditas,* and the house specialty, *carnitas* (little meats). A tray of condiments—salsas, avocado dip, onion, chiles, cilantro, and radishes— accompanies menu selections. Handmade tortillas and a hearty bean soup are an added treat. This is great Mexican food at great prices. *$; Cash only; lunch, dinner every day; no alcohol; no reservations; between Carranza and Alvaro Obregón.*

Casa Rafael's / ★★★⯪

CALLE PLAYA EL MÉDANO AND CAMINO AL HOTEL HACIENDA, CABO SAN LUCAS; 624/143-0739, FAX 624/143-1679 Food for a gourmet's palate, service for royalty, and a wine list that's impeccable are all suitable descriptions for Casa Rafael's. Though the setting is not opulent, it has an ambience all its own. Housed in a hot-pink hacienda lush with landscaping and whimsical decor, the dining areas are situated in a series of intimate indoor/outdoor locations. Starters include such items as fresh smoked *dorado* pâté, fried prawns in bisque sauce, or escargots with shallots and blue cheese. Progress to the excellent hearts of palm salad with raspberry vinaigrette or Rafael's Greek salad. Entree specialties include lobster medallions in an Oriental black bean sauce, Chicken Allison, and, for beef lovers, Black Angus filet mignon with morel mushrooms. Satisfy your sweet tooth with a treat from the evening's selection of freshly made desserts. After dinner, mosey over to the piano bar for a nightcap. *$$$$; AE, MC, V; traveler's checks OK; dinner every day; full bar, reservations required; casarafa@cabonet.net.mx; www.allabout cabo.com/casarafaels.htm; near the beach.*

El Bistro / ★★⯪

CALLES ZARAGOZA AND NINOS HEROES, CABO SAN LUCAS; 624/143-8999 Warm and unassuming, El Bistro charms you in with its tasteful decor, wood-beamed ceiling, Mexican tile flooring, and indoor/outdoor dining rooms. The creation of Michel and Valerie Cicéron, restaurateurs who recently migrated from Lyon, France, this casual eatery is friendly and affordable. Michel oversees the preparation of Mexican, Italian, and French cuisine in the kitchen while Valerie interacts with customers. Start with *escargots à la France* or Mediterranean bruschetta—toasted and topped with olive oil, ratatouille, and fresh Parmesan. The jambalaya à la New Orleans with chicken, shrimp, chorizo, and exotic rice is a taste pleaser, as are the sautéed shrimp in a light curry sauce. Bistec Arrachera, a fork-tender steak, was cooked exactly as ordered. The wine selection is varied and affordable. If you have room, finish with an old-fashioned banana split or a Mexican café, flambéed at your table. *$–$$; MC, V; traveler's checks OK; dinner Mon–Sat; full bar; reservations recommended; 1 block up from Aramburo supermarket.*

La Dolce / ★★⯪

CALLE HIDALGO AND ZAPATA, CABO SAN LUCAS; 624/143-4122 OR 624/143-9653 Arrive early or make sure you have a reservation, because this authentic Italian eatery always has a full house. Dedicated to customer satisfaction, proprietor/chef Stefano Miotto, originally from Treviso, Italy, learned to cook from his mother and then gained experience from different Italian chefs as he cooked his way around the world. Settling in Mexico 11 years ago, he started his first La Dolce in Puerto Vallarta in 1995. There are now three successful branches in the country—Puerto Vallarta, Cabo San Lucas, and San José del Cabo. Miotto's menu takes advantage of the fresh seafood and vegetables available in the region. Try one of the thin-crusted pizza creations or calzones from their wood-burning oven. Cannellonis, raviolis, and lasagne are made fresh daily, and if you're not in the mood for pizza or pasta, try the fillet of fish, prepared in your choice of lime or white wine sauce. Top it off with tiramisu or a rich Italian coffee. *$; MC, V; traveler's checks OK; dinner every day Dec–June, Mon–Sat only July–Nov; full bar; reservations recommended; ladolce@cabotel.co.mx; next to Pancho's.*

Mama's Royal Café / Felix / ★★☆

CALLE MIGUEL HIDALGO AND ZAPATA, CABO SAN LUCAS; 624/143-4290 This colorful indoor/outdoor eatery has a dual personality. During the morning and early afternoon, it's known as Mama's Royal Cafe. In the evening, however, Mama takes a siesta, as the eatery is transformed into a dinner house known simply as Felix. A father-and-son team of Spencer Moores own and operate these restaurants with a motto of "No Lard, No MSG, and No BS." Dine indoors or beneath the bamboo ramada amid colorful tables and potted plants. Both restaurants are famous for their elaborate salsa bar, boasting anywhere from 25 to 40 different salsas on any given day. Try Mama's stuffed French toast, bulging with cream cheese, topped with bananas and pecans, and flambéed in orange liqueur. The expansive breakfast menu also includes traditional Mexican or American dishes, and some nontraditional specialties such as crab Benedict. As the sun slips to the west, Felix emerges with a host of Mexican specialties not found in most places. Try the *pozole*, a hearty stew of meat cooked until it falls off the bone, then served in a large bowl with a rich, flavorful meat broth with hominy, accompanied by chopped cilantro, oregano, fresh limes, and toasted pumpkin seeds. Other favorites include shrimp in jalapeño cream sauce, chicken Monterrey, and their vegetarian stir-fry. Meals here are educational and the owners are happy to share recipes with customers. *$–$$; MC, V; traveler's checks OK; breakfast, dinner every day; full bar; no reservations; www.felix cabosanlucas.com; between Zapata and Madero.*

Mi Casa / ★★★☆

AV CABO SAN LUCAS, CABO SAN LUCAS; 624/143-1933 If you're in the mood for *muy auténtico*, traditional Mexican food, Mi Casa is a must. This extremely popular restaurant was established more than a decade ago by Keisha Valdez. Using recipes from her grandmother's cookbook, Valdez was forced to expand in order to appease her growing number of loyal customers—locals, return visitors, and celebrities. The fiesta begins in the open-air, terraced courtyard with colorful folk art, banners, table linens, and brightly painted chairs. Busy waiters scurry to and fro and the air is thick with the aroma of scrumptious, full-bodied tortillas made on the spot. Choose your tequila and order up a huge margarita while you listen to the lone guitarist singing ballads as traditional as the menu. Try one of Mexico's most notable dishes from the culinary capital of Puebla—*chiles en nogada*, a mouth-watering presentation of flavorful poblano chiles stuffed with sautéed beef or pork, covered with a walnut cream sauce; or try the *mancha mantele*—a tropical dish originating in the Yucatán, with chicken or pork sautéed in a burnished, red pepper *guajillo* sauce and smothered with tropical fruits. Seafood dishes are popular, but don't order the *langosta entera* (whole lobster) unless you are prepared to handle an enormous plate-size crustacean. For dessert, the *pastel de tres leches* (three-milk cake) is so moist and delicious you'll be tempted to order a second piece. *$–$$; AE, MC, V; traveler's checks OK; lunch Mon–Sat, dinner every day; full bar; reservations required; across from plaza.*

Nick-San Japanese Restaurant / ★★

BLVD MARINA, PLAZA DE LA DANZA, LOCAL 2, CABO SAN LUCAS; 624/143-4484 Nick-San is the place for melt-in-your-mouth sashimi and the freshest sushi in town. With a loyal following of locals and seasonal tournament fishermen, sushimeister Angel Carbajal creates tasty specialties, many directly from the Sea of Cortez. Start off with the sashimi salad, sliced tuna and sea bass with Angel's tangy, sesame-based dressing. Or try the baked scallops served with mango sauce, a deliciously light yet filling meal or appetizer. This popular eatery can fill up during lunch hours and evenings, but don't let that scare you off—service is fast and attentive. *$$; MC, V; traveler's checks OK; lunch, dinner Tues–Sat; full bar; no reservations; under stairway in plaza.*

The Office / ★

CALLE PLAYA EL MÉDANO, CABO SAN LUCAS; 624/143-3464 OR 624/143-4919 Certainly not like the office you're familiar with back home, the only concentrated work here is the study of throngs and thongs milling on Médano Beach. This popular restaurant/bar is not only beachfront, but literally *on* the beach with umbrellas and tables set in the sand. A longtime Cabo favorite, the Office was established in 1987, setting the pace for copycats ever since. During the day, this is a casual, come-as-you-are barefoot and bathing suit scene—and it's always crowded! Breakfast fare features Mexican traditionals such as huevos rancheros or Mexican omelets along with fresh-squeezed orange juice and great coffee. Lunch offerings include enchiladas, burritos, meal-size salads, seafood specials, and even American hamburgers. Evening selections are more upscale, including steamed lobster tail, jumbo shrimp, and steak. Get in on "the Office Party" every Thursday, Sunday, and Monday evening beginning at 6:30pm, when they stage a Mexican fiesta. Colorful *folklóric* dancers, mariachis, and music accompany this lively dinner. Reservations are required for these special evenings. *$$; AE, MC, V; traveler's checks OK; breakfast, lunch, dinner every day; full bar; reservations recommended; foot of Paseo del Pescador.*

Pancho's / ★☆

CALLE HIDALGO AND ZAPATA, CABO SAN LUCAS; 624/143-2891 Pancho's is a colorful Mexican eatery that is quite popular and centrally located. Chiles rellenos stuffed with Chihuahua cheese are a house specialty. Although the menu boasts "Authentic Mexican food at authentic Mexican prices," the prices are more reflective of an expensive Mexican restaurant in the United States. What makes Pancho's unique is that 10 years ago, owner John Bragg developed an interest in tequila, which drew him deep into the tequila regions of mainland Mexico. He has since collected more than 450 labels, and is a recognized international authority—a *tequilero,* giving lectures and tequila tastings throughout the United States and Mexico. If you can bring John an unopened bottle of tequila that he doesn't have, he'll buy the bottle and your dinner. Sign up for his weekly tequila tasting and get an education on *pulque,* the milky, unrefined beverage developed by the Aztecs; mezcal, the next stage in agave fermentation; and the four categories of tequila. If you have the nerve or the need, sip a sampling from the glass receptacle on the bar. It holds *tequila con cascabel*— rattlesnakes immersed in homemade tequila, a purported cure for arthritis and an aphrodisiac! *$$; MC, V; traveler's checks OK; breakfast, lunch, dinner every day; full bar; no reservations; bragg@panchos.com; www.panchos.com; 1 block from marina.*

Sancho Panza Wine Bistro / ★★★↘

PLAZA LAS GLORIAS, LOCAL D10-22, CABO SAN LUCAS; 624/143-3212
Named after Don Quixote's pudgy sidekick who was preoccupied with food and drink, this stylish jewel is one of the hottest restaurants in Cabo. Sancho Panza's owners, Monica Hidalgo and Ron Kleist, have filled the need for a trendy place to enjoy fine food, select wines, and great music. And they know what they're doing. This twosome has been importing fine wines to Baja since 1994. With some 200 labels to choose from and more than 4,000 cases stored in temperature-controlled warehouses, they sell to many of the Cape's upscale restaurants and major hotels. Chef Monica, who is originally from Cuernavaca and studied in Switzerland, likes to describe her dinner creations as "Mediterranean with a Latin flair." She changes the menu every few days, reflecting current inspirations and seasonal ingredients. Her signature dish, the grilled *ahi* tuna, was served with a tempting pasilla and tomatillo salsa one week and a fresh sage, lemon, and garlic *chimichurri* the next. There's live jazz and blues every night to dance away the calories, wine tasting on Wednesday, and tequila sampling on Thursday, with some of the more popular tequilas in Mexico. Check their sophisticated web site for more information and special events. *$$$; MC, V; traveler's checks OK; dinner Mon–Sat; full bar; reservations recommended; wine@sanchopanza.com; www.sanchopanza.com; behind lighthouse tower.*

Señior Greenberg's Mexicatessen / ★★

BLVD MARINA, PLAZA NÁUTICA, CABO SAN LUCAS; 624/143-5630, FAX 624/143-5620 Señior G's doors are open 24 hours, convenient after a night on the town. American-Jewish with a touch of Mexico, this airy deli offers an almost unending array of menu options. Breakfasts include traditional Mexican selections such as huevos rancheros, *chilaquiles* and eggs, or *puntas encebolladas* (tasty beef strips with sautéed onions), as well as cheese blintzes, sticky buns, and cinnamon rolls. For lunch, go Asian with the Thai chicken salad or choose a giant-size deli sandwich. Burgers, burritos, and chiles rellenos are available at all hours. For kids, choose from a less expensive children's menu. Satisfy your sweet tooth with New York cheesecake, carrot cake, or an ice cream sundae. Items are on the pricey side, as is generally true in Cabo, but portions are generous. *$; MC, V; traveler's checks OK; breakfast, lunch, dinner every day; beer and wine; no reservations; just off the marina.*

Taquería El Paisa I and II

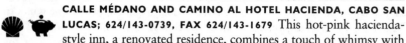

REVOLUCIÓN, CABO SAN LUCAS; LEONA VICARIO, CABO SAN LUCAS Schedule a visit to either of the Paisa locations for savory grilled carne asada tacos, *papas rellenos mixtas* (baked potatoes stuffed with meat and cheese), quesadillas, Mexican beans, and tasty grilled onions. These open-air sidewalk cafes operate on Cabo nightlife time—6pm–4am—and can be crowded in the evenings with both locals and tourists. Service is relatively prompt; the attraction is authentic Mexican grilled beef and good prices. *$; Cash only; dinner every day; no alcohol; no reservations; Revolución between Morelos and Leona Vicario; Leona Vicario on corner of 20th de Noviembre.*

LODGINGS

Casa Rafael's / ★★★

CALLE MÉDANO AND CAMINO AL HOTEL HACIENDA, CABO SAN LUCAS; 624/143-0739, FAX 624/143-1679 This hot-pink hacienda-style inn, a renovated residence, combines a touch of whimsy with excellence at an affordable price. Owners Raphael and Allison Arraut refer to their creation as a "boutique hotel" where fine attention to detail is exhibited within their 10 charming guest rooms. Comfortable and roomy with pleasing decor, each tiled room offers such amenities as hair dryers, coffeemakers, fluffy terry-cloth robes, furnished sitting areas, air conditioning, and open-air balconies. The lushly landscaped grounds incorporate aviaries of songbirds, saltwater aquariums with colorful tropical fish, fountains, outdoor patios and sundecks, a swimming pool, and a hot tub. The romantic Casa Rafael's restaurant (see review), with its charming piano bar and superb wine collection, is an area attraction. One block off Médano Beach, so you're an easy walk to town and a multitude of activities. *$$; AE, MC, V; traveler's checks OK; casarafa@ cabonet.net.mx; take Camino al Hotel Hacienda from Lázaro Cárdenas to intersection with Calle Medano.*

Hotel Finisterra / ★★☆

BLVD MARINA, CABO SAN LUCAS; 624/143-3333 OR 800/347-2252 US, FAX 624/143-0590 The original Hotel Finisterra, built in the early '70s, clung to the upper cliffs of the rocky ridge separating Bahiá San Lucas from the Pacific. Today these rooms are nearly overshadowed by the hotel's latest addition—a massive nine-story tower rising from the beach. A walking bridge spans the distance between this newer annex and the cliff-top location of the original section. The older rooms have recently been renovated, still offering impressive views of the Pacific, Cabo San Lucas harbor, and central Cabo. The combined complex now occupies 700 acres on the Pacific Ocean, with 280 rooms and 125 junior suites. A magnificent beachfront Tahitian-style *palapa* centers serpentine pools with swim-up bars and hot tubs. On-site facilities include a fitness center and spa, lighted tennis courts, two restaurants, and three bars (service can be inconsistent). Order a drink at the famous Whale Watcher's Bar, now reopened after suffering damage from Hurricane Juliette in September 2001, and a favorite observation area for spotting whales and watching vivid sunsets. The junior suites offer a 600-square-foot layout with marble baths, tile floors, sitting areas, minibars, and ocean-view terraces. Satellite TV and air conditioning are standard in all rooms. The expansive ocean beach is relatively uncrowded, but it's unsuitable for swimming due to a strong undertow. *$$$–$$$$; AE, MC, V; traveler's checks OK; finister@cabonet.net.mx; www.finisterra.com; Finisterra turnoff on Pacific side.*

Hotel Hacienda Beach Resort / ★★★↾

HACIENDA BLVD, CABO SAN LUCAS; 624/143-4466 OR 800/733-2226 US Capture the feeling of early-day Cabo at this subtropical resort situated on a peninsula forming the south end of Playa El Médano. Hosting guests for more than four decades, this was the first grand resort on beachfront Cabo. Mission-style architecture amid lush landscaping, flagstone pathways winding down to the beach, and private cabanas opening directly onto the sand are signatures of this alluring retreat. Shielded from the commercialism of the marina and central Cabo, the 115 units are a combination of suites, beach cabanas, studios, and town houses. All have private balconies or patios, most with fantastic views of Land's End. The units here are not as modern as the newer, more ostentatious neighboring resorts, but this resort exudes Mexican charm. Five restaurants, including an open-air dining terrace, are on the premises, as well as five bars, a large free-form swimming pool, lighted tennis courts, an exercise room, a water-sports center, and a full-service dive center. The marina and central Cabo are just steps away. *$$$–$$$$; AE, MC, V; traveler's checks OK; hhbr@cabonet.net.mx; www.haciendacabo.com; from Lázaro Cárdenas, take Hacienda Blvd to Playa el Médano.*

Hotel Santa Fé / ★

IGNACIO ZARAGOZA AND ALVARO OBREGÓN, CABO SAN LUCAS; 624/143-4401 OR 624/143-4402, FAX 624/143-2552 Relatively new on the scene, this studio-unit hotel is located in the heart of Cabo San Lucas, offering 46 air-conditioned units with kitchenettes, queen-size beds and sofa beds, satellite TV, and telephones. Added bonuses include a swimming pool, ample parking, 24-hour security, a small coffee shop, and laundry facilities. A restaurant and minimarket are also located on the premises. Located within walking distance of most attractions, Santa Fe caters to budget-minded families, as children under 18 are free if staying in the same room as their parents. *$$; AE, MC, V; traveler's checks OK; santafe@cabonet.net.mx; www.hotel santafecabo.com; downtown.*

Hotel Solmar Suites Resort / ★★★

AV SOLMAR 1, CABO SAN LUCAS; 624/143-3535 OR 800/344-3349 US Removed from the bustle of central Cabo, the Solmar conveys a certain serenity—something lacking at many of Cabo's hotels. The sprawling Pacific-side resort, just a mile from the heart of Cabo, is tucked against Land's End. Low-profile buildings of white stucco seem to blend with the sands of the expansive Playa Solmar, the rhythm of surf nearby. Flagstone surrounds the large oceanfront swimming pool, with its shaded swim-up *palapa* bar. Resort facilities include an on-site restaurant, "La Roca," two swimming pools, a heated aquaerobic pool, a 15-person hot tub, indoor/outdoor dining areas, and tennis courts. The 176 units vary in size and come complete with king- or queen-size beds, satellite TV, minibars, telephones, coffeemakers, tile bathrooms with shower and tub, ground-floor beach-entry patios, and second-floor private balconies. They also have a reputable dive operation, and the Solmar fishing fleet is one of the best and largest in the region. Unfortunately, timeshare solicitors are allowed to approach guests here. *$$$–$$$$; AE, MC, V; traveler's checks OK; www.solmar.com; off south end of Blvd Marina.*

Mar De Cortez Hotel / ★

LÁZARO CÁRDENAS AND VICENTE GUERRERO, CABO SAN LUCAS; 624/143-0032 OR 800/347-8821 US, FAX 624/143-0232 Exceptionally popular in the '60s and '70s, this colonial-style hotel has been attracting guests since Cabo was a quaint fishing village. Family-owned and -operated, this two-story complex is very well kept and situated in the heart of town. Although most rooms are not modern, recent renovations, upkeep, and service make this a smart, affordable choice. The 90 rooms—which include a recent addition—feature a choice of beds (king, queen, doubles, and twins), private baths, and air conditioning, and surround an interior patio and large swimming pool. The hotel also operates the convenient indoor/outdoor restaurant and the bar, Spencer's, where live entertainment is not unusual. Convenient parking behind the complex is an added plus in congested downtown Cabo, and shopping, restaurants, and nightlife are at your front door. *$; MC, V; traveler's checks OK; www.mardecortez.com; in downtown Cabo.*

CHANGING BAJA

For centuries only natives, Spanish *padres*, miners, and adventurous explorers took an interest in the narrow strip of land with the seemingly endless coastline. With the paving of Mexico 1 in the 1970s, however, Baja opened itself to anyone with an automobile or bus fare. The construction of international airports and overflow of cruise ships created a need for hotels, with mega-resorts following in hot pursuit. In the past few years, media attention, word of mouth, and the growing popularity of the Internet spread the news of this unspoiled recreational haven. The increase in visitors has led to an increase in development that, some feel, if left unchecked might compromise Baja's very essence.

During the 1980s, tourism exploded along the southern tip, with the once-quaint fishing village of Cabo San Lucas at its epicenter. "Cabo" is now better known as a party town, and its transformation has triggered a trend toward commercialization in Baja. Peaceful La Paz, noted for its colonial architecture and traditional Mexican eateries, recently opened its doors to a Burger King. Farther south, on a stretch of previously tourist-ignored beaches, a gigantic resort is under construction. The project will feature its own desalination plant, and golf courses will soon blanket the arid terrain. Like many privately backed developments in Baja, this one received full support from the Mexican government, including the official renaming of the bay from Bahía de los Muertos (Bay of the Dead) to Bahía de los Sueños (Bay of Dreams) on the premise that dreams sell much better than death on the World Wide Web.

Government-initiated tourist enterprises have not always been successful. Puerto Escondido, a natural harbor south of Loreto (see the Mid-South chapter), was slated for development several years ago by FONATUR, the government's official tourism department. Today, all that remains of the planned marina, hotels, and restaurants are weed-ridden parking lots and dilapidated structures.

The government's current venture, dubbed the "Nautical Ladder," could result in the construction of 22 ports lining both sides of the peninsula. (See "The Phantom Escalera Náutica" sidebar in the North-Central chapter.) The completed project would bring tourist dollars to several low-income regions. Conservation groups, both Mexican and American, are examining the plan, trying to anticipate its environmental effects.

Many of Baja's marine creatures are disappearing as development increases. Gray whales, however, which breed in Baja's Pacific lagoons, seem to be on the rebound due to strictly enforced boating regulations and the protection of the lagoons. The whales' popularity with tourists actually helped save Laguna San Ignacio from development in 1999 when the Mexican government, under pressure from conservation groups worldwide, refused to grant Mitsubishi permission to construct a salt evaporation plant at the remote site. Ironically, the bay leading into this same lagoon has been slated for development by the Mexican government as part of the Nautical Ladder.

The more popular the peninsula becomes, the more developers see dollar signs in its blue waters, jagged mountains, and stark desert scenery—and the more conservationists fight to protect its natural beauty and wildlife, as do many locals and visitors who also hope to preserve Baja's character. The need to find a balance between tourism, the culture, and the environment is not unique to Baja, but it is a relatively new phenomenon for the narrow strip of land whose coastline no longer seems quite so endless.

For more information visit these websites: www.escaleranautica.com.mx; www.fonatur.gob.mx; Sea of Cortez Foundation—http://mexicofile.com/seaofcortezfoundation; www.planeta.com/ecotravel/mexico/baja/baja.html.

—*Carrie Robertson*

Todos Santos

Sandwiched between the Pacific Ocean and the dramatic heights of the Sierra de la Laguna, Todos Santos sits on the Tropic of Cancer. This idyllic community strives to retain its Mexican heritage, low-key ambience, and cultural diversity, while embracing an ever-increasing population. Among those seeking residence here are numerous artists, sculptors, writers, and entertainers from the United States, Canada, Europe, and mainland Mexico. Its reputation as a center for locally produced art is steadily growing.

This oasis with freshwater lagoons, lush palm groves, and abundant fruit trees is a great place to shed the frantic pace of Cabo. Linger a while and indulge in fine foods, browse the art galleries and artisan shops, and study the historic brick buildings.

The first known permanent settlement here was a Jesuit outpost mission, established in 1723 to take advantage of the rich soil and water supply, a rarity in the arid Baja terrain. Fruits, vegetables, wine, and sugarcane were produced and transported to the mother mission in La Paz. Although Misión Nuestra Señora del Pilar de Todos Santos was elevated to full-fledged mission status, over time Indian rebellions, religious/government conflicts, and the demise of the Indian population through disease led to its close in 1840. The lands previously under church rule became farmland and cattle ranches, attracting mainland immigrants. The thriving sugarcane industry became the mainstay of the economy.

By the early 1900s, the pueblo was a growing community of hotels, theaters, municipal offices, and handsome brick homes. The area fell on hard times in the 1950s, when water, essential to the production of sugarcane, was in short supply. Although water is once again plentiful, provided by underground streams from the Sierra de la Laguna, the water-intensive sugarcane industry never recovered. Today's historic structures—along with the decaying sugarcane mills—are from this era, while the current economy thrives on organic farming, orchards, fishing, ranching, and an increasing number of tourists. The 1986 opening of Mexico 19—the paved road from San Pedro to Cabo San Lucas—was an invitation for travelers to discover the charm of Todos Santos and its nearby beaches. Today the population hovers around 6,000.

ACCESS AND INFORMATION

The primary means of access to Todos Santos is by **CAR** via Mexico 19. From La Paz, head south on Mexico 1 through San Pedro to the Mexico 19 junction. The route is well marked by signs indicating "Cabo San Lucas." Todos Santos is 35 miles south of this junction; Cabo San Lucas lies another 48 miles south of Todos Santos. The nearest airport is the **MÁRQUEZ DE LEÓN INTERNATIONAL AIRPORT** in La Paz (see Access and Information in the La Paz section). **LOS CABOS INTERNATIONAL AIRPORT** is farther away, but offers more scheduled flights (see Access and Information at the beginning of this chapter).

AIRPORT SHUTTLES are available from either airport, albeit expensive. **RENTAL CARS** are a more popular choice for getting to Todos Santos, and are also available at both airports. **BUS TRANSPORTATION** is available from both La Paz and Cabo. Autotransportes Águila (612/122-7898) operates the two-hour trip from either location. Tickets are purchased as you board and cost $3 US for a one-way fare. Bus stops are located on Colegio Militar (the main road to La Paz) between Degollado and Zaragoza near the park.

A fleet of **BLUE VANS** is operated within Todos Santos by Union Costa Azul (612/145-0063), providing sightseeing, beach runs, or return trips to the airport (they do not pick up). **TAXIS** are located next to the park at the foot of Zaragoza. Budget Car Rental (35 Calle Juárez; 612/145-0219) is new in town. Clients can pick up at the airport and drop off here, or vice versa.

There are no formal visitor information centers within this small community. The best source of both historical and current information is the popular bookstore **EL TECOLOTE LIBROS** (Calle Juárez and Hidalgo; 612/145-0295). The *Todos Santos Book,* co-authored by owner Janet Howey, is excellent for visitors who intend to remain in the area for several days or weeks, and a must for those considering residency. The monthly publication **EL CALENDARIO DE TODOS SANTOS** is also chock full of useful information and offered free in area shops. The **TODOS SANTOS INTERNET CAFE** (Calle Juárez and Topete; 612/145-0219) offers five-station, high-speed Internet service with basic rates of 1 peso a minute.

EXPLORING

The only way to truly enjoy this intimate Mexican community is to stroll the local streets. Start at the **CENTRAL PLAZA** (one block off Calle Juárez, between Centenario and Legaspi), a hub for civic and cultural events. The mission church, **IGLESIA NUESTRA SEÑORA DEL PILAR,** fronts the plaza and is definitely worth a visit. **TEATRO CINE GRAL. MANUEL MÁRQUEZ DE LEÓN** is an age-old theater housed in the large building flanking the north side of the plaza. From the '40s until the early '90s, this was the only live-production theater in Baja Sur, hosting music, dance, and dramatic performances staged by traveling theater troupes. Today it's again seeing increased use, but remains closed between performances; if the doors are open, don't hesitate to peek inside. Centenario, Legaspi, Calle Juárez, and Colegio Militar are all dotted with restored **HISTORIC BRICK BUILDINGS,** many functioning today as shops, cafes, art galleries, or private homes.

CENTRO CULTURAL PROFESSOR NÉSTOR AGÚNDEZ MARTÍNEZ (Topete and Obregón) is the refurbished brick building commonly referred to as **CASA DE LA CULTURA** or the **MUSEUM,** recently renamed to honor a local teacher and poet. The entry of this former elementary school features wall murals from the industrial 1930s era. A series of exhibit rooms display modern and contemporary art, Indian and historic artifacts, photographs, and a more current color representation of today's community. Art festivals, plays, and other cultural events are often staged here. Open Monday–Friday (8am–5pm), with shorter hours on the weekends; admission is free.

Locals often congregate at **TACOS CHILAKOS** (Calle Juárez and Hidalgo) for exceptional carne asada tacos with a nice selection of toppings. On Mexico 19, one block south of the Pemex station, choose between **THE HAPPY FISH** (Zaragoza and Colegio Militar) for fish and shrimp tacos, and **CARNITAS BARAJAS** (Degollado and Cuauhtémoc), specializing in mouth-watering shredded pork or *carnitas.*

Although Mexican arts and crafts have traditionally come from mainland villages, today Todos Santos is an emerging exception. This vibrant art colony boasts nearly a dozen small **ART GALLERIES** featuring artwork in various media—wood and metal sculpture, ceramics and pottery, watercolors, oils, pastels, woven basketry, and stained glass—including creations by well-known Mexican and local regional artists.

First on the scene was **GALERÍA DE TODOS SANTOS** (Legaspi and Topete; 612/145-0050), established in 1995 by Michael and Pat Cope, providing an exhibition site for a few solitary artists. Today the Copes display exceptional exhibits, which change every three or four weeks in the winter season. Visit the original gallery and their newer **GALLERY ANNEX** (Centenario and Hidalgo). Other galleries to explore in this area include **GALLERÍA LA CORONELA** (Legaspi between Hidalgo and Topete; 612/145-0505), displaying paintings and pottery created by Mexican artists; **GALLERÍA ORSAY** (Topete and Centenario; 612/145-0514), owned by multimedia Mexican artist Gabo and featuring his work as well as the work of popular La Paz artist Leonardo Diaz; **THE CHARLES STEWART GALLERY** (Centenario and Obregón; 612/145-0265), the home and studio of Charles Stewart, a former Taos, New Mexico, artist known for his distinctive style and wood carvings; **GALLERÍA LOGAN** (Calle Juárez and Morelos; 612/145-0151), featuring oils and acrylics by artist Joan Logan, whose contemporary impressionist subjects range from bold, brilliant landscapes to sensuous female figures; **GALLERÍA WALL** (Calle Juárez between Márquez de León and Hidalgo; 612/145-0527), which exhibits original oils in Mexican themes by Catherine Wall; and **GALLERÍA FIDENCIO** (Colegio Militar between Márquez de León and Hidalgo) featuring Fidencio's religious wood carvings, along with sculpture and furniture crafted by other local artists.

SHOPPING

Artisan shops also offer noteworthy selections and beckon as you stroll around town. Be sure to visit **CASA FRANCO** (Calle Juárez between Zaragoza and Morelos; 612/145-0356) for its wonderful selection of Mexican pottery, arts, crafts, and rustic furniture. **FÉNIX DE TODOS SANTOS** (Calle Juárez between Hidalgo and Topete; 612/145-0028) specializes in handcrafted Mexican art, jewelry, leather bags, hand-woven fabrics, *equipal* furniture, and decorative tinware. **LA SONRISA** (Calle Juárez between Topete and Obregón; 612/145-0472) features unique iron art such as accent wall pieces, garden sculpture, and furniture. **EL PERICO AZUL** (Centenario and Topete; 612/145-0222) is an upscale boutique featuring designer clothes and accessories from Mexico, South America, and Asia. **MANGOS MEXICANAS** (Centenario between Topete and Obregón) offers a selection of Mexican folk art, ceramics, metal sculpture, and Guatemalan textiles. Keep in mind that these small shops and galleries often keep short hours, typically 10am–4pm, with Sunday closures.

ADVENTURES

PACIFIC BEACHES / From Todos Santos, Mexico 19 heads south, threading its way between the Pacific shore and coastal farmlands for some 50 miles. Wide sandy beaches, remote and unspoiled, stretch for miles without shoreline interruptions by condos or high-rise resorts. Since the Pacific beaches are accessible only by poorly marked dirt roads, they have remained well-kept secrets shared by more adventurous off-roaders, surfing enthusiasts, or avid surf fishermen. Challenging surf crashing against the shoreline with steep dropoffs creates strong currents and undertows, rendering most of the shore unsuitable and unsafe for swimmers. Even beach walkers and waders are warned to keep a constant vigil for an unexpected "rogue" wave, which could sweep them into churning waters. Fortunately, there are a few locations where swimming is recommended and surfing is great for beginners, while other areas provide beachside camping, surf fishing, and shell collecting accompanied by the rhythm of the ocean.

Visit **PLAYA PUNTA LOBOS** (km 54 Mexico 19) between 1 and 3pm to witness the exciting return of fisherman who expertly "surf" the waves while bringing their *pangas* ashore. Boat launching is not permitted, and the beach often has dangerous currents that make it unsafe for swimming, but it's said to be good for surf fishing. You can sometimes barter with local fishermen for a day of fishing or a whale-watching expedition in a *panga*. If all else fails, purchase some fresh fish. The dirt access road for Lobos is located just over a mile south of Todos Santos, and is currently marked by a real estate sign advertising beach lots overlooking Punta Lobos.

PLAYA SAN PEDRO (km 59 Mexico 19) offers the best facilities of the Pacific beaches. The expansive, sandy beach is unsuitable for swimmers, but popular with **SURFERS** at the north end. **SAN PEDRITO RV PARK RESTAURANT AND BAR** (621/108-4316) is located on this popular beach, offering tent sites with *palapa* shelters, full RV hookups, showers, flush toilets, laundry facilities, rental cabanas with private baths, and a swimming pool. The restaurant/bar offers an extensive selection of freshly prepared seafood and a variety of Mexican specialties, as well as several versions of the ever-popular *hamburguesa*. San Pedro is easily accessed via dirt road located at the km 59 sign, about 5 miles south of Todos Santos.

Commonly referred to as Playa Las Palmas, **PLAYA SAN PEDRITO** (km 56–57 Mexico 19) is home to a thick grove of palms that fringe a nearby salt marsh—home to a variety of plants, birds, and wildlife. The wide, sandy beach is secluded and scenic, with rocky headlands at each end. Swimming is acceptable only in the center of the sweeping cove, as the ends are notorious for riptides. The landlord of this privately owned area allows public visitation, but no beach camping. Access is by an unmarked dirt road across from Campo Experimental. When entering, look for the ruins of an old sugar mill, and stay to the left at all road forks. Follow this section that curves around the south end of the palm orchard—otherwise, you will find yourself separated from the beach by the marsh. Gates are open 6am–6pm.

One of the few Pacific beaches usually safe for swimming, **PLAYA LOS CER-RITOS** (km 64) boasts miles of scenic coastline. If the waves aren't too big, this is a great spot for novice surfers and boogie boarders. A northwest swell brings in a nice point break near the northern rocks. Climb the rocky ledge for a panoramic vista and a chance to spot migrating whales. If there are whales in the area, put your head underwater and sometimes you can hear their songs. An older, unkempt campground attracts self-contained campers and RVs, as electricity and water are not available at this time. The turnoff is located about 9 miles south of Todos Santos.

GUIDES AND OUTFITTERS

Many of the Pacific surfing locations are for experts only. Breaks are usually best during the northwest swell, December through March. Check out the **TODOS SANTOS SURF SHOP** (Mexico 19 and Rangel; 612/145-0003; teampaty1@hotmail.com) for rental equipment and an update on surf conditions. **PESCADERO SURF CAMP** (km 64 Mexico 19; 612/145-0288 or 800/847-5921 US/Canada; info@pescaderosurf.com; www.pescadersosurf.com/surfcamp.htm) offers board and boogie rentals, surfing instructions, and "Surfaris"—guided surfing expeditions to the best locations in Baja Sur. Camp facilities include rental cabanas, as well as *palapa* or tent camping. Showers, private baths, outdoor kitchens, and electricity and water hookups are available.

FESTIVALS AND EVENTS

Each year in February or early March, Todos Santos stages the **TODOS SANTOS FIESTA DEL ARTE,** one or two weeks of cultural festivals. One series is dedicated to the performing arts, featuring colorful Mexican dance troupes, music, and theater performances staged in the historic theater fronting the plaza and at the Cultural Center. Local galleries sponsor another festival, with exhibitions featuring paintings, sculpture, ceramics, and other artwork by locals as well as regional artists. Usually in conjunction with one of these events, the cultural center sponsors an Historic Homes Tour. This is a once-a-year opportunity to see inside the numerous historic buildings that have been artfully restored as private residences surrounding intimate interior gardens. For exact dates or more information, contact any of the local galleries (see Exploring).

The entire population turns out for the gala **FIESTA TODOS SANTOS** (www.todossantos-baja.com), which honors the town's patron saint, Our Lady of Pilar of Zaragoza. Staged the week of October 12, festival activity centers around the town plaza, with the appearance of colorful Mexican folk performers, serenading mariachi bands, carnival rides, and street vendors selling their wares, foods, and Mexican confections. Cockfights, horse races, and theater performances are also held, along with the blessing of flower-bedecked fishing boats at Punta Lobos. The 17th-century image of the virgin is carried during nightly processions in honor of the saint.

Beginning on December 12 (the Day of Our Lady of Guadalupe), nightly candlelight processions called **POSADAS** wind through the streets, ending at the plaza church. These and other colorful celebrations of the season permeate the pueblo atmosphere during the two-week holiday season. The *Posada* celebrations culminate in a midnight mass on Christmas Eve.

RESTAURANTS

Café Santa Fé / ★★★

CENTENARIO 4, TODOS SANTOS; 612/145-0340, FAX 612/145-0340

Housed in a 150-year-old hacienda, Café Santa Fé is marked by one scripted word, "Restaurant," appearing over gigantic wooden doors at the entrance. Inside, Mexican tile flooring, vanilla walls, and small tables adorned in white linens are a pleasant backdrop for the focal point, an interior garden courtyard canopied by a *palapa* and fringed with large ferns, mature trees, and clay-potted plants. Indoor/outdoor dining attracts both locals and visitors drawn by the exceptional northern Italian cuisine prepared under the strict supervision of the owners, Ezio and Paula Colombo. The menu features homemade pastas, locally grown vegetables, fresh fish and shellfish, premium meat selections, and wood-fired pizzas. Pasta dishes with tantalizing sauces include Raviola Aragosta, prepared with lobster and ricotta cheese, served in a light cream sauce with basil, chopped tomatoes, vodka, and freshly grated Parmesan. Succulent grilled New Zealand rack of lamb is marinated in olive oil, garlic, rosemary, and sage. Popular first-course choices are fresh steamed clams in a savory sauce, antipasto, octopus salad, or a crisp organic garden salad. Sip espresso with tiramisu for dessert. Service is friendly and prompt. *$$$; AE, MC, V; traveler's checks OK; lunch, dinner Wed–Mon (closed Sept–Oct); full bar; reservations recommended; colombo@cabonet.net.mx; facing town plaza on southeast side.*

Caffé Todos Santos / ★★

CENTENARIO, TODOS SANTOS; 612/145-0300 Cafe central for locals, who gather here to talk and sip espresso, cappuccino, or herb tea over freshly baked cinnamon rolls. Colorful, hand-painted chairs adorn the indoor dining area, but the attraction of an intimate, brick-walled patio with subtropical plants and a honeysuckle-covered ramada makes it hard to opt for inside dining. For breakfast choose a regular or Mexican-style omelet, or a bagel teamed with a fresh-fruit smoothie. Hearty deli sandwiches, hamburgers, and enchiladas are lunchtime favorites. The Mexican specialty chicken flautas are particularly tasty: chicken marinated in coconut milk with a hint of curry, wrapped in a flour tortilla and fried, then served with mango salsa, sliced avocado, and chopped tomato and lettuce. The kid's menu includes frothy milkshakes. Service is cheerful, but can be on the slow side. *$; Cash only; breakfast, lunch every day, dinner Tues–Sun; beer and wine; no reservations; between Topete and Obregón.*

Fonda El Zaguán / ★

CALLE JUÁREZ BETWEEN HIDALGO AND TOPETE, TODOS SANTOS; 612/145-0217 Tucked away behind its giant, wooden-door entrance, this small hallway restaurant is very unassuming. The attraction is reasonably priced, fresh, but simple seafood dishes prepared according to authentic Mexican tradition. Daily specials vary, but usually include a shrimp of the day, catch of the day, and some version of the house's special seafood stew. Fish and shrimp tacos come wrapped in fresh, handmade tortillas with an array of condiments. Add an ice-cold beer with *limón,* a margarita, or a Mexican soft drink to complete this Mexican *comida* experience. *$; Cash only; lunch, dinner every day; full bar; no reservations; near El Tecolote Libros.*

Restaurante El Gusto! / ★★★

OFF MEXICO 19 (POSADA LA POZA), TODOS SANTOS; 612/145-0400, FAX 612/145-0475 Sunset and ocean views are undeniably breathtaking at this upscale eatery, which claims to offer the only beachfront dining in Todos Santos. The glass-enclosed dining room and two terraces look out over a sand beach and the palm-fringed lagoon setting of the Posada La Poza resort. The Ballena Deck is appropriately named as patrons digest glimpses of passing *ballenas* (whales) along with their appetizers and cocktails. Appointed with comfortable high-backed teak chairs, quality linen-clothed tables, and soft lighting, the dining room is small but airy, its amber walls highlighted with original paintings by Libusche, one of the owners. Mexican chef Carlos Reynoso Calixto comes to El Gusto from the exclusive Las Ventanas al Paraiso resort on the Corridor. Menu offerings here are simple, with an emphasis on locally grown, organic vegetables, fresh seafood, meats, and poultry. *Queso-* (cheese-) stuffed chicken breast is a delight, combining three cheeses and a touch of *camote* (sweet potato). The baby rack of lamb is fork-tender, drizzled with a raspberry sauce. Choose Swiss chocolate mousse as a grand finale. The wine list is appropriate, and service is attentive but not intrusive. *$$; AE, MC, V; traveler's checks OK; lunch, dinner Mon–Sat; full bar; reservations recommended; contact@la poza.com; www.lapoza.com; from Mexico 19 head west on Olochea and follow signs on winding, rugged dirt road.*

Restaurante Santanas / ★

LEGASPI 3 (HOTEL TODOS SANTOS), TODOS SANTOS; 612/145-0009, FAX 612/145-0098 This funky outdoor restaurant occupies the flagstone patio behind the Hotel Todos Santos, overlooking a distant ocean and adjacent garden terrace. Shaded by a large *palapa* roof and decorated with hanging surfboards and barstools sporting U.S. license plates, Santanas is popular with locals and the active set. The menu includes a variety of hearty, freshly prepared pizzas, calzones, subs, and salads. Brad Baer, the owner, is in the process of expanding menu offerings to include pastas, seafood selections, and traditional Mexican dishes. *$; AE, MC, V; traveler's checks OK; lunch, dinner Tues–Sun; full bar; no reservations; reservations@hoteltodossantos.com; www.hoteltodossantos.com; on town square.*

Suki's / ★★

HIDALGO BETWEEN RANGEL AND CUAUHTÉMOC, TODOS SANTOS; 612/145-0619 Suki settled in Todos Santos in the late '90s, bringing her Asian cooking craft and her love of Thai food to this receptive artist community. Recently opened Suki's Restaurant won immediate fans, wooed by such creative dishes as phad thai, Ginger Chicken with Ruby Curry, and the ever favorite Korean dish Beef Bul Go Gu—beef strips marinated in 15 spices, then stir-fried with fresh vegetables. Suki and her husband, Mat, are hands-on mom-and-pop businessfolk, running the whole show with the help of only one other employee. The quaint restaurant is situated in a tranquil setting, with an outdoor patio amid gardens and winding brick walkways. The service here is friendly and impeccable. *$; Cash only; lunch Tues–Sat; no alcohol; no reservations; 2 blocks from historic district.*

LODGINGS

Hacienda Inn Todos Santos / ★

CALLE B. JUÁREZ 21, TODOS SANTOS; 612/145-0193, FAX 612/145-0002 This large, hacienda-style brick building overlooks Todos Santos, the valley, and the ocean from its hilltop perch. Spacious rooms come with views of the lush, landscaped courtyard and swimming pool or distant ocean, and include fireplaces, television, air conditioning, and comfortable furnishings. Plush terry-cloth robes and a complimentary bottle of wine await guests, and a continental breakfast is included in the room rate. The inn has 14 guest facilities, including rooms with king-size and double beds. Junior and larger suites come with kitchenettes. The interior is somewhat dark, but the staff is friendly and accommodating. Proprietor Manuel Valdez also owns the Tequila Sunrise Restaurant/Bar (Calle Juárez between Morelos and Márquez de León; 612/145-0073). Since the Hacienda Inn is difficult to find, Valdez provides transportation from centrally located Tequila Sunrise or detailed directions via phone or email if you choose to drive. *$; AE, MC, V; traveler's checks OK; hacienda@cabonet.net.mx; take Topete leading northwest of town via unmarked dirt roads—limited signs.*

Hotel Todos Santos / ★

LEGASPI 3, TODOS SANTOS; 612/145-0009 OR 866-225-2786 US, FAX 612/145-0098 Situated in the heart of the historic district, Hotel Todos Santos occupies one of the estates built during the heyday of sugar production. The original adobe structure has been artfully restored. The building's vaulted ceilings, with their sturdy, black-palm beams, are typical construction of that period. Spacious guest rooms offer a choice of one or two double beds and provide views of the historic plaza or the Pacific. Centrally located, you're at the doorstep of art galleries, artisan shops, and local attractions. The casual Restaurante Santanas (see review) occupies a garden setting in back of the building. *$; AE, MC, V; traveler's checks OK; reservations@hoteltodossantos.com; www.hoteltodossantos. com; fronting town plaza next to historic theater.*

Posada La Poza / ★★★⯪

LA POZA DISTRICT, TODOS SANTOS; 612/145-0400, FAX 612/145-0475 Europeans Juerg and Libusche Wiesendanger are the owners, operators, and designers of this elegant seaside retreat. Arriving in 1998 from their Swiss homeland, they fell in love with this neighborhood. As you step into their virtual oasis, that love affair is contagious. Tucked behind a rocky point, the resort encompasses an expansive lagoon and palm-studded estuary, fronting a sprawling white-sand beach pounded by Pacific surf. The intimate resort, with several ultra-posh suites, captures the ambience of this natural setting. Low-profile buildings in earthy tones frame magnificent views through arched windows or from large view terraces. Attention to detail is evident, from the hand-tied palm supports and colorful accent tiles to the sculptured sand and rock garden with its native plants and winding walkways. Examples of Libusche's artwork grace the walls of each tastefully decorated suite. The hotel's Restaurante El Gusto! (see review) has become a magnet for locals and visitors with its ambience, fine cuisine, and great ocean views. Access roads to this resort are a bit of a maze, but the rewards are here upon arrival. *$$$; AE, MC, V; traveler's checks OK; contact@lapoza.com; www.lapoza.com; from Mexico 19, head west on*

Olachea and follow signs while traversing a winding, rugged dirt road; or take one-way Topete out of town, turn left on La Cachora Rd, and follow signs toward La Poza District.

Todos Santos Inn / ★★★

LEGASPI 33, TODOS SANTOS; 612/145-0040 PHONE AND FAX Innkeeper Robert Whiting has done an impeccable job of transforming an historic adobe-brick building into this enchanting inn. Although situated in the heart of Todos Santos, street activity and the pace of this century are far removed once you step inside the Mexican-tiled foyer with its painted wall mural of a bygone era. From this vantage point, brick archways magnificently frame the interior grounds, revealing a stone-paved, multilevel terrace and garden. The inn offers quiet privacy for its guests in spacious rooms with high-beamed ceilings, Saltillo tile flooring, and French-style wooden doors and windows exposing garden views. Furnishings are tastefully simple, mostly Mexican-colonial with some antiques, oriental rugs, gauze-white curtains, and beds canopied in sheer white mosquito netting. Upper-level rooms overlook the terrace, while larger suites have private garden-view patios. The inn is small and intimate, offering only two rooms and four suites. Centrally located, from the inn the interesting attractions of this small Mexican community are only a short walk away. *$$; No credit cards; traveler's checks (and checks) OK; closed Aug–Sept; todossantosinn@yahoo.com; www.todossantosinn.com; between Topete and Obregón.*

VACATION RENTALS

In keeping with the relaxed, intimate style of this hospitable artistic community, local residents have created a proliferation of small, homey accommodations for visitors. Ranging from traditional in-home bed-and-breakfast quarters to clusters of small *casitas* and on-premise guest houses, the variety and innovative style of overnight and seasonal rentals is astounding. Information and bookings for many of these rentals can be obtained through **SU CASA** (Degollado #69; 612/145-0657; sucasarentals@hotmail.com).

GLOSSARY

GLOSSARY

abarrotes
groceries

aeropuerto
airport

agua caliente
hot water

a la plancha
grilled

al vapor
steamed

almejas
clams

almejas rancheras
clams in tomato sauce with onions and peppers

almendrado
almond-based mole

almuerzo
lunch

alto
stop

arrechera
steak

arroyo
river bed, wash

artesanía
craftsmanship

artesano
craftsman, artist

avenida
avenue (abbreviated as Av in addresses throughout this book)

banco
bank

baño
bathroom

basura
garbage

bistec ranchero
beefsteak with tomato, onion, and pepper

bo-bo
tiny biting gnats aka jejénes

boleo
ball

bolillo
thick, crusty roll

bolgonesa
thick meat sauce

bombón glacé
a caramel-centered scoop of vanilla ice cream smothered with chocolate and topped with nuts

boojum
nickname of cirio cactus

bronca
quarrel, dispute

¡buen provecho!
good appetite

burrito
flour tortillas wrapped around a wide range of fillings

butano
propane

caballero
gentleman

cabrilla
sea bass

café Diablo
coffee, tequila, and whipped cream

cajas permanentes
ATMs, permanent boxes

calles
streets

callo de hacha
the adductor muscle of the hatchet shell

callos empanizadas
scallops, wrapped in foil and cooked on the grill

camarónes
shrimp

camarónes al mojo de ajo
shrimp cooked in garlic sauce

camarónes barracho
drunken shrimp

camarónes rellenos
stuffed shrimp

campo
camp

canastas
baskets

cardón
the world's tallest cactus species and cousin to the saguaro

cardonal
a thick grove of cardón cactus

caribe
thorny thistle plant aka mala mujer

carnaval
carnival; celebration held in port cities beginning nine days before Ash Wednesday

carne asada
marinated and grilled strips of beef served in tacos, burritos, or as an entree

carne tampiqueña
beef piled high with beans, guacamole, lettuce, and chiles

carnicería
meat market

carnitas
marinated pork served in tacos and burritos

casa de cambio
house of exchange

cascarones
colored, hollowed-out eggshells stuffed with confetti

caseta de teléfono
telephone booth

casita
small house

la cena
dinner

centavo
cent

cervecería
beer depot

cerveza
beer

ceviche de pescado
firm, white fish "cooked" by marinating in lime juice with tomatoes, onions, cilanto, and spices

charreadas
amazing displays of horsemanship inadequately translated as "Mexican rodeos"

charrería
the sport of charreadas

charros
Mexican cowboys

chilaquiles
tortilla chips smothered with chile sauce

chilaquiles con huevos
chilaquiles topped with two fried eggs

chiles rellenos
large semi-spicy green chile stuffed with cheese, coated with batter, fried, and covered with sauce.

chile verde
green chile; often a spicy sauce

chimichurri
a thick sauce made from olive oil, garlic, parsley, and herbs (Argentina)

chinicuiles
fried maguey worms

chubasco
violent storm

churro
long sticks of fried, sweet dough rolled in coarse white sugar

cirio
tall, tapering cactus which resemble upside-down carrots; found south of El Rosario

cocina
kitchen

cockteles
seafood cocktails

la cola
the tail; a task performed in charreadas involving the flipping of a bull by its tail

coleadero

see la cola

colectivos
shared vans

combinacíon
combination

cordinador
coordinator

la comida
food

corridas de toros
bullfight

corbina
slender, dark grey surf croaker (fish) with chin barbel; very tasty

corvina
migratory, soft-mouthed croaker (fish); very tasty

crema
sour cream

cuarto
fourth, quarter

curva peligrosa
dangerous curve

dama
lady, woman

delicioso
delicious

dentista
dentist

desayuno
breakfast

desayuno vegetariano
vegetarian breakfast

dinero
money

dorado
golden; gamefish also known as mahi mahi

drogas o armas
drugs or guns

dulces
sweets

ejido
cooperative property

enchiladas
corn tortillas wrapped around cheese, chicken, or beef and baked in a semi-spicy sauce.

enchiladas suizas de pollo
Swiss-style enchiladas filled with chicken and a creamy sauce

entero
whole

elote
ear of corn

equipale
pigskin; popular woven wood and leather furniture

Escalera Náutica
the Nautical Ladder

esqina
corner

farmacia
pharmacy

ferretería
hardware store

filete adobado
fillet marinated in chipotle chile sauce

flan
custard-like dish with a caramel flavor, sometimes prepared with tropical fruits or fancy sauces.

folklórica
folk music

fugazzeta
a double-layer pizza filled with ham, cheese, and onions

glorieta
traffic circle, roundabout

gorditas
fat little corncakes slathered with butter and cheese and heaped with salsa, sour cream, and meat

granjas
farms

guacamole
mashed avocados mixed with lime, onions, tomatoes, cilantro, and other ingredients

guajillo
long, thin, smooth-skinned chile

guayabera
embroidered dress shirts

güera
amber

hamburguesa
hamburger

harina
flour

helado
ice cream

hielo
ice

hombre
man

huachinango
red snapper

huaraches
woven leather sandals with rubber soles

huevos a la mexicana
eggs scrambled wth salsa

huevos rancheros
fried eggs on corn tortillas topped with a spicy, tomato-based sauce

huitlacoche
black fungus grown on corn, with a taste like an earthy mushroom

jaiba
blue crab

jefe
chief

jejénes

tiny, biting gnats; also called bobos

jugo de zanahoria
carrot juice

langosta
lobster

langosta asar con ajo
lobster roasted with garlic

larga distancia
long distance

lienzo charro
key-shaped arena used for charreadas

limón
lemon

llantera
tire repair

lonchería
snack bar

lunada
moonlight picnic

machaca
air-dried, shredded meat

magna sin
unleaded gas

maíz
Indian corn

mala mujer
bad woman—nickname for thorny
thistle plant

malecón
waterfront walkway

manda
personal promise

maquiladoras
manufacturing plants

mariscos
seafood

medio
middle; half

medio kilo
half kilogram

mercado
market

mezcal
clear, potent liquor produced from
several species of agave; bottles often
contain a maguey worm

Milanesa
Italian-style breaded veal

mole
blend of spices used for sauces on
chicken, pork, and enchiladas comes in
several varieties; black mole includes
bitter chocolate and chilies; yellow mole
is seasoned with pumpkin seeds

la mordida
little bite; bribe

morena
brown, dark

museo
museum

muy auténtico
very authentic

nopal
prickly pear cactus pad

norteño
northern

padre
father, priest

palapa
palm-thatched roof or shelter

paleta
fruit popsicles

palo verde
indigenous tree with stiff green branches

panadería
bakery

pan dulce
sweet breads sold in bakeries

panga
fiberglass skiff, boat

pangero
panga driver

panqueque
Argentina's caramel crepes

papas
potatoes

papas rellenos mixtas
baked potatoes stuffed with meat and
cheese

pargo
snapper

el paso de la muerte
charreada task in which the charro
moves from his horse to an unbroken
steed at full gallop

pastel de tres leches
three-milk cake

pescado
fish

piales
charreada task involving the roping of
the back legs of a galloping horse

playa
beach

policía
police

pollo en mole
chicken in mole sauce

prima
first; prime

propina
tip, gratuity

pulque
the milky, sweet, unrefined stage of
agave fermentation

puente
bridge

puro marisco
pure seafood

queso
cheese

queso fundido
melted cheese

ranchero
rancher

rojo
red

rompope
eggnog-type liqueur

salmon fresco
fresh salmon

salpiconitas de jaiba
shredded crab with onions, tomatoes,
garlic, olives, and lettuce

salsa ranchera
sauce used for huevos rancheros

sangrita
Spanish/Mexican drink of tomato juice,
lemon and orange juice, chiles, and a
shot of tequila

sanitario
toilet

sarapes
brightly colored woven ponchos

sierra
schooling, white-fleshed member of the
mackerel family; makes excellent
ceviche

sincronizadas
ham and cheese quesadillas

sopa de mariscos
seafood soup or stew

sopa de siete mares
seven seas soup

sopa de tortilla
tortilla soup

sopes
small gorditas with beans, lettuce, and
tomato

suertes
moves performed in a charreada

superpanga
A 26+ foot panga with center console,
steering, and a bimini top

taco
fried or soft corn tortillas stuffed with
ingredients

taco de carne asada
grilled beef tacos

taco del pastor
pork tacos with adobo sauce and
pineapple

taco del pulpo al mojo de ajo
garlic octopus tacos

tacone
wrap

tamales
Cornmeal paste stuffed with beef, pork,
chicken, veggies, or fruit and then
wrapped in corn husks and steamed

tamarindo
the sweet and sour fruit or pod of the
tamarind tree used for seasoning and
drinks; also a key ingredient in
Worcestershire sauce

tampiqueña
meat piled high with beans, guacamole, lettuce, and chiles

taquerías
taco stands

taquero
taco maker

taquitos
rolled, deep-fried tacos

tarjetas de crédito
credit cards

tarjetas de telefóno
phone cards

temezcal
a sauna made of a stick frame covered in reed mats

tequila con cascabel
tequila with rattlesnake

tequilero
tequila expert or authority

tienda
store

topes
speedbumps

torta
sandwich made on a bolillo

tortillería
tortilla factory

traje de faena
work outfit worn in charreadas

tranquilo
tranquil, quiet

turista
tourist; also nickname for the intestinal bug frequently caught by visitors to Mexico

untramarinos
mini-market

vado
dip

vado peligroso
dangerous dip

vaquero
cowboy

a la veracruzana
sautéed with tomato sauce, onions, and olives

zócalo
public square

zona de ganado
livestock zone

Index

We Stand By Our Reviews

Sasquatch Books is proud of *Best Places Baja*. Our editors and contributors go to great lengths and expense to see that all of the restaurant and lodging reviews are as accurate, up-to-date, and honest as possible. If we have disappointed you, please accept our apologies; however, if a recommendation in this 1st edition of *Best Places Baja* has seriously misled you, Sasquatch Books would like to refund your purchase price. To receive your refund:

1. Tell us where and when you purchased your book and return the book and the book-purchase receipt to the address below.
2. Enclose the original restaurant or lodging receipt from the establishment in question, including date of visit.
3. Write a full explanation of your stay or meal and how *Best Places Baja* misled you.
4. Include your name, address, and phone number.

Refund is valid only while this 1st edition of *Best Places Baja* is in print. If the ownership, management, or chef has changed since publication, Sasquatch Books cannot be held responsible. Tax and postage on the returned book is your responsibility. Please allow six to eight weeks for processing.

Please address to Satisfaction Guaranteed, *Best Places Baja*, and send to:
Sasquatch Books
119 South Main Street, Suite 400
Seattle, WA 98104

Best Places Baja Report Form

Based on my personal experience, I wish to nominate the following restaurant, place of lodging, shop, nightclub, sight, or other as a "Best Place"; or confirm/correct/disagree with the current review.

_____

_____

_____

_____

(Please include address and telephone number of establishment, if convenient.)

REPORT

Please describe food, service, style, comfort, value, date of visit, and other aspects of your experience; continue on another piece of paper if necessary.

_____

_____

_____

_____

_____

_____

_____

_____

I am not concerned, directly or indirectly, with the management or ownership of this establishment.

_____

SIGNED

_____

ADDRESS

_____

_____

_____

PHONE   **DATE**

Please address to Best Places Baja and send to:
SASQUATCH BOOKS
119 SOUTH MAIN STREET, SUITE 400
SEATTLE, WA 98104
Feel free to email feedback as well: **BOOKS@SASQUATCHBOOKS.COM**

Best Places Baja Report Form

Based on my personal experience, I wish to nominate the following restaurant, place of lodging, shop, nightclub, sight, or other as a "Best Place"; or confirm/correct/disagree with the current review.

_____

_____

_____

_____

(Please include address and telephone number of establishment, if convenient.)

REPORT

Please describe food, service, style, comfort, value, date of visit, and other aspects of your experience; continue on another piece of paper if necessary.

_____

_____

_____

_____

_____

_____

_____

I am not concerned, directly or indirectly, with the management or ownership of this establishment.

SIGNED

ADDRESS

PHONE   **DATE**

Please address to Best Places Baja and send to:
SASQUATCH BOOKS
119 SOUTH MAIN STREET, SUITE 400
SEATTLE, WA 98104
Feel free to email feedback as well: **BOOKS@SASQUATCHBOOKS.COM**

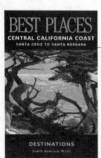